Creating Surplus Populations

Creating Surplus Populations

The Effects of Military and Corporate Policies on Indigenous Peoples

edited by

Lenora Foerstel

Maisonneuve Press
Washington, D.C. 1996

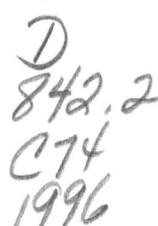

Lenora Foerstel, ed. *Creating Surplus Populations: The Effects of Military of Military and Corporate Policies on Indigenous Peoples*

© 1996 Maisonneuve Press
P.O. Box 2980, Washington, D.C. 20013-2980

All rights reserved. Brief quotations used in articles, books, or reviews are encouraged provided clear acknowledgment to this book and the publisher is given. For any other reproduction, please contact the publisher.

Maisonneuve Press is a division of the Institute for Advanced Cultural Studies, a non-profit organization devoted to social change through cultural analysis and education.

Printed in the United States by BookCrafters, Fredricksburg, VA
printed on long-life acid-free paper

Library of Congress Cataloging-In-Publication Data

Creating surplus populations : the effects of military and corporate
         policies on indigenous peoples / edited by Lenora Foerstel
      p.   cm.
      Includes bibliographical references.
1. Military history, Modern--20th century--Congresses. 2. Refugees, Political--History--20th Century--Congresses. I. Lenora Foerstel, 1929–
D842.2.C74 1996   96-12961
325'.21--dc20   CIP

ISBN 0-944624-31-6 paperback

Cover photos: *Background*, Refugees from Rwanda fleeing to Tanzania, May 1994 (UNHCR / 24069 / P. Moumtzis). *Left*, Hungarian children receive schooling at Gerovo refugee camp, Yugoslavia, June 1957 (UN photo 54486 / pcd). *Right*, Nuer children from Southern Sudan learn their lessons at a refugee camp near Nasir, August 1990 (UN photo 157694 / M. Grant).

Contents

Lenora Foerstel, Introduction	1
Margarita Papandreou, Refugees and the Power Elite	7
Lenora Foerstel, Refugees: Root Causes from an Historical Viewpoint	9
Ward Churchill, Like Sand in the Wind: The Making of an American Indian Diaspora	19
Amartya Sen, Population: Delusion and Reality	53
Teresa Gutierrez, Cuba: The Real Causes of Emigration	80
Jocelyn McCalla, Better than Fiction: The Odyssey of the Haitian Refugees	92
Lilia Velasquez, The Effect of U.S. Foreign Policy on Asylum Applicants	109
Amy Goodman, A First-Hand Account of the Role of Power in East Timor and Haiti	128
Yvonne Deutsh, Israeli Women and the Occupation of Palestine	136
Roni Ben Efrat, After Oslo: The Roots of the Israeli-Palestine Conflict Still Unresolved	141
Sean Gervasi, The Drift Toward Military Intervention in the Balkans: Another Vietnam?	147
Sara Flounders, Bosnian Refugees—Pawns in the "Great Game": A new U.S.-CIA War	174
Jemera Rone, Displacement Related to Human Rights Abuses and Aid Manipulation by the Military Parties to the War in Southern Sudan	188

Jeff Drumtra, Genocide in Rwanda	204
Nick Papandreou, Inequality and the Emergence of a New Global Underclass: The Refugee Woman	217
Julia Clones, Environment, Refugees, and Displaced Persons: The Gender Perspective	225
Sissy Farenthold, The Militarization of U.S. Foreign Policy	231
Georgina Ritchie, From Powerlessness to Empowerment: Turning Refugee Experience into a Movement for Human Rights	240
Robert Merrill, Theory and Progress of Human Rights: The UN Declaration on the Rights of Indigenous Peoples	249

Appendix
    1. Excerpts from International Instruments on Refugee Status   270
    2. UN Declaration on the Rights of Indigenous People   277
    3. Women for Mutual Security   285
    4. Contributors to this book   289

Acknowledgments

Women for Mutual Security (WMS) would like to thank the organizations and individuals who helped to make the conference "Dialogue on Refugee and Displaced Women in Times of Conflict," a great success. It was this conference which stimulated the papers compiled in this book. The following organizations played a major role in the conference: Sisterhood is Global Institute (SIGI); Refugee Women in Development (REFWID); and Women's International League for Peace and Freedom (WILPF).

Supporters of the conference were: Doctors Without Frontiers, International Organization of Refugees, Amnesty International, Women's Bureau, General Association of Greek Workers, Greek Housewives Organization, Intervention (Greece), Planned Parenthood Association, Women's Movement (POGO) Greece, Women's Association PROTOPORIA, GODIK (Greece) Equal Rights-Equal Responsibilities, Socialist Women's Movement (Greece).

The conference, held in Greece on September 15-17, 1994, was also supported by local organizations and, in particular, we wish to thank the Center for Research and Action on Peace and the Athens Office of the UN High Commission on Refugees.

Without financial and facility support, the conference could not have taken place. We are, therefore, very grateful to the following organizations: Ministry of Foreign Affairs, Onasis Foundation, Global Fund for Women, Shaler-Adams Foundation, International Planned Parenthood Federation, the General Board of Global Ministries, and especially Elizabeth Calvin, Executive Secretary of the Ministry of Women and Children, The World Council of Churches, and in particular, Stella Jungo, Administrative Assistant for Women and Development, and the Commercial Bank of Greece. We also wish to thank John G. Kessanis, Manager of Support Services for Olympic Airways, and Marie E. Vicente, Group Self Assistant, for their patience and cooperation in bringing participants to the conference.

The success of every project depends on the work and dedication of many individuals. To Roxani Agrevi, Pepi Christaki, Vivian Dragona, Denise Dufault, Mary Economou, Madeline Gilchrist, Eleni Gizi, Elia Kanaki, Annita Kontoyiannis, Pepi Markopoulou, Anna Panagopoulou, Christos Pantazis, Vassilis Poulpouloglou, Aristotelis Sarikostas, Elli Sirmopoulou, Lila Stavridou, and Aliki Tsapara we offer special thanks. To the individuals who organized the art exhibit and gave the proceeds to refugee women, we also express our thanks. To Christine Killingbeck of the United Nations photo library and to Barbara Francis, Ann Lau-Hansen, and Eve Weisberg of the UNHCR Photo Library we wish to express our gratitude for helping us in the selection of the book's photographs.

The editor of this book would like to thank her daughter, Karen Foerstel, and her husband, Herbert Foerstel, for their editorial assistance. Finally, WMS is deeply grateful to Robert Merrill of Maisonneuve Press for his advice and assistance in the development of this book.

Creating Surplus Populations

"I spent 33 years and four months in active service as a member of the Marine Corps. . . . And during that period, I spent most of my time being a high-class muscle man for Big Business. . . . Thus I helped make Mexico and especially Tampico safe for American oil interests in 1914. I helped make Haiti and Cuba a decent place for the National City Bank to collect revenues in. . . . I helped purify Nicaragua for the international banking house of Brown Brothers* in 1909 and 1912. I brought light to the Dominican Republic for American sugar interests in 1916. I helped make Honduras 'right' for American fruit companies in 1903."

—Major General Smedley Butler, 1935

(*George Bush's father, Prescott, was a partner. *ed.*)

Lenora Foerstel

Introduction

The opportunity for compiling the papers for this book rose out of a conference, "Dialogue on Refugee and Displaced Women in Times of Conflict." Women from Cyprus, Bosnia, Croatia, Armenia, Palestine, Iraq, Kurdistan, South Africa and Azerbaijan were among the many who met in Athens, Greece, to describe the horrors of being uprooted from their homes, separated from their families, and plunged into a poverty which denied proper food and medication for their children. Scores of other books have described the unprecedented crisis of refugees in the developing world, but what makes this book unique is that the authors reveal the root causes, which, in a world population of 5.5 billion, have made one in every 130 people a refugee.

The United States and European nations have, through their mass media, represented ethnic wars as a major cause of the global refugee crisis. What is often ignored in their presentations is the historical role of Europe and the United States in dividing the Third World into artificial states in order to control their natural resources. Beginning in the sixteenth century, Spain, Portugal, Britain, France, and to some extent Holland and Denmark, carved up the Americas under colonialism. Those citizens who resisted the authority of their colonial masters soon found themselves jailed or deported. Malnutrition, environmental degradation, and genocide became common place, leading to further displacement of the population. In his paper, "Like Sand in the Wind," Ward Churchill (Cree/Cherokee Métis), a coordinator of the Colorado chapter of the American Indian Movement, describes how Native Americans fought, suffered and died to preserve their people's residency in the portions of North America which had been theirs since "time immemorial."

In the 1870s, Germany and Italy joined the ranks of the imperial states, shifting their military forces toward Africa in order to claim their vast land masses and natural resources for their own. Again, artificial boundaries were drawn between nations of people. "Most new African states consisted of culturally diverse social groups, mistakenly labeled as tribes, that were combined into distinct territorial entities by European colonial entrepreneurs in response to the dictates of

This page is
intentionally blank

imperial rivalries in the late nineteenth century" (Zolberg, Suhrke, Aguaya, p. 40-41). The colonizers established their laws over those of the indigenous authorities, destroying cultural traditions which had encouraged beneficial trade and intercultural relationships between African "nations." Under colonialism, the remnants of the "Traditional" societies developed into what are today called "ethnic groups."

Europe's need to control its colonies required the use of soldiers from within the occupied nations, and Great Britain established the model for military recruitment during its occupation of India. After a mutiny by the Sepoys of the Bengal army in 1857, the British realized the need to create a local military force made up of ethnically homogeneous units. "When the Peel Commission investigated the mutiny, it concluded that the way to a secure military force was to create a counterpoise of natives against natives. The result was a policy of ethnic balance in the armed forces. Units in India, the Sudan, and Burma were composed in a heterogeneous fashion, their component companies proudly bearing their ethnic designations" (Horowitz, p. 446).

After World War II with the departure of the colonizers, the local military structure degenerated into ethnic conflict. The civilian population sought to reclaim its land, and the armed forces, treated as a tool of the colonizer, became the enemy. Part of the legacy of the colonial period was the imposition of western education as a prerequisite for officer's training. This created a military elite divided along ethnic lines, from which grew ethnic political parties and a political structure vulnerable to recurring military coups.

Since its independence in 1956, the Sudan has suffered two major waves of refugees. Early struggle for colonial control of this country, first by the British and then by Arab imperialists, have played a role in dividing the Northern part of the country from the South. Jemera Rone's paper, "Displacement Related to Human Rights Abuses and Aid Manipulation by the Military Parties to the War in Southern Sudan," provides the reader with a better understanding of the events which have generated 380,000 Sudanese refugees and some 60,000 internally displaced people in the southern Sudan.

Jeff Drumtra's paper, "Genocide in Rwanda," clearly demonstrates how colonial rule in Rwanda, particularly under the Belgians, enforced a "divide and rule" strategy which led to a rigid pseudo-racial hierarchy. This division eventually produced a violent confrontation which caused the murder of one million people and the displacement of another 900,000.

The same "divide and rule" strategy is currently being used by the United States and European powers. "Yugoslavia has for some time been the target of a covert policy waged by the West, primarily Germany, the United States, Britain, Turkey and Saudi Arabia, as well as Iran, to divide Yugoslavia into ethnic components, dismantle it, and eventually recolonize it." In his essay, "The Drift toward

Military Intervention in the Balkans: Another Vietnam?" Sean Gervasi warns that the American intervention in the Balkan conflict will lead the U.S. down the same disastrous road it traveled in Vietnam. In her paper, "Bosnia Refugees: Pawns in the Great Game," Sara Flounder examines the role Western nations played in stimulating the civil war which led to the destruction of Yugoslavia.

Though ethnic conflict is acknowledged as a major cause of refugee flow, there are those who believe that the growth of Third World populations plays a large part in forcing their people to emigrate to the developed countries. In his paper, "Population: Delusion and Reality," Dr. Amartya Sen rejects this view, stating that to use over-population as a explanation for the increases in immigration "is to close one's eyes to the deep changes that have occurred and are occurring in the world in which we live, and the rapid internationalization of its cultures and economics that accompanies these changes." His research leads him to conclude that the increased migratory pressures in the Third World derive more from the dynamics of international capitalism than the growing size of their populations. Papers by Nicolas Papandreou, Julia Clones, Robert Merrill and Lenora Foerstel further examine the dynamics of international capitalism and its relationship to immigration and the refugee flow.

Haiti's economic policies have been controlled by the United States since American marines landed on the island in 1915. The invasion was intended to prop up the Haitian dictators and their military forces, and it marked the beginnings of almost 75 years of US support for Haitian military governments. Not until December 16, 1990, did the election of Jean Bertrand Aristide as Haiti's first democratically elected president end the succession of US-supported military dictators. But in 1991, when a military coup replaced Aristide, some 40,000 Haitians fled their country seeking asylum in the United States.

Papers by Lilia Velasquez, Jocelyn McCalla and Amy Goodman analyze the problems facing Haitian refugees today. The American press paints a picture of the World Bank, the National Endowment for Democracy (NED), and other American funded groups as the source of money and "development" projects to stabilize Haiti economy. However, there are those who fear that "their goal is to impose a neo-liberal economic agenda, to undermine grass roots participatory democracy, to create political stability conducive to a good business climate, and to bring Haiti into the 'new world order' appendaged to the U.S. as a source for markets and cheap labor" (Regan, p. 12).

When the manipulation of international aid proved ineffective in dictating the domestic policies of the Cuban government, the Eisenhower Administration initiated a blockade against the Cuban people in 1960. Defying the United Nations Declaration on Human Rights, which includes economic as well as political rights, successive American administrations have maintained the blockade against Cuba for thirty-five years. In the last four years alone, 25,000 Cubans have fled their country in search of economic relief. Teresa Gutierrez, in her paper, "Cuba: The Real Causes of Emigration," points out that the United Nations has continually voted against the blockade, with the most recent vote on September 24, 1994 showing 101 nations opposing the blockade and only two, the United States and Israel supporting it. European nations and other allies of the U.S. have begun a campaign to block the new anti-Cuban legislation, the "Cuban Liberty and Solidarity Act of 1995, introduced by Sen. Jesse Helms (R.-NC.) and Rep. Dan Burton (R-IN). European governments have objected to provisions of the Act which go beyond U.S. jurisdiction and impose on the sovereignty of other nations. It is feared that "the collective effects of these provisions have the potential to cause grave and damaging effects to bilateral EU-U.S. relations" (*NY Times*, 4/13/95).

The inhuman and often counterproductive impact of blockades and economic sanctions has been examined by former U.S. Attorney General Ramsey Clark. In an interview, Clark gave to a delegation of women from Women for Mutual Security, he described the results of the Gulf War and the effects of subsequent economic sanctions against the nation of Iraq. Although there are no exact figures available, it is estimated that some two million Iraqi people have been forced to live abroad. The sanctions imposed on Iraq since 1990 have been responsible for the deaths of 400,000 Iraqi children, and continued sanctions would threaten an estimated 1.5 million additional children.

In papers presented by Yvonne Deutsh and Roni Ben Efrat, attention is directed to other parts of the world where the struggle of refugees for their human rights and common security is rarely revealed in the mass media. Some areas of the world are scrutinized closely by the media, while other regions are seldom mentioned. There is, for example, a great deal of misinformation about the conflicts in the three former Soviet republics, Armenia, Azerbaijan and Georgia. Few realize that the Caucuses contains one of the largest concentrations of refugees and displaced persons in the world, creating nearly two million refugees and displaced persons in the three nations. No matter what are the basic causes for internal conflict within a nation, outside military forces, supported by foreign interests always seem to become involved. "Mercenaries and profiteers are making a killing in the six-year Azerbaijan-Armenian war. One U.S. company, with connections to Richard Secord is training soldiers under cover of oil deals" (Rowell, p. 23). General Richard Secord is an international arms dealer with long-time ties to the CIA.

Outside interference in the national and economic affairs of Third World nations has become a huge factor intensifying Third World conflicts. In her paper "The Militarization of United States Foreign Policy," Sissy Farenthold writes that "the United States is the leading supplier of weapons to the developing world, providing in 1993 73% of all weapons sold for a total of $4.8 billion." In spite of the end of the Cold War, the fall of the Berlin Wall and the dissolution of the Warsaw Pact Treaty, the military industrial complex continues to grow in the United States. The origins of the military industrial complex appeared shortly after the New Deal, when an alliance was formed between big business, organized labor and the government. "Military corporations grew up as a variance of the broader form of economic corporations that developed during the last stages of the Great Depression and became accepted after World War II" (Bischak, p. 134). The defense industry continues to dominate the U.S. economy and plays a major role in determining US foreign policy.

A policy sub-government or as Gordon Adams, director of the Washington-based Defense Budget project, states, an iron triangle has emerged. Adam's reference to the "iron triangle" identifies the cooperative relationship between the Pentagon, key members of Congress, and the private sector. As a result of this linkage, modern industries are geared to produce military weapons. The military industrialist have little concern for the destructive consequences of weapons production, including regional wars and refugee problems, yet they enjoy the profits of such conflicts.

Those who profit from the military industries have also overlooked the cost to the civilian sector throughout the United States. Roads, bridges and basic infrastructures are deteriorating and simultaneously we find the engineering, construction, and architectural industries withering. The results is the loss of millions of jobs. These and other social ills derive from the diversion of resources, especially in the realm of science and technology, from the civilian to the military sector.

When concerned Congressional leaders try to pass legislation for "economic conversion," which would phase the military economy into a civilian economy, they are accused of promoting "Big Government." A growing class of poor, politically conservative white males, many trained by the armed forces, have taken up the cause of the military industrialist by advancing a "states rights" philosophy within a militia movement. These proliferating militias, blame the federal government for transforming the U.S. into a second rate industrial economy, but they do not recognize how military spending drains the civilian economy, diverting vital capital, technical and human resources away from productive uses.

Economic conversion would reverse a U.S. military economy into a civilian peace economy, and the U.S. would no longer be dependent on wars for its economic existence. War is the greatest cause for creating the refugee situation. Some 22 million people have been killed in wars since 1945. Some 24 million people have become displaced people within their own countries while still another 18 million have become refugees. As Nicolas Papandreou concluded in his paper "Inequality and the Emergence of a New Under Class: The Refugee Woman."

In an age when millions of working people throughout the developing world are hired by transnational corporations, while other migrate in search of work, others languish without employment, and still others become refugees, where does the locus of civil rights and obligations reside? The dramatic political and economic changes occurring around the world argue for a different concept of citizenship, of rights and obligations, a concept that puts emphasis on basic human rights regardless, with a special emphasis for those who are the weakest and most vulnerable.

References

Adams, G. *The Iron Triangle: The Politics of Defense Contracting.* New York: The Council on Economic Priorities, 1983.

Bischak, G. A. "The Obstacles to Real Security: Military Corporation and the Cold War State" in *Real Security,* Kevin J. Cassidy and Gregory A. Bischak, eds. Albany: State University of New York Press, 1993.

Gervasi, S. "Germany, US and Yugoslav Crisis," *Covert Action Quarterly* 43 (Winter, 1992).

Horowitz, D. L. *Ethnic Groups in Conflict.* Berkeley: University of California Press, 1985.

Johnson, B. R. and G. Button. "Human Environmental Rights Issues and the Multinational Corporations: Industrial Development in the Free Trade Zone" in *Who Pays the Price,* Barbara Rose Johnston, ed. Washington, DC: Island Press, 1994.

Rowell, A. "US Mercenaries Fight in Azerbaijan,"*Covert Action Quarterly* 48 (Spring 1994).

Yudken, J. "Economic Development, Technology and Defense Conversion: A National Policy Perspective" in *Real Security,* Cassidy and Bischak, eds. Albany: State University of New York Press, 1993.

Zolberg, A. R., A. Suhke, and S. Agwayo. *Escape from Violence: Refugee Crisis in the Developing World.* London: Oxford University Press, 1989.

Margarita Papandreou

Refugees and the Power Elite

Everyday we hear the cries of millions of people worldwide fleeing from war and famine. The twentieth century's historic struggles surrounding colonialism and the East/West cold war have given way to today's conflicts resulting form a varying mix of population/economic development imbalances, environmental degradation, and acute poverty. These are conditions which humans have managed to create, particularly those in positions of power.

The purpose of this book is to ask the questions why, how, and what are the conditions which create shifts in population: voluntarily, as in migration, and involuntarily, as in refugee flight. The latter case is the most poignant because people are forced to leave their traditional home in order to save their lives. Families with whatever possessions they can carry are scattered like leaves, branches, papers in an ongoing hurricane, scudding before a powerful wind of death and destruction. These images flash horrors beyond our comprehension and open wounds on the global conscience. Every day we see refugees being stripped of their humanity; endless lines of women, men, and children with skinny, sick, starving, dying blank stares of hopeless dull eyes staring at us from shriveled, parched faces. Human catastrophes like these are going on in many parts of the world, either in small or biblical dimensions.

Because of the frequency of these pictures, we are in danger of becoming immune to the unbearable suffering refugees experience. The mass media in developed nations (especially the United States) talk incessantly about "compassion fatigue," as if Americans are now exhausted from having to spend a few minutes each week contemplating the horror their government has caused around the world. We must not lose our humanity by turning off our emotions. For those whose strength to cry out has been sapped or who are too stunned to rebel, we must be their voices until they are able to speak for themselves. This book will be raising questions on their behalf to the international community: "Why do you give only band-aid support?" "Why are industrialized nations unable to deal with the poverty and upheaval of the South in a coordinated fashion?" " Why not acknowledge that famine and violence are manipulated by those who expect to benefit from them?" "Why push countries into austerity programs and force them to pay their debt instead of committing domestic income to poverty, uneven development, and crumbling national infrastructures?" "Why continue to sell arms to corrupt and brutal governments, increasing the risk of violence and reducing the amount of money given to care for the people?" " Why such indifference to the women refugees and their very special problems of exploitation?"

In this book, we will look at the humanitarian protection aspects of the refugee problem. The world's refugees deserve an immediate response from all of us and from the institutions and organizations set up for this purpose. But we will also be looking at the ways we can stem this worldwide tragedy. The medicine offered by the developed northern hemisphere for all of these woes is nothing more than the global free market, which is generally, in fact, indifferent to the needs of the people and more often than not deeply corrupt. The global free market, as free markets always have, puts profit before people—precisely the problem it is being offered as a cure for. The so-called free market is only free to large corporations or wealthy individuals who have no connection to a geographic region or the community of people who live there and can shift capital around the world at will. Instead of free markets, we should be concentrating on two human realities: 1.- human populations are part of the earth's ecosystem and therefore have natural rights in ways that economic institutions do not, and 2.- the greed and competition inherent in the free market system have made money values and monetary institutions more important concerns of governmental policy than even people.

We women are searching for a new public policy that truly empowers the people—particularly women—promoting authentic self-government and a sense of community. We want a comprehensive peace plan that allows for cooperative management of social, economic, and environmental problems before they metastasize into ethnic passions and more floods of refugees. In searching for a therapy for a violent world, we are hampered by a power-elite who exert their considerable influence to insure that social policies will derive from a patriarchal mentality—male values, male culture, and male needs. We are missing desperately the influence of feminist values and feminist culture.

We hope this book will contribute to the thinking on these basic and difficult problems.

Lenora Foerstel

Refugees:
Root Causes from an Historical Viewpoint

Racism, nationalism, cultural imperialism, and the free market economy, now under the umbrella of the General Agreement on Tariffs and Trade (GATT), are ideologies and practices historically used by the United States and European powers to invade and control the land and resources of other nations. The politics of creed and color are increasingly used by the West today against the Third World, the Middle East, and particularly against those nations which practice the Muslim religion. Within the United States, the struggle which took place between the English colonists, Native Americans, and African slaves led to the formulation of laws that protected the rights and privileges of the Anglo-Saxons over people of other cultures. "The idea expressed by Cotton Mather in the seventeenth century that the Indians were the devil's minions, damned from birth by God and incapable of redemption, shifted in the nineteenth century to the conviction that the Indians were damned by biology—that they were inherently incapable of taking the first step toward civilization" (Gossett, p. 229). This process is now being globalized.

By the 1870s, the currents of racism were running strongly on both sides of the Atlantic. In England, as in Germany, Teutonic origin theories were prevalent and carried with them nationalist implications. In France, the nobility developed racist theories to explain the special privileges of their class. This is a message still being heard in Europe and the United States today. Since German unification in 1990, three phenomena have characterized Germany: an economic crisis, an expansionist stand toward Europe, a rise in extreme nationalism and neo-Nazism.

Immigrants and refugees have been made the scapegoat for economic insecurity. Germany went so far in May 1993 as to reverse its constitution in order to limit the flow of immigrants and refugees. Like Germany, France is seeking to become a "zero immigration" country.

A similar attitude toward immigrants has developed in the United States. It is therefore not surprising that in 1994, Proposition 187, a California proposal to cut off social services to non-documented immigrants, was supported by the majority of Californian voters. The proposition is now being challenged in court, but if enacted, it would threaten public health by reducing immunization for aliens and putting 300,000 children of immigrants out of school and onto the streets. The proposal violates California laws as well as the U.S. Constitution, which provide protection for non-citizens, non-permanent residents and visitors. Latin American leaders have begun to criticize what they call a growing U.S nativism. They see Proposition 187 as a racist act which violates human rights, particularly the rights of children. The "refugee and the migrant worker share a common characteristic: they are vulnerable and powerless, their human rights are frequently violated and they are often treated without dignity" (Downing and Kushner, p. 152).

Racist theories become more prevalent when a country experiences economic insecurity and the dominant population is threatened by unemployment and other financial problems. In the United States, the immigrant is blamed for stealing white jobs and people of color are accused of draining the economy. Charles Murray and his now deceased co-author Richard Hernstein argued in their book, *The Bell Curve*, that intellectuals and policy-makers have largely overlooked the role intelligence plays in determining wealth, poverty and social status. Traditionally, racists have used genetics to rationalize economic instability.

In the bibliography of the *Bell Curve*, the authors make a special mention of seventeen researchers from whom their essential theories derive. Of the seventeen cited, ten are present or former contributors or members to *Mankind Quarterly*. "This is interesting because *Mankind Quarterly* is a notorious journal of 'racial history' founded and funded by men who believe in the genetic superiority of the white race" (Lane, p. 14). Those who have supported and still endorse eugenic theories are largely white, Anglo-Saxon and protestant, drawn from the upper and middle classes, who fear immigrants and people of color will somehow dilute and destroy their culture.

> The genetic model has endured not because it has any scientific basis, but because it is useful. Around the turn of the century, eugenics took the ethnically-diverse U.S. by storm. It provided a 'scientific' justification for stigmatizing African-Americans, Asians and Eastern and Southern European immigrants and forced them to work for less. (Horn, p. 33)

Racism and nationalism were easily merged. Both are modern phenomena developed first in Europe. As Gossett has shown in *Race: The History of an Idea*, "Before the eighteenth century, physical difference among people were so rarely referred to as a matter of great importance that something of a case can be made for the proposition that race consciousness is largely a modern phenomenon" (p. 3). Concepts of nationalism rose up as a reaction to industrialization—a period when people were being uprooted from their local communities. "In this historical context, a need arises for a new kind of ideology capable of creating cohesion and loyalty among individuals participating in social systems on a large scale. Nationalism was able to satisfy these requirements" (Eriksen, p. 104).

With the rise of European nationalism in late nineteenth century, citizens quickly developed attitudes of "them" vs. "us," which developed the belief that Europeans and their culture are superior to all others. Historians and anthropologists, influenced by industrial capitalism and their own European culture, participated in the myth of white superiority by ignoring and distorting the great accomplishments and scientific achievements of non-European peoples. Anthropologists were involved in romanticizing "exotic" cultures in Africa and Asia, studying village life exclusively and ignoring the existence of empires and the impact of colonialism on non-European nations.

Cultural traits that did not fit easily into European systems of behavior or were not synonymous with the European patriarchal system of rational understanding were often characterized as primitive or savage. The philosophical views of Friedrich Nietzche and Martin Heidegger and the psychobiological theories of Sigmund Freud and Carl Jung helped to reinforce racist and nationalist views. Jung, drawing from Nietzche's philosophy, saw the wealthy upper class European male as the center of human progress, placed there through biology and destiny.

The framers of the U.S. Constitution held a similar attitude. For them the poor were "inferior" and should not exert political influence. They felt that the emerging American nation needed "to promote the expansion of a private economy independent from what the "inferior people might think is in their best interest" (Fresia, p. 49). The citizens of the United States, writes Dr. Fresia have unreflectively accepted the idea that freedom means the right of a few individuals to control the lives of millions of people by virtue of their private ownership of community, national, and international resources (p. 87).

The journalist Charles Krauthammer recently confirmed this view in a column that charged Democrats with waging class warfare by describing Republicans as the party of the rich. "Unfortunately," stated Krauthammer, "it doesn't work. One reason for the current conservative ascendancy is its grasp of a fundamental truth about the American middle class: It may harbor the occasional envy tinged resentment of the rich, but what class animus it has is directed against the poor." This is not only the sentiment of the U.S. citizen, but it also holds true for the European middle classes. Krauthammer only fails to note that the animus against the poor or the non-European is not new; it is synonymous with modern industrialism and has been promoted with great energy by writers like Krauthammer himself.

It was this attitude that allowed for uncontrolled corporate growth and a shift to a corporate global economy after World War II. While the war weakened the European nations, the U.S. emerged as the dominant world power. It was clear that, economically, European nations could no longer maintain their colonies. A strategy for a new economic relationship between Europe, the United

States, and the Third World had to be formulated. In 1944, at the Breton Woods Conference in New Hampshire, the new economic structure was created.

It was at this conference that the World Bank and the International Monetary Fund (IMF) were founded. The architects of these agreements, among them, John Mayard Keynes, originally visualized a new world order built on the foundation of full employment, prosperity, and cooperation. The World Bank and the IMF were to be accountable to the United Nations. As emerging Third World nations joined the United Nations and accepted the international finance, a new enthusiasm developed as both sides felt that economic cooperation would lead to economic equity. Leaders in the Third World did not repudiate the debts or treaty obligations that their former colonizers had committed them to. They decided to work within the boundaries of the free market policies and conditions placed upon them. Third World nations also agreed to allow foreign investors complete freedom in their countries, with the additional assurance that they would not nationalize foreign enterprises. A new nation seeking to bring all sections of its economy under its control by nationalization could do so only at the risk of crippling economic retaliation.

In the mid 1950s, the World Bank and the IMF, with the backing of the United States, announced that their policies would no longer be accountable to the United Nations. This gave the two organizations arbitrary power over the economic policies of the Third World. The U.S.-dominated and Eurocentric World Bank now represented itself as a specialized organization able to define the needs of the Third World, whether in areas of agriculture, health, water needs, or education. The World Bank's new "Structural Adjustment" policies defined a reduced role for Third World nations in building their own economies, allowing only that spending which the World Bank considered necessary. In Africa, this meant sharp reductions in future education and social services and the removal of tariffs protecting emerging industries which the World Bank considered inefficient as compared to U.S. or European industries.

The IMF argued that "Africa should continue doing what it apparently does best: the production of cheap raw materials for the developed world in exchange for more expensive processed goods. This means turning the clock back to a colonial relationship which independence was supposed to eradicate" (Anyadike, p. 28). Civil rights leader, Jessie Jackson, denounced the effects of what he calls economic colonialism on the developing world: "they no longer use bullets and ropes," he stated. "they use the World Bank and International Monetary Fund" (cited by Rich, p. 25).

Throughout the Third World, foreign investors promoted new industries. With the growth of these industries, villagers and farmers who had earlier maintained self sufficiency through democratic and cooperative economies soon found themselves plunged into poverty. This was caused by the subordination of agricultural development to the interests of export-oriented industries. The new entrepreneurial class, holding contracts with Northern corporations and governments, maintained agricultural commodity prices and workers wages at a depressed level that ensured cheap and competitive exports. As a result, working the land became unsustainable throughout much of the Third World, forcing many farmers and laborers to migrate to over-crowded cities and to live in slum conditions. Today, those migrants have become refugees within their own nation.

Other problems facing poor communities of the South, especially farmers, are their reliance on foreign companies for their supply of seeds, fertilizers, and other products. Traditionally, farm cultures have used biological diversity as a practice for survival. But biotechnological corporations have made the South's biological resources their private property. Under the General Agreement on Tariffs and Trade (GATT) and the North American Free Trade Agreement (NAFTA), Third World nations will continue to lose their resources and knowledge without protection. However, the corporations of the industrialized North have taken aggressive action to protect their own technology from the Third World. GATT includes a set of national laws called Trade Related Intellectual Property Rights (TRIP). The major consequences of TRIP would be to limit the possibility of technologically imitative development by the nations of the South, preventing even the adaptation of foreign technology to local conditions.

Children at a refugee camp school in Chiapas, Mexico, July 1991 (photo: Jeff Ponting)

The face of the new colonizer is marked by a trinity: the IMF, the World Bank and GATT. This trinity dominates the world economy. With the ability to move production from one country to another, corporations hold no allegiance to any nation. Early in American history, Thomas Jefferson spoke despairingly of the merchant class, saying, "They have no ties with the soil. All they are interested in is the source of their profits" (Barnet, and Muller, 77). Both the Republican and Democratic parties in the U.S. strongly support corporate interests and needs. However, there are some members of the U.S. House of Representatives who are concerned over the economic disparity that GATT will create, not only in the Third World, but also in the United States. Senator Hollings from South Carolina points out that we are moving our jobs to Mexico and the Pacific Rim where labor is cheaper and profits are higher for corporate stockholders. Hollings says that nations measure their wealth by what they export, not by what they import, and the United States is importing far more than it exports. "Exports create jobs, but imports lose the jobs," he states, "and we are losing them at $100 billion a year. And according to their [the Government] own measures, every billion dollars represents 20,000 jobs. So, we are losing two million jobs a year." In 1994, the U.S. had a $150-$160 billion trade deficit. That is three million jobs lost" (Hollings, *Congressional Record*, 515084).

Senator Metzenbaum from Ohio agrees with Senator Hollings, and adds that the GATT treaty ignores the problem of 200 million children around the world who are being employed under slave conditions in the manufacturing of cheap goods for the U.S. and other developed markets. By ignoring this problem, employers will continue to exploit the children of the Third World (*Congressional Record*, S-15086).

The case against free trade and the globalization of corporate powers has also been taken up by consumer advocate Ralph Nader. "Global commerce without commensurate democratic global law may be the dream of corporate chief executive officers, "he states, "but it would be a disaster for the rest of the world with its ratcheting downwards of workers, consumer, and environmental standards" (Nader, pp. 2-3).

As more and more children are moved into slave labor and farmers are forced off their lands, we find the break-up of families and the destruction of social stability. The structure which the GATT is managing to create will remove two billion people from former jobs and force them to migrate. Sir James Goldsmith predicts that GATT will create mass migrations of refugees on a scale a thousand times greater than the two million people forced to flee the tragic events in Rwanda: "We will have profoundly and tragically destabilized the world's population" (p. 39).

Corporate profits, not political ideologies have become the defining principle of the present era. When Third World nations threaten the economic interests of Western corporations, they inevitably find themselves caught up in war.

"Desert Storm," the American war against Iraq, was openly justified in terms of Western oil interests. Many of the nations of Africa have been fighting "civil wars" for thirty years, wars which were either fomented, maintained, or expanded through the intervention of foreign interests. Such foreign interests in Africa's internal affairs can be found in Angola, Mozambique, Ethiopia, Somalia, Zaire, Rwanda and the Western Sahara. Since 1975, American high technology weapons have targeted the nomadic peoples of the Western Sahara in order to save a monarchy and a phosphate monopoly. The result has been the killing of thousands of people and the creation of hoards of refugees.

A residential neighborhood in Basra, Iraq destroyed by the U.S. bombing campaign during the Persian Gulf War which was about the control of Middle East oil resouces.

The troubled political history of Zaire provides an excellent example of how foreign corporations and the IMF can conspire with local military leaders to subvert the national interest. Zaire has a rich agricultural base and vast mineral deposits, including one-fourth of all the world's diamonds and large supplies of copper and zinc. Most of its minerals are concentrated in the area of Shaba, formally known as Katanga province. Following independence from Belgium in the early 1960s, western corporate interests and local business men soon conspired with Shaba military leaders to secede from the Congo Republic and declare independence. "These Europeans and American advisors feared that the central government might try to nationalize mineral resources, and they hoped to secure continued Western ownership of the minerals through an alliance with an independent Shaba" (Kwitny, p. 13).

However, when Patrice Lumumba, the first Prime Minister of the newly independent Congo Republic, (now Zaire) made it clear that he did not intend to become a puppet of foreign interests, his fate was sealed. The same foreign investors who had urged rebellion in Shaba now shifted their support to a united Zaire under a hand-picked pro-Western leadership. Because such a newly constituted union would be more beneficial to foreign economic interests, it was necessary to quell the rebellion in Shaba. Western interests quickly searched for a cooperative military leader to replace Lumumba. Colonel Mobutu Sese Seko, Chief of Staff of the Zairian army, was a pro-Western leader who had demonstrated his hostility to Lumumba. A Mobutu-led government would prevent the nationalization of Shaba's mineral resources while supporting America's broader strategic interests.

On September 14, 1960, the coup took place. "Two State Department officials who worked intensely in Congo-Zaire policy have said that the U.S. designed the September 14 coup and selected Mobutu for the job" (Kwitny, p. 66). After the coup, the U.S. urged Mobutu to create the facade of a parliamentary government, and Mobutu publicly announced that he would retain control over the government only until January 1, 1961, at which time democratic elections would be held. Mobutu, himself, was not eligible to become prime minister because he had never been elected to parliament or any other elective office. But Mobutu never held the promised elections and over the next several years he controlled a series of interim prime ministers, each of whom acknowledged the real power behind the government—Mobutu and his cohort Colonel Leonard Mulamba. In 1965, Mobutu, tiring of the revolving prime ministers, created another coup d'etat which made Mulamba the permanent Prime Minister and himself Head of State.

Yet, in spite of Mobutu's heavy-handed control of government, armed conflict continued in Shaba. One rebellion broke out in 1977 and another in 1978. These rebellions were put down with the aid of French and Belgian paratroopers, using U.S. military transportation and logistical support. It was also in 1978 that an IMF team arrived in Zaire, establishing its quarters in Zaire's central bank. The IMF became a mini-government, dispatched to Zaire by the U.S. and Western Europe to run Zaire's economy during Mobutu's dictatorial rule.

"The IMF operates such mini-governments in about forty countries" (Kwitney, p. 15). Indeed, this pattern under which foreign parties either create civil wars or provide support for military governments to advance their own interests can be found around the world. "Under the U.S. Military Assistance Program (MAP) and the International Military Education and Training Program (IMET), the Fijian, Papua New Guinean, and Tongan militaries are being prepared for their role in international defense, that is, how to wage war efficiently on their own people to facilitate a more intensified process of capitalist accumulation" (Duratalo, p. 214). For example, when the people of Bougainville rebelled against Papua New Guinea because of the misuse of their land by foreign firms, the Papua New Guinea government, with foreign military aid, crushed the Bougainville rebels.

Western nations seeking to open up new markets in Eastern Europe helped to stimulate the dismemberment of Yugoslavia. The first moves were made by the German government in 1991, when it overtly and covertly conspired with ultra-right wing nationalist forces in Croatia and Slovenia to break away from the Socialist Federation of Yugoslavia. Subsequently, Germany and other Western powers financed and armed ethnic militias in an effort to further divide Yugoslavia.

Within the Third World, the new colonialism, like the old, works with the military to suppress dissident groups which hinder corporate interests. Using the myth of economic aid under the umbrella of the World Bank and the IMF, Western nations have brought the Third World and former Eastern Block countries under their control. When local protest and armed rebellions occur, countless people are killed or turned into refugees. In a world population of 5.5 billion, roughly one in every 130 people has been forced into flight (UNHCR, I). In 1993 alone, 18.2 million people around the world were made refugees. Today, one half of the world's refugee population are located in Africa.

The citizens of the United States, Europe and the Third World can no longer accept the idea that political and economic power is to be controlled by a few. If they do not recast the world's economic system, refugee populations will continue to multiply, and few will benefit from the earth's riches, except the transnational institutions.

References

Anyadike, O. "Structural Adjustment: No light at the End of Tunnel," *Third World Resurgence: Reconquest of the South*, #28, KDN: January 1992, p. 28.
Barnet, R. J. and R. E. Muller. *Global Reach: The Power of the Multinational Corporations*. New York: Simon and Schuster, 1974.
Downing, T. E. and G. Kushner. *Human Rights and Anthropology*. Cambridge, MA: Cultural Survival Inc., 1988.
Durutalo, S. "Anthropology and Authoritarianism in the Pacific Islands,"*Confronting the Margaret Mead Legacy: Scholarship, Empire and the South Pacific*, L. Foerstel and A. Giliam, eds. Philadelphia: Temple University Press, 1992.
Eriksen, T. H. *Ethnicity and Nationalism: Anthropological Perspectives*. London: Pluto Press, 1993.
Fresia, J. *Toward an American Revolution: Exposing the Constitution and Other Illusions*. Boston: South End Press, 1988.
Goldsmith, J. *The Trap*. New York: Carroll and Graf Publishers, Inc., 1993.
Gossett, T. F. *Race: The History of an Idea in America*. New York: Schocken Books, 1973.

Hollings, E. F. *Congressional Record: Proceedings and Debate of the 103rd Congress*, Second Session, Vol. 140, #148, November 30, 1994, pp. S15084.

Horn, G. "Race Backwards: Genes, Violence, Race, and Genocide,"*Covert Action Quarterly*, 43 (Winter 1992-93).

Krauthammer, C. "General Gephardt's Class War,"*Washington Post*, December 23, 1994: A15.

Kwitny, J. *Endless Enemies*. New York: Congdon and Weed, 1984.

Rich, B. "50 years of World Bank Outrages,"*Third World Resurgence*, 49 (January 1994), p. 25.

Lane, C. "The Tainted Sources of *The Bell Curve*," *The New York Review of Books*, December 1, 1994.

Metzenbaum, H. M. *Congressional Record: Proceedings and Debate of the 103rd Congress*, Second Session, Vol. 140, #148, November 30, 1994, p. 5 15086.

Nader, R. "Introduction: Free Trade and the Decline of Democracy,"*The Case Against Free Trade: GATT, NAFTA, and the Globalization of Corporate Power*. Ralph Nader, William Greider, and Margaret Atwood, eds. San Francisco: Earth Island Press and North Atlantic Books, 1993.

United Nations High Commissioner for Refugees,*The State of the World's Refugees: The Challenge of Protection*, 1993, p. 1.

Ward Churchill

Like Sand in the Wind:
The Making of an American Indian
Diaspora in the United States

> They are going away! With a visible reluctance which nothing has overcome but the stern necessity they feel impelling them, they have looked their last upon the graves of their sires—the scenes of their youth, and have taken up the slow toilsome march with their household goods among them to their new homes in a strange land. They leave names to many of our rivers, towns, and counties, and so long as our State remains the Choctaws who once owned most of her soil will be remembered.
>
> —*Vicksburg Daily Sentinel*
> February 25, 1832

> We told them that we would rather die than leave our lands; but we could not help ourselves. They took us down. Many died on the road. Two of my children died. After we reached the new land, all my horses died. The water was very bad. All our cattle died; not one was left. I stayed till one hundred and fifty-eight of my people had died. Then I ran away.
>
> —Standing Bear
> January 1876

Within the arena of Diaspora Studies, the question of whether the field's analytical techniques might be usefully applied to the indigenous population of the United States is seldom raised. In large part, this appears to be due to an unstated presumption on the part of diaspora scholars that because the vast bulk of the native people of the U.S. remain inside the borders of that nation-state, no population dispersal comparable to that experienced by Afroamericans, Asian Americans, Latinos—or, for that matter, Euroamericans—is at issue. Upon even minimal reflection, however, the fallacy imbedded at the core of any such premise is quickly revealed.

To say that a Cherokee remains essentially "at home" so long as s/he resides within the continental territoriality claimed by the U.S. is equivalent to arguing that a Swede displaced to Italy, or a Vietnamese refugee in Korea, would be at home simply because they remain in Europe or Asia. Native Americans, no less than other peoples, can and should be understood as identified with the specific geographical settings by which they came to identify themselves as peoples. Mohawks are native to the upstate New York/southern Québec region, not Florida or California. Chiricahua Apaches are indigenous to southern Arizona and northern Sonora, not Oklahoma or Oregon. The matter is not only cultural, although the dimension of culture is crucially important, but political and economic as well.

Struggles by native peoples to retain use and occupancy rights over their traditional territories, and Euroamerican efforts to supplant them, comprise the virtual entirety of U.S./Indian relations since the inception of the republic. All forty of the so-called "Indian Wars" recorded by the federal government were fought over land.[1] On more than 370 separate occasions between 1778 and 1871, the Senate of the United States ratified treaties with one or more indigenous peoples by which the latter ceded portions of their landbase to the U.S. In every instance, a fundamental *quid pro quo* was arrived at: Each indigenous nation formally recognized as such through a treaty ratification was simultaneously acknowledged as retaining a clearly demarcated national homeland within which it might maintain its sociopolitical cohesion and from which it could draw perpetual sustenance, both spiritually and materially.[2]

At least five succeeding generations of American Indians fought, suffered and died to preserve their peoples' residency in the portions of North America which had been theirs since "time immemorial." In this sense, the fundamental importance they attached to continuing their linkages to these areas seems unquestionable. By the same token, the extent to which their descendants have been dislocated from these defined, or definable, landbases is the extent to which it can be observed that the conditions of diaspora have been imposed upon the population of Native North America. In this respect, the situation is so unequivocal that a mere sample of statistics deriving from recent census data will be sufficient to tell the tale:

By 1980, nearly half of all federally-recognized American Indians lived in off-reservation locales, mostly cities. The largest concentration of indigenous people in the country—90,689—was in the Los Angeles Metro Area.[3] By 1990, the proportion of urban-based Indians is estimated to have swelled to approximately fifty-five percent.[4]

All federally-unrecognized Indians—a figure which may run several times that of the approximately 1.6 million the U.S. officially admits still exist within its borders—are effectively landless and scattered everywhere across the country.[5]

Texas, the coast of which was once one of the more populous locales for indigenous people, reported a reservation-based Native American population of 859 in 1980.[6] The total Indian population of Texas was reported as being 39,740.[7] Even if this number were included only members of peoples native to the area (which it does not), it would still represent a reduction from about 1.5 million at the point of first contact with Europeans.[8]

A veritable vacuum in terms of American Indian reservations and population is now evidenced in most of the area east of the Mississippi River, another region once densely populated by indigenous people. Delaware, Illinois, Indiana, Kentucky, Maryland, New Hampshire, New Jersey, Ohio, Pennsylvania, Rhode Island, Tennessee, Vermont, Virginia, West Virginia show no reservations at all.[9] The total Indian population reported in Vermont in 1980 was 968. In New Hampshire, the figure was 1,297. In Delaware, it was 1,307; in West Virginia, 1,555. The reality is that a greater number of persons indigenous to the North American mainland now live in Hawaii, far out in the Pacific Ocean, than in any of these easterly states.[10]

The ways in which such deformities in the distribution of indigenous population in the U.S. have come to pass were anything but natural. To the contrary, the major causative factors have consistently derived from a series of official policies implemented over more than two centuries by the federal government of the United States. These have ranged from forced removal during the 1830s, to concentration and compulsory assimilation during the 1880s, to coerced relocation beginning in the late 1940s. Interspersed through it all have been periods of outright liquidation and dissolution, continuing into the present moment. The purpose of this essay is to explore these policies and their effects on the peoples targeted for such exercises in "social engineering."

The Postrevolutionary Period

During the period immediately following the American Revolution, the newly formed United States was in a "desperate financial plight . . . [and] saw its salvation in the sale to settlers and land companies of western lands" lying outside the original thirteen colonies.[11] Indeed, the revolution had been fought in significant part in order to negate George III's Proclamation of 1763, an edict restricting land acquisition by British subjects to the area east of the Appalachian Mountains and thereby voiding certain speculative real estate interests held by the U.S. Founding Fathers. During the war, loyalty of rank-and-file soldiers, as well as major creditors, had been maintained through warrants advanced by the Continental Congress with the promise that rebel debts would be retired through issuance of deeds to parcels of Indian land once the revolution had succeeded.[12] A substantial problem for the fledgling republic was that in the immediate aftermath, it possessed neither the legal nor the physical means to carry through on such commitments.

In the Treaty of Paris, signed on September 3, 1783, England quit-claimed its rights to all present U.S. territory east of the Mississippi. Contrary to subsequent Americana, this action conveyed no bona fide title to any of the Indian lands lying within the area.[13] Rather, it opened the way for the United States to replace Great Britain as the sole entity entitled under prevailing international law to *acquire* Indian land in the region through negotiation and purchase.[14] The U.S.—already an outlaw state by virtue of its armed rejection of lawful Crown authority—appears to have been emotionally prepared to seize native property through main force, thereby continuing its initial posture of gross illegality.[15] Confronted by the incipient indigenous alliance espoused by Tecumseh in the Ohio River Valley (known at the time as the "Northwest Territory") and to the south by the powerful Creek and Cherokee confederations, however, the U.S. found itself militarily stalemated all along its western frontier.[16]

The Indian position was considerably reinforced when England went back on certain provisions of the Treaty of Paris, refusing to abandon a line of military installations along the Ohio until the U.S. showed itself willing to comply with minimum standards of international legalism, "acknowledging the Indian right in the soil" long since recognized under the Doctrine of Discovery.[17] To the south, Spanish Florida also aligned itself with native nations as a means of holding the rapacious settler population of neighboring Georgia in check.[18] Frustrated, federal authorities had to content themselves with the final dispossession and banishment of such peoples as the Huron (Wyandot) and Delaware (Lenni Lanape)—whose homelands fell within the original colonies, and who had been much weakened by more than a century of warfare—to points beyond the 1763 demarcation line. There, these early elements of a U.S.-precipitated indigenous diaspora were taken in by stronger nations such . . . as the Ottawa and Shawnee.[19]

Meanwhile, George Washington's initial vision of a rapid and wholesale expulsion of all Indians east of the Mississippi, expressed in June 1783,[20] was tempered to reflect a more sophisticated process of gradual encroachment explained by General Philip Schuyler of New York in a letter to Congress the following month:

> As our settlements approach their country, [the Indians] must, from the scarcity of game, which that approach will induce, retire farther back, and dispose of their lands, unless they dwindle to nothing, as all savages have done . . . when compelled to live in the vicinity of civilized people, and thus leave us the country without the expense of purchase, trifling as that will probably be.[21]

As Washington himself was to put it a short time later, "[P]olicy and economy point very strongly to the expediency of being on good terms with the Indians, and the propriety of purchasing their Lands in preference to attempting to drive them by force of arms out of their Country. . . . The gradual extension of our Settlements will certainly cause the Savage as the Wolf to retire. . . . In a word there is nothing to be gained by an Indian War but the Soil they live on and this can be had by purchase at less expense."[22] By 1787, the strategy had become so well-accepted that the U.S. was prepared to enact the Northwest Ordinance (1 *Stat.* 50), codifying a formal renunciation of what it had been calling its "Rights of Conquest" with respect to native peoples: "The utmost good faith shall always be observed towards the Indian; their land shall never be taken from them without their consent; and in their property, rights, and liberty, they shall never be invaded or disturbed—but laws founded in justice and humanity shall from time to time be made, for wrongs done to them, and for preserving peace and friendship with them."[23]

The Era of Removal

By the early years of the nineteenth century, the balance of power in North America had begun to shift. To a certain extent, this was due a burgeoning of the Angloamerican population, a circumstance actively fostered by government policy. In other respects, it was because of an increasing consolidation of the U.S. state and a generation-long erosion of indigenous strength resulting from the factors delineated in Schuyler's policy of gradual expansion.[24] By 1810, the government was ready to resume what Congress described as the "speedy provision of the extension of the territories of the United States" through means of outright force.[25] Already, in 1803, provision had been made through the Louisiana Purchase for the massive displacement of all eastern Indian nations into what was perceived as the "vast wasteland" west of the Mississippi.[26] The juridical groundwork was laid by the Supreme Court with Chief Justice John Marshall's opinion in *Fletcher v. Peck* (10 U.S. 87), a decision holding that the title of U.S. citizens to parcels of Indian property might be considered valid even though no Indian consent to cede the land had been obtained.[27]

With the defeat of Great Britain in the War of 1812, the subsequent defeat of Tecumseh's confederation in 1813, and General Andrew Jackson's defeat of the Creek Red Sticks in 1814, the "clearing" of the east began in earnest.[28] By 1819, the U.S. had wrested eastern Florida from Spain, consummating a process begun in 1810 with assaults upon the western ("panhandle") portion of the territory.[29] Simultaneously, the first of a pair of "Seminole Wars" was begun on the Florida peninsula to subdue an amalgamation of resident Miccosukees, "recalcitrant" Creek refugees, and runaway chattel slaves naturalized as free citizens of the indigenous nations.[30] In 1823, John Marshall reinforced the embryonic position articulated in *Peck* with *Johnson v. McIntosh* (21 U.S. 98 Wheat. 543), an opinion inverting conventional understandings of indigenous status in international law by holding that U.S. sovereignty superseded that of native nations, even within their own territories. During the same year, President James Monroe promulgated his doctrine professing a unilateral U.S. "right" to circumscribe the sovereignty all other nations in the hemisphere.[31]

In this environment, a tentative policy of Indian "removal" was already underway by 1824, although not codified as law until the Indian Removal Act (ch. 148, 4 *Stat.* 411) was passed in 1830. This was followed by John Marshall's opinions, rendered in *Cherokee v. Georgia* (30 U.S. (5 Pet.) 1 (1831)) and *Worcester v. Georgia* (31 U.S. (6 Pet.) 551 (1832)), that Indians comprised "domestic dependent nations," the sovereignty of which was subject to the "higher authority" of the federal government.[32] At that point, the federal program of physically relocating entire nations of people from their eastern homelands to what was then called the "Permanent Indian Territory of Oklahoma" west of the Mississippi became full-fledged and forcible.[33] The primary targets were the prosperous "Five Civilized Tribes" of the Southeast: the Cherokee, Creek, Chickasaw, Choctaw and Seminole nations. They were rounded up by troops, concentrated in camps until their numbers were sufficient to make efficient their being force-marched at bayonet-point, typically without adequate food, shelter or medical attention, often in the dead of winter, as much as 1,500 miles to their new "homelands."[34]

There were, of course, still those who attempted to mount a military resistance to what was happening. Some, like the Sauk and Fox nations of Illinois, who fought what has come to be known as the "Black Hawk War" against those dispossessing them in 1832, were simply slaughtered *en mass*.[35] Others, such as the "hard core" of Seminoles who mounted the second war bearing their name in 1835, were forced from the terrain associated with their normal way of life. Once ensconced in forbidding locales like the Everglades, they became for all practical intents and purposes invincible—one group refused to make peace with the U.S. until the early 1960s—but progressively smaller and more diffuse in their demography.[36] In any event, by 1840 removal had been mostly accomplished (although it lingered as a policy until 1855), with only "the smallest, least offensive, and most thoroughly integrated tribes escaping the pressure to clear the eastern half of the continent from its original inhabitants."[37] The results of the policy were always catastrophic for the victims. For instance, of the approximately 17,000 Cherokees subjected to the removal process, about 8,000 died of disease, exposure and malnutrition along what they called the "Trail of Tears."[38] In addition:

> The Choctaws are said to have lost fifteen percent of their population, 6,000 out of 40,000; and the Chickasaw . . . surely suffered severe losses as well. By contrast the Creeks and Seminoles are said to have suffered about 50 percent mortality. For the Creeks, this came primarily in the period immediately after removal: for example, 'of the 10,000 or more who were resettled in 1836-37 . . . an incredible 3,500 died of "bilious fevers."'[39]

Nor was this the only cost. Like the Seminoles, portions of each of the targeted peoples managed through various means to avoid removal, remaining in their original territories until their existence was once again recognized by the U.S. during the twentieth century. One consequence was a permanent sociocultural and geographic fragmentation of formerly cohesive groups; while the bulk of the identified populations of these nations now live in and around Oklahoma, smaller segments reside on the tiny "Eastern Cherokee" Reservation in North Carolina (1980 population 4,844); "Mississippi Choctaw" Reservation in Mississippi (pop. 2,756); the Miccosukee and "Big Cypress," "Hollywood" and "Brighton" Seminole Reservations in Florida (pops. 213, 351, 416 and 323, respectively).[40]

An unknown but significant number of Cherokees also went beyond Oklahoma, following their leader, Sequoia, into Mexico in order to escape the reach of the U.S. altogether.[41] This established something of a precedent for other peoples such as the Kickapoos, a small Mexican "colony" of whom persists to this day.[42] Such dispersal was compounded by the fact that throughout the removal process varying numbers of Indians escaped at numerous points along the route of march, blending into the surrounding territory and later intermarrying with the incoming settler population. By-and-large, these people have simply slipped from the historical record, their descendants today inhabiting a long arc of mixed-blood communities extending from northern Georgia and Alabama, through Tennessee and Kentucky, and into the southernmost areas of Illinois and Missouri.[43]

Worse was yet to come. At the outset of the removal era proper, Andrew Jackson—a leading proponent of the policy who had ridden into the White House on the public acclaim deriving from his role as commander of the 1814 massacre of the Redsticks at Horseshoe Bend and a subsequent slaughter of noncombatants during the First Seminole War—offered a carrot as well as the stick he used to compel tribal "cooperation."[44] In 1829, he promised the Creeks that:

> Your father has provided a country large enough for all of you, and he advises you to remove to it. There your white brothers will not trouble you; they will have no claim to the land, and you can live upon it, you and all your children, as long as the grass grows or the water runs, in peace and plenty. It will be yours forever.[45]

Jackson was, to put it bluntly, lying through his teeth. Even as he spoke, he was aware that the Mississippi, that ostensible border between the U.S. and Permanent Indian Territory proclaimed by Thomas Jefferson and others, had already been breached by the rapidly consolidating states of Louisiana, Arkansas and Missouri in the south, Iowa, Wisconsin and Minnesota in the north.[46] Nor could Jackson have been unknowing that his close friend, Senator Thomas Hart Benton of Missouri, had stipulated as early as 1825 that the Rocky Mountains rather than the Mississippi should serve as an "everlasting boundary" of the U.S.[47] By the time the bulk of removal was completed a decade later, Angloamerican settlement was reaching well into Kansas. Their cousins who had infiltrated the

Mexican province of Texas had revolted, proclaimed themselves an independent republic, and were negotiating for statehood. The eyes of empire had also settled on all of Mexico north of the Río Grande, and the British portion of Oregon as well.[48]

Peoples such as the Shawnee and Potawatomi, Lenni Lanape and Wyandot, Peoria, Sac, Fox, and Kickapoo, already removed from their eastern homelands, were again compulsorily relocated as the western Indian Territory was steadily reduced in size.[49] This time, they were mostly shifted southward into an area eventually conforming to the boundaries of the present state of Oklahoma. Ultimately, sixty-seven separate nations (or parts of nations), only six of them in truly indigenous to the land at issue, were forced into this relatively small dumping ground.[50] When Oklahoma, too, became a state in 1907, most of the territorial compartments reserved for the various Indian groups were simply dissolved. Today, although Oklahoma continues to report the second largest native population of any state, only the Osage retain a reserved landbase which is nominally their own.[51]

Subjugation in the West

The U.S. "Winning of the West" which began around 1850—that is, immediately after the northern half of Mexico was taken in a brief war of conquest—was, if anything, more brutal than the clearing of the east.[52] Most of the U.S. wars against native people were waged during the following thirty-five years under what has been termed an official "rhetoric of extermination."[53] The means employed in militarily subjugating the indigenous nations of California and southern Oregon, the Great Plains, Great Basin, and northern region of the Sonora Desert devolved upon a lengthy series of wholesale massacres. Representative of these are the slaughter of about 150 Lakotas at Blue River (Nebraska) in 1854, some five hundred Shoshones at Bear River (Idaho) in 1863, as many as 250 Cheyennes and Arapahos at Sand Creek (Colorado) in 1864, perhaps three hundred Cheyennes on the Washita River (Oklahoma) in 1868, 175 Piegan noncombatants at the Marias River (Montana) in 1870, and at least a hundred Cheyennes at Camp Robinson (Nebraska) in 1878. The parade of official atrocities was capped off by the butchery of another three hundred unarmed Lakotas at Wounded Knee (South Dakota) in 1890.[54]

Other means employed by the government to reduce its native opponents to a state of what it hoped would be abject subordination included the four-year internment of the entire Navajo (Diné) Nation in a concentration camp at the Bosque Redondo, outside Fort Sumner, New Mexico, beginning in 1864. The Diné, who had been force-marched in what they called the "Long Walk," a four hundred mile trek from their Arizona homeland. They were then held under abysmal conditions, with neither adequate food nor shelter, and died like flies. Approximately half had perished before their release in 1868.[55] Similarly, if less dramatically, food supplies were cut off to the Lakota Nation in 1877—militarily defeated the year before, the Lakotas were being held under army guard at the time—until starvation compelled its leaders to "cede" the Black Hills area to the U.S.[56] The assassination of resistance leaders such as the Lakotas' Crazy Horse (1877) and Sitting Bull (1890) was also a commonly used technique.[57] Other recalcitrant figures like Geronimo (Chiricahua) and Satanta (Kiowa) were separated from their people by being imprisoned in remote facilities like Fort Marion, Florida.[58]

In addition to these official actions, which the U.S. Census Bureau acknowledged in an 1894 summary as having caused a minimum of 45,000 native deaths, there was an even greater attrition resulting from what were described as "individual affairs."[59] These took the form of Angloamerican citizens at large killing Indians, often systematically, under a variety of quasi-official circumstances. In Dakota Territory, for example, a $200 bounty for Indian scalps was paid in the territorial capitol of Yankton during the 1860s; the local military commander, General Alfred Sully, is known to have privately contracted for a pair of Lakota skulls with which to adorn the city.[60] In Texas, first as a republic and then as a state, authorities also "placed a bounty upon the scalp of any Indian brought in to a government office—man, woman, or child, no matter what 'tribe'—no questions asked."[61] In California and Oregon, "the enormous decrease [in the native population of 1800] from about a quarter-million to less than 20,000 [in 1870 was] due chiefly to the cruelties and wholesale massacres perpetrated by the miners and early settlers."[62]

> Much of the killing in California and southern Oregon Territory resulted, directly and indirectly, from the discovery of gold in 1848 and the subsequent influx of miners and settlers. Newspaper accounts document the atrocities, as do oral histories of the California Indians today. It was not uncommon for small groups or villages to be attacked by immigrants . . . and virtually wiped out overnight.[63]

It has been estimated that Indian deaths resulting from this sort of direct violence may have run as high as a half-million by 1890.[64] All told, the indigenous population of the continental United States, which may still have been as great as two million when the country was founded, had been reduced to well under 250,000 by 1900.[65] As the noted demographer Sherburn F. Cook has observed, "The record speaks for itself. No further commentary is necessary."[66]

Under these conditions, the U.S. was able to shuffle native peoples around at will. The Northern Cheyennes and closely allied Arapahos, for instance, were shipped from their traditional territory in Montana's Powder River watershed to the reservation of their southern cousins in Oklahoma in 1877. After the Cheyenne remnants, more than a third of whom had died in barely a year of malaria and other diseases endemic to this alien environment, made a desperate attempt to return home in 1878, they were granted a reservation in the north country. But not before the bulk of them had been killed by army troops. Moreover, they were permanently separated from the Arapahos, who were "temporarily" assigned to the Wind River Reservation of their hereditary enemies, the Shoshone, in Wyoming.[67]

A faction of the Chiricahua Apaches who showed signs of continued "hostility" to U.S. domination by the 1880s were yanked from their habitat in southern Arizona and "resettled" around Fort Sill, Oklahoma.[68] Hinmaton Yalatkit (Chief Joseph) of the Nez Percé and other leaders of that people's legendary attempt to escape the army and flee to Canada were also deposited in Oklahoma, far from the Idaho valley they'd fought to retain.[69] Most of the Santee Dakotas of Minnesota's woodlands ended up on the wind-swept plains of Nebraska, while a handful of their relatives remained behind on tiny plots which are now called the "Upper" and "Lower Sioux" reservations.[70] A portion of the Oneidas, who had fought on the side of the rebels during the revolution, were moved to a small reservation near Green Bay, Wisconsin.[71] An even smaller reserve was provided in the same area for residual elements of Connecticut's Mahegans, Mohegans, and other peoples, all of them lumped together under the heading "Stockbridge-Munsee Indians."[72] On and on, it went.

Allotment and Assimilation

With the native ability to militarily resist U.S. territorial ambitions finally quelled, the government moved first to structurally negate any meaningful residue of national status on the part of indigenous peoples, and then to dissolve them altogether. The opening round of this drive came in 1871, with the attachment of a rider to the annual congressional appropriations act (ch. 120, 16 *Stat.* 544, 566) suspending any further treaty-making with Indians. This was followed, in 1885, with passage of the Major Crimes Act (ch. 341, 24 *Stat.* 362, 385), extending U.S. jurisdiction directly over reserved Indian territories for the first time. Beginning with seven felonies delineated in the initial statutory language, and combined with the Supreme Court's opinion in *U.S. v. Kagama* (118 U.S. 375 (1886)) that Congress possessed a unilateral and "incontrovertible right" to exercise its authority over Indians as it saw fit. The 1885 act opened the door to subsequent enactment of the more than five thousand federal laws presently regulating every aspect of reservation life and affairs.[73]

In 1887, Congress passed the General Allotment Act (ch. 119, 24 *Stat.* 388), a measure designed expressly to destroy what was left of the basic indigenous socioeconomic cohesion by eradicating traditional systems of collective land holding. Under provision of the statute, each Indian identified as such by demonstrating "one-half or more degree of Indian blood" was to be issued an individual deed to a specific parcel of land—160 acres per family head, eighty acres per orphan or single person over eighteen years of age, and forty acres per dependent child—within existing reservation boundaries. Each Indian was required to accept U.S. citizenship in order to receive his or her allotment. Those who refused, such as a substantial segment of the Cherokee "full-blood" population, were left landless.[74]

Generally speaking, those of mixed ancestry whose "blood quantum" fell below the required level were summarily excluded from receiving allotments. In many cases, the requirement was construed by officials as meaning that an applicant's "blood" had to have accrued from a single people; persons who whose cumulative blood quantum derived from intermarriage between several native peoples were thus often excluded as well. In other instances, arbitrary geographic criteria were also employed; all Cherokees, Creeks and Choctaws living in Arkansas, for example, were not only excluded from allotment, but permanently denied recognition as members of their respective nations.[75] Once eligible Indians had been assigned their allotments within a given reservation—all of them from the worst land available therein—the remainder of the reserved territory was declared "surplus" and opened to non-Indian homesteaders, corporate acquisition, and conversion into federal or state parks and forests.[76]

> Under the various allotment programs, the most valuable land was the first to go. Settlers went after the rich grasslands of Kansas, Nebraska, and the Dakotas; the dense black-soil forests of Minnesota and Wisconsin; and the wealthy oil and gas lands of Oklahoma. In 1887, for example, the Sisseton Sioux of South Dakota owned 918,000 acres of rich virgin land on their reservation. But since there were only two thousand of them, allotment left more than 600,000 acres for European American settlers. . . . The Chippewas of Minnesota lost their rich timber lands; once each member had claimed [their] land, the government leased the rest to timber corporations. The Colvilles of northeastern Washington lost their lands to cattlemen, who fraudulently claimed mineral rights there. In Montana and Wyoming the Crows lost more than two million acres, and the Nez Percés had to cede communal grazing ranges in Idaho. All sixty-seven of the tribes in Indian Territory underwent allotment. . . . On the Flathead Reservation [in Montana—which included Flatheads, Pend Oreilles, Kutenais, and Spokanes . . . —the federal government opened 1.1 million acres to settlers. A similar story prevailed throughout the country.[77]

By the time the allotment process had run its course in 1930, the residue of native land holdings in the U.S. had been reduced from approximately 150 million acres to less than fifty million.[78] Of this, more than two-thirds consisted of arid or semi-arid terrain deemed useless for agriculture, gazing, or other productive purposes. The remaining one-third had been leased at extraordinarily low rates to non-Indian farmers and ranchers by local Indian agents exercising "almost dictatorial powers" over remaining reservation property.[79]

Indians across the country were left in a state of extreme destitution as a result of allotment and attendant leasing practices. Worse, the situation was guaranteed to be exacerbated over succeeding generations insofar as what was left of the reservation landbase, already insufficient to support its occupants at a level of mere subsistence, could be foreseen to become steadily more so as the native population recovered from the genocide perpetrated against it during the nineteenth century.[80] A concomitant of allotment was thus an absolute certainty that ever-increasing numbers of Indians would be forced from what remained nominally their own land during the twentieth century, dispersed into the vastly more numerous American society-at-large. There, it was predictable (and often predicted) that they would be "digested," disappearing once and for all as anything distinctly Indian in terms of sociocultural, political, or even racial identity. The record shows that such outcomes were anything but unintentional.

> The purpose of all this was "assimilation," as federal policymakers described their purpose, or—to put the matter more unabashedly—to bring about the destruction and disappearance of American Indian peoples as such. In the words of Francis E. Leupp, Commissioner of Indian Affairs from 1905 through 1909. The Allotment Act in particular should be viewed as a "mighty pulverizing engine for breaking up the tribal mass" which stood in the way of complete Euroamerican hegemony in North America. Or, to quote Indian Commissioner Charles Burke a decade later, "[I]t is not desirable or consistent with the general welfare to promote tribal characteristics and organization."[81]

The official stance was consecrated in the Supreme Court's determination in the 1903 *Lonewolf v. Hitchcock* decision (187 U.S. 553)—extended from John Marshall's "domestic dependent nations" thesis of the early 1830s—that the U.S. possessed "plenary" (full) power over all matters involving Indian affairs. In part, this meant the federal government was unilaterally assigning itself perpetual "trust" prerogatives to administer or dispose of native assets, whether these were vested in land, minerals, cash, or any other medium, regardless of Indian needs or desires.[82] Congress then consolidated its position with passage of the 1906 Burke Act (34 *Stat*. 182), designating the Secretary of Interior as permanent trustee over Indian Country. In 1924, a number of lose ends were cleaned up with passage of the Indian Citizenship Act (ch. 233, 43 *Stat*. 25) imposing U.S. citizenship upon all native people who had not otherwise been naturalized. The law was applied across-the-board to all Indians, whether they desired citizenship or not, and thus included those who had forgone allotments rather than accept it.[83]

Meanwhile, the more physical dimensions of assimilationist policy were coupled to a process of ideological conditioning designed to render native children susceptible to dislocation and absorption by the dominant society. In the main, this assumed the form of a compulsory boarding school system administered by the Interior Department's Bureau of Indian Affairs (BIA) wherein large numbers of indigenous children were taken, often forcibly, to facilities remote from their families and communities. Once there, the youngsters were prevented from speaking their languages, practicing their religions, wearing their customary clothing or wearing their hair in traditional fashion, or in any other way overtly associating themselves with their own cultures and traditions. Instead, they were indoctrinated—typically for a decade or more—in Christian doctrine and European values such as the "work ethic." During the summers, they were frequently "farmed out" to Euroamerican "foster homes" where they were further steeped in the dominant society's views of their peoples and themselves.[83]

> Attendance was made compulsory [for all native children, aged five to eighteen] and the agent was made responsible for keeping the schools filled, by persuasion if possible, by withholding rations and annuities from the parents, and by other means if necessary. . . . [Students] who were guilty of misbehavior might either receive corporal punishment or be imprisoned in the guardhouse [a special "reform school" was established to handle "incorrigible" students who clung to their traditions]. . . . A sincere effort was made to develop the type of school that would destroy tribal ways.[84]

The intention of this was, according to federal policymakers and many of its victims alike, to create generations of American Indian youth who functioned intellectually as "little white people," facilitating the rapid dissolution of traditional native cultures desired by federal policymakers.[85] In combination with a program in which native children were put out for wholesale adoption by Euroamerican families, the effect upon indigenous peoples was devastating.[86] This systematic transfer children not only served to accelerate the outflow of Indians from reservation and reservation-adjacent settings, but the return of individuals mentally conditioned to conduct themselves as non-Indians escalated the rate at which many native societies unraveled within the reservation contexts themselves.[87]

The effects of the government's allotment and assimilation programs are reflected in the demographic shifts evidenced throughout Indian Country from 1910 through 1950. In the former year, only 0.4 percent of all identified Indians lived in urban locales. By 1930, the total had grown to 9.9 percent. As of 1950, the total had grown to 13.4 percent. Simultaneously, the displacement of native people from reservations to off-reservation rural areas was continuing apace.[88] In 1900, this involved only about 3.5 percent of all Indians. By 1930, the total had swelled to around 12.5 percent and, by 1950, it had reached nearly eighteen percent.[89] Hence, in the latter year, nearly one-third of the federally-recognized Indians in the United States had been dispersed to locales other than those the government had defined as being "theirs."

Reorganization and Colonization

It is likely, all things being equal, that the Indian policies with which the United States ushered in the twentieth century would have led inexorably to a complete eradication of the reservation system and corresponding disappearance of American Indians as distinct peoples by some point around 1950. There can be no question but that such a final consolidation of its internal landbase would have complemented the phase of transoceanic expansionism into which the U.S. entered quite unabashedly during the 1890s.[90] That things did not follow this course seems mainly due to a pair of ironies, one geological and the other unwittingly imbedded in the bizarre status of "quasi-sovereignty" increasingly imposed upon native nations by federal jurists and policymakers over the preceding hundred years.

As regards the first of these twin twists of fate, authorities were becoming increasingly aware by the late 1920s that the "worthless" residue of territory to which indigenous people were consigned was turning out to be extraordinarily endowed with mineral wealth. Already, in 1921, an exploratory team from Standard Oil had come upon what it took to be substantial fossil fuel deposits on the Navajo Reservation.[91] During the next three decades, it would be discovered just how great a proportion of U.S. "domestic" resources lay within American Indian reservations. For example:

> Western reservations in particular . . . possess vast amounts of coal, oil, shale oil, natural gas, timber, and uranium. More than 40 percent of the national reserves of low sulfur, strippable coal, 80 percent of the nation's uranium reserves, and billions of barrels of shale oil exist on reservation land. On the 15-million-acre Navajo Reservation, there are approximately 100 million barrels of oil, 25 trillion cubic feet of natural gas, 80 million pounds of uranium, and 50 billion tons of coal. The 440,000-acre Northern Cheyenne Reservation in Montana sits atop a 60-foot-thick layer of coal. In New Mexico, geologists estimate that the Jicarilla Apache Reservation possesses 2 trillion cubic feet of natural gas and as much as 154 million barrels of oil.[92]

This led directly to the second quirk. The more sophisticated federal officials, even then experiencing the results of opening up Oklahoma's lush oil fields to unrestrained corporate competition, realized the extent of the disequilibriums and inefficiencies involved in this line of action when weighed against the longer-term needs of U.S. industrial development.[93] Only by retaining its "trust authority" over reservation assets would the government be in a continuing position to dictate which resources would be exploited, in what quantities, by whom, at what cost, and for what purpose, allowing the North American political economy to evolve in ways preferred by the country's financial élite.[94] Consequently, it was quickly perceived as necessary that both Indians and Indian Country be preserved, at least to some extent, as a facade behind which the "socialistic" process of central economic planning might occur.

For the scenario to work in practice, it was vital that the reservations be made to appear "self-governing" enough to exempt themselves from the usual requirements of the U.S. "free market" system whenever this might be convenient to their federal "guardians." On the other hand, they could never become independent or autonomous enough to assume control over their own economic destinies, asserting demands that equitable royalty rates be paid for the extraction of its ores, for example, or that profiting corporations underwrite the expense of environmental clean-up once mining operations had been concluded.[95] In effect, the idea was that many indigenous nations should be maintained as outright internal colonies of the United States rather than being liquidated out-of-hand.[96] All that was needed to accomplish this was the creation of a mechanism through which the illusion of limited Indian self-rule might be extended.

The vehicle for this purpose materialized in 1934, with passage of the Indian Reorganization Act (ch. 576, 48 *Stat.* 948), or "IRA," as it is commonly known. Under provision of this statute, the traditional governing bodies of most indigenous nations were supplanted by "Tribal Councils," the structure of which were devised in Washington, D.C., functioning within parameters of formal constitutions written by BIA officials.[97] A democratic veneer was maintained by staging a referendum on each reservation prior to its being reorganized, but federal authorities simply manipulated the outcomes to achieve the desired results.[98] The newly-installed IRA councils were patterned much more closely upon the model of corporate boards than of governments, and possessed little power other than to sign-off on business agreements. Even at that, they were completely and "voluntarily" subordinated to U.S. interests: "All decisions of any consequence (in thirty-three separate areas of consideration) rendered by these 'tribal councils' were made 'subject to the approval of the Secretary of Interior or his delegate,' the Commissioner of Indian Affairs."[99]

One entirely predictable result of this arrangement has been that an inordinate amount of mining, particularly that related to "energy development," has occurred on Indian reservations since the late mid-to-late 1940s. *All* uranium mining and milling during the life of the U.S. Atomic Energy Commission's (AEC) ore buying program (1954-1981) occurred on reservation land; Anaconda's Jackpile Mine, located at the Laguna Pueblo in New Mexico, was the largest open pit uranium extraction operation in the world until it was phased out in 1979.[100] Every year, enough power is generated by Arizona's Four Corners Power Plant alone—every bit of it from coal mined at Black Mesa, on the Navajo Reservation—to light the lights of Tucson and Phoenix for two decades, and present plans include a four-fold expansion of Navajo coal production.[101] Throughout the West, the story is the same.

On the face of it, the sheer volume of resource "development" in Indian Country over the past half-century should—even under disadvantageous terms—have translated into *some* sort of "material improvement" in the lot of indigenous people. Yet the mining leases offered to selected corporations by the BIA "in behalf of" their native "wards"—and duly endorsed by the IRA councils—have consistently paid such a meager fraction of prevailing market royalty rates that no such advancement has been discernible. Probably the best terms were those obtained by the Navajo Nation in 1976, a contract paying a royalty of fifty-five cents per ton for coal; this amounted to eight percent of market price at a time when Interior Secretary Cecil Andrus admitted the *minimum* rate paid for coal mined in off-reservation settings was 12.5 percent (more typically, it was upwards of fifteen percent).[102] Simultaneously, a 17.5 cents per ton royalty was being paid for coal on the Crow Reservation in Montana, a figure which was raised to forty cents—less than half the market rate—only after years of haggling.[103] What are at issue here are not profits, but the sort of "super-profits" usually associated with U.S. domination of economies elsewhere in the world.[104]

Nor has the federally-coordinated corporate exploitation of the reservations translated into wage income for Indians. As of 1989, the government's own data indicated that reservation unemployment nation-wide still hovered in the mid-sixtieth percentile, with some locales running persistently running in the ninetieth.[105] Most steady jobs involved administering or enforcing the federal order, reservation by reservation. Such "business-related" employment as existed tended to be temporary, menial, and paid the minimum wage, a matter quite reflective of the sort of transient, extractive industry—which brings its cadre of permanent, skilled labor with it—the BIA had encouraged to set up shop in Indian Country.[106] Additionally, the impact of extensive mining and associated activities had done much to disrupt the basis for possible continuation of traditional self-sufficiency occupations, destroying considerable acreage which held potential as grazing or subsistence garden plots.[107] In this sense, U.S. governmental and corporate activities have "underdeveloped" Native North America in classic fashion.[108]

Overall, according to a federal study completed in 1988, reservation-based Indians experienced every indice of extreme impoverishment: by far the lowest annual and lifetime incomes of any North American population group, highest rate of infant mortality (7.5 times the national average), highest rates of death from plague disease, malnutrition and exposure, highest rate of teen suicide, and so on. The average life expectancy of a reservation-based Native American males is 44.6 years, that of females less than three years longer.[109] The situation is much more indicative of a Third World context than of rural areas in a country that claims to be the world's "most advanced industrial state." Indeed, the poignant observation of many Latinos regarding their relationship to the U.S., that "your wealth is our poverty," is as appropriate to the archipelago of Indian reservations in North America itself as it is to the South American continent. By any estimation, the "open veins of Native America" created by the IRA have been an incalculable boon to the maturation of the U.S. economy, while Indians continue to pay the price by living in the most grinding sort of poverty.[110]

And there is worse. One of the means used by the government to maximize corporate profits in Indian Country over the years—again rubber-stamped by the IRA councils—has been to omit clauses requiring corporate reclamation of mined lands from leasing instruments. Similarly, the cost of doing business on reservations has been pared to the bone (and profitability driven up) by simply waiving environmental protection standards in most instances.[111] Such practices have spawned ecological catastrophe in many locales. As the impact of the Four Corners plant, one of a dozen coal-fired electrical generation facilities currently "on-line" on the Navajo reservation, has been described elsewhere:

> The five units of the 2,075 megawatt power plant has been churning out city-bound electricity and local pollution since 1969. The plant burns ten tons of coal per minute—five million tons per year—spewing three hundred tons of fly-ash and other waste particulates into the air each day. The black cloud hangs over ten thousand acres of the once-pristine San Juan River Valley. The deadly plume was the only visible evidence of human enterprise as seen from the Gemini-12 satellite which photographed the earth from 150 miles in space. Less visible, but equally devastating is the fact that since 1968 the coal mining operations and power plant requirements have been extracting 2,700 gallons from the Black Mesa water table each minute—60 million gallons per year—causing extreme desertification of the area, and even the sinking of some ground by as much as twelve feet.[112]

Corporations engaged in uranium mining and milling on the Navajo Reservation and at Laguna were also absolved by the BIA of responsibility for cleaning-up upon completion of their endeavors, with the result that hundreds of tailings piles were simply abandoned during the 1970s and eighties.[113] A fine sand retaining about 75 percent of the radioactive content of the original ore, the tailings constitute a massive source of wind-blown carcinogenic/mutogenic contaminants effecting all persons and livestock residing within a wide radius of each pile.[114] Both ground and surface water has also been heavily contaminated with radioactive by-products throughout the Four Corners region.[115] In the Black Hills region, the situation is much the same.[116] At its Hanford Nuclear Weapons Facility, located on the Yakima Reservation in Washington State, the AEC itself secretly discharged some 440 billion gallons of plutonium, strontium, celsium, tritium and other high level radioactive contaminants into the local aquifer between 1955 and 1989.[117]

Given that the half-life of the substances involved is as long as 125,000 years, the magnitude of the disaster inflicted upon Native North America by IRA colonialism should not be underestimated. The Los Alamos National Scientific laboratory observed in its February 1978 *Mini-Report* that the only "solution" its staff could conceive to the problems presented by wind-blown radioactive contaminants would be "to zone the land into uranium mining and milling districts so as to forbid human habitation." Similarly:

> A National Academy of Sciences (NAS) report states bluntly that [reclamation after any sort of mining] cannot be done in areas with less than 10 inches of rainfall a year; the rainfall over most of the Navajo Nation [and many other western reservations] ranges from six to ten inches a year. The NAS suggests that such areas be spared development or honestly labeled "national sacrifice areas."[118]

Tellingly, the two areas considered most appropriate by the NAS for designation as "national sacrifices"—the Four Corners and Black Hills region—are those containing the Navajo and "Sioux Complex" of reservations, the largest remaining blocks of acknowledged Indian land and concentrations of landbased indigenous population in the U.S. For this reason, many American Indian activists have denounced both the NAS scheme, and the process of environmental destruction which led up to it, as involving not only National Sacrifice Areas, but "National Sacrifice Peoples" as well.[119] At the very least, having the last of their territory zoned "so as to forbid human habitation" would precipitate an ultimate dispersal of each impacted people, causing its disappearance as a "human group" per se.[120] As American Indian Movement leader Russell Means has put it, "It's genocide . . . no more, no less."[121]

Regardless of whether a policy of national sacrifice is ever implemented in the manner envisioned by the NAS, it seems fair to observe that the conditions of dire poverty and environmental degradation fostered on Indian reservations by IRA colonialism have contributed heavily to the making of the contemporary native diaspora in the United States. In combination with the constriction of the indigenous landbase brought about through earlier policies of removal, concentration, allotment and assimilation, they have created a strong and ever-increasing pressure upon reservation residents to "cooperate" with other modern federal programs meant to facilitate the outflow and dispersal of Indians from their residual landbase. Chief among these have been termination and relocation.

Termination and Relocation

As the IRA method of administering Indian Country took hold, the government returned to such tasks as "trimming the fat" from federal expenditures allocated to support Indians, largely through manipulation of the size and disposition of the recognized indigenous population.

> By 1940, the . . . system of colonial governance on American Indian reservations was largely in place. Only the outbreak of World War II slowed the

pace of corporate exploitation, a matter that retarded initiation of maximal 'development' activities until the early 1950s. By then, the questions concerning federal and corporate planners had become somewhat technical: what to do with those indigenous nations which had refused reorganization? How to remove the portion of Indian population on even the reorganized reservations whose sheer physical presence served as a barrier to wholesale strip mining and other profitable enterprises anticipated by the U.S. business community?[122]

The first means to this end was found in a partial resumption of nineteenth century assimilationist policies, focused this time on specific peoples, or parts of peoples, rather than upon Indians as a whole. On August 1, 1953, Congress approved House Resolution 108, a measure by which the federal legislature empowered itself to enact statutes "terminating" (i.e., withdrawing recognition from, and thus unilaterally dissolving) selected native peoples, typically those which had rejected reorganization, or who lacked the kind of resources necessitating their maintenance under the IRA.[123]

> Among the [nations] involved were the comparatively large and wealthy Menominee of Wisconsin and the Klamath of Oregon—both owners of extensive timber resources. Also passed were acts to terminate . . . the Indians of western Oregon, small Paiute bands in Utah, and the mixed-bloods of the Uintah and Ouray Reservations. Approved, too, was legislation to transfer administrative responsibility for the Alabama and Coushatta Indians to the state of Texas. . . . Early in the first session of the Eighty-Fourth Congress, bills were submitted to [terminate the] Wyandotte, Ottawa, and Peoria [nations] of Oklahoma. These were enacted early in August of 1956, a month after passage of legislation directing the Colville Confederated Tribes of Washington to come up with a termination plan of their own. . . . During the second administration of President Dwight D. Eisenhower, Congress enacted three termination bills relating to . . . the Choctaw of Oklahoma, for whom the termination process was never completed, the Catawba of South Carolina, and the Indians of the southern California *rancherias*.[124]

It is instructive that the man chosen to implement the policy was Dillon S. Myer, an Indian Commissioner whose only apparent "job qualification" was in having headed up the internment program targeting Japanese Americans during the Second World War.[125] In total, 109 indigenous nations encompassing more than 35,000 people were terminated before the liquidation process had run its course during the early 1960s.[126] Only a handful, like the Menominee and the Siletz of Oregon, were ever "reinstated."[127] Suddenly landless, mostly poor and largely unemployed, those who were not terminated mostly scattered like sand in the wind.[128] Even as they went, they were joined by a rapidly swelling exodus of people from unterminated reservations, a circumstance fostered by yet another federal program.

Passed in 1956, the "Relocation Act" (P.L. 959) was extended in the face of a steady diminishment throughout the first half of the decade in federal allocations to provide assistance to people living on reservations. The statute provided funding to underwrite the expenses of any Indian agreeing to move to an urban area, establish a residence, and undergo a brief period of job training. The *quid pro quo* was that each person applying for such relocation was required to sign an agreement that s/he would never return to his or her reservation to live. It was also specified that all federal support would be withdrawn after relocatees had spent a short period —often no more than six weeks—"adjusting" to city life.[129] Under the conditions of near-starvation on many reservations, there were many takers; nearly 35,000 people signed up to move to places like Los Angeles, Minneapolis, San Francisco, Chicago, Denver, Phoenix, Seattle and Boston during the period 1957-1959 alone.[130]

Although there was ample early indication that relocation was bearing disastrous fruit for those who underwent it—all that was happening was that relocatees were exchanging the familiar squalor of reservation life for that of the alien Indian ghettos that shortly emerged in most major cities—the government accelerated the program during the 1960s. Under the impact of termination and relocation during the fifties, the proportion of native people who had been "urbanized" rose dramatically, from 13.5 percent at the beginning of the decade to 27.9 percent at the end. During the sixties, relocation alone drove the figure upwards to 44.5 percent. During the 1970s, as the program began to be phased out, the rate of Indian urbanization decreased sharply, with the result that the proportion had risen to "only" forty-nine percent by 1980.[131] Even without a formal federal relocation effort on a national scale, the momentum of what had been set in motion over an entire generation carried the number into the mid-fiftieth percentile by 1990, and there is no firm indication the trend is abating.[132]

Despite much protestation to the contrary, those who "migrated" to the cities under the auspices of termination and relocation have already begun to join the legions of others, no longer recognized as Indians even by other Indians, who were previously discarded and forgotten along the tortuous route from 1776 to the present.[133] Cut off irrevocably from the centers of their sociocultural existence, they have increasingly adopted arbitrary and abstract methods to signify their "Indianness." Federally-sanctioned "Certificates of Tribal Enrollment" have come to replace tangible participation in the political life of their nations as emblems of membership. Federally-issued "Certificates of Degree of Indian Blood" have replaced discernible commitment to Indian interests as the ultimate determinant of identity.[134] In the end, by embracing such "standards," Indians are left knowing no more of being Indian than do non-Indians. The process is a cultural form of what, in the physical arena, has been termed "autogenocide."[135]

Conclusion

The Indian policies undertaken by the United States during the two centuries since its inception appear on the surface to have been varied, even at times contradictory. Openly genocidal at times, they have more often been Elli Sirmopoulou, Elli Sirmopoulou, garbed, however thinly, in the attire of "humanitarianism." In fact, as the matter was put by Alexis de Tocqueville, the great French commentator on the early American experience, it would occasionally have been "impossible to destroy men with more respect to the laws of humanity."[136] Always, however, there was an underlying consistency in the sentiments which begat policy: to bring about the total dispossession and disappearance of North America's indigenous population. It was this fundamental coherence in U.S. aims, invariably denied by responsible scholars and officials alike, which caused Adolf Hitler to ground his own notions of *lebensraumpolitik* ("politics of living space") in the U.S. example.[137]

> Neither Spain nor Britain should be the models of German expansion, but the Nordics of North America, who had ruthlessly pushed aside an inferior race to win for themselves soil and territory for the future. To undertake this essential task, sometimes difficult, always cruel—this was Hitler's version of the White Man's Burden.[138]

As early as 1784, A British observer remarked that the intent of the fledgling United States with regard to American Indians was that of "extirpating them totally from the face of the earth, men, women and children."[139] In 1825, Secretary of State Henry Clay opined that U.S. Indian policy should be predicated in a presumption that the "Indian race" was "destined to extinction" in the face of persistent expansion by "superior" Anglo-Saxon "civilization."[140] During the 1870s, General of the Army Phil Sheridan is known to have called repeatedly for the "complete extermination" of targeted native groups as a means of making the West safe for repopulation by Euroamericans.[141] Subsequent assimilationists demanded the disappearance of any survivors through cultural and genetic absorption by their conquerors.[142] Well into the twentieth century, Euroamerica as a whole typically referred—often hopefully—to indigenous people as "the vanishing race," decimated and ultimately subsumed by the far greater number of invaders who had moved in upon their land.[143]

Many of the worst U.S. practices associated with these sensibilities have long since been suspended (arguably, because their goals were accomplished). Yet, large-scale and deliberate dislocation of native people from their land is anything but an historical relic. Probably the most prominent current example is that of the Big Mountain Diné, the largest remaining enclave of traditionally-oriented Indians in the United States. Situated astride an estimated twenty-four billion tons of the most accessible low sulfur coal in North America, the entire 13,000 person population of the Big Mountain area are even now being forcibly expelled to make way for the Peabody corporation's massive shovels. There being no place left on the remainder of the Navajo Reservation in which to accommodate their sheep-herding way of life, the refugees, many of them elderly, are being "resettled" in off-reservation towns like Flagstaff, Arizona.[144] Some have been sent to Phoenix, Denver, and Los Angeles. All suffer extreme trauma and other maladies resulting from the destruction of their community and consequent "transition."[145]

Another salient illustration is that of the Western Shoshone. Mostly resident to a vast expanse of the Nevada desert secured by the ancestors in the 1863 Treaty of Ruby Valley, the Shoshones have suffered the fate of becoming the "most bombed nation on earth" by virtue of the U.S. having located the majority of its nuclear weapons testing facilities in the southern portion of their homeland since 1950. During the late seventies, despite its being unable to demonstrate that it had ever acquired valid title to the territory the Shoshones call Newe Segobia, the government began to move into the northern area as well, stating an intent to construct the MX missile system there. While the MX plan has by now been dropped, the Shoshones are still being pushed off their land, "freeing" it for use in such endeavors as nuclear waste dumps like the one scheduled to be built at Yucca Mountain over the next few years.[146]

In Alaska, where nearly two hundred indigenous peoples were instantly converted into "village corporations" by the 1971 Alaska Native Claims Settlement Act (85 *Stat.* 688), there is a distinct possibility that the entire native population of about 22,000 will be displaced by the demands of tourism, North Slope oil extraction, and other "developmental" enterprises by some point early in the next century. Already, their landbase has been constricted to a complex of tiny "townships" and their traditional economy mostly eradicated by the impacts of commercial fishing, whaling, and sealing, as well as the effects of increasing Arctic industrialization on region caribou herds and other game animals.[147] Moreover, there is a plan—apparently conceived in all seriousness—to divert the water flow of the Yukon River southward all the way to the Río Grande, an expedient to supporting continued non-Indian population growth in the arid regions of the "lower forty-eight" states and creating the agribusiness complex in the northern Mexican provinces of Sonora and Chihuahua envisioned in a "free trade agreement" recently enacted by the Clinton administration.[148] It seems certain that no traditional indigenous society can be expected to stand up against such an environmental onslaught.

Eventually, if such processes are allowed to run their course, the probability is that a "Final Solution of the Indian Question" will be achieved. The key to this will rest, not in an official return to the pattern of nineteenth century massacres or emergence of some Auschwitz-style extermination center, but in the erosion of sociocultural integrity and confusion of identity afflicting any people subjected to conditions of diaspora. Like water flowing from a leaking bucket, the last self-consciously Indian people will pass into oblivion silently, unnoticed and unremarked. The deaths of cultures destroyed by such means usually occur in this fashion, with a faint whimper rather than resistance and screams of agony.

There are, perhaps, glimmers of hope flickering upon the horizon. One of the more promising is the incipient International Convention on the Rights of Indigenous Peoples. Drafted over the past decade by the United Nations Working Group on Indigenous Populations, the instrument is due for submission to the General Assembly during the summer of 1996. When it is ratified by the latter body—on the 504th anniversary of the Columbian expedition which unleashed the forces discussed herein—the Convention will at last extend to native peoples the essential international legal protections enjoyed by their colonizers the world over.[149] Should it be adhered to by this "nation of laws," the instrument will effectively bar the United States from completing its quietly ongoing drive to obliterate the remains of Native North America. If not—and the U.S. has historically demonstrated a truly remarkable tendency to simply ignore those elements of international legality it finds inconvenient—the future of American Indians looks exceedingly grim.[150]

Notes

1. U.S. Bureau of the Census, *Report on Indians Taxed and Indians Not Taxed in the United States (except Alaska) at the Eleventh United States Census: 1890* (Washington, D.C.: U.S. Government Printing Office, 1894, pp. 637-8).

2. Texts of 371 ratified treaties may be found in Charles J. Kappler, comp.,*Indian Treaties, 1778-1883* (New York: Interland Publishing Co., [2nd ed.] 1973).

3. U.S. Bureau of the Census, *1980 Census of the Population, Vol. I: Characteristics of the Population*, Table 69, "Persons by Race and Sex for Areas and Places: 1980" (Washington, D.C.: U.S. Government Printing Office, 1983, pp. 201-12).

4. National Congress of the American Indian (NCAI) Briefing Paper (Washington, D.C.: NCAI, April 1991).

5. See Jack D. Forbes, "Undercounting Native Americans: The 1980 Census and Manipulation of Racial Identity in the United States,"*Wicazo Sa Review*, Vol. VI, No. 1, Spring 1990, pp. 2-26.

6. U.S. Bureau of the Census, *1980 Census of the Population, Supplementary Report: American Indian Areas and Alaska Native Villages, 1980* (Washington, D.C.: U.S. Government Printing Office, PC80-S1-13, 1984, p. 24).

7. *Ibid.*, Table I, p. 14.

8. Henry F. Dobyns, *Their Numbers Become Thinned: Native American Population Dynamics in Eastern North America* (Knoxville: University of Tennessee Press, 1983, p. 41).

9. Francis Paul Prucha, *Atlas of American Indian Affairs* (Lincoln: University of Nebraska Press, 1990, pp. 151-7).

10. *1980 Census of the Population, Supplementary Report*, Table I,*op. cit.* The American Indian population reported for Hawaii in 1980 was 2,655.

11. Reginald Horseman, *Expansion and American Indian Policy, 1783-1812*(Ann Arbor: University of Michigan Press, 1967, pp. 6-7).
12. See Thomas Perkins Abernathy, *Western Lands and the American Revolution* (Albuquerque: University of New Mexico Press, 1979).
13. The complete text of the 1783 Treaty of Paris may be found in Hunter Miller, ed., *Treaties and Other International Acts of the United States of America*(Washington, D.C.: U.S. Government Printing Office, 1931, pp. 151-7).
14. This interpretation corresponds to conventional understandings of contemporaneous international law ("Discovery Doctrine"). See Robert A. Williams, Jr.*The American Indian in Western Legal Thought: The Discourses of Conquest*(London/New York: Oxford University Press, 1990).
15. Reflections on initial U.S. stature as a legal pariah are more fully developed in Vine Deloria, Jr., "Sovereignty," in Roxanne Dunbar Ortiz and Larry Emerson, eds.*Economic Development in American Indian Reservations*(Albuquerque: Native American Studies Center, University of New Mexico, 1979).
16. On the Northwest Territory, see Randolph C. Downes, *Council Fires on the Upper Ohio: A Narrative of Indian Affairs on the Upper Ohio until 1795* (Pittsburgh: University of Pittsburgh Press, 1940). On the situation further south, see R. S. Cotterill,*The Southern Indians: The Story of the Five Civilized Tribes Before Removal* (Norman: University of Oklahoma Press, 1954).
17. A. L. Burt, *The United States, Great Britain, and British North America, from the Revolution to the Establishment of Peace after the War of 1812*(New Haven, CT: Yale University Press, 1940, pp. 82-105).
18. Arthur P. Whitaker, *The Spanish-American Frontier, 1783-1795*(Boston: ???, 1927). Also see John W. Caughey,*McGillivray of the Creeks*(Norman: University of Oklahoma Press, 1938).
19. David R. Edmunds, *Tecumseh and the Quest for American Indian Leadership* (Boston: Little Publishers, 1984).
20. Horseman, *op. cit.*, p. 7.
21. Letter from Schuyler to Congress, July 29, 1783, in *Papers of the Continental Congress, 1774-1789* (Washington, D.C.: National Archives, Item 153, III, pp. 601-7).
22. Letter from Washington to James Duane, September 7, 1783, in John C. Fitzpatrick, ed., *The Writings of George Washington from Original Manuscript Sources, 1745-1799* (Washington, D.C.: U.S. Government Printing Office, 1931-1944, Vol. XXVII, pp. 133-40).
23. In actuality, legitimate Conquest Rights never had bearing on the U.S. relationship to indigenous nations, exercise of such rights being restricted to the very confined parameters of what was at the time defined as being prosecution of a "Just War." For details, see Williams, *op. cit.*
24. For analysis, see Bernard W. Sheehan,*Seeds of Extinction: Jeffersonian Philanthropy and the American Indian* (Chapel Hill: University of North Carolina Press, 1973).
25. Quoted from "Report and Resolutions of October 15, 1783,"*Journals of the Continental Congress, Vol. XXV* (Washington, D.C.: U.S. Government Printing Office, no date, pp. 681-93).
26. The idea accords quite perfectly with George Washington's notion that all eastern Indians should be pushed into the "illimitable regions of the West," meaning what was then Spanish territory beyond the Mississippi (letter from Washington to Congress, June 17, 1783, in Fitzpatrick, *op. cit.*, pp. 17-8). In reality, however, the U.S. understood that it possessed no lawful right to unilaterally dispose of the territory in question in this or any other fashion. In purchasing the rights of France (which had gained them from Spain in

1800) to "Louisiana" in 1803, the U.S. plainly acknowledged indigenous land title in its pledge to Napoleon Bonaparte that it would respect native "enjoyment of their liberty, property and religion they profess." Hence, the U.S. admitted it was not purchasing land from France, but rather a monopolistic French right within the region to acquire title over specific areas through the negotiated consent of individual Indian nations.

27. Further elaboration on the implications of the cases mentioned herein may be found in Ward Churchill, "Perversions of Justice: Examining the Doctrine of U.S. Rights to Occupancy in North America," in *Struggle for the Land: Indigenous Resistance to Genocide, Ecocide and Expropriation in Contemporary North America* (Monroe, ME: Common Courage Press, 1992). It should be noted here, however, that Marshall was hardly a disinterested party in the issue he addressed in *Peck*. Both the Chief Justice and his father were holders of the deeds to 10,000 acre parcels in present-day West Virginia, awarded for services rendered during the revolution but falling within an area never ceded by its aboriginal owners. See L. Baker, *John Marshall: A Life in Law* (New York: Macmillan Publishers, 19??, p. 80).

28. On the War of 1812, see Sidney Lens, *The Forging of the American Empire* (New York: Thomas Y. Crowell Co., 1971, pp. 40-61). On Tecumseh, see John Sugden, *Tecumseh's Last Stand* (Norman: University of Oklahoma Press, 1985). On the Red Sticks, see Joel W. Martin, *Sacred Revolt: The Muskogees' Struggle for a New World* (Boston: Beacon Press, 1991).

29. C.C. Griffin, *The United States and the Disruption of the Spanish Empire, 1810-1822* (New York: Columbia University Press, 1937).

30. Edwin C. McReynolds, *The Seminoles* (Norman: University of Oklahoma Press, 1957).

31. Frederick Merk, *The Monroe Doctrine and American Expansionism* (New York: Alfred A. Knopf Publishers, 1967). Also see Albert K. Weinberg, *Manifest Destiny* (New York: Quadrangle Books, 1963, pp. 73-89).

32. This was the ultimate in playing both ends against the judicial middle. Thereafter, Indians could always be construed as sovereign for purposes of alienating their lands to the United States, thus validating U.S. title to territory it desired, but never sovereign enough to refuse federal demands. See generally, Vine Deloria, Jr., and Clifford M. Lytle, *American Indians, American Justice* (Austin: University of Texas Press, 1983).

33. See generally, Grant Foreman, *Advancing the Frontier, 1830-1860* (Norman: University of Oklahoma Press, 1933).

34. Gloria Jahoda, *The Trail of Tears: The Story of the American Indian Removals, 1813-1855* (New York: Holt, Rinehart and Winston Publishers, 1975). Also see Grant Foreman, *Indian Removal: The Immigration of the Five Civilized Tribes* (Norman: University of Oklahoma Press, 1953).

35. Driven from Illinois, the main body of Sauks were trapped and massacred—men, women and children alike—at the juncture of the Bad Axe and Mississippi Rivers in Wisconsin. See Cecil Eby, *"That Disgraceful Affair": The Black Hawk War* (New York: W. W. Norton Publishers, 1973, pp. 243-61).

36. In many ways, the Seminole "hold outs" were the best guerrilla fighters the U.S. ever faced. The commitment of 30,000 troops for several years was insufficient to subdue them. Ultimately, the U.S. broke off the conflict, which was stalemated, and in which it was costing several thousand dollars for each Indian killed. See Fairfax Downey, *Indian Wars of the United States Army, 1776-1865* (New York: Doubleday Publishers, 1963, pp. 116-7).

37. Wilcomb E. Washburn, *The Indian in America* (New York: Harper Torchbooks, 1975, p. 169).

38. Russell Thornton, "Cherokee Losses During the Trail of Tears: A New Perspective and a New Estimate," *Ethnohistory*, No. 31, 1984, pp. 289-300.

39. *Ibid.*, p. 293.

40. *1980 Census of the Population, Supplementary Report, op. cit.*

41. Duane H. King, *The Cherokee Nation: A Troubled History* (Knoxville: University of Tennessee Press, 1979, pp. 103-9).

42. Angie Debo, *A History of the Indians of the United States* (Norman: University of Oklahoma Press, 1977, p. 157).

43. Very little work has been done to document this proliferation of communities, although their existence has been increasingly admitted since the 1960s.

44. Marquis James, *Andrew Jackson: Border Ruffian* (New York: Grossett and Dunlap Publishers, 1933). Jackson's stated goal was not simply to defeat the Red Sticks, but to "exterminate" them. At least 557 Indians, many of them noncombatants, were killed after being surrounded at the Horseshoe Bend of the Tallapoosa River, in northern Alabama.

45. The text of Jackson's talk of March 23, 1829 was originally published in *Documents and Proceedings relating to the Formation and Progress of a Board in the City of New York, for the Emigration, Preservation, and Improvement of the Aborigines of America* (New York: Indian Board for the Emigration, Preservation and Improvement of the Aborigines of America, 1829, p. 5).

46. Frederick Merk, *Manifest Destiny and Mission in American History* (New York: Alfred A. Knopf Publisher, 1963).

47. Quoted in Lens, *op. cit.*, p. 100.

48. Actually, this transcontinental gallop represents a rather reserved script. As early as 1820, Luis de Onis, former Spanish governor of Florida, observed that, "The Americans . . . believe that their dominion is destined to extend, now to the Isthmus of Panama, and hereafter over all the regions of the New World. . . . They consider themselves superior to the rest of mankind, and look upon their republic as the only establishment upon earth founded on a grand and solid basis, embellished by wisdom, and destined one day to become the sublime colossus of human power, and the wonder of the universe (quoted in Lens, *op. cit.*, pp. 94-5). It is a matter of record that William Henry Seward, Secretary of State under Lincoln and Johnson in the 1860s, advanced a serious plan to annex all of Canada west of Ontario, but was ultimately forced to content himself with acquiring Alaska Territory. See R. W. Van Alstyne, *The Rising American Empire* (London/New York: Oxford University Press, 1960).

49. A map delineating the "permanent" territories assigned these peoples after removal is contained in Jack D. Forbes, *Atlas of Native History* (Davis, CA: D-Q University Press, no date).

50. The federal government recognizes less than half (32) of these nations as still existing; see John W. Morris, Charles R. Goins, and Edward C. McReynolds, *Historical Atlas of Oklahoma* (Norman: University of Oklahoma Press, [3rd ed.] 1986, Map 76).

51. According to *1980 Census of the Population, Supplementary Report* (Table I, *op. cit.*) Oklahoma's Indian population of 169,292 is second only to California's 198,275. The Osage Reservation evidences a population of 4,749 Indians, 12.1 percent of its 39,327 total inhabitants (*ibid.*, p. 22).

52. On the War with Mexico, see George Pierce Garrison, *Westward Expansion, 1841-1850* (New York: Harper Publishers, 1937).

53. David Svaldi, *Sand Creek and the Rhetoric of Extermination: A Case-Study in Indian-White Relations*, (Washington, D.C.: University Press of America, 1989).

54. Much of this is covered in Ralph K. Andrist, *The Long Death: The Last Days of the Plains Indians* (New York: Collier Books, 1964). Also see Paul Andrew Hutton, *Phil*

Sheridan and His Army (Lincoln: University of Nebraska Press, 1985).

55. L. R. Bailey, *The Long Walk: A History of the Navajo Wars, 1846-68*(Pasadena, CA: Westernlore Publications, 1978).

56. This episode is covered adequately in Edward Lazarus,*Black Hills, White Justice: The Sioux Nation versus the United States, 1775 to the Present*(New York: Harper Collins Publishers, 1991, pp. 71-95).

57. See Robert Clark, ed., *The Killing of Chief Crazy Horse* (Lincoln: University of Nebraska Press, 1976), and the concluding chapter of Stanley Vestal's*Sitting Bull: Champion of the Sioux* (Norman: University of Oklahoma Press, 1957).

58. The imprisonment program is described in some detail in the memoirs of the commandant of Marion Prison, later superintendent of the Carlisle Indian School. See Richard Henry Pratt, *Battlefield and Classroom: Four Decades with the American Indian, 1867-1904* (New Haven, CT: Yale University Press, [reprint] 1964).

59. *Report on Indians Taxed and Indians Not Taxed*, op. cit., pp. 637-8.

60. Lazarus, op. cit., p. 29. It should be noted that, contrary to myth, scalping was a practice introduced to the Americas by Europeans, not native people. It was imported by the British—who had previously used it against the Irish—during the seventeenth century. See Nicholis P. Canny, "The Ideology of English Colonialism: From Ireland to America," *William and Mary Quarterly*, 3rd Series, XXX, 1973, pp. 575-98.

61. Lenore A. Stiffarm and Phil Lane, Jr., "The Demography of Native North America: A Question of American Indian Survival," in M. Annette Jaimes, ed.,*The State of Native America: Genocide, Colonization and Resistance* (Boston: South End Press, 1992, p. 35). It is instructive that the Texas state legislature framed its Indian policy as follows: "We recognize no title in the Indian tribes resident within the limits of the state to any portion of the soil thereof; and . . . we recognize no right of the Government of the United States to make any treaty of limits with the said Indian tribes without the consent of the Government of this state" (quoted in Washburn, op. cit., p. 174). In other words, extermination was intended to be total.

62. James M. Mooney, "Population," in Frederick W. Dodge, ed.,*Handbook of the Indians North of Mexico, Vol. 2* (Washington, D.C.: Bureau of American Ethnology, Bulletin No. 30, Smithsonian Institution, 1910, pp. 286-7).

63. Sherburn F. Cook, *The Conflict Between the California Indian and White Civilization* (Berkeley: University of California Press, 1976, pp. 282-4).

64. Russell Thornton, *American Indian Holocaust and Survival: A Population History Since 1492* (Norman: University of Oklahoma Press, 1987, p. 49).

65. Thornton (ibid.) estimates the aboriginal North American population to have been about 12.5 million, most of it within what is now the continental U.S. Dobyns (op. cit.) estimates it as having been as high as 18.5 million. Kirkpatrick Sale, in his*The Conquest of Paradise: Christopher Columbus and the Columbian Legacy* (New York: Alfred A. Knopf, 1990) splits the difference, placing the figure at 15 million. Extreme attrition due to disease and colonial warfare had already occurred prior to the American War of independence. Something on the order of two million survivors in 1776 therefore seems a reasonable estimate. Whatever the exact number in that year, it had been reduced to 237,196 according to U.S. census data for 1900. See U.S. Bureau of the Census,*Fifteenth Census of the United States, 1930: The Indian Population of the United States and Alaska*, Table 2, "Indian Population by State, 1890-1930" (Washington, D.C.: U.S. Government Printing Office, Washington, 1937, p. 3).

66. Cook, op. cit., p. 284.

67. Donald J. Berthrong, *The Cheyenne and Arapaho Ordeal: Reservation and Agency Life in the Indian Territory, 1875-1907* (Norman: University of Oklahoma Press, 1976).

Also see Mari Sandoz, *Cheyenne Autumn* (New York: Avon Books, 1964).

68. Dan L. Thrapp, *The Conquest of Apacheria* (Norman: University of Oklahoma Press, 1967).

69. Merril Beal, *I Will Fight No More Forever: Chief Joseph and the Nez Percé War* (Seattle: University of Washington Press, 1963).

70. Kenneth Carley, *The Sioux Uprising of 1862* (St. Paul: Minnesota Historical Society, 1961).

71. Edmund Wilson, *Apology to the Iroquois* (New York: Farrar, Strauss, and Cudahy Publishers, 1960).

72. As of 1980, a grand total of 582 members of these amalgamated peoples were reported as living on the Stockbridge Reservation. See *1980 Census of the Population, Supplementary Report*, Table I, op. cit.

73. The next major leap in this direction was passage of the Assimilative Crimes Act (30 *Stat.* 717) in 1898, applying state, territorial, and district criminal codes to "federal enclaves" such as Indian reservations. See generally, Robert N. Clinton, "Development of Criminal Jurisdiction on Reservations: A Journey Through a Jurisdictional Maze,"*Arizona Law Review*, Vol. 18, No. 3, 1976, pp. 503-83.

74. Overall, see Janet A. McDonnell, *The Dispossession of the American Indian, 1887-1934* (Bloomington/Indianapolis: Indiana University Press, 1991).

75. As is stated in the current procedures for enrollment provided by the Cherokee Nation of Oklahoma, "Many descendants of the Cherokee Indians can neither be certified nor qualify for tribal membership in the Cherokee Nation because their ancestors were not enrolled during the final enrollment [during allotment, 1899-1906]. Unfortunately, these ancestors did not meet the [federal] requirements for the final enrollment. The requirements at the time were . . . having a permanent residence within the Cherokee Nation (now the 14 northeastern counties of Oklahoma). If the ancestors had . . . settled in the states of Arkansas, Kansas, Missouri, or Texas, they lost their citizenship within the Cherokee Nation at that time."

76. D. S. Otis, *The Dawes Act and the Allotment of Indian Land* (Norman: University of Oklahoma Press, 1973).

77. James S. Olson and Raymond Wilson, *Native Americans in the Twentieth Century* (Urbana: University of Illinois Press, 1984, pp. 82-3).

78. Kirk Kicking Bird and Karen Ducheneaux, *One Hundred Million Acres* (New York: Macmillan Publishers, 1973).

79. The powers of individual agents in this regard accrued from an amendment (26 *Stat.* 794) made in 1891. The language describing these powers comes from Deloria and Lytle, op. cit., p. 10.

80. This is known as the "Heirship Problem," meaning that if a family head with four children began with a 160 acre parcel of marginal land in 1900, his/her heirs would each inherit forty acres somewhere around 1920. If each of these heirs, in turn, had four children, then their heirs would inherit ten acres, circa 1940. Following the same formula, their heirs would have inherited 2.5 acres each in 1960, and their heirs would have received about one-half acre each in 1980. In actuality, many twentieth century families have been much larger during the twentieth century—as is common among peoples recovering from genocide—and contemporary descendants of the original allottees often find themselves measuring their "holdings" in square inches. For a fuller discussion of the issue, and a description of the material circumstances otherwise confronting Indians during the early twentieth century, see the opening chapters of Vine Deloria, Jr., and Clifford M. Lytle, *The Nations Within: The Past and Future of American Indian Sovereignty* (New York: Pantheon Books, 1984).

81. Rebecca L. Robbins, "Self-Determination and Subordination: The Past, Present and Future of American Indian Governance," in *The State of Native America, op. cit.*, p. 93. The quote from Leupp comes from his book, *The Indian and His Problem* (New York: Charles Scribner and Sons, Publishers, 1910, p. 93); that from Burke from a letter to William Williamson on September 16, 1921 (William Williamson Papers, Box 2, File—Indian Matters, Misc., I. D. Weeks Library, University of South Dakota).

82. Among other things, the decision meant that the U.S. had decided it could unilaterally absolve itself of any obligation or responsibility it had incurred under provision of any treaty with any indigenous nation while simultaneously considering the Indians to still be bound by *their* treaty commitments. See Ann Laquer Estin, "Lonewolf v. Hitchcock: The Long Shadow," in Sandra L. Cadwallader and Vine Deloria, Jr., eds., *The Aggressions of Civilization: Federal Indian Policy Since the 1880s* (Philadelphia: Temple University Press, 1984, pp. 215-45). This was an utterly illegitimate posture under international custom and convention at the time, a matter amply reflected in contemporary international black letter law. See Sir Ian Sinclair, *The Vienna Convention on the Law of Treaties* (Manchester: Manchester University Press, [2nd ed.] 1984).

83. Much of this is covered—proudly—in Pratt, *op. cit.* Also see Estelle Fuchs and Robert J. Havighurst, *To Live on this Earth: American Indian Education* (Garden City, NY: Anchor Books, 1973).

84. Evelyn C. Adams, *American Indian Education: Government Schools and Economic Progress* (Morningside Heights, NY: King's Crown Press, 1946, pp. 55-6, 70).

85. The phrase used was picked up by the author in a 1979 conversation with Floyd Red Crow Westerman, a Sisseton Dakota who was sent to a boarding school at age six. For a broader statement of the same theme, see Vine Deloria, Jr., "Education and Imperialism," *Integrateducation*, Vol. XIX, Nos. 1-2, January 1982, pp. 58-63. For ample citation of the federal view, see J. U. Ogbu, "Cultural Discontinuities and Schooling," *Anthropology and Education Quarterly*, Vol. 12, No. 4, 1982, pp. 1-10.

86. On adoption policies, including those pertaining to so-called "blind" adoptions (where children are prevented by law from ever learning their parents' or tribe's identities), see Tillie Blackbear Walker, "American Indian Children: Foster Care and Adoptions," in U.S. Office of Education, Office of Educational Research and Development, National Institute of Education, *Conference on Educational and Occupational Needs of American Indian Women* (Washington, D.C.: U.S. Government Printing Office, 1980, pp. 185-210.

87. The entire program involving forced transfer of Indian children is contrary to Article II (d) of the United Nations 1948 Convention on Punishment and Prevention of the Crime of Genocide. See Ian Brownlie, *Basic Documents on Human Rights* (Oxford: Clarendon Press, 1994, p.3).

88. *American Indian Holocaust and Survival, op. cit.*, p. 227.

89. These estimates have been arrived at by deducting the reservation population totals from the overall census figures deployed in Prucha (*op. cit.*), and then subtracting the urban population totals used by Russell Thornton (see note 88, above).

90. The U.S., as is well known, undertook the Spanish-American War in 1898 primarily to acquire oversees colonies, notably the Philippines and Cuba (for which Puerto Rico was substituted at the last moment). It also took the opportunity to usurp the government of Hawai'i, about which it had been expressing ambitions since 1867, and to obtain a piece of Samoa in 1899. This opened the door to its assuming "protectorate" responsibility over Guam and other German colonies after World War I, and many of the Micronesian possessions of Japan after World War II. See Julius Pratt, *The Expansionists of 1898* (Baltimore: Johns Hopkins University Press, 1936). Also see Richard O'Connor, *Pacific Destiny: An Informal History of the U.S. in the Far East, 1776-1968* (Boston: Little, Brown and Co., 1969).

91. Anita Parlow, *Cry, Sacred Ground: Big Mountain, USA* (Washington, D.C.: Christic Institute, 1988, p. 30).

92. Olson and Wilson, *op. cit.*, p. 181.

93. For a good overview, see Craig H. Miner, *The Corporation and the Indian: Tribal Sovereignty and Industrial Civilization in Indian Territory, 1865-1907* (Columbia: University of Missouri Press, 1976).

94. This is brought out in thinly veiled fashion in official studies commissioned at the time. See, for example, U.S. House of Representatives, Committee of One Hundred,*The Indian Problem: Resolution of the Committee of One Hundred Appointed by the Secretary of Interior and Review of the Indian Problem* (Washington, D.C.: H. Doc. 149, Ser. 8392, 68th Cong., 1st Sess., 1925). Also see Lewis Meriam,*et al.*, *The Problem of Indian Administration* (Baltimore: Johns Hopkins University Press, 1928).

95. This was standard colonialist practice during the same period. See Mark Frank Lindsey, *The Acquisition and Government of Backward Territory in International Law*, (London: Longmans Green Publishers, 1926).

96. For what may be the first application of the term "internal colonies" to analysis of the situation of American Indians in the U.S., see Robert K. Thomas, "Colonialism: Classic and Internal," *New University Thought*, Vol. 4, No. 4, Winter 1966-67.

97. For the best account of how the IRA "package" was assembled, see the relevant chapters of *The Nations Within, op. cit.*

98. The classic example of this occurred at the Hopi Reservation, where some 85 percent of all eligible voters actively boycotted the IRA referendum in 1936. Indian Commissioner John Collier then counted these abstentions as "aye" votes, making it appear as if the Hopis had been nearly unanimous in affirming reorganization rather than overwhelmingly rejecting it. See Oliver LaFarge, *Running Narrative of the Organization of the Hopi Tribe of Indians* (unpublished manuscript in the LaFarge Collection, University of Texas at Austin). In general, the IRA referendum process was similar to—and served essentially the same purpose as—those more recently orchestrated abroad by the State Department and CIA; see Edward S. Herman and Frank Brodhead,*Demonstration Elections. U.S.-Staged Elections In the Dominican Republic, Vietnam, and El Salvador*(Boston: South End Press, 1984).

99. Robbins, *op. cit.*, p. 95.

100. See generally, Ward Churchill and Winona LaDuke, "Native North America: The Political Economy of Radioactive Colonization," in *The State of Native America*,*op. cit.*, pp. 241-66.

101. Alvin Josephy, "Murder of the Southwest," *Audubon Magazine*, September 1971, p. 42.

102. Bruce Johansen and Roberto Maestas,*Wasi'chu: The Continuing Indian Wars* (New York: Monthly Review Press, 1979, p. 162. The minimum rate was established by the Federal Coal Leasing Act of 1975, applicable everywhere in the U.S. except Indian reservations.

103. Olson and Wilson, *op. cit.*, p. 200.

104. The term "super-profits" is used in the manner defined by Richard J. Barnet and Ronald E. Müller in their*Global Reach: The Power of the Multinational Corporations* (New York: Touchstone Books, 1974).

105. U.S. Department of Interior, Bureau of Indian Affairs,*Indian Service Population and Labor Force Estimates* (Washington, D.C.: U.S. Government Printing Office, 1989). The study shows one-third of the 635,000 reservation-based Indians survey had an annual income of less than $7,000.

106. U.S. Senate, Committee on Labor and Human Resources,*Guaranteed Job*

Opportunity Act: Hearing on S. 777 (Washington, D.C.: 100th Cong., 1st Sess., 23 March 1987, Appendix A).

107. The classic image of this is that of Emma Yazzie, an elderly and very traditional Diné who subsists on her flock of sheep, standing forlornly before a gigantic Peabody coal shovel which is digging up her scrubby grazing land on Black Mesa. The coal is to produce electricity for Phoenix and Las Vegas, but Yazzie has never had electricity (or running water) in her home. She gains nothing from the enterprise. To the contrary, her very way of life is being destroyed before her eyes. See Johansen and Maestas, *op. cit.*, p. 141.

108. The term "underdevelopment" is used in the sense defined by Andre Gunder Frank in his *Capitalism and Underdevelopment in Latin America* (New York: Monthly Review Press, 1967).

109. U.S. Bureau of the Census, *A Statistical Profile of the American Indian Population* (Washington, D.C.: U.S. Government Printing Office, 1984). Also see U.S. Department of Health and Human Services, *Chart Series Book* (Washington, D.C.: Public Health Service HE20.9409.988, 1988).

110. The terminology accrues from Eduardo Galeano, *The Open Veins of Latin America: Five Centuries of the Pillage of a Continent* (New York: Monthly Review Press, 1973).

111. Thus far, the only people which has been able to turn this around have been the Northern Cheyenne, which won a 1976 lawsuit to have Class I environment protection standards applied to their reservation, thereby halting construction of two coal-fired generating plants before it began. The BIA had already waived such protections in the Cheyennes' "behalf." See Johansen and Maestas, *op. cit.*, p. 174.

112. Rex Weyler, *Blood of the Land: The U.S. Government and Corporate War Against the American Indian Movement* (New York: Everest House Publishers, 1982, pp. 154-5).

113. Tom Barry, "Bury My Lungs at Red Rock," *The Progressive*, February 1979, pp. 1979.

114. On tailings and associated problems such as radon gas emissions, see J. B. Sorenson, *Radiation Issues: Government Decision Making and Uranium Expansion in Northern New Mexico* (Albuquerque: San Juan Regional Study Group, Working Paper 14, 1978). On carcinogenic/mutogenic effects, see J. M. Samet, *et al.*, "Uranium Mining and Lung Cancer in Navajo Men," *New England Journal of Medicine*, No. 310, 1984, pp. 1481-4. Also see Harold Tso and Laura Mangum Shields, "Navajo Mining Operations: Early Hazards and Recent Interventions," *New Mexico Journal of Science*, Vol. 20, No. 1, June 1980.

115. Richard Hoppe, "A stretch of desert along Route 66—the Grants Belt—is chief locale for U.S. uranium," Engineering and Mining Journal, November 1978. Also see Nancy J. Owens, "Can Tribes Control Energy Development?" in Joseph Jorgenson, ed., *American Indians and Energy Development* (Cambridge, MA: Anthropology Resource Center, 1978).

116. Amelia Irvin, "Energy Development and the Effects of Mining on the Lakota Nation," *Journal of Ethnic Studies*, Vol. 10, No. 2, Spring 1982.

117. Elouise Schumacher, "440 billion gallons: Hanford wastes would fill 900 King Domes," *Seattle Times*, April 13, 1991.

118. Johansen and Maestas, *op. cit.*, p. 154. They are referring to Thadis Box, *et al.*, *Rehabilitation Potential for Western Coal Lands* (Cambridge, MA: Ballinger Publishing Co., 1974). The book is the published version of a study commissioned by the National Academy of Sciences and submitted to the Nixon administration in 1972.

119. Russell Means, "Fighting Words on the Future of Mother Earth," *Mother Jones*, December 1980, p. 27.

120. Bringing about the destruction of an identifiable "human racial, ethnical or racial group" as such, is and always has been the defining criterion of genocide. As the matter was framed by Raphael Lemkin, who coined the term: "Generally speaking, genocide does not necessarily mean the immediate destruction of a nation,*except when* accomplished by mass killing of all the members of a nation. It is intended rather to signify a coordinated plan of different actions aimed at destruction of the essential foundations of the life of national groups, with the aim of annihilating the groups themselves. The objective of such a plan would be disintegration of the political and social institutions, of culture, language, national feelings, religion, and the economic existence of national groups, and the destruction of personal security, liberty, health, dignity, and the lives of individuals belonging to such groups. Genocide is the destruction of the national group as an entity, and the actions involved are directed against individuals, not in their individual capacity but as members of the national group (emphasis added)"; see Raphael Lemkin, *Axis Rule in Occupied Europe* (Concord, NH: Carnegie Endowment for International Peace/Rumford Press, 1944, p. 79). The view is reflected in the 1948 Convention on Punishment and Prevention of the Crime of Genocide; see Brownlie, *op. cit.*

121. Means, *op. cit.*

122. Robbins, *op. cit.*, p. 97.

123. The complete text of House Resolution 108 appears in Part II of Edward H. Spicer's *A Short History of the United States* (New York: Van Nostrum Publishers, 1968).

124. James E. Officer, "Termination as Federal Policy: An Overview," in Kenneth R. Philp, ed., *Indian Self-Rule: First-Hand Accounts of Indian-White Relations from Roosevelt to Reagan* (Salt Lake City: Howe Brothers Publishers, 1986, p. 125).

125. Richard Drinnon, *Keeper of Concentration Camps: Dillon S. Myer and American Racism* (Berkeley: University of California Press, 1987).

126. Raymond V. Butler, "The Bureau of Indian Affairs Activities Since 1945,"*Annals of the Academy of American Academy of Political and Social Science*, No. 436, 1978, pp. 50-60. The last dissolution, that of the Oklahoma Ponca, was delayed in committee and was not consummated until 1966.

127. See generally, Nicholas Poroff, *Menominee DRUMS: Tribal Termination and Restoration, 1954-1974* (Norman: University of Oklahoma Press, 1982).

128. Oliver LaFarge, "Termination of Federal Supervision: Disintegration and the American Indian," *Annals of the American Academy of Political and Social Science*, No. 311, May 1975, pp. 56-70.

129. See generally, Donald L. Fixico, *Termination and Relocation: Federal Indian Policy, 1945-1960* (Albuquerque: University of New Mexico Press, 1986).

130. Sharon O'Brien, *American Indian Tribal Governments* (Norman: University of Oklahoma Press, 1989, p. 86).

131. U.S. Bureau of the Census, *General Social and Economic Characteristics: United States Summary* (Washington, D.C.: U.S. Government Printing Office, 1983, p. 92). Also see *American Indian Holocaust and Survival*, *op. cit.*, p. 227.

132. NCAI Briefing Paper, *op. cit.*

133. For use of the term "migration" to describe the effects of termination and relocation, see James H. Gundlach, Nelson P. Reid and Alden E. Roberts, "Native American Migration and Relocation,"*Pacific Sociological Review*, No. 21, 1978, pp. 117-27. On the "discarded and forgotten," see American Indian Policy Review Commission, Task Force Ten, *Report on Terminated and Nonfederally Recognized Tribes*(Washington, D.C.: U.S. Government Printing Office, 1976).

134. Alan L. Sokin, *The Urban American Indian* (Lexington, MA: Lexington Books, 1978).

135. The term was coined in the mid-1970s to describe the self-destructive behavior

exhibited by the Khmer Rouge regime in Kampuchea (Cambodia) in response to genocidal policies earlier extended against that country by the United States. For analysis, see Noam Chomsky and Edward S. Herman, *After the Cataclysm: Postwar Indochina and the Reconstruction of Imperial Ideology* (Boston: South End Press, 1979).

136. Alexis de Tocqueville, *Democracy in America* (New York: Harper and Row Publishers, 1966, p. 312).

137. "Hitler's concept of concentration camps as well as the practicality of genocide owed much, so he claimed, to his studies of British and United States history. He admired the camps for Boer prisoners in South Africa and for the Indians in the wild West; and often praised to his inner circle the efficiency of America's extermination—by starvation and uneven combat—of the red savages who could not be tamed by captivity." John Toland, *Adolf Hitler* (New York: Doubleday and Co., 1976, p. 802).

138. Norman Rich, *Hitler's War Aims: Ideology, the Nazi State, and the Course of Expansion* (New York: W. W. Norton Publishers, 1973, p. 8). Rich is relying primarily on the secret but nonetheless official policy position articulated by Hitler during a meeting on November 5, 1937 and recorded by his adjutant, Freidrich Hossbach. The "Hossbach Memorandum" is contained in *Trial of the Major War Criminals before the International Military Tribunal, Proceedings and Documents, Vol. 25* (Nuremberg: 1947-1949, pp. 402-6).

139. John F. D. Smyth, *A Tour of the United States of America* (London: Privately Published, 1784, p. 346).

140. Quoted in Reginald Horsman, *Race and Manifest Destiny: The Origins of Racial Anglo-Saxonism* (Cambridge, MA: Harvard University Press, 1981, p. 198).

141. See the various quotes in Hutton, *op. cit.*

142. Henry E. Fritz, *The Movement for Indian Assimilation, 1860-1890* (Philadelphia: University of Pennsylvania Press, 1963).

143. The classic articulation, of course, is Joseph K. Dixon's 1913 *The Vanishing Race*, recently reprinted by Bonanza Books, New York. An excellent examination of the phenomenon may be found in Stan Steiner's *The Vanishing White Man* (Norman: University of Oklahoma Press, 1976).

144. Parlow, *op. cit.* Also see Jerry Kammer, *The Second Long Walk: The Navajo-Hopi Land Dispute* (Albuquerque: University of New Mexico Press, 1980).

145. Thayer Scudder, et al., *No Place to Go: Effects of Compulsory Relocation on Navajos* (Philadelphia: Institute for the Study of Human Issues, 1982).

146. Dagmar Thorpe, *Newe Segobia: The Western Shoshone People and Land* (Battle Mountain, NV: Western Shoshone Sacred Lands Association, 1981). Also see Glenn T. Morris, "The Battle for Newe Segobia: The Western Shoshone Land Rights Struggle," in Ward Churchill, ed., *Critical Issues in Native North America, Vol. II* (Copenhagen: IWGIA Document 68, 1991, pp. 86-98).

147. M. C. Barry, *The Alaska Pipeline: The Politics of Oil and Native Land Claims* (Bloomington/Indianapolis: Indiana University Press, 1975). Also see Thomas R. Berger, *Village Journey: The Report of the Alaska Native Review Commission* (New York: Hill and Wang Publishers, 1985).

148. The plan is known by the title of its sponsoring organization, the North American Water and Power Association (NAWAPA). It is covered in Mark Reisner's *Cadillac Desert: The American West and Its Disappearing Water* (New York: Viking Press, New York, 1986).

149. For analysis, see S. James Anaya, "The Rights of Indigenous Peoples and International Law in Historical and Contemporary Perspective," in Robert N. Clinton, Nell Jessup Newton and Monroe E. Price, *American Indian Law: Cases and Materials*

(Charlottesville, VA: Michie Co., 1991, pp. 1257-69. Also see Glenn T. Morris, "International Law and Politics: Toward a Right to Self-Determination for Indigenous Peoples," in *The State of Native America, op. cit.*, pp. 55-86.

150. This includes a rather large array of covenants and conventions pertaining to everything from the binding effect of treaties to the Laws of War. It also includes Ronald Reagan's postulation, advanced in October 1985, that the International Court of Justice hold's no authority other than in matters of trade. A detailed examination of U.S. posturing in this regard may be found in Lawrence W. LeBlanc, *The United States and the Genocide Convention* (Durham, NC: Duke University Press, 1991).

Amartya Sen

Population: Delusion and Reality

Few issues today are as divisive as what is called the "world population problem." The International Conference on Population and Development held in Cairo in September 1994 and organized by the United Nations served to exacerbate these divisions among experts who received enormous attention and generated considerable heat in the mass media around the world. There is a danger that in the confrontation between apocalyptic pessimism, on the one hand, and a dismissive smugness, on the other, a genuine understanding of the nature of the population problem may be lost.[1]

Visions of impending doom have been increasingly aired in recent years, often presenting the population problem as a "bomb" that has been planted and is about to "go off." These catastrophic images have encouraged a tendency to search for emergency solutions which treat the people involved not as reasonable beings, allies facing a common problem, but as impulsive and uncontrolled sources of great social harm, in need of strong discipline.

Such views have received serious attention in public discussions, not just in sensational headlines in the popular press, but also in seriously argued and widely read books. One of the most influential examples was Paul Ehrlich's *The Population Bomb*, the first three sections of which are headed "Too Many People," "Too Little Food," and "A Dying Planet."[2] A more recent example of a chilling diagnosis of imminent calamity is Garrett Hardin's *Living within Limits*.[3] The arguments on which these pessimistic visions are based deserve serious scrutiny.

If the propensity to foresee impending disaster from overpopulation is strong in some circles, so is the tendency, in others, to dismiss all worries about population size. Just as alarmism builds on the recognition of a real problem and then magnifies it, complacency may also start off from a reasonable belief about the history of population problems and fail to see how they may have changed by now. It is often pointed out, for example, that the world has coped well enough with fast increases in population in the past, even though alarmists had expected otherwise. Malthus anticipated terrible disasters resulting from population growth and a consequent imbalance in "the proportion between the natural increase of population and food."[4] At a time when there were fewer than a billion people, he was quite convinced that "the period when the number of men surpass their means of subsistence has long since arrived." However, since Malthus first published his famous *Essay on Population* in 1798, the world population has grown nearly six times larger, while food output and consumption per person are considerably higher now, and there has been an unprecedented increase both in life expectancies and in general living standards.[5]

The fact that Malthus was mistaken in his diagnosis as well as his prognosis two hundred years ago does not, however, indicate that contemporary fears about population growth must be similarly erroneous. The increase in the world population has vastly accelerated over the last century. It took the world population millions of years to reach the first billion, then 123 years to get to the second, 33 years to the third, 14 years to the fourth, 13 years to the fifth billion; with a sixth billion to come, according to one UN projection, in another 11 years.[6] During the last decade, between 1980 and 1990, the number of people on earth grew by about 923 million, an increase nearly the size of the total world population in Malthus' time. Whatever may be the proper response to alarmism about the future, complacency based on past success is no response at all.

Parents and children waiting for food in Macuacua Camp for Mozambicans displaced by the prolonged drought and the Mozambican civil war (with substantial weapons support going to the rebel RENAMO from South Africa and the U.S.): Emergency food and water supplies are a first priority, but long term political and developmental solutions must also be addressed. (photo: UN 153649 / Paul Neath Hoeffel)

Immigration and Population

One current worry concerns the regional distribution of the increase in world population, about 90 percent of which is taking place in the developing countries. The percentage rate of population growth is fastest in Africa—3.1 percent per year over the last decade. But most of the large increases in population occur in regions other than Africa. The largest absolute increases in numbers are taking place in Asia, which is where most of the world's poorer people live, even though the rate of increase in population has been slowing significantly there. Of the worldwide increase of 923 million people in the 1980s, well over half occurred in Asia—517 million in fact (including 146 million in China and 166 million in India).

Beyond concerns about the well-being of these poor countries themselves, a more self-regarding worry causes panic in the richer countries of the world and has much to do with the current anxiety in the West about the "world population problem." This is founded on the belief that destitution caused by fast population growth in the third world is responsible for the severe pressure to emigrate to the developed countries of Europe and North America. In this view, people impoverished by overpopulation in the "South" flee to the "North." Some have claimed to find empirical support for this thesis in the fact that pressure to emigrate from the South has accelerated in recent decades, along with a rapid increase in the population there.

There are two distinct questions here: first, how great a threat of intolerable immigration pressure does the North face from the South, and second, is that pressure closely related to population growth in the South, rather than to other social and economic factors? There are reasons to doubt that population growth is the major force behind migratory pressures, and I shall concentrate here on that question. But I should note in passing that immigration is now severely controlled in Europe and North America, and insofar as Europe is concerned, most of the current immigrants from the third world are not "primary" immigrants but dependent relatives—mainly spouses and young children—of those who had come and settled earlier. The United States remains relatively more open to fresh immigration, but the requirements of "labor certification" as a necessary part of the immigration procedure tend to guarantee that the new entrants are relatively better educated and more skilled. There are, however, sizable flows of illegal immigrants, especially to the United States and to a lesser extent to southern Europe, though the numbers are hard to estimate.

What causes the current pressures to emigrate? The "job-worthy" people who get through the immigration process are not seen as impoverished and destitute migrants created by the sheer pressure of population. Even the illegal immigrants who manage to evade the rigors of border control are typically not starving wretches but those who can make use of work prospects in the North.

The explanation for the increased migratory pressure over the decades owes more to the dynamism of international capitalism than to just the growing size of the population of the third world countries. The immigrants have allies in potential employers, and this applies as much to illegal farm laborers in California as to the legally authorized "guest workers" in automobile factories in Germany. The economic incentive to emigrate to the North from the poorer Southern economies may well depend on differences in real income. But this gap is very large anyway, and even if it is presumed that population growth in the South is increasing the disparity with the North—a thesis I shall presently consider—it seems unlikely that this incentive would significantly change if the Northern income level were, say, twenty times that of the Southern as opposed to twenty-five times.

The growing demand for immigration to the North from the South is related to the "shrinking" of the world (through revolutions in communication and transport), reduction in economic obstacles to labor movements (despite the increase in political barriers), and the growing reach and absorptive power of international capitalism (even as domestic politics in the North has turned more inward looking and nationalistic). To try to explain the increase in immigration pressure by the growth rate of total population in the third world is to close one's eyes to the deep changes that have occurred—and are occurring—in the world in which we live, and the rapid internationalization of its cultures and economics that accompanies these changes.

1. Fears of Being Engulfed

A closely related issue concerns what is perceived as a growing "imbalance" in the division of the world population, with a rapidly rising share belonging to the third world. That fear translates into worries of various kinds in the North, especially the sense of being overrun by the South. Many Northerners fear being engulfed by people from Asia and Africa, whose share of the world population increased from 63.7 percent in 1950 to 71.2 percent by 1990, and is expected, according to the estimates of the United Nations, to rise to 78.5 percent by 2050 AD.

It is easy to understand the fears of relatively well-off people at the thought of being surrounded by a fast growing and increasingly impoverished Southern population. As I shall argue, the thesis of growing impoverishment does not stand up to much scrutiny, but it is important to address first the psychologically tense issue of racial balance in the world (even though racial composition as a consideration has only as much importance as we choose to give it). Here it is worth recollecting that the third world is right now going through the same kind of demographic shift—a rapid expansion of population for a temporary but long stretch—

that Europe and North America experienced during their industrial revolution. In 1650 the share of Asia and Africa in the world population is estimated to have been 78.4 percent, and it stayed around there even in 1750.[7] With the industrial revolution, the share of Asia and Africa diminished because of the rapid rise of population in Europe and North America; for example, during the nineteenth century while the inhabitants of Asia and Africa grew by about 4 percent per decade or less, the population of "the area of European settlement" grew by around 10 percent every decade.

Even now the combined share of Asia and Africa (71.2 percent) is considerably below what its share was in 1650 or 1750. If the United Nations' prediction that this share will rise to 78.5 percent by 2050 comes true, then the Asians and the Africans would return to being proportionately almost exactly as numerous as they were before the European industrial revolution. There is, of course, nothing sacrosanct about the distributions of population in the past, but the sense of a growing "imbalance" in the world, based only on recent trends, ignores history and implicitly presumes that the expansion of Europeans earlier on was natural, whereas the same process happening now to other populations unnaturally disturbs the "balance."

2. Collaboration versus Override

Other worries involving the relation of population growth to food supplies, income levels, and the environment reflect more serious matters.[8] Before I take up those questions, a brief comment on the distinction between two rival approaches to dealing with the population problem may be useful. One involves voluntary choice and a collaborative solution, and the other overrides voluntarism through legal or economic coercion.

Alarmist views of impending crises tend to produce a willingness to consider forceful measures for coercing people to have fewer children in the third world. Imposing birth control on unwilling people is no longer rejected as readily as it was until quite recently, and some activists have pointed to the ambiguities that exist in determining what is or is not "coercion."[9] Those who are willing to consider—or at least not fully reject—programs that would use some measure of force to reduce population growth often point to the success of China's "one child policy" in cutting down the national birth rate. Force can also take an indirect form, as when economic opportunities are changed so radically by government regulations that people are left with very little choice except to behave in ways the government would approve. In China's case, the government may refuse to offer housing to families with too many children—thus penalizing the children as well as the dissenting adults.

In India the policy of compulsory birth control that was initiated during the "emergency period" declared by Mrs. Gandhi in the 1970s was decisively rejected by the voters in the general election in which it—along with civil rights—was a major issue. Even so, some public health clinics in the northern states (such as Uttar Pradesh) insist, in practice, on sterilization before providing normal medical attention to women and men beyond a certain age. The pressures to move in that direction seem to be strong, and they are reinforced by the rhetoric of "the population bomb."

I shall call this general approach the "override" view, since the family's personal decisions are overridden by some agency outside the family—typically by the government of the country in question (whether or not it has been pressed to do so by "outside" agencies, such as international organizations and pressure groups). In fact, overriding is not limited to an explicit use of legal coercion or economic compulsion, since people's own choices can also be effectively overridden by simply not offering them the opportunities for jobs or welfare that they can expect to get from a responsible government. Override can take many different forms and can be of varying intensity (with the Chinese "one child policy" being something of an extreme case of a more general approach).

A central issue here is the increasingly vocal demand by some activists concerned with population growth that the highest "priority" should be given in third-world countries to family planning over other public commitments. This demand goes much beyond supporting family planning as a part of development. In fact, proposals for shifting international aid away from development in general to family planning in particular have lately been increasingly frequent. Such policies fit into the general approach of "override" as well, since they try to rely on manipulating people's choices through offering them only some opportunities (the means of family planning) while denying others, no matter what they would have themselves preferred. Insofar as they would have the effect of reducing health care and educational services, such shifts in public commitments will not only add to the misery of human lives, they may also have, I shall argue, exactly the opposite effect on family planning than the one intended, since education and health care have a significant part in the voluntary reduction of the birth rate.

The "override" approach contrasts with another, the "collaborative" approach, that relies not on legal or economic restrictions but on rational decisions of women and men, based on expanded choices and enhanced security, and encouraged by open dialogue and extensive public discussions. The difference between the two approaches does not lie in government's activism in the first case as opposed to passivity in the second. Even if solutions are sought through the decisions and actions of people themselves, the chance to take reasoned decisions with more knowledge and a greater sense of personal security can be increased by public policies, for example, through expanding educational facilities, health care, and economic well-being, along with providing better access to family planning. The central political and ethical issue concerning the "override" approach does not lie in its insistence on the need for public policy but in the ways it significantly reduces the choices open to parents.

3. The Malthus—Condorcet Debate

Thomas Robert Malthus forcefully argued for a version of the "override" view. In fact, it was precisely this preference that distinguished Malthus from Condorcet, the eighteenth-century French mathematician and social scientist from whom Malthus had actually derived the analysis of how population could outgrow the means of living. The debate between Malthus and Condorcet in some ways marks the origin of the distinction between the "collaborative" and the "override" approaches, which still compete for attention.[10]

In his *Essay on Population*, published in 1798, Malthus quoted—extensively and with approval—Condorcet's discussion, in 1795, of the possibility of overpopulation. However, true to the Enlightenment tradition, Condorcet was confident that this problem would be solved by reasoned human action: through increases in productivity, through better conservation and prevention of waste, and through education (especially female education) which would contribute to reducing the birth rate.[11] Voluntary family planning would be encouraged, in Condorcet's analysis, by increased understanding that if people "have a duty toward those who are not yet born, that duty is not to give them existence but to give them happiness." They would see the value of limiting family size "rather than foolishly . . . encumber the world with useless and wretched beings."[12]

Even though Malthus borrowed from Condorcet his diagnosis of the possibility of overpopulation, he refused to accept Condorcet's solution. Indeed, Malthus' essay on population was partly a criticism of Condorcet's enlightenment reasoning, and even the full title of Malthus' famous essay specifically mentioned Condorcet. Malthus argued that

> there is no reason whatever to suppose that anything beside the difficulty of procuring in adequate plenty the necessaries of life should either indispose this greater number of persons to marry early, or disable them from rearing in health the largest families.[13]

Malthus thus opposed public relief of poverty: he saw the "poor laws" in particular as contributing greatly to population growth.[14] Malthus was not sure that any public policy would work, and whether "overriding" would in fact be possible: "The perpetual tendency in the race of man to increase beyond the means subsistence is one of the great general laws of animated nature which we have no reason to expect change."[15] But insofar as any solution would be possible, it could not come from voluntary decisions of the people involved, or acting from a position strength and economic security. It must come from overriding their preferences through the compulsions economic necessity, since their poverty was the only thing that could "indispose the greater number of persons to marry early, or disable them from rearing in health the largest families."

4. Development and Increased Choice

The distinction between the "collaborative" approach and the "overriding" approach thus tends to correspond closely to the contrast between, on the one hand, treating economic and social development as the way to solve the population problem and, on the other, expecting little from development and using, instead, legal and economic pressures to reduce birth rate. Among recent writers, those such as Gerard Piel[16] who have persuasively emphasized our ability to solve problems through reasoned decisions and actions have tended—like Condorcet—to find the solution of the population problem in economic and social development. They advocate a broadly collaborative approach, in which governments and citizens would together produce economic and social conditions favoring slower population growth. In contrast, those who have been thoroughly skeptical of reasoned human action to limit population growth have tended to go in the direction of "override" in one form or another, rather than concentrate on development and voluntarism.

Has development, in fact, done much to reduce population growth? There can be little doubt that economic and social development, in general, has been associated with major reductions in birth rates and the emergence of smaller families as the norm. This is a pattern that was, of course, clearly observed in Europe and North America as they underwent industrialization, but that experience has been repeated in many other parts of the world.

In particular, conditions of economic security and affluence, wider availability of contraceptive methods, expansion of education (particular female education), and lower mortality rates have had—and are currently having—quite substantial effects in reducing birth rates in different parts of the world.[17] The rate of world population growth is certainly declining, and even over the last two decades its percentage growth rate has fallen from 2.2 percent per year between 1970 and 1980 to 1.7 percent between 1980 and 1992. This rate is expected to go steadily down until the size of the world's population becomes nearly stationary.[18]

There are important regional differences in demographic behavior; for example, the population growth rate in India peaked at 2.2 percent a year (in the 1970s) and has since started to diminish, whereas most Latin American countries peaked at much higher rates before coming down sharply, while many countries in Africa currently have growth rates between 3 and 4 percent, with an average for sub-Saharan Africa of 3.1 percent. Similarly, the different factors have varied in their respective influence from region to region. But there can be little dispute that economic and social development tends to reduce fertility rates. The regions of the third world that lag most in achieving economic and social development, such as many countries in Africa, are, in general, also the ones that have failed to reduce birth rates significantly. Malthus' fear that economic and social development could only encourage people to have more children has certainly proved to be radically wrong, and so have all the painful policy implications drawn from it.

This raises the following question: in view of the clear connection between development and lower fertility, why isn't the dispute over how to deal with population growth fully resolved already? Why don't we reinterpret the population problem simply as a problem of underdevelopment and seek a solution by encouraging economic and social development (even if we reject the over-simple slogan "development is the most reliable contraceptive")?

In the long run, this may indeed be exactly the right approach. The problem is more complex, however, because a "contraceptive" that is "reliable" in the long run may not act fast enough to meet the present threat. Even though development may dependably work to stabilize population if it is given enough time, there may not be, it is argued, time enough to give. The death rate often falls very fast with more widely available health care, better sanitation, and improved nutrition, while the birth rate may fall rather slowly. Much growth of population may meanwhile occur.

This is exactly the point at which apocalyptic prophecies add force to the "override" view. One claim, then, that needs examination is that the world is facing an imminent crisis, one so urgent that development is just too slow a process to deal with it. We must try right now, the argument goes, to cut down population growth by drastic and forceful means if necessary. The second claim that also needs scrutiny is the actual feasibility of adequately reducing population growth through these drastic means, without fostering social and economic development.

Population and Income

It is sometimes argued that signs of an imminent crisis can be found in the growing impoverishment of the South, with falling income per capita accompanying high population growth. In general, there is little evidence for this. As a matter of fact, the average population of "low-income" countries (as defined by the World Bank) has been not only enjoying a rising gross national product (GNP) per head, but a growth rate of GNP per capita (3.9 percent per year for 1980-1992) that is much faster than those for the "high-income" countries (2.4 percent) and for the "middle-income" ones (O percent).[19]

The growth of per capita GNP of the population of low-income countries would have been even higher had it not been for the negative growth rates of many countries in sub-Sahan Africa, one region in which a number of countries have been experiencing economic decline. But the main culprit causing this state of affairs is the terrible failure of economic production in sub-Saharan Africa (connected particularly with political disruption, including wars and military rule), rather than population growth, which is only a subsidiary factor. Sub-Saharan Africa does have high population growth, but its economic stagnation has contributed much more to the fall in its per capita income.

With its average population growth rate of 3.1 percent per year, had sub-Saharan Africa suddenly matched China's low population growth of 1.4 percent (the lowest among the low income countries), it would have gained roughly 1.7 percent in per capita GNP growth. The real income per person would still have fallen, even with that minimal population growth for many countries in the region. The growth of GNP per capita is *minus* 1.9 percent for Ethiopia, *minus* 1.8 percent for Togo, *minus* 3.6 percent for Mozambique, *minus* 4.3 percent for Niger, *minus* 4.7 percent for Ivory Coast, not to mention Somalia, Sudan, and Angola, where the political disruption has been so serious that no reliable GNP estimates even exist. A lower population growth rate could have reduced the magnitude of the fall in per capita GNP, but the main roots of Africa's economic decline lie elsewhere. The complex political factors underlying the troubles of Africa include, among other things, the subversion of democracy and the rise of combative military rulers, often encouraged by the cold war (with Africa providing "client states" from Somalia and Ethiopia to Angola and Zaire for the superpowers, particularly from the 1960s onward). The explanation of sub-Saharan Africa's problems has to be sought in these political troubles, which affect economic stability, agricultural and industrial incentives, public health arrangements, and social services—even family planning and population policy.

There is indeed a very powerful case for reducing the rate of growth of population in Africa, but this problem cannot be dissociated from the rest of the continent's woes. Sub-Saharan Africa lags behind other developing regions in economic security, in health care, in life expectancy, in basic education, and in political and economic stability. It should be no great surprise that it lags behind in family planning as well. To dissociate the task of population control from the politics and economics of Africa would be a great mistake and would seriously mislead public policy.

1. Population and Food

Malthus' exact thesis cannot, however, be disputed by quoting statistics of income per capita, for he was concerned specifically with food supply per capita, and he had concentrated on "the proportion between the natural increase of population and food." Many modern commentators, including Paul Ehrlich and Garrett Hardin, have said much about this, too. When Ehrlich says, in his *Population Bomb*, "too little food," he does not mean "too little income," but specifically a growing shortage of food.

Is population beginning to outrun food production? Even though such an impression is often given in public discussions, there is, in fact, no serious evidence that this is happening. While there are some year-to-year fluctuations in the growth of food output (typically inducing, whenever things slacken a bit, some excited remarks by those who anticipate an impending doom), the worldwide trend of food output per person has been firmly upward. Not only over the two centuries since Malthus' time, but also during recent decades, the rise in food output has been significantly and consistently outpacing the expansion of world population.[21]

Table I
Indices of Food Production Per Capita

	1979-1981 Base Period	1991-1993
World	100	103
Europe	100	102
North America	100	95
Africa	100	94
Asia	100	122
including		
India	100	123
China	100	139

source: FAO Quarterly Bulletin of Statistics

But the total food supply in the world as a whole is not the only issue. What about the regional distribution of food? If it were to turn out that the rising ratio of food to population is mainly caused by increased production in richer countries (for example, if it appeared that US wheat output was feeding the third world, in which much of the population expansion is taking place), then the neo-Malthusian fears about "too many people" and "too little food" may have some plausibility. Is this what is happening?

In fact, with one substantial exception, exactly the opposite is true. The largest increases in the production of food—not just in the aggregate but also per person—are actually taking place in the third world, particularly in the region that is having the largest absolute increases in the world population, that is, in Asia.

The many millions of people who are added to the populations of India and China may be constantly cited by the terrorized—and terrorizing—advocates of the apocalyptic view, but it is precisely in these countries that the most rapid rates of growth in food output per capita are to be observed. For example, between the three-year averages of 1979-1981 and 1991-1993, food production per head in the world moved up by 3 percent, while it went up by only 2 percent in Europe and went down by nearly 5 percent in North America. In contrast, per capita food production jumped up by 22 percent in Asia generally, including 23 percent in India and 39 percent in China.[22] (See Table 1.)

During the same period, however, food production per capita went down by 6 percent in Africa, and even the absolute size of food output fell in some countries (such as Malawi and Somalia). Of course, many countries in the world—from Syria, Italy, and Sweden to Botswana in Africa—have had declining food production per head without experiencing hunger or starvation since their economies have prospered and grown; when the means are available, food can be easily bought in the international market if it is necessary to do so. For many countries in sub-Saharan Africa, the problem arises from the fact that the decline in food production is an integral part of the story of overall economic decline, which I have discussed earlier.

Difficulties of food production in sub-Saharan Africa, like other problems of the national economy, are not only linked to wars, dictatorships, and political chaos. In addition, there is some evidence that climatic shifts have had unfavorable effects on parts of that continent. While some of the climatic problems may be caused in part by increases in human settlement and environmental neglect, that neglect is not unrelated to the political and economic chaos that has characterized sub-Saharan Africa during the last decades. The food problem of Africa must be seen as one part of a wider political and economic problem of that region.[23]

2. The Price of Food

To return to "the balance between food and population," the rising food production per capita in the world whole, and in the third world in general, contradicts some of the pessimism that characterized the gloomy predictions of the past. Prophecies of imminent disaster during the last decades have not proved any more accurate than Malthus' prognostications nearly two hundred years ago. As for new prophecies of doom, they cannot of course, be contradicted until future arrives. There was no way of refuting the theses of W. Paddock and P.

Paddock's popular book *Famine 1975!*, published in 1968, which predicted a terrible cataclysm for the world as a whole by 1975 (writing off India, in particular, as a basket case) until 1975 actually arrived. The new prophets have learned not to attach specific dates to the crises they see, and past failures do not seem to have reduced the popular appetite for this creative genre.

Milk being distributed to refugee children in Somalia. The government has estimated that there are some 1.3 million refugees in some 40 special camps and more than half of a million outside the camps. About 60% of the refugees are children. (photo: UN 146 504 / Peter Magubane)

However, after noting the rather dismal forecasting record of doom sayers, we must also accept the general methodological point that present trends in output do not necessarily tell us much about the prospects of further expansion in the future. It could, for example, be argued that maintaining growth in food production may require proportionately increasing investments of capital, drawing them away from other kinds of production. This would tend to make food progressively more expensive if there are "diminishing returns" in shifting resources from other fields into food production. And, ultimately, further expansion of production may become so expensive that it would be hard to maintain the trend of increasing food production without reducing other outputs drastically.

But is food production really getting more and more expensive? There is, in fact, no evidence for that conclusion either. In fact, quite the contrary. Not only is food generally much cheaper to buy today, in constant dollars, than it was in Malthus' time, but it also has become cheaper during recent decades. As a matter of fact, there have been increasing complaints among food exporters, especially in the third world, that food prices have fallen in relation to other commodities. For example, in 1992 a United Nations report recorded a 38 percent fall in the relative prices of "basic foods" over the last decade.[24] This is entirely in line with the trend, during the last three decades, toward declining relative prices of particular food items, in relation to the prices of manufactured goods.

The World Bank's adjusted estimates of the prices of particular food crops, between 1953-1955 and 1983-1985, show similarly steep declines for such staples as rice (42 percent), wheat (57 percent), sorghum (39 percent), and maize (37 percent).[25] Not only is food getting less expensive, but we also have to bear in mind that the current increase in food production (substantial and well ahead of population growth, as it is) is itself being kept in check by the difficulties in selling food profitably, as the relative prices of food have fallen. Those neo-Malthusians who concede that food production is now growing faster than population often point out that it is growing "only a little faster than population," and they are inclined to interpret this as evidence that we are reaching the limits of what we can produce to keep pace with population growth.

But that is surely the wrong conclusion to draw in view of the falling relative prices of food, and the current difficulties in selling food, since it ignores the effects of economic incentives that govern production. When we take into account the persistent cheapening of food prices, we have good grounds to suggest that food output is being held back by a lack of effective demand in the market. The imaginary crisis in food production, contradicted as it is by the upward trends of total and regional food output per head, is thus further debunked by an analysis of the economic incentives to produce more food.

3. Deprived Lives and Slums

I have examined the alleged "food problem" associated with population growth in some detail because it has received so much attention both in the traditional Malthusian literature and in the recent writings of neo-Malthusians. In concentrating on his claim that growing populations would not have enough food, Malthus differed from Condorcet's broader presentation of the population question. Condorcet's own emphasis was on the possibility of "a continual diminution of happiness" as a result of population growth, a diminution that could occur in many different ways—not just through the deprivation of food, but through a decline in living conditions generally. That more extensive worry can remain even when Malthus' analysis of the food supply is rejected.

Indeed, average income and food production per head can go on increasing even as the wretchedly deprived living conditions of particular sections of the population get worse, as they have in many parts of the third world. The living conditions of backward regions and deprived classes can decline even when a country's economic growth is very rapid on the average. Brazil during the 1960s and 1970s provided an extreme example of this. The sense that there are just "too many people" around often arises from seeing the desperate lives of people in the large and rapidly growing urban slums—*bidonvilles*—in poor countries, sobering reminders that should not take too much comfort from aggregate statistics of economic progress.

But in an essay addressed mainly to the population problem, what we have to ask is not whether things are just fine in the third world (they obviously are not), but whether population growth is the root cause of the disasters that people suffer. The question is whether the particular instances of deep poverty we observe derive mainly from population growth rather than from other factors that lead to unshared prosperity and persistent and possibly growing inequality. The tendency to see in population growth an explanation for every calamity that afflicts poor people is now fairly established in some circles, and message that gets transmitted constantly is the opposite of the old picture postcard: "Wish you weren't here."

To see in population growth the main reason for the growth of over-crowded and very poor slums in large cities, for example, is not empirically convincing. It does not help to explain why the slums of Calcutta and Bombay have grown worse at a faster rate than those of Karachi and Islamabad (India's population growth rate is 2.1 percent per year, Pakistan's 3.1), why Jakarta has deteriorated faster than Ankara or Istanbul (Indonesia's population growth is 1.8 percent, Turkey's 2.3), or why the slums in Mexico City have become worse more rapidly than those of San José (Mexico's population growth rate is 2.0, Costa Rica's 2.8), or why Harlem can seem more and more deprived when compared with the poorer districts Singapore (US population growth rate is 1.0, Singapore's is 1.8). Many causal factors affect the degree of deprivation in particular parts of a country—rural as well as urban—and to try to see them all as resulting from over population is the negation of social analysis.

This is not to deny that population growth may well have an effect on deprivation, but only to insist that any investigation of the effects of population growth must be part of the analysis of economic and political processes, including the effects of other variables. It is the isolationist view of population growth that should be rejected.

4. Threats to the Environment

In his concern about "a continual diminution of happiness" from population growth, Condorcet was a pioneer in considering the possibility that natural raw materials might be used up, thereby making living conditions worse. In his characteristically rationalist solution, which relied partly on voluntary and reasoned measures to reduce the birth rate, Condorcet also envisaged the development of less improvident technology: "The manufacture of articles will be achieved with less wastage in raw materials and will make better use of them."[26]

The effects of a growing population on the environment could be a good deal more serious than the food problems that have received so much attention in the literature inspired by Malthus. If the environment is damaged by population pressures this obviously affects the kind of life we lead, and the possibilities of a "diminution in happiness" can be quite considerable. In dealing with this problem, we have to distinguish once again between the long and the short run. The short-run picture tends to be dominated by the fact that the per capita consumption of food, fuel, and other goods by people in third world countries is often relatively low; consequently, the impact of population growth in these countries is not, in relative terms, so damaging to the global environment. But the problems of the local environment can, of course, be serious in many developing economies. They vary from the "neighborhood pollution" created by unregulated industries to the pressure of denser populations on rural resources such as fields and woods.[27] (The Indian authorities had to close down several factories in and around Agra, since the façade of the Taj Mahal was turning pale as a result of chemical pollution from local factories.) But it remains true that one additional

As peasant families lose land to agri-business, they move to slum areas near large cities. Images of crowed slums help create ideas about third-world over population. (photo: UN 157 160)

American typically has a larger negative impact on the ozone layer, global warmth, and other elements of the earth's environment than dozens of Indians and Zimbabweans put together. Those who argue for the immediate need for forceful population control in the third world to preserve the global environment must first recognize this elementary fact.

This does not imply, as is sometimes suggested, that as far as the global environment is concerned, population growth in the third world is nothing to worry about. The long-run impact on the global environment of population growth in the developing countries can be expected to be large. As the Indians and the Zimbabweans develop economically, they too will consume a great deal more, and they will pose, in the future, a threat to the earth's environment similar to that of people in the rich countries today. The long-run threat of population to the environment is a real one.

Women's Deprivation and Power

Since reducing the birth rate can be slow, this and other long-run problems should be addressed right now. Solutions will no doubt have to be found in the two directions to which, as it happens, Condorcet pointed: (1) developing new technology and new behavior patterns that would waste little and pollute less, and (2) fostering social and economic changes that would gradually bring down the growth rate of population.

On reducing birth rates, Condorcet's own solution not only included enhancing economic opportunity and security, but also stressed the importance of education, particularly female education. A better-educated population could have a more informed discussion of the kind of life we have reason to value; in particular, it would reject the drudgery of a life of continuous child bearing and rearing that is routinely forced on many third-world women. That drudgery, in some ways, is the most immediately adverse consequence of high fertility rates.

Central to reducing birth rates, then, is a close connection between women's well-being and their power to make their own decisions and bring about changes in the fertility pattern. Women in many third-world countries are deprived by high birth frequency of the freedom to do other things in life, not to mention the medical dangers of repeated pregnancy and high maternal mortality, which are both characteristic of many developing countries. It is thus not surprising that reductions in birth rates have been typically associated with improvement of women's status and their ability to make their voices heard—often the result of expanded opportunities for schooling and political activity.[28]

There is nothing particularly exotic about declines in the birth rate occurring through a process of voluntary rational assessment, of which Condorcet spoke. It is what people do when they have some basic education, know about family planning methods and have access to them, do not readily accept a life of persistent drudgery, and are not deeply anxious about their economic security. It is also what they do when they are not forced by high infant and child mortality rates to be so worried that no child will survive to support them in their old age that they try to have many children. In country after country, the birth rate has come down with more female education, the reduction of mortality rates, the expansion of economic means and security, and greater public discussion of ways of living.

1. Development versus Coercion

There is little doubt that this process of social and economic change will over time cut down the birth rate. Indeed the growth rate of world population is already firmly declining—it came down from 2.2 percent in the 1970s to 1.7 percent between 1980 and 1992. Had imminent cataclysm been threatening, we might have had good reason to reject such gradual progress and consider more drastic means of population control, as some have advocated. But that apocalyptic view is empirically baseless. There is no imminent emergency that calls for a breathless response. What is called for is systematic support for people's own decisions to reduce family size through expanding education and health care, and through economic and social development.

It is often asked where the money needed for expanding education, health care, etc., would be found. Education, health services, and many other means of improving the quality of life are typically highly labor-intensive and are thus relatively inexpensive in poor countries (because of low wages).[29] While poor countries have less money to spend, they also need less money to provide these services. For this reason many poor countries have indeed been able to expand educational and health services widely without waiting to become prosperous through the process of economic growth. Sri Lanka, Costa Rica, Indonesia, and Thailand are good examples, and there are many others. While the impact of these social services on the quality and length of life have been much studied, they are also major means of reducing the birth rate.

By contrast with such open and voluntary developments, coercive methods, such as the "one child policy" in some regions, have been tried in China, particularly since the reforms of 1979. Many commentators have pointed out that by 1992 the Chinese birth rate has fallen to 19 per 1,000, compared with 29 per 1,000 in India, and 37 per 1,000 for the average of poor countries other than China and India. China's total fertility rate (reflecting the number of children born per woman) is now at "the replacement level" of 2.0, compared with India's 3.6 and the weighted average of 4.9 for low-income countries other than China and India.[30] Hasn't China shown the way to "solve" the population problem in other developing countries as well?

China's Population Policies

The difficulties with this "solution" are of several kinds. First, if freedom is valued at all, the lack of freedom associated with this approach must be seen to be a social loss in itself. The importance of reproductive freedom has been persuasively emphasized by women's groups throughout the world.[31]

The loss of freedom is often dismissed on the grounds that because of cultural differences, authoritarian policies that would not be tolerated in the West are acceptable to Asians. While we often hear references to "despotic" Oriental traditions, such arguments are no more convincing than a claim that compulsion in the West is justified by the traditions of the Spanish Inquisition or of the Nazi concentration camps. Frequent references are also made to the emphasis on discipline in the "Confucian tradition"; but that is not the only tradition in the "East," nor is it easy to assess the implications of that tradition for modern Asia (even if we were able to show that discipline is more important for Confucius than it is for, say, Plato or Saint Augustine).

Only a democratic expression of opinion could reveal whether citizens would find a compulsory system acceptable. While such a test has not occurred in China, one did in fact take place in India during "the emergency period" in the 1970s, when Indira Gandhi's government imposed compulsory birth control and suspended various legal freedoms. In the general elections that followed, the politicians favoring the policy of coercion were overwhelmingly defeated. Furthermore, family planning experts in India have observed how the briefly applied programs of compulsory sterilization tended to discredit voluntary birth control programs generally, since people became deeply suspicious of the entire movement to control fertility.

Second, apart from the fundamental issue of whether people are willing to accept compulsory birth control, its specific consequences must also be considered. Insofar as coercion is effective, it works by making people do things they would not freely do. The social consequences of such compulsion, including the ways in which an unwilling population tends to react when it is coerced, can be appalling. For example, the demands of a "one child family" can lead to the neglect—or worse—of a second child, thereby increasing the infant mortality rate. Moreover, in a country with a strong preference for male children—a preference shared by China and many other countries in Asia and North Africa—a policy of allowing only one child per family can easily lead to the fatal neglect of a female child. There is much evidence that this is fairly widespread in China, with very adverse effects on infant mortality rates. There are reports that female children have been severely neglected as well as suggestions that female infanticide occurs with considerable frequency. Such consequences are hard to tolerate morally, and perhaps politically also, in the long run.

Third, what is also not clear is exactly how much additional reduction in the birth rate has been achieved through these coercive methods. Many of China's long-standing social and economic programs have been valuable in reducing fertility, including those that have expanded education for women as well as men, made health care more generally available, provided more job opportunities for women, and stimulated rapid economic growth. These factors would themselves have reduced the birth rates, and it is not clear how much "extra lowering" of fertility rates has been achieved in China through compulsion.

For example, we can determine whether many of the countries that match (or outmatch) China in life expectancy, female literacy rates, and female participation in the labor force actually have a higher fertility rate than China. Of all the countries in the world for which data are given in the *World Development Report 1994*, there are only three such countries: Jamaica (2.7), Thailand (2.2), and Sweden (2.1)—and the fertility rates of two of these are close to China's (2.0). Thus the additional contribution of coercion to reducing fertility in China is by no means clear, since compulsion was superimposed on a society that was already reducing its birth rate and in which education and jobs outside the home were available to large numbers of women. In some regions of China, the compulsory program needed little enforcement, whereas in other—more backward—regions, it had to be applied with much severity, with terrible consequences in infant mortality and discrimination against female children. While China may get too much credit for its authoritarian measures, it gets far too little credit for the other, more collaborative and participatory, policies it has followed, which have themselves helped to cut down the birth rate.

1. China and India

A useful contrast can be drawn between China and India, the two most populous countries in the world. If we look only at the national averages, it is easy to see that China with its low fertility rate of 2.0 has achieved much more than India has with its average fertility rate of 3.6. To what extent this contrast can be attributed to the effectiveness of the coercive policies used in China is not clear, since we would expect the fertility rate to be much lower in China in view of its higher percentage of female literacy (almost twice as high), higher life expectancy (almost ten years more), larger female involvement (by three quarters) in the labor force, and so on. But India is a country of great diversity, whose different states have very unequal achievements in literacy, health care, and economic and social development. Most states in India are far behind the Chinese provinces in educational achievement (with the exception of Tibet, which has the lowest literacy rate of any Chinese or Indian state), and the same applies to other factors that affect fertility. However, the state of Kerala in southern India provides an interesting comparison with China, since it too has high levels of basic education, health care, and so on. Kerala is a state within a country, but with its 29 million people, it is larger than most per 1,000, and its fertility rate is 1.8 for 1991, compared with China's 2.0 for 1992. These low rates have been achieved without any state coercion.[32]

The roots of Kerala's success are to be found in the kinds of social progress Condorcet hoped for, including among others, a high female literacy rate (86 percent, which is substantially higher than China's 68 percent). The rural literacy rate is in fact higher in Kerala—for women as well as men—than in every single province in China. Male and female life expectancies at birth in China are respectively 67 and 71 years; the provisional 1991 figures for men and women in Kerala are 71 and 74 years. Women have been active in Kerala's economic and political life for a long time. A high proportion do skilled and semi-skilled work and a large number have taken part in educational movements.[33] It is perhaps of symbolic importance that the first public pronouncement of the need for widespread elementary education in any part of India was made in 1817 by Rani Gouri Parvathi Bai, the young queen of the princely state of Travancore, which makes up a substantial part of modern Kerala. For a long time public discussions in Kerala have centered on women's rights and the undesirability of couples marrying when very young.

Table 2
Fertility Rates in China, Kerala, and Tamil Nadu

	1979	1991
China	2.8	2.0
Kerala	3.0	1.8
Tamil Nadu	3.5	2.2

Sources: For China, Xihe Peng, *Demographic Transition in China* (Oxford University press, 1991), Li Chengrui, *A Study of China's Population* (Beijing: Foreign Language Press, 1992), and *World Development Report 1994*. For India, *Sample Registration System 1979-80* (New Delhi: Ministry of Home Affairs, 1982) and *Sample Registration: Fertility and Mortality Indicators 1991* (New Delhi: Ministry of Home Affairs, 1993).

This political process has been voluntary and collaborative, rather than coercive, and the adverse reactions that have been observed in China, such as infant mortality, have not occurred in Kerala. Kerala's low fertility rate has been achieved along with an infant mortality rate of 16.5 per 1,000 live births (17 for boys and 16 for girls), compared with China's 31 (28 for boys and 33 for girls). And as a result of greater gender equality in Kerala, women have not suffered from higher mortality rates than men in Kerala, as they have in the rest of India and in China. Even the ratio of females to males in the total population in Kerala (above 1.03) is quite close to that of the current ratios in Europe and America (reflecting the usual pattern of lower female mortality whenever women and men receive similar care). By contrast, the average female to male ratio in China is 0.94 and in India as a whole 0.93.[34] Anyone drawn to the Chinese experience of compulsory birth control must take note of these facts.

The temptation to use the "override" approach arises at least partly from impatience with the allegedly slow process of fertility reduction through collaborative, rather than coercive, attempts. Yet Kerala's birth rate has fallen from 44 per 1,000 in the 1950s to 18 by 1991—not a sluggish decline. Nor is Kerala unique in this respect. Other societies, such as those of Sri Lanka, South Korea, and Thailand, which have relied on expanding education and reducing mortality rates—instead of on coercion—have also achieved sharp declines in fertility and birth rates.

It is also interesting to compare the time required for reducing fertility in China with that in the two states in India, Kerala and Tamil Nadu, which have done most to encourage voluntary and collaborative reduction in birth rates (even though Tamil Nadu is well behind Kerala in each respect)." Table 2 shows the fertility rates both in 1979, when the one-child policy and related programs were introduced in China, and in 1991. Despite China's one-child policy and other coercive measures, its fertility rate seems to have fallen much less sharply than those of Kerala and Tamil Nadu. The "override" view is very hard to defend on the basis of the Chinese experience, the only systematic and sustained attempt to impose such a policy that has so far been made.

2. Family Planning

Even those who do not advocate legal economic coercion, sometimes suggest a variant of the "override" approach—the view, which has been getting increasing support, that the highest priority should be given simply to family planning, even if this means diverting resources from education and health care as well as other activities associated with development. We often hear claims that enormous declines in birth rates have been accomplished through making family planning services available, without waiting for improvements in education and health care.

The experience of Bangladesh is sometimes cited as an example of such success. Indeed, even though the female literacy rate in Bangladesh is only around

22 percent and life expectancy at birth no higher than 55 years, fertility rates have been substantially reduced there through the greater availability of family planning services, including counseling.[36] We have to examine carefully what lessons can, in fact, be drawn from this evidence.

First, it is certainly significant that Bangladesh has been able to cut its fertility rate from 7.0 to 4.5 during the short period between 1975 and 1990, an achievement that discredits the view that people will not voluntarily embrace family planning in the poorest countries. But we have to ask further whether family planning efforts may themselves be sufficient to make fertility come down to really low levels, without providing for female education and the other features of a fuller collaborative approach. The fertility rate of 4.5 in Bangladesh is still quite high—considerably higher than even India's average rate of 3.6. To begin stabilizing the population, the fertility rates would have to come down closer to the "replacement level" of 2.0, as has happened in Kerala and Tamil Nadu, and in many other places outside the Indian subcontinent. Female education and the other social developments connected with lowering the birth rate would still be much needed.

Contrasts between the records of Indian states offer some substantial lessons here. While Kerala, and to a smaller extent Tamil Nadu, have surged ahead in achieving radically reduced fertility rates, other states in India in the so-called "northern heartland" (such as Uttar Pradesh, Bihar, Madhya Pradesh, and Rajasthan), have very low levels of education, especially female education, and of general health care (often combined with pressure on the poor to accept birth control measures, including sterilization, as a qualifying condition for medical attention and other public services). These states all have high fertility rates—between 4.4 and 5.1. The regional contrasts within India strongly argue for the collaborative approach, including active and educated participation of women.

The threat of an impending population crisis tempts many international observers to suggest that priority be given to family planning arrangements in the third world countries over other commitments such as education and health care, a redirection of public efforts that is often recommended by policy-makers and at conferences. Not only will this shift have negative effects on people's well-being and reduce their freedoms, it can also be self-defeating if the goal is to stabilize population. The appeal of such slogans as "family planning first" rests partly on misconceptions about what is needed to reduce fertility rates, but also on mistaken beliefs about the excessive cost of social development, including education and health care. As has been discussed, both these activities are highly labor intensive, and thus relatively inexpensive even in very poor economies. In fact, Kerala, India's best performer in expanding education and reducing both death rates and birth rates, is among the poorer Indian states. Its domestically produced income is quite low—lower indeed in per capita terms than even the Indian average—even if this is somewhat deceptive, for the greatest expansion of Kerala's earnings derives from citizens who work outside the state. Kerala ability to finance adequately both educational expansion and health coverage depends on both activities being labor-intensive; they can be made available even in a low-income economy when there is the political will to use them. Despite its economic backwardness, an issue which Kerala will undoubtedly have to address before long (perhaps by reducing bureaucratic controls over agriculture and industry, which have stagnated), its level of social development has been remarkable, and that has turned out to be crucial in reducing fertility rates Kerala's fertility rate of 1.8 not only compares well with China's 2.0, but also with the US's and Sweden's 2.1, Canada's 1.9, and Britain's and France's 1.8.

The population problem is serious, certainly, but neither because of "the proportion between the natural increase of population and food" nor because of some impending apocalypse. There are reasons for worry about the long-term effects of population growth on the environment; and there are strong reasons for concern about the adverse effects of high birth rates on the quality of life, especially of women. With greater opportunities for education (especially female education), reduction of mortality rates (especially of children), improvement in economic security (especially in old age), and greater participation of women in employment and in political action, fast reductions in birth rates can be expected to result through the decisions and actions of those whose lives depend on them.

This is happening right now in many parts of the world, and the result has been a considerable slowing down of world population growth. The best way of dealing with the population problem is to help to spread these processes elsewhere. In contrast, the emergency mentality based on false beliefs in imminent cataclysms leads to breathless responses that are deeply counterproductive, preventing the development of rational and sustainable family planning. Coercive policies of forced birth control involve terrible social sacrifices, and there is little evidence that they are more effective in reducing birth rates than serious programs of collaborative action.

Notes

This essay is reprinted with permission from the *New York Review of Books*, September 22, 1994. Thanks to the *NYRB*.

1. This paper draws on my lecture arranged by the "Eminent Citizens Committee for Cairo '94" at the United Nations in New York on April 18, 1994 and also on research supported by the National Science Foundation.
2. Paul Ehrlich, *The Population Bomb* (Ballantine, 1968). More recently Paul Ehrlich and Anne H. Ehrlich have written *The Population Explosion* (Simon and Schuster, 1990).
3. Garrett Hardin, *Living within Limits* (New York: Oxford University Press, 1993).

4. Thomas Robert Malthus, *Essay on the Principle of Population As It Affects the Future Improvement of Society with Remarks on the Speculation of Mr. Godwin, M. Condorcet, and Other Writers* (London: J. Johnson, 1798), Chapter 8 in the Penguin Classics edition, *An Essay on the Principle of Population* (1982), p. 123.

5. See Simon Kuznets, *Modern Economic Growth* (New Haven: Yale University Press, 1966).

6. Note by the Secretary-General of the United Nations to the Preparatory Committee for the International Conference on Population and Development, Third Session, A/Conf. 171/PC/5, February 18, 1994, p. 30.

7. Philip Morris Hauser's estimates are presented in the National Academy of Sciences publication, *Rapid Population Growth: Consequences and Policy Implications*, Vol. 1 (Baltimore: Johns Hopkins University Press, 1971). See also Simon Kuznets,*Modern Economic Growth*, Chapter 2.

8. For an important collection of papers on these and related issues, see Sir Francis Graham-Smith, F.R.S., ed., *Population—The Complex Reality: A Report of the Population Summit of the World's Scientific Academies*, issues by the royal Society and published in the U.S. by North American Press, Golden, CO. See also D. Gale Johnson and Ronald D. Lee, ed., *Population Growth and Economic Development, Issues and Evidence* (Madison: University of Wisconsin Press, 1987).

9. Hardin, *Living within Limits*, p. 274.

10. Paul Kennedy, who has discussed important problems in the distinctly "social" aspects of population growth, has pointed out that this debate "has, in one form or another, been with us since then," and "it is even more pertinent today than when Malthus composed his essay" in*Preparing for the Twenty-First Century*(New York: Random House, 1993), pp. 5-6.

11. On the importance of "enlightenment" traditions in Condorcet's thinking, see Emma Rothschild, "Condorcet and the Conflict of Values," *The Historical Journal* .

12. Marie Jean Antoine Nicholas de Caritat Marquis de Condorcet's*Esquisse d'un Tableau Historique des Progrès de l'Esprit Humain, Xe Epoque* (1795). English translation by June Barraclough, *Sketch for a Historical Picture of the Progress of the Human Mind*, with an introduction by Stuart Hampshire (Weidenfeld and Nicolson, 1955), pp. 187-192.

13. T. R. Malthus, *A Summary View of the Principle of Population* (London: John Murray, 1930); in the Penguin Classics edition (1892), p. 243; italics added.

14. On practical policies, including criticism of poverty relief and charitable hospitals, advocated for Britain by Malthus and his followers, see William St. Clair,*The Godwins and the Shelleys: A Biography of a Family* (New York: W. W. Norton, 1989).

15. Malthus, Essay on the Principle of Population, Chapter 17; in the Penguin Classics edition, An Essay on the Principle of Population, pp. 198-199. Malthus showed some signs of weakening in this belief as he grew older.

16. Gerard Piel, Only One World: Our Own to Make and to Keep (Freeman, 1992).

17. For discussions of these empirical connections, see R. A. Easterlin, ed., Population and Economic Change in Developing Countries (Chicago: University of Chicago Press, 1980); T. P. Schultz, Economics of Population (Addison-Wesley, 1981); J. C. Caldwell, Theory of Fertility Decline (Academic Press, 1982); E. King and M. A. Hill, eds., Women's Education in Developing Countries (Baltimore: Johns Hopkins University Press, 1992); Nancy Birdsall, "Economic Approaches to Population Growth," The Handbook of Development Economics, H. B. Chenery and T. N. Srinivasan, eds. (Amsterdam: North Holland, 1988); Robert Cassen, et al., Population and Development: Old Debates, New Conclusions (New Brunswick: Overseas Development Council/Transaction Publishers, 1994).

18. World Bank, World Development Report, 1994 (Oxford University Press, 1994), Table 25, pp. 210-211.

19. World Bank, World Development Report, 1994, Table 2.

20. These issues are discussed in my joint book with Jean Drèze, Hunger and Public Action (Oxford University Press, 1990), and also in my paper "Economic Regress: Concepts and Features," Proceedings of the World Bank Annual Conference on Development Economics 1993 (World Bank, 1994).

21. This is confirmed by, among other statistics, the food production figures regularly presented by the United Nations Food and Agricultural Organization (see the FAO Quarterly bulletin of Statistics, and also the FAO Monthly Bulletins).

22. For a more detailed picture and references to data sources, see my "Population and Reasoned Agency: Food, Fertility, and Economic Development," Population, Economic Development, and the Environment, Kerstin Lindahl-Kiessling and Hans Landberg, eds. (Oxford University Press, 1994); see also the other contributions to this volume. The data presented here have been slightly updated from later publication of the FAO.

23. On this, see my Poverty and Famines (Oxford University Press, 1981).

24. See UNCTAD VIII, Analytical Report by the UNCTAD Secretariat to the Conference (United Nations, 1992), Table V-S, p. 235. The period covered is between 1979-1981 to 1988-1990. these figures and related ones are discussed in greater detail in my paper, "Population and Reasoned Agency."

25. World Bank, Price Prospects for Major Primary Commodities, vol. II (World Bank, March 1993), Annex Tables 6, 12, and 18.

26. Condorcet, Esquisse d'un Tableau Historique des Progrès de L'Esprit Humain; in the 1987 reprint, p. 187.

27. The importance of "local" environmental issues is stressed and particularly explored by Partha Dasgupta in An Inquiry into Well-Being and Destitution (Oxford University Press, 1993).

28. Jean Drèze and myself in "India: Economic Development and social Opportunities," discuss the importance of women's political agency in rectifying some of the more serious lapses in Indian economic and social performance—not just pertaining to the deprivation of women themselves.

29. See Jean Drèze and Amartya Sen, Hunger and Public Action (Oxford University Press, 1989), which also investigates the remarkable success of some poor countries in providing widespread educational and health services.

30. World Bank, World Development Report 1994, p. 212; and Sample Registration System: Fertility and Mortality Indicators 1991 (New Delhi: Ministry of Home Affairs, 1993).

31. See the discussions, and the literature cited, in Gita Sen, Adrienne German, and Lincoln Chen, eds., Population Policies Reconsidered: Health, Empowerment, and Rights (Harvard Center for Population and Development Studies/International Women's Health Coalition, 1994).

32. On the actual processes involved, see T. N. Krishnan, "Demographic Transition in Kerala: Facts and Factors," Economic and Political Weekly, Vol. 11 (1976); and P. N. Mari Bhat and S. I. Rajan, "Demographic Transition in Kerala Revisited," Economic and Political Weekly, Vol. 25 (1990).

33. See, for example, Robin Jeffrey, "Culture and Governments: How Women Made Kerala Literate," Pacific Affairs, Vol. 60 (1987).

34. On this, see my "More Than 100 Million Women Are Missing," New York Review of Books, December 20, 1990; Ansley J. Coale, "Excess Female Mortality and the Balance of the Sexes: An Estimate of the Number of 'Missing Females,'" Population and Development Review, No. 17 (1991); Amartya Sen, "Missing Women," British Medical

Journal, No. 304 (March 1992); Stephen Klasen, "Missing Women Reconsidered," World Development, .

35. Tamil Nadu has benefited from an active and efficient voluntary program of family planning, but these efforts have been helped by favorable social conditions as well, such as a high literacy rate (the second highest among the sixteen major states), a high rate of female participation in work outside the home (third highest), a relatively low infant mortality rate (the third lowest), and a traditionally higher age of marriage. See also T. V. Antony, "The Family Planning Programme—Lessons from Tamil Nadu's Experience," Indian Journal of Social Science, Vol. 5 (1992).

36. World Bank and Population Reference Bureau, Success in a Challenging Environment: Fertility Decline in Bangladesh (World Bank, 1993).

Teresa Gutierrez

Cuba: The Real Causes of Emigration

In August 1994, 25,000 Cubans dramatically left their homes in Cuba in a seeming race. The development was presented in the U.S. media as a sudden and spontaneous "rush to freedom" by thousands of Cubans fleeing from "political repression." But this explanation simply is not true. It is political distortion designed to provide justification for further U.S. aggression against Cuba.

In reality, the long-term cause of the August crisis was the unrelenting 34-year long U.S. blockade of Cuba. The short term causes were U.S.-inspired provocations. A news article in the *San Francisco Chronicle* on June 17, 1994, confirms this view. On June 17, the *Chronicle* carried a front-page story titled "Secret Plan to Meet Mass Immigration: U.S. Strategy to Handle Sudden Influx from Cuba." The article revealed the existence of "Operation Distant Shore," a classified plan involving 37 federal agencies including the Department of Defense, CIA, FBI and Immigration and Naturalization Service.

Although work on the plan began in 1981, the pace had recently been stepped up: "After top-level meetings at the White House, officials are expected to complete the plan within days," the *Chronicle* reported. It is clear from the article that the plan's authors viewed a "mass migration" as the result of counter-revolutionary developments in Cuba.

This question must be asked: why after 13 years of preparation was there a sudden rush to finish this plan? Was it that the U.S. intelligence agencies had become suddenly clairvoyant, and knew that a crisis was about to break out in Cuba? Or were they already implementing plans to create a crisis? Anyone with a knowledge of the CIA's history—particularly its long record of subversion, assassination and attempted destabilization in Cuba—would have to believe the latter explanation. The CIA has never been very good at predicting anything but its own actions.

That the CIA has had its hand in destabilization attempts against Cuba is more than well documented. Several hundred CIA assassination attempts against Fidel Castro and other Cubans are widely recorded in books such as *The Cuban*

Revolution and the United States: A Chronological History by Jane Franklin (Ocean Press, 1992).

In her "ZR Rifle: The Plot to Kill Kennedy and Castro," Claudia Furiati shows how and why it was the CIA, not Cuba, that planned and orchestrated the Kennedy assassination. In *Deadly Secrets: The CIA-Mafia War Against Castro and the Assassination of J.F.K.* (Thunders Mouth Press, 1992), Warren Hinckle and William Turner (one of them a former FBI agent) detail a 30-year long CIA war against Cuba that include the collaboration of multi-millionaire E. Howard Hunt and former CIA Director George Bush.

The U.S. Blockade

The fundamental cause of the August 1994 emigration crisis is the U.S. blockade of Cuba. To begin to understand this, the question about why did the U.S. government imposed this blockade must be answered. In 1959, a rebel army under the leadership of Cuba's current president, Fidel Castro, took power. The revolution drove out one of the most hated dictators in Latin America, Fulgencio Batista. A creature of the U.S., Batista had built up an apparatus to make the island a paradise for U.S. multinational corporations and organized crime. Sugar companies, mining companies, real-estate barons, hotel owners, gangsters, and pimps virtually dominated the nation as Ramon Eduardo Ruiz points out in *Cuba: The Making of a Revolution* (Norton & Company, 1970). U.S. Treasury Department sources reveal that during the 1950s U.S. corporations doing business in Cuba made $329 million in profits.

Within a short time after the revolution triumphed, conditions in Cuba changed. Rents were reduced by 50%. The eviction of peasants by landlords was stopped. Previously private beaches were opened to the public. Educational campaigns and agricultural reforms that dramatically improved the life of the people were carried out. All these progressive public policies are detailed in Jane Franklin's *The Cuban Revolution and the United States: A Chronological History*.

The Eisenhower Administration initiated the blockade in 1960. On February 3, 1962, the Kennedy Administration announced a total trade embargo with Cuba to take affect on February 7, 1962. It was imposed as an attempt to strangle the Cuban Revolution, as an attempt to stop the gains the government was making for the Cuban people. Before the Revolution, ninety percent of Cuba's trade was with the U.S. Washington believed that by imposing a blockade, it could quickly destroy the Revolution. Instead, Cuba established economic relations with the Soviet Union and other socialist countries.

Over the next 30 years, Cuba withstood attempted invasions, assassination, and economic warfare by the U.S. The island flourished, developing health care, education, and other institutions that set a standard for developing countries. Various independent organizations—from the American Public Health Association to UNICEF to the World Health Organization—report that Cuba has one of the highest standards of health care in the world. Cuba's infant mortality rate in 1992 was 10.2 deaths per 1,000 live births. Compare this to the rate in the rest of the Caribbean, which is 48 deaths per 1,000 live births. However, the collapse of the Soviet Union and Eastern Europe—Cuba's main trading partners between 1989 and 1991—caused an extremely sharp decline in Cuba's economy. Many of the gains advanced by the Cuban Revolution were in jeopardy. Imports shrank from over $8 billion in 1990 to $1.7 billion in 1993, or nearly 80%. Nothing this severe has ever happened to the U.S., not even during the Great Depression.

Cuba has suffered severe shortages of food, medicines, raw materials, spare parts and most critically, fuel. In June 1993 the, APHA led a fact-finding trip to Cuba. The following is an excerpt from its report "The Politics of Suffering: The Impact of the U.S. Embargo on the Health of the Cuban People":

> The past several years have been difficult for the Cuban people. . . . The U.S. embargo was tightened to include trade—mostly in food and medicines. The March 1993 'Storm of the Century' . . . caused an estimated $1 billion in damage to Cuba. A mysterious disease known as neuropathy, which can affect vision, appeared in late 1991 and has spread. All this has created a situation of scarcity and uncertainty that has affected . . . [Cuba's] health care system.
>
> The strains . . . are visible everywhere. Almost everything, from paper to shampoo, is in short supply. The food supply has diminished. Medicines and medical supplies . . . are scare. The huge reduction in the availability of oil has emptied the streets of cars, caused periodic power shortages, disrupted factory production, and increased unemployment and underemployment.
>
> All these difficulties threaten the health of the Cuban people. Cuba entered this period having achieved the health profile of an advanced country. The diseases so rampant in the rest of the developing world have been overcome. Cuba's infant mortality rate . . . rivals that of advanced industrialized countries. Through a complete restructuring of its health care system after the revolution of 1959, Cuba has developed an exemplary national health system which provides . . . health care to the entire population without charge.
>
> The embargo's interference in the Cuban people's access to food and medicine is tantamount to the use of food and medicine as a weapon in the U.S. arsenal against Cuba.

In any other country in Latin America or the Caribbean such a drastic change in the economy would have at once resulted in dramatic social upheaval. Throughout the southern continent, example after example of people rising up against such intolerable conditions can be cited. One illustration is Mexico. The U.S.

government has historically portrayed Mexico as one of the most stable societies in Latin America. Yet on January 1, 1994, there emerged an indigenous army in the southern province of Chiapas that profoundly challenged the Mexican government. Since then, hundreds of thousands of peasants and others have demonstrated, occupied government buildings, and carried out strikes around the country. This kind of challenge has not emerged in Cuba since the triumph of the Cuban Revolution. Why? The facts show that the vast majority of the Cuban people both support their government and see the blockade as the principal problem in the economy.

The U.S. government and its accomplices in the mainstream press, however, would have people believe that the reason an upheaval in Cuba has not occurred is because the Cuban state is so repressive that people are too afraid to dissent or rebel. But if repression or fear were enough to prevent resistance, history would never change and we would not have the examples of rebellion all over Latin America where truly repressive governments prevail. During the 1970s and 1980s, El Salvador was a country where repression, torture, and murder were perfected. Yet a mass movement fought back and a people's army was organized to challenge the death squads that dominated the country. The rebellion escalated to a full-scale civil war during the 1980s.

In August 1994, when thousands left Cuba for the U.S., 600,000 Cubans took to the streets of Havana to defend their country. These people are not mentioned in the pages of the *New York Times*. It is true that there are those in Cuba who are critical of the Revolution. Others are unhappy about the shortages and the power outages. But most understand that had it not been for the revolution, Cuba's standard of living would not be as high as it is. Many who leave Cuba say that it is because things are just too hard.

Those in Washington who go to great lengths to rationalize U.S. policy to-

Cuban emigrants in Washington, D.C. February 26, 1994 call for the end of the U.S. blockade of Cuba. Action organized by the Association of Cuban Workers, Miami, FL.

ward Cuba maintain that there is wide dissent in Cuba, highly political in character. Yet a Top Secret memo sent from the U.S. Interest Section in Havana to the State Department shows once again how this is an intentional distortion (see below for text). The memo, written in January 1994, stated:

> The process of refugee applicants continues to show weak cases. Most people apply more because of the deteriorating economic situation than a real fear of persecution. Cases presented by human rights activists proved particularly difficult for USINT officers and INS members. . . . Human rights cases represent the weakest category of the refugee program.

There you have it. Straight from the horse's mouth. In November 1994, an artistic performer said:

> All the Cubans are struggling to end the blockade. We are capable of resolving our own problems without anyone criticizing us.

A medical student stated:

> Unlike in many other countries, students and youth here in Cuba are in the front lines of defending our government. Yes, there are shortages but we have our sovereignty and our dignity and we fight to keep that." (Author's interviews)

As a result of the shortages, the Cuban government was forced to adopt measures known as the "Special Period" (war-like conditions of rationing, etc., during peacetime). In order to guarantee people the basic means of life, rationing was instituted while still preserving the education and health-care systems. Because of Cuba's socialist system of equal distribution of goods for all, this assures that no one is left hungry or homeless.

The U.S. government's response to the economic crisis confronting the Cuban people was to tighten the screws—or "ratchet up the suffering" as it is called in the hallowed halls of Congress. In hopes of causing a rebellion inside Cuba, a bipartisan effort supported by both former President Bush and President Clinton pushed the Torricelli Bill into law in October 1992, just days before the presidential election. The law reads in part:

> . . . pass the bill to promote a peaceful transition to democracy in Cuba through a trade embargo against foreign subsidiaries of U.S. companies that trade or assist Cuba until it has held free and fair elections and is moving toward a free market economy.

Cynically misnamed the Cuban Democracy Act, the law requires foreign subsidiaries of U.S. corporations to end trade with Cuba. This trade, amounting to approximately $700 million in 1991, declined precipitously to under $2 million in 1993. Ninety percent of this trade was in food and medicines. These statistics come from the U.S. government that claims to be concerned about human rights. No one can say that politicians in Washington do not know the effects of their policies. The purpose of the blockade was never simply to stop all trade between the U.S. and Cuba. Historically, Washington has actively sought to disrupt and destroy economic relations between Cuba and all other countries. And since the collapse of the USSR, the U.S. government has further tightened the blockade in hopes of strangling the revolution.

Andrew Zimbalist of Smith College writing in *Foreign Policy* points out:

> Cuba's efforts to enter the 'free trade' of world capitalism have been blocked . . . by U.S. efforts to prevent Cuba from trading with companies from other countries. First, the U.S. government prohibits the importation of goods into the United States that contain even trace amounts of Cuban input. Thus . . . the French conglomerate Le Cruesot Loire was told that it could not sell steel containing Cuban nickel in the U.S. The company then canceled its contract with Cuba.
>
> Second, companies operating outside the U.S. are not allowed to sell Cuba goods that contain more than 20% U.S. inputs. Third, the U.S. government prohibits foreign banks . . . from maintaining dollar-denominated accounts for Cuba. . . . Fifth, ships docking at Cuban ports are not allowed to enter U.S. ports for six months. Although that restriction was part of the October 1992 Cuban Democracy Act, it was actually put into practice by presidential decree in April 1992.
>
> Sixth, threats and other pressures have been employed against other countries to deter economic relations with Cuba. Sometimes the threats are embodied in legislative initiatives . . . sometimes the pressure takes the form of letters or phone calls indicating that the U.S. would look unfavorably upon Cuban participation.

Children in the U.S. gather school supplies for Cuban children. (photo: Bill Hackwell)

On November 24, 1992, the United Nations General Assembly voted 59 to three to condemn the extraterritorial provision in the Cuban Democracy Act as an attempt to violate trade sovereignty and international law. The following year, it voted 88 to four to call on the U.S. to end the blockade. Again on September 24, 1994, the UN voted 101 to two against the blockade. Even Washington's closest allies oppose the law. In October 1992, Canada issued a blocking order and imposed fines on companies complying with the Torricelli Law.

The U.S. has argued that the UN has no business taking up the blockade as it is a matter of relations between two countries. It argues that it carries out an embargo, not a blockade. But the facts confirm that U.S. policy toward Cuba is thoroughly extraterritorial and therefore clearly a blockade.

U.S. Immigration Policy

At the same time as it has sought to cause maximum hardship and suffering inside Cuba, the U.S. has pursued a destabilizing and dishonest immigration policy. In 1966, the Cuban Adjustment Act became law. This law allows any Cuban who lands on U.S. soil to be granted asylum and gain permanent resident status within a year. This is a special status, unlike that granted in law to immigrants from any other country in the world. The purpose of this act is to entice highly skilled engineers, doctors, scientists and others to leave, as well as to politically embarrass Cuba for propaganda purposes.

In 1984, the U.S. and Cuba signed an immigration treaty. The treaty provides for 20,000 Cubans a year to lawfully emigrate to the U.S. In the eight years the treaty has been in effect, however, Washington has allowed only 11,000 Cubans to legally immigrate to this country; 93% of all applications have been rejected by the U.S. Interest Section in Havana. During the same period, every Cuban who made it to U.S. shores, even if they hijacked a plane or ship, was accepted, given benefits and legal status. No one was ever prosecuted, even if they committed murder in the act of leaving. Underscoring the double standard that exists for these refugees, the press automatically characterizes these incidents as "freedom flights" or hijackings. But as the Haiti Commission for the Inquiry into the September 30 Coup in Haiti pointed out December 30, 1993 after a Cuban pilot hijacked a plane from Cuba: "Tens of thousands of Haitians try to enter the U.S. everyday in an attempt to gain freedom from flagrant economic and political repression, yet these refugees are immediately turned back to face extreme conditions in their country."

Such sophisticated acts on the high seas could not successfully occur without the full backing of the U.S. government. In 1983 the Bush Administration set up Radio Marti—a radio station broadcasting from Miami, Florida, directly to

Cuba. On more than one occasion, this radio station has filled the airwaves with inflammatory anti-communist rhetoric. The funding for Radio Marti has continued in spite of severe cutbacks on government spending by Republicans. In 1994, the House/Senate Conference Committee awarded $21 million of taxpayers' money to Radio and T.V. Marti (*Cuba Action*, Fall 1994). This money has been well spent in encouraging Cubans to either rise up in arms against the Cuban government or leave the island at any cost and be guaranteed a hero's welcome. The U.S. government-funded Radio Marti and many other radio stations in south Florida, which are easily heard in Cuba, have for years reported on the hero's welcome and benefits accorded to those who flee Cuba in boats or planes, regardless of whether they committed violent acts in the process.

No other immigrant to the United States has ever received the kind of treatment that Cubans receive in this country. Millions of Mexicans, Salvadorans, and other Latin Americans are harshly treated, often cruelly deported, and in essence live as second-class citizens. Witness the recent passage of Proposition 187 in the state of California, which legalizes the denial of education and social services to immigrants and their children. Yet Cuban Americans not only experience a higher standard of living in the U.S., they wield an extreme amount of political influence in Washington and reap plenty. The U.S. policy before August 16, 1994, can be summarized in this way: cause the greatest possible hardship in Cuba, refuse in practice to honor the immigration treaty between the two countries, and encourage refugees to leave illegally.

The August Crisis

In July and August 1994, violent hijackings of at least four boats and ferries by people armed with guns, grenades, and other weapons took place. A police officer and a navy lieutenant were killed and several people who resisted the hijackings were thrown overboard at sea. Incidents like this are very rare in Cuba; that four of them happened in less than a month cannot have been a coincidence. The hijackers who killed the Cuban naval officer were allowed into the U.S. with no charges against them, and their welcome was reported on Radio Marti and other south Florida stations. On August 5, rumors that another boat was going to leave Havana brought several hundred people to the waterfront. When no ship materialized, part of the crowd attacked stores in the downtown area. Thousands of Cuban workers poured into the streets and stopped this riot. Two days later, 600,000 people demonstrated in Havana in support of the government.

After these incidents, the Cuban government announced that unless there were negotiations with the U.S. it would "stop protecting U.S. borders" by patrolling Cuban shores and would allow Cubans to leave if they so desired. By mid-

August, 500 people per day were leaving. On August 18, President Bill Clinton announced a big change in U.S. policy: From now on, Cuban rafters would not be allowed into the U.S., but instead be taken to the U.S. Naval base at Guantanamo Bay and held indefinitely. On August 20, Clinton announced new punitive measures designed to further heighten the economic and political pressure on Cuba, including cutting off cash gifts from Cuban Americans to family members in Cuba, reducing charter flights to Cuba, increasing hostile radio broadcasts, and seeking UN condemnation of Cuba.

The next day, White House Chief of Staff Leon Panetta and other government officials said a naval blockade of Cuba was "an option." By this time, the number of Cuban refugees being picked up had reached 2,000 a day. The White House announced that virtually all flights to Cuba were being ended. The Clinton administration has rejected Cuba's proposal to enter into wide-ranging talks to resolve the crisis. The direction of U.S. policy is clearly more aggressive and hostile. It is designed to deepen the crisis. Given the record of the U.S. government, its hostility toward Cuba could lead to direct military intervention at any time. Witness U.S. policy toward Panama. Here was a country with which the U.S. was not at war and had a known working relationship with its head of state, General Manuel Noriega—yet suddenly in 1988, the U.S. imposed sanctions. It then invaded the country a year later in the middle of the night five days before Christmas, overthrew the government, arrested Noriega, and installed a U.S. puppet regime.

Shortly after the November 8, 1994, U.S. elections, Sen. Jesse Helms (R-NC) emboldened by the victory of the right-wing Republicans, said that troops should have been sent not to Haiti but to Cuba to get Castro out of Cuba once and for all. With the republican victory in the legislature, Helms assumed the chairmanship of the powerful Senate Foreign Relations Committee. For over 35 years the powerful and rich of this country have sought to return Cuba back to the days before 1959, when inequality and exploitation dominated the island. The multinational corporations want to return Cuba back to the status of a U.S. neo-colony. Because the Cuban government and people have resisted this aggression, the most aggressive and right-wing forces in this country are promoting crisis after crisis in Cuba.

This is what is behind the refugee situation in Cuba.

The following pages reproduce a "top secret" memo from the U.S. Interest Section in Havana to the Secretary of State, the CIA, and the Immigration and Naturalization Service. The memo makes clear that the U.S. government's charges that human rights violations cause Cuban migration is a conscious fraud. In spite of the U.S. government's best efforts to cultivate complaintants, "human rights cases represent the weakest category of the refugee program."

```
                                            TOP SECRET

FROM      :    US INT. SECT. HAVANA

TO        :    SEC. STATE, WASHINGTON
               CIA
               INS

DATE      :    JANUARY 94

REFERENCE :    H/18422/693-4

SUBJECT   :    UPDATE ON THE CUBAN REFUGEE PROGRAM
```

I. <u>OVERVIEW</u>

THE PROCESSING OF REFUGEE APPLICANTS CONTINUES TO SHOW WEAK CASES. MOST PEOPLE APPLY MORE BECAUSE OF THE DETERIORATING ECONOMIC SITUATION THAN A REAL FEAR OF PERSECUTION. CASES PRESENTED BY HUMAN RIGHTS ACTIVISTS PROVED PARTICULARLY DIFFICULT FOR USINT OFFICERS AND INS MEMBERS. ALTHOUGH WE HAVE TRIED HARD TO WORK WITH THOSE HUMAN RIGHTS ORGANIZATIONS ON WHICH WE EXERT GREATER CONTROL TO IDENTIFY ACTIVISTS TRULY PERSECUTED BY THE GOVERNMENT, HUMAN RIGHTS CASES REPRESENT THE WEAKEST CATEGORY OF THE REFUGEE PROGRAM.

APPLICATIONS BY HUMAN RIGHTS GROUPS MEMBERS ARE MARKED BY GENERAL AND IMPRECISE DESCRIPTIONS OF ALLEGED HUMAN RIGHTS ACTIVITY. LACK DEMONSTRABLE EVIDENCE OF PERSECUTION, AND DO NOT MEET THE BASIC CRITERIA FOR PROCESSING IN THE PROGRAM. COMMON ALLEGATIONS OF FRAUDULENT APPLICATIONS BY ACTIVISTS AND OF THE SALE OF TESTIMONIALS BY HUMAN RIGHTS LEADERS HAVE CONTINUED IN RECENT MONTHS. DUE TO THE LACK OF VERIFIABLE DOCUMENTARY EVIDENCE, AS A RULE USINT OFFICERS AND INS MEMBERS HAVE REGARDER HUMAN RIGHTS CASES AS THE MOST SUSCEPTIBLE TO FRAUD.

II. <u>ASSESSMENT</u>

THE DECREASE IN THE NUMBER OF POLITICAL PRISONERS WITH LED THE STATE DEPARTMENT AND THE INS THREE YEARS AGO TO WORK TOGETHER IN EXPANDING THE CATEGORIES FOR PROCESSING IN THE CUBAN REFUGEE PROGRAM. PROFESSIONALS DISMISSED FROM THEIR JOBS, HUMAN RIGHTS ACTIVISTS, AND MEMBERS OF RELIGIOUS FAITHS SUFFERING PERSECUTION WERE INTRODUCED AS NEW CATEGORIES. WITH PROCCESING GUIDELINES

```
                      TOP SECRET
```

TOP SECRET

THE LEADER OF ONE GROUP SAID THAT SEVERAL PEOPLE LEFT HIS ORGANIZATION WHEN THEY KNEW THAT IT DOES NOT GIVE TESTIMONIALS TO MEMBERS. HE COMPLAINED OF PRESSURES FROM MEMBERS TO OBTAIN STRONG TESTIMONIALS OF THEIR HUMAN RIGHTS ACTIVITY.

THE LATEST INS VISITS HAVE WITNESSED REPEATED INCIDENCES OF FRAUD AND ALLEGATIONS OF FRAUD BY HUMAN RIGHTS ACTIVISTS. USINT HAS ATTEMPTED TO ADDRESS THE PROBLEM THROUGH A REVISION OF INTERNAL PROCEDURES TO IDENTIFY STRONG HUMAN RIGHTS CASES. IN ADDITION, IT MET WITH HEADS OF HUMAN RIGHTS ORGANIZATIONS TO DETERMINE THE OBJECTIVES, SIZE AND OTHER ASPECTS OF THE MAJOR HUMAN RIGHTS GROUPS. USINT RESTRICTED AS WELL THE TESTIMONIALS ACCEPTED FROM THE GROUPS TO THOSE FROM LEADERS WE TRUST, AWARE THAT PAST DIVISIONS WITHIN HUMAN RIGHTS GROUPS HAVE PRODUCED ALLEGATIONS OF UNAUTHORIZED AND FRAUDULENT ISSUANCES OF TESTIMONIALS.

TO OUR REGRET, NOT EVEN THESE STEPS HAVE PREVENTED ALLEGATIONS OF FRAUD AND BITTER RECRIMINATIONS AMONG TOP HUMAN RIGHTS LEADERS. SHORTLY BEFORE THE INS DECEMBER VISIT, GUSTAVO ARCOS AND JESUS YANEZ OF THE COMITE CUBANO PRO-DERECHOS HUMANOS, ACCUSED AIDA VALDES OF SELLING FRAUDULENT AVALS. SHE, IN TURN, ACCUSES ARCOS AND YANEZ OF SIMILAR PRACTICES FOR ECONOMIC PROFITS.

THIS SITUATION INCREASES THE GENERAL CONCERN REGARDING THE DANGER OF RELYING ON THE TESTIMONIALS. THE DEEP RIVALRIES AND INFIGHTING AMONG THE HUMAN RIGHTS GROUPS MAKE IT SIMPLY INEVITABLE FOR THE RECURRENCE OF CHARGES OF FRAUD NOT TO PREVAIL.

PROMINENT ACTIVISTS HAVE CONFESSED THEIR WORRIES THAT THE REFUGEE PROGRAM IS ROBBING THEM OF THE FEW DEDICATED MEMBERS WHILE AT THE SAME TIME IT HAS BECOME A MAGNET FOR OPPORTUNISTS. DURING A MEETING WITH USINT AND THE INS, FELIX BONNE, THE HEAD OF THE GROUP "CORRIENTE CIVICA", CALLED THE REFUGEE PROGRAM "THE PRIMARY FOCUS OF MANY HUMAN RIGHTS LEADERS AND ORGANIZATIONS".

THE INVOLVEMENT BY SOME OF THE BEST-KNOWN HUMAN RIGHTS LEADERS IN CUBA IN THESE SERIOUS ALLEGATIONS CLEARLY ILLUSTRATES THAT OUR REFUGEE PROGRAM HAS BECOME A DIVISIVE AND INCREASINGLY CONTROVERSIAL FOCUS OF ATTENTION FOR MANY HUMAN RIGHTS GROUPS, WHOSE LEADERS APPEAR ALMOST OBSESSED WITH THE PROGRAM. USINT HAS EVEN RECEIVED APPEALS TO GIVE HUMAN RIGHTS ORGANIZATIONS A FORMAL ROLE IN THE REFUGEE PROGRAM.

OUT OF THE 225 CASES PRESENTED BY USINT TO INS DURING ITS

TOP SECRET

TOP SECRET

DECEMBER VISIT, 47 CLAIMED INVOLVEMENT IN HUMAN RIGHTS ACTIVITY ALTHOUGH MANY FELL INTO OTHER CATEGORIES, LIKE PROFESSIONALS DISMISSED FROM THEIR JOBS AND PERSONS ATTEMPTING TO COMMITT ILLEGAL EXITS. ALTHOUGH THIS WAS OUR BEST EFFORT TO WORK WITH HUMAN RIGHTS GROUPS TO PRESENT THE STRONGEST CASES, INTERVIEWS CLEARLY SHOWED THE WEAKNESS OF MOST CASES.

OF ALL 47 HUMAN RIGHTS CASES, ONLY ONE CLAIMED A TOTAL OF MORE THAN 30 DAYS DETENTION OVER THE LAST FIVE YEARS FOR HUMAN RIGHTS ACTIVITY, AN EVEN HE COULD NOT PROVIDE EVIDENCE OF THE DETENTIONS. THE REST IN GENERAL, ONLY CLAIMED HOUSE SEARCHES OR A FEW UNDOCUMENTED SUMMONS TO POLICE STATIONS. MOST ACTIVISTS GAVE ONLY VAGUE DESCRIPTIONS OF THEIR INVOLVEMENT IN HUMAN RIGHTS GROUPS. AND ONLY 19 WERE FINALLY APPROVED.

DESPITE BEING ONLY 20 PERCENT OF THE TOTAL, HUMAN RIGHTS CASES REPRESENTED MORE THAN HALF OF THE DENIALS. THE OVERALL REFUSAL RATE FOR THE DECEMBER VISIT AS A RESULT WAS 22 PERCENT. THIS RATE, ALTHOUGH SIGNIFICANTLY HIGHER THAN IN PAST INS VISITS, HAS ON THE SIDELINE THE ADVANTAGE OF HOPEFULLY RESULTING IN A HIGHER LEVEL OF ACTIVITY BY THE GROUPS.

CONSIDERATIONS

IN THE FACE OF A GENERAL DECLINE IN THE QUALITY OF THE CASES, INCLUDING THOSE INVOLVING EX-POLITICAL PRISONERS, USINT WILL NEED TO WORK HARDER IN IDENTIFYING THE BEST CASES. WITH A VIEW TO HELP IN THIS EFFORT, IT WILL INTRODUCE ADDITIONAL CHANGES IN THE PROCESSING OF CASES.

THE PROBLEMS ENCOUNTERED IN THE PROCESSING OF THE BULK OF THE HUMAN RIGHTS CASES POINT TO THE NEED FOR USINT TO CONTINUE ITS CLOSE WORK WITH THE INS TO SELECT STRONG CASES.

HOWEVER, THE USINT WILL MAINTAIN THE FLEXIBILITY TO PRESENT CASES THAT MAY NOT MEET ALL OF THE CRITERIA BUT THAT GIVEN THEIR NATURE MAY PROVE USEFUL FOR US INTERESTS.

GIVEN CIA'S EXPRESSED INTERESTS IN THE SUBJECT OF HUMAN RIGHTS, AND ITS GREATER INVOLVEMENT WITH AND BETTER KNOWLEDGE OF THE DIFFERENT GROUPS, WE SUGGEST A CLOSER COOPERATION WITH USINT IN LINE WITH OUR COMMON GOALS.

SULLIVAN

Jocelyn McCalla

Better than Fiction:
The Odyssey of the Haitian Refugees

The words rolled off the page in a booming, brutal, military voice. The message was simple. After intervening in Haiti to restore the controversial Father Jean-Bertrand Aristide to his President's office in Haiti, the United States would no longer tolerate a Haitian refugee presence at the Guantanamo Bay naval base. The 3,000 Haitian refugees still at the base, almost three months after the second American military intervention in their small Caribbean nation, would simply be told that they had five days to return without coercion. Otherwise they would be put on Coast Guard cutters by force. As an incentive, the United States promised both to double the amount of money that each returnee would receive from the Haitian Red Cross upon disembarkment—from U.S. $20 to U.S. $40—and to put them first on the job line. But there would be no exceptions.

The Administration stood firm on its commitment to block their entry into the United States, regardless of their circumstances. Nevertheless, it felt the need to placate criticism from advocates of Haitian refugees, who kept demanding that those claiming fear of persecution be heard. The administration decided that If the Haitians insisted, they would be given a hearing, but that the best they could hope for would be the opportunity to remain isolated in a refugee camp in Guantanamo Bay, Cuba. In other words, internment would be their reward for convincing an INS asylum officer[1] that, despite the presence of U.S. troops and other international peacekeeping forces in Haiti, despite the near-complete disintegration of the dreaded Haitian military and the disappearance of its ruthless paramilitary allies, despite the restoration of the Aristide government, and the return of Aristide himself, they had a well-founded fear of persecution.

Fewer than 500 Haitians jumped at the U.S. offer by the end of the five-day deadline. That meant that the Marines had to move the recalcitrants from the base to Port-au-Prince, Haiti, swiftly and in large numbers, allowing no legal injunction to stand in the way. The Coast Guard planned for and executed a mission that included the transportation of up to 600 Haitian refugees a day. At dockside, the U.S. command assembled a multi-national military contingent that, with their guns drawn and aimed at the Haitians descending from the gangplank, provided a humiliating welcome to the men, women and children who had risked their lives to flee the most brutal Caribbean dictatorship in recent memory. Except for two low-level government employees, who came to the docks as if on cue to take down the names and fingerprints of the returnees—just as they had done months earlier on orders of the Haitian military—there were no representatives of the Aristide government. No grand hero's welcome.

And so it came to pass that the Haitians, whose desperate flight to freedom brought the U.S. to take two unprecedented steps—establish a safe haven and intervene on behalf of a popular democratic leader against the "better" counsel of Pentagon and CIA officials—once again became the victims of politically-expedient measures.

The timing of this forced repatriation no doubt came with an eye towards the Republican Party's take-over of both houses of Congress on January 4, 1995. On that day, there remained about 700 Haitians, among them 345 unaccompanied minors and others with active tuberculosis. Not enough fodder for the Republicans.

The White House may have postponed the inevitable attempt by his opponents to deny the Democratic President even the satisfaction of having done well by Haitian democracy, but it missed a unique opportunity to set the United States on the path of adhering to the United Nations Protocol Relating to the Status of Refugees. Indeed, advocates for Haitian refugees counseled application of the well-founded fear of persecution standard as the best way to insure impartiality and fairness. They noted that, while the political situation had by all accounts improved, there were areas which remained under the control of local chieftains opposed to democratic rule. They argued that under these circumstances, a strict application of the refugee screening standard would yield a small number of refugees eligible for resettlement in the United States or a third country. The gain for the U.S. would be that the safe haven and refugee screening would have proven itself. Resorting to *refoulement* on the other hand could simply lead to more policy-on-the-go.

Could it in fact have been any different? Did the policies of the Clinton Administration differ much from those of Presidents Reagan, Bush, or even Carter? If they did, how?

The Failure of U.S. Policy in Haiti

U.S. policy in Haiti has long been designed to insure Haiti's short-term "stability" and the Haitian government's cooperation in controlling migration to the

United States. Migration control, however, focused primarily on stopping the flow of refugees to the United States.

Haitian refugees first arrived by boat on the U.S. mainland in 1972. They were immediately jailed and denied asylum. For most of the 1970's, the U.S. response to the growing number of Haitians seeking desperately to leave the Duvalier[3] dictatorship behind consisted of denying the reality of persecution in Haiti, jailing, swift expulsion from the U.S., taking expeditious measures in contravention of the procedures guaranteeing due process under American laws, and throwing up a multitude of barriers to prevent assistance from lawyers and advocates.

In 1980 however, the Carter Administration faced an influx of both Haitian and Cuban refugees. Carter could not bring himself to repatriate the Haitians while the Cubans were welcomed with open arms, and in fact were being fetched from deep within Cuban territorial waters. The contrasting treatment would have been too great, even for his most fervent supporters. With re-election in mind, Carter adopted a policy that sought to win support both from African-Americans and the anti-Castro Cuban community. He conferred on both groups of refugees a hitherto new status: "Entrant." Neither refugees, nor asylees. What became of them, he promised, would eventually be decided by legislation. And so it was that 18,000 Haitians and 125,000 Cubans became Cuban-Haitian Entrants.

Asylum-seekers fleeing Haiti by boat, January 1992. (photo: Maud Weiss)

That year, Ronald Reagan won the November presidential elections by a huge margin, partly because of Carter's inability to handle deftly the Caribbean refugees. Reagan promised not to be as generous as his predecessor, declaring border control, at least when it came to the Haitians, to be an absolute priority of his administration.

Despite the awful human rights record of the Duvalier regime, the Reagan administration continued to support it with economic and military assistance. In exchange it got the Duvaliers to relinquish sovereign rights over Haiti's borders and its citizens. In September 1981, Reagan established the Haitian Migrant Interdiction Operation (HMIO), according to which U.S. Coast Guard cutters patrolling the high seas and Haitian waters had the right to intercept Haitians and return them to their homeland. In addition, the U.S. President promised Haitians able to escape Coast Guard scrutiny lengthy detention in federal penitentiaries and INS detention centers.

The executive order which launched interdiction at sea contained passing reference to the obligation of the Unites States—as a state party to the Protocol Relating to the Status of Refugees—to not forcibly return Haitians claiming fear of persecution before their claims could be judged on their merit. By all accounts, however, the reference to the Protocol was just that: passing. The U.S. rigged the process in a manner forbidding Haitians from asserting their claims. Indeed the agreement reached with the Government of Haiti provided for Haitian military officers to be posted on board patrolling U.S. Coast Guard cutters. In addition, there was no attempt to put the rescued at ease, allow for rest after an undoubtedly dangerous journey on a makeshift boat unfit for deep sea travel, or provide for individual interviews. Immigration inspectors assembled the refugees as a group to ask them of their possible fear, while they were surrounded by Coast Guardsmen and faced the Haitian officer. Invariably, the refugees, expecting certain return, failed to speak out.

And in huge numbers they were returned, handed over to Duvalier's "Macoutes" militia and military. The policy failed to deter Haitians from leaving because the basic cause of Haitian flight had not been addressed. Yet the Reagan Administration considered it a success, since it removed the "Haitian problem" from American public scrutiny,

It was only when the demise of the Duvalier dynasty became certain the Reagan administration distanced itself, cutting off aid. But as soon as a military junta affirmed itself as Haiti's new government, the U.S. rushed to give it a ringing endorsement. The Reagan administration claimed that the "National Governing Council's (CNG) most radical break with the Duvalier past has come in the area of human rights and democracy. The CNG moved quickly to clean up Haiti's severely tarnished human rights record."

From 1986 to 1990, four military governments held power in Haiti. Each one promised to put Haiti on an irreversible path to democracy. Each one violated these vows. Each time, a new one came to the fore, U.S. government officials heralded it as Haiti's best hope for democracy, neglecting the obvious: Haitian democratic leaders with a proven track record of accomplishments in civilian life and concern for their fellow citizens had been consistently denied the opportunity to prove that they could do better than the existing power structure.

Meanwhile, more than 23,000 Haitian refugees had been intercepted at sea by U.S. Coast Guard cutters since 1981. Of these, only 6 were ever presumed refugees. All the others, except those needing emergency medical assistance, were promptly returned to Haiti and turned over to the authorities.

This apparent success on the high seas had not been matched by similar political gains in Haiti. Instead, the Haitian establishment's capacity to prevent the erosion of its power had significantly diminished. In March 1990, Lt.-General Prosper Avril, a trusted American ally, was forced to give up the reins of government in favor of secured asylum in the United States. Afterwards, the U.S. embraced free and fair elections under UN. supervision, prompting progressive and popular opposition figures to throw their hats into the ring. Among them was Father Jean-Bertrand Aristide.

Aristide was elected on December 16, 1990 in elections that were free, fair and peaceful. On that historic day in Haiti—it was this country's first-ever democratic election since gaining independence in 1804—Mr. Aristide, an advocate of the poor, won by a landslide. A late-comer into the race, Aristide quickly outpaced his competitors; the measure of support gained was unexpected even by the coalition of political parties which urged him to run. That coalition was known as the Front National pour le Changement et la Démocratie (National Front for Change and Democracy) or FNCD and included three groupings: the Parti du Congrés des Mouvements Démocratiques (Congress of Democratic Movements) or KONAKOM, the Confédération de l'Unité Démocratique (Confederation of Democratic Unity) or KID, and the Parti National Démocratique Progressiste d'Haïti (National Democratic and Progressive Party of Haiti) or PNDPH.

Each of these organizations was a major group in its own right. The KONAKOM, founded in 1987, included some 300 organizations with its membership primarily rooted in Haiti's heartland. The KID, an urban-based mass organization founded in 1986, was comprised of neighborhood committees established in Port-au-Prince's shantytowns. Though smaller than its partners, the PNDPH had a long history of struggle for democracy in Haiti going back to the time when Haiti was ruled by Jean-Claude Duvalier, a self-proclaimed "President-for-Life."

The enthusiastic reception given Aristide's bid for the presidency contributed to the creation of a truly mass movement. That movement became known as LAVALAS (the flood) and included members of Christian base communities (primarily Roman catholic), trade union and peasant organizations, professional associations and student organizations. A cursory review of the groups openly supporting Aristide's candidacy indicates that they included but were not limited to the Movement des Paysans de Papayes (Papayes Peasant Movement) or MPP, the Centrale Autonome des Travailleurs Haïtiens (Independent Federation of Haitian Workers) or CATH, the Confédération Nationale des Enseignants Haïtiens (National Confederation of Haitian Teachers) or CNEH, the Ti-Kominote Legliz (Little Church Communities) or TKL, Tèt Ansanm (Heads Together), and the Fédération Nationale des Etudiants Haïtiens (National Federation of Haitian Students) or FENEH. As the vote neared, the Haitian Chamber of Commerce and three Roman Catholic Bishops endorsed Aristide's candidacy. Supporters of President Aristide have since been known as Lavalas.

Aristide's policies in power never matched the populist rhetoric that sowed so much fear in the hearts of the people who despised and opposed him. In fact, except for a token effort at military reform, and more open displays of the President's religious embrace of the poor, little had changed in the conduct of Haitian politics. Still, the people of Haiti were more hopeful than ever that their basic wretched conditions would improve since they were subjected to far fewer abuses than in any previous years. That hope was reflected in the number of refugees interdicted by the U.S. Coast Guard. Prior to September 1991, as it was true of 1990, that number was never more than 1,200, three times less than the number of refugees intercepted in each of the years 1987, 1988, and 1989. Such significance was lost on Washington which, equating Aristide with radical left politics, failed to support him when the Haitian military moved to destroy his presidency.

The September 30, 1991 military coup caught everyone by surprise. President Aristide who was extremely popular before he was sworn in had become even more so following his trip to the United Nations where he met with world leaders and with large crowds of Haitian supporters in New York City and Miami. Upon his return to Haiti, he was given a massive and enthusiastic welcome by Haitians in Port-au-Prince. His popularity was unquestionable, leading his government to believe that no military force in Haiti would dare depose him, and to downplay insistent rumors of a coup d'état.

Even as the Haitian military stepped up attacks on the president's residence in Tabarre, on the northern outskirts of Port-au-Prince, shut down most radio station within hours, and positioned heavily armed units at key locations in Port-au-Prince with orders to shoot protesters, Aristide's prime minister, Rene Preval, believing it to be a minor soldiers' revolt, sought to play down the conflict (there had been three such rebellions since Aristide's inauguration). Aristide's flight into exile and the killings that were perpetrated in Port-au-Prince and rapidly spread to other parts of the country as Haitians everywhere mobilized against the putschists, showed otherwise. The September 30th coup far surpassed the military coups of the last five years, in terms of the numbers of Haitians killed, the widespread resistance which organized and unorganized Haitians tried to mobilize and the disruption of political and social life in the country.

As gunshots from semi-automatic weapons thundered during the days and nights following the coup, as the army stepped up search and destroy missions to flush out activists and resistance organizers, as the death toll mounted with no end in sight, it became increasingly clear that the Haitian army and its supporters were determined to exterminate every form of known and potential opposition to its rule. Soldiers acted with a ruthlessness unseen since François (Papa Doc) Duvalier unleashed the Tontons Macoutes on the people of Haiti.

Haitians fearing for their lives and hoping against all odds that President Aristide would soon be restored initially moved out of their households, leaving for rural areas which were presumably safer and less violent and where they could wait out the crisis. It has been estimated that in the early days of the coup d'état Port-au-Prince, a city of one million residents lost 10% of its population. Other cities such as Gonaives, Cap-Haitien, Jacmel, Jeremie, St. Marc, and Port-de-Paix experienced a similar population decrease. However, military-sponsored repression followed them there too, leaving them no place to hide. Because of the widespread nature of the repression, the United States, France, Canada among others urged all their nationals (development and relief workers, technical assistants and advisers) to leave Haiti immediately for they could not guarantee their safety under the circumstances. Seventeen American medical missionaries caught in the crisis in rural areas, commandeered three boats and fled the country immediately, underscoring the danger that even non-Haitians faced under military rule.

In response to the military coup in Haiti, the Organization of American States called on its members to impose trade sanctions on Haiti. Mexico and Venezuela immediately complied by suspending oil shipments. The U.S. followed suit by imposing sanctions that were to take effect on October 28 and be in full force by December 5, 1991. These sanctions were imposed on Haiti's military junta to force it to negotiate in good faith and facilitate the restoration of the Aristide government and the return of Aristide himself. Far from complying with these sanctions however, Haiti's de facto government continued to demonstrate that it was willing to go to any length to assure dictatorial order.

By late 1991, the Bush administration, faced with the largest flood of seafaring Haitian refugees since the 1980 Cuban boat lift, had virtually abandoned all but token efforts to restore Aristide to office. The U.S. was hesitant at first to return to their country Haitians intercepted at sea, seeking instead to convince countries in the Americas to offer them a safe harbor. These efforts appearing to bear little fruit, the U.S. decided to ship back the fleeing Haitians it had plucked from the ocean and transferred to its cutters.

However, a day after the U.S. resumed repatriation of the Haitian asylum-seekers in its custody, a federal district judge in Florida imposed a temporary restraining order on such actions, halting for the first time in 10 years a policy that had overcome several similar challenges. The Bush administration then decided to transfer the Haitians to the nearby Guantanamo naval base where they were screened for credible fear of persecution.

Thereafter, the U.S. administration focused its efforts on justifying its interdiction and refoulement of Haitian refugees in the hope of preventing them from becoming a major liability during the 1992 electoral campaign. President Bush adopted a policy that consisted of:

1.- Downplaying the severity of human rights abuses perpetrated by the Haitian military and insisting that Haitians' woes were due chiefly to poverty and lack of economic opportunities;

2.- Lifting trade sanctions against American business interests in Haiti:

3.- Equating Aristide's human rights record with his opponents:

4.- Opposing all attempts to honor Haitian refugees' pleas for asylum in a manner guaranteeing a fair process;

5.- Insisting on the swift refoulement of all Haitian refugees with rejected claims;

6.- Opposing the involvement of the UN High Commissioner for Refugees in Haitian refugee processing, but welcoming its support in finding other countries willing to provide asylum to the refugees.

In February 1992, faced with growing public criticism and congressional pressure, the Bush Administration established an in-country processing (ICP) program through the U.S. embassy in Port au Prince. That month, the Supreme Court lifted the ban on repatriation, allowing the Bush administration to promptly resume the practice.

Meanwhile, although welcomed as Haiti's legitimate authority wherever he traveled, Aristide, Haiti's most famous refugee, had to defend his record from accusations, coming mostly from the United States, that he used illegal and violent means to suppress dissent and that he planned to rule Haiti with an iron hand. Aristide's response was to imply strongly that the United States had engineered his fall, and that all it would take to reverse the coup would be "one phone call" from the White House. In addition, mistrustful of governments, he went on urging independent human rights groups and international supporters to undertake frequent visits to Haiti to report on human rights violations committed by the military regime, and to show solidarity with the Haitian people.

The parameters of the refugee debate were changed irrevocably when, on May 24 1992, President Bush ordered all Haitians interdicted on the high seas and summarily returned to Haiti, with no prior screening for refugees fearing persecution. Refugee processing in-country, conducted in close proximity of army barracks, became the only option for victims of the repressive military regime. Bush aimed to prevent the Haitian refugees from becoming a major issue in the electoral campaign. He succeeded, despite Bill Clinton's best efforts.

During the campaign, Clinton strongly criticized Bush for his administration's Haiti policy and implied that he would adopt a tough stand against the country's military rulers, reverse the refugee policy, and push hard for democracy and the restoration of Aristide. Aristide and his congressional supporters naturally expected a far greater commitment to their cause. While they were willing to concede to Clinton that it might take more than "one phone call" to get Lt.-General Raoul Cedras out of the way, they still insisted on "a date certain" for the President's return.

No sooner had Clinton won the elections than he began a rapid conversion to the policies of the Bush and Reagan administrations on Haitian refugees, forfeiting an early opportunity to rectify an illegal and irresponsible interdiction measure. His administration justified the President's reversal by a) raising the specter of a huge uncontrollable invasion of the United States by opportunistic job-seeking black Haitians with fraudulent claims of persecution once the President took office, and b) claiming that since the Haitians put themselves at risk of drowning, the U.S. had a responsibility to adopt rescue at sea and life-saving measures.

Additionally, it moved to still further criticism by taking steps to achieve President Aristide's return in conjunction with other members of the international community. Having secured President Aristide's support, together Bill Clinton and George Bush agreed to strengthen U.S. capacity to catch Haitians floating on the high seas with an unprecedented naval net outside Haiti's territorial waters: fifteen Coast Guard cutters, five Navy ships and several helicopters were dispatched under Operation White Picket Fence (Able Manner) to impede refugee flight.

In short, U.S. policy in Haiti consisted of two simple propositions:

1.- Contain Haitian migration to the United States at all costs;

2.- However great the inequalities in Haiti, however repugnant the elite and its military shield, U.S. interests were best served by an alliance with the established political order.

Haitian Refugee Policy Unravels

By January 1993, the struggle on behalf of Haitian refugees appeared to have been all but lost. President Clinton had turned his back on the Haitians, but had managed to get away with it because Aristide went along. Pundits profusely praised the President for taking the tough road and abandoning the "foolish ideas" that he had trumpeted during the campaign. Aristide supporters in the United

States, including the Congressional Black Caucus, followed his lead, bargaining their silence on Haitian refugees for a distant promise that Aristide's return to Haiti would be prompt.

Except that there remained more than 300 Haitian refugees in Guantanamo, quarantined there because they were found to be carrying the AIDS virus. These refugees refused to accept their condition and became very combative. Their supporters refused to give up as well.

The National Coalition for Haitian Refugees had adopted a strategy that sought to unravel Clinton's overall Haiti policy one bit at a time. Immediately following the Democrat's electoral win, its members had drafted and submitted to the president-elect a comprehensive plan for resolving both Haiti's political crisis and the U.S. refugee problem. NCHR had recommended among other things that Clinton:

1.- Designate a special envoy on Haiti who could bring U.S. and international pressure to bear on Haiti's military rulers;

2.- End the automatic repatriation of Haitian refugees;

3.- Establish for a 6-months period regional safe havens in the Caribbean, including in Guantanamo Bay, Cuba, in cooperation with governments in the region;

4.- Release the quarantined Haitian refugees and allow them to pursue their asylum claims on U.S. soil just like their 11,000 brothers and sisters who had been admitted earlier;

5.- Expand the number of sites within Haiti where refugees could be processed.

NCHR had realized early on that safe havens were the key element of the proposal but perhaps the most difficult to achieve. Indeed, the conventional wisdom at the highest levels of the Clinton Administration dictated that the administration seek at all cost to not give the Haitians an incentive to migrate in great numbers to the United States. It followed from this rationale that leniency toward Haitian refugees should not be tolerated because it could be such an incentive and could prompt thousands of Haitians to seek entry into the U.S. The bottom line was that State Department, National Security Council, Immigration Service and Defense Department officials blurred the lines between refugees and immigrants and preferred to consider all Haitians to be opportunistic job-seekers.

NCHR recognized that for its recommendations to be at least seriously considered, it had to meet administration's concerns part of the way. And so NCHR recommended that safe haven be coupled with an aggressive effort to settle Haiti's political crisis in a manner that met Haitians' expectations that democracy would reign in their country. And that while efforts were actively being pursued in this regard, its agencies would cooperate with the administration in communicating to the beneficiaries of safe haven that sheltering them was temporary and would not, for at least a 6-month period, lead to admission of any kind to the United States, even if the refugee could meet international refugee criteria.

This was undoubtedly a concession to the conservative and reactionary forces within the administration and Congress, but a necessary concession. Yet, except for the recommendations pertaining to the special envoy and the increase in the number of refugee processing sites in Haiti, the administration had rejected NCHR's primary recommendation. NCHR had no other choice but to try to make Clinton's Haiti policy as much of a domestic issue as any other issue deserving of the American public's attention.

Soon after President Clinton took office, the refugees declared a hunger strike in Guantanamo, challenging both President Clinton and President Aristide to keep their word and succeeding in re-focusing international, and most importantly national attention to their plight. In solidarity with the refugees, college students across the United States engaged in hunger strikes, teach-ins and picket lines. Celebrities followed suit with public appearances decrying the internment of the Haitian refugees. And refugee advocates stepped up their efforts to influence Clinton's politics.

By March 1993, Clinton's support among African-American members of Congress had slipped to a considerable degree. That month, his defense of the automatic return policy before the Supreme Court of the United States forced the Congressional Black Caucus to rally around the striking refugees. Still, they were willing to publicly challenge the President on the refugee issue only to a small degree, while focusing on Clinton's promise to deliver Aristide's return in a short time-frame. It fell primarily to the refugees' lawyers and policy advocates to keep pursuing their release.

In May 1993, Judge Sterling Johnson of the Federal District Court in Brooklyn, NY ordered that all Haitians at Guantanamo Bay, Cuba be brought in so that they could be provided the medical assistance they needed. A month later, the Supreme Court ruled almost unanimously—Justice Blackmun was the sole dissenter—that the President of the United States could order the repatriation of Haitian refugees without being constrained by treaty obligations.

Justice Stevens, writing on behalf of the majority said that "Although gathering fleeing refugees and returning them to the one country they had desperately sought to escape may violate the spirit of Article 33, general humanitarian intent cannot impose uncontemplated obligations on treaty signatories. Although not dispositive, the Convention's negotiating history—which indicates, inter alia, that the right of non-refoulement applies only to aliens physically present in the host country, that the term "refouler" was included in Article 33 to avoid concern about an inappropriately broad reading of the word "return," and that the Convention's limited reach resulted from a hard-fought bargain—solidly supports the foregoing conclusion."

By then, however, sufficient momentum had built up against the White House's strategy of appeasement of Haiti's military rulers at Aristide's expense. Compelled to act, Washington agreed to threaten the military's supporters in the business community with an effective embargo, prompting them in turn to force Lieutenant-General Cedras to the negotiating table.

Asylum-seekers at the U.S. military base at Guantanomo Bay, Cuba. (photo: National Coalition for Haitian Refugees)

In July 1993, the UN convened the two antagonists at Governors Island in NY where they finally agreed that by October 30, 1993, the General would step down and the President would return to head a coalition government in Port-au-Prince. Meanwhile, the international community pledged to provide both the military and economic support necessary to create an environment facilitating a peaceful return of democratic rule This promise implied the use of force if necessary, an option that none of the four friends of Haiti at the UN (the U.S., France, Canada and Venezuela) were initially ready to exercise on their own or support through UN mechanisms.

The Haitian military saw things differently however, and almost as soon as its leadership returned to Port-au-Prince, sought to create an environment in which only terror prevailed, the insertion of multilateral forces in Haiti would proceed on its terms if at all, and Aristide's return would be postponed if not foiled altogether.

By mid-October 1993, the International Civilian Mission (ICM) of the UN and the OAS was reporting a crescendo of politically-motivated killings. Despite occasionally strong statements by the UN. Secretary-General's Special Envoy to Haiti, Mr. Dante Caputo, against General Cedras and Colonel Michel Francois, chief of the Port-au-Prince Police, the international community as a whole maintained that the Governors Island Agreement was on track and that they expected the Haitian military to relinquish power. Meanwhile, the latter was repeatedly reassured that its leaders would be granted a blanket amnesty, might be posted abroad or reassigned to a different command post, but that they would not lose their rank and that military reforms would not necessarily lead to a diminution of the army's influence.

Although it appeared that Haiti's military was winning the upper hand with such a strategy, they were forcing the Clinton administration to decisively choose between them and Aristide, failing to realize that this was precisely what would give credence to the refugees' claims and help expose their plight to an ever-broader American audience.

They handed Clinton a humiliating defeat when the U.S. troops to be deployed in Haiti in accordance with the Governors Island Agreement failed to land when the White House, reacting to tragic events in Somalia in which several American soldiers were killed, ordered the troops' return after a two-day standoff with Haitian paramilitaries. Clinton's Republican opposition, aided by officials in the CIA and the Pentagon, seized the opportunity to pound further on the President, bringing to the fore Aristide's alleged psychological instabilities to force the President to abandon the objective of returning him to office.

Publicly, Haiti's President remained supportive of Clinton, hoping that he would maintain his goal of facilitating the removal of the military leadership. He could not however ignore these developments. As Clinton appeared to walk away from Haiti altogether as an impregnable third-world enigma—Secretary of State

Warren Christopher began to lay down the justification for such a policy by referring to Haiti as a failed state—Aristide began to pay attention to the refugee advocates who had counseled a public and strong stand on behalf of Haitian refugees as the way to his own salvation. NCHR had recommended that Haiti give the required 6-months notice to the United States that it would no longer give them the authority to intercept boatloads of Haitian refugees as per the 1981 interdiction agreement. Shortly before Christmas 1993, President Aristide threw the Clinton administration into turmoil by issuing a strong statement condemning automatic repatriation, in light of Haiti's abysmal human rights record.

It took the Haitian President another four months before he formally gave the required notice. By that time however, much had been done to bring the refugee issue to the fore of Clinton's domestic agenda. Randall Robinson, head of TransAfrica, had joined with refugee advocates in focusing attention to the plight of the refugees and the gross human rights violations that were prevalent in Haiti, rather than the simple return of Aristide. Robinson initiated a hunger strike, vowing to end it only when the Administration took steps to provide fair hearing to Haitians fleeing terror in their homeland. The Congressional Black Caucus engaged in civil disobedience to achieve the same goal. Meanwhile, NCHR took the Administration to task for failing to address both the human rights and refugee crisis in Haiti. A month later, on May 8, Clinton announced the desired change in refugee policy, pleading for time so that he could establish the environment necessary to conduct the refugee hearings.

To most of the advocates, this was undoubtedly a stunning reversal and a victory to be relished. They were willing to concede to the administration the respite it requested. NCHR believed however that while hearings were a progressive step, they were nonetheless a half-measure that merited to be made complete.

Government spokespersons were openly predicting that some 95% of Haitian refugees' claims would be denied, thereby signifying that the vast majority would continue to be returned to the terror in Haiti. In this context, NCHR stepped up both its private and public efforts to promote safe havens as the only viable step forward, given the situation of generalized violence that prevailed in Haiti. More importantly, NCHR argued that refugee processing would undoubtedly yield more migration, not less, regardless of the efforts developed to restrict the number of eventual beneficiaries. In the end, NCHR's views prevailed.

Shipboard refugee processing was launched on June 17, 1994 off the coast of Jamaica, but news that asylum claims would be considered had rapidly spread throughout Haiti. Largely as a result, thousands of Haitians, seeking to escape the escalating violence of an increasingly isolated army, chose to take to sea. On U.S. Independence Day alone, some 3,247 Haitians were interdicted, a number far surpassing the U.S. government's predictions and overwhelming the capacity of the single U.S. naval vessel designated for shipboard screenings. With more than 10,000 Haitians intercepted in a ten-day period, it became clear that even the reopening of facilities at the U.S. naval base at Guantanamo Cuba would prove incommensurate to the task. Succumbing both to the unanticipated number of desperate asylum-seekers and to the persistence of the scrutiny of its screening procedures by NCHR and other allied agencies—on July 5, upon consultation with NCHR and others in the refugee advocacy community, the Clinton government announced its plan for a network of safe haven zones for Haitians. Almost immediately afterwards, the exodus of Haitian refugees slowed and finally stopped. Instead, Haitians awaited the freedom they had been promised.

Epilogue

President Aristide returned to Haiti on the wings of the United States military two weeks after the formal end of the Haitian Migrant Interdiction Operation. The U.S. no longer has the diplomatic fig leaf it needed in 1981 to initiate high seas interception and refoulement. It has however a Supreme Court decision that grants the President almost blanket license to do for refugees as he pleases. Unless of course, Congress decides to adopt legislation limiting the President's authority in this area.

Such is not likely to occur however. Under significant domestic pressure, the Clinton establishment cracked, and momentarily set aside its prejudices to act upon the recommendations of the refugees' advocates. In the process, it has discovered "safe haven." And the lesson it retained was that safe haven cut the flow of refugees. Faced with a sudden exodus of Cuban rafters, Clinton quickly allowed that they would not be given a free ride to Florida and that instead they would be granted shelter in Guantanamo Bay and Panama. He wasted no time afterwards in conferring on the Cubans the status that had been reserved the Haitians for decades: opportunistic job-seeking migrants seeking to jump in the front of the immigration line. The Administration has once again reverted to type, denying that among these Cubans are refugees who cannot avail themselves of the protection of their government, thereby blurring the lines between refugees and immigrants.

The international refugee protection regime, erected in the aftermath of World War II, was not able to adequately respond to the Haitian refugee dilemma when governments refused to abide by its rules. Although a party to the Protocol relating to tile status of Refugees and once a vehement opponent of the forcible refoulement of Vietnamese refugees by countries in Southeast Asia, the U.S. absolutely refused to comply with the Protocol's provisions with respect to Haitian refugees. The U.S. sought instead to compromise the protection mission of the

UN High Commissioner for Refugees. That this institution did not completely give in to U.S. pressure signals perhaps that the system has not completely collapsed.

The lesson of the 13-year struggle on behalf of Haitian refugees is, however, simple: any struggle on behalf of persons alien to the country in which this struggle is being waged has to be part of the domestic battleground. Otherwise, no efforts however valiant will succeed.

Notes

1. The United States fashioned new, politically-expedient standards by which to judge Haitians' claims to fear of persecution. U.S. asylum officers were told that their determination that a Haitian deserved the protection of the U.S. in a safe haven such as that established at Guantanamo would have to be based on the belief that "notwithstanding the changed circumstances in Haiti, the migrant will face serious harm. for reasons related to the migrant's individual circumstances but not related to personal disputes, if he or she is returned to Haiti."

2. François Duvalier came to power in 1957 and immediately set out to destroy his political opponents, first with the assistance of the Haitian military—which had traditionally been the power-broker since the end of the U.S. occupation of Haiti in 1934—and secondly by creating a large militia, the Tontons Macoutes, who answered only to his command. Several democrats were killed, or died in prison. Those who escaped fled into exile. The unprecedented level of repression in Haiti led to the migration of a substantial number of Haiti's middle class to the United States, Canada, France and African countries. In some cases, this migration was even encouraged, as when the Duvalier government negotiated with the United Nations for the emigration of hundreds of Haitian teachers to newly independent countries in Africa. Today, there are more Haitian doctors practicing abroad than in Haiti. Several Haitian teachers occupy high-level positions in higher education establishments-, some chair the Caribbean or Afro-American programs of well-known universities. Haitians can also be found in positions of high responsibility in international financial institutions.

The Haitian parliament was dissolved, and when it was reinstated. Duvalier cronies put a legal face on otherwise illegal government policies. The Courts were also staffed by Duvalier loyalists who ratified arbitrary appropriation of land and property. Most of the high-ranking officers in the Haitian military who had acquired their position prior to the establishment of the dictatorship were removed from the ranks and replaced by Duvalierists, some of whom had no military training. Finally, the Roman Catholic Church itself became subservient to Duvalier rule, when following a series of expulsions of priests and bishops, Duvalier gained the right to appoint the Bishops through an agreement with the Vatican.

During this time, trade unions and peasant associations which had began to develop in the late 1950's were banned, and their leaders forced into exile. No political party, except the government party, was allowed the freedom of association.

François Duvalier died in 1971, leaving the presidency in the hands of his son Jean-Claude who was then just 18 years old.

3. INS was not empowered to automatically grant asylum to a Haitian refugee, who convincingly made a plea for asylum on a Coast Guard cutter. Instead, still subject to exclusion under U.S. immigration laws, the Haitian would be paroled into the mainland

and granted the opportunity to state his case before an immigration judge with the assistance of an attorney. Therefore, while the Haitian jumped over the initial hurdle of Coast Guard screening, he could still end up in Haiti.

4. Upon his inauguration, President Aristide publicly shamed the high command into giving up power by choosing retirement. Months later, he issued an executive order dismissing the section chiefs whose abuse of the Haitian citizenry had become legendary. No measures however were taken to improve prison conditions, reform the administration of justice and quickly establish a police force independent of the military. Neither was support given to local civilian councils, composed of democratically-elected officials who nevertheless depended on the central government support to carry out democratic reforms. Instead, Aristide endlessly called for a marriage of the army and the people, without fundamentally challenging the army itself. Thus, by September 1991, he had sown the seeds of his own demise.

Americans protesting against the U.S. government's refugee policy outside of the White House, July 1992. (photo: National Coalition for Haitian Refugees)

Lilia S. Velasquez

The Effect of U.S. Foreign Policy on Asylum Applicatants

Introduction

The United States has a history of applying its asylum law with "ideological selectivity."[1] The effect of this selectivity for potential refugees is that the political relationship between the originating country and the United States will be a substantial factor in determining whether asylum will be granted. Because refugee policy can be used to embarrass and destabilize other governments, the United States is wary of granting asylum to a person from a country with which it has amicable relations.[2] However, applying asylum law with ideological selectivity is a blatant violation of the international instruments and the United States' Refugee Act of 1980, which bar these types of political considerations in the asylum process.[3]

As in other countries, immigration and asylum laws have recently gained widespread publicity in the united States. This publicity was precipitated by the recent attempt of thousands of Cuban and Haitian refugees to enter the United States by boat across the high seas.[4] Though the need and desperation of these people is unquestionable, the United States government is vigorously attempting to restrict the number of refugees entering the country. Like many other countries, the United States is developing a closed-door policy to foreigners and immigrants.[5] Growing anti-immigrant sentiment and unstable domestic economies have had an important role in this policy change, however, foreign and domestic political considerations continue to be the driving force in the application of asylum laws.[6]

This article will discuss asylum law in general with a focus on the disparity of application to different groups of people depending on the relationship the United States has with the government of the originating country. Part one will provide a general overview of the two main international instruments governing the treatment of refugees by receiving countries, specifically, the 1951 Convention Relating to the Status of Refugees[7] and its 1967 Protocol.[8] Part two explains how foreign policy considerations have resulted in the disparate treatment and application of asylum laws to different groups of applicants, specifically, refugees from Central America and the Caribbean. Part three will discuss the future of asylum law in the United States with a focus on the proposed Expedited Exclusion and Alien Smuggling Enhanced Penalties Act of 1994, which is currently pending in Congress. In conclusion, this article will offer some recommendations to improve and expand the interpretation of asylum law. These will include, pressure upon the government for a more neutral and objective application of asylum law, the international condemnation of interdiction practices, similar to that promulgated in the Kennebunkport Order,[9] and the addition of gender-based persecution to the definition of refugee. The proposed recommendations will aid in bringing asylum law up to date and provide greater protection to refugees around the world.

1. International Instruments Governing the Treatment of Refugees

International awareness of the need for guidelines concerning the treatment of refugees came to the forefront in the late 1940's.[10] The dramatic increase in the number of displaced people following World War II demanded this attention from the international community, since no existing international instruments addressed a refugee situation of this dimension.[11] A committee of representatives from thirteen nations was appointed by the United Nations Economic and Social Committee to draft the 1951 Convention Relating to the Status of Refugees (1951 Convention).[12]

The 1951 Convention is significant in that it outlined who is eligible to receive asylum protections. Article I of the 1951 Convention defines the term "refugee" as follows:

A. For the purposes of the present Convention, the term "refugee," shall apply to any person who;

(1) Has been considered a refugee under the Arrangements of 12 May 1926 and 30 June 1928 or under the Conventions of 28 October 1933 and 10 February 1938, the Protocol of 14 September 1939 or the Constitution of the International Refugee organization;

(2) As a result of events occurring before 1 January 1951 and owing to well-founded fear of being persecuted for reasons of race, religion, nationality, membership of a particular social group or political opinion, is outside the country of his nationality and is unable or, owing to such fear, is unwilling to avail himself of the protection of that country; or who, not having a nationality and being outside the country of his former habitual residence as a result of such events, is unable or, owing to such fear, is unwilling to return to it.[13]

Even if a person met this strict definition of "refugee," she would not be guaranteed "asylum." Although there are references to asylum in the Preamble to the 1951 Convention, the granting of asylum is not dealt with in that Convention.[14]

Since the implementation of the 1951 Convention, the non-*refoulement* obligation specified in Article 33, paragraph 1, has been the single most significant protection given to refugees.[15] Non-refoulement refers to the obligation that no refugee may be returned against his will to a territory "where his life or freedom would be threatened on account of his race, religion, nationality, membership of a particular social group or political opinion."[16] Therefore, because the 1951 Convention expressly prohibits the refoulement of refugees, one would expect parties to the 1951 Convention to be obligated to admit refugees into their territory.

Although the United States is not a party to the 1951 Convention, it is under similar international obligations because it ratified the 1967 Protocol Relating to the Status of Refugees (the 1967 Protocol).[17] The 1967 Protocol incorporated the terms of the 1951 Convention by reference and expanded its application.[18] The time and place limitations of the 1951 Convention were eliminated and its protections were expanded to apply to all refugees worldwide, regardless of when or where they fled.[19] Unfortunately, like the 1951 Convention, it did not deal with the granting of asylum.[20]

Haitian refugees under U.S. Coast Guard custody being returned to the docks in Port-au-Prince, Haiti, February 1992 (photo: Maud Weiss)

In the United States, the 1951 Convention and the 1967 Protocol are given effect through the Immigration and Nationality Act (INA).[21] The United States government enacted the Refugee Act of 1980 to amend the INA so that it conformed to the 1967 protocol.[22] Since amendment, the INA has been construed as living up to the terms of the 1967 Protocol and the 1951 Convention.[23]

The standard used by the United States Immigration and Naturalization Service (INS)[24] in determining refugee status is whether the person is outside the country of his nationality and is unwilling to return to it due to past persecution or due to a well-founded fear of future persecution on the basis or race, religion, nationality, membership in a particular social group, or political opinion.[25] Even if a person can prove that she meets these requirements, the INS can still refuse to grant asylum in its discretion.[26] In 1993, 150,386 people from 154 countries submitted asylum applications to the INS.[27] Only 18,100 applications were actually processed by the INS and of those processed, approximately 5,100 people were granted asylum.[28] As these statistics show, this standard is not easily met. However, there is irrefutable evidence that other political factors, not sanctioned by law or treaty, are playing a part in the determination of whether or not an asylum applicant meets the definition of refugee and can be granted asylum.

2. The Discriminatory Application of Asylum Law in the United States

The United States enforces its asylum law with ideological selectivity because its refugee determinations are influenced by the relationship that the United States government has with the government of the persons' originating country.[29] Since 1980, the approval rate of asylum claims for refugees from countries with which the United States has not historically had amicable relations, such as Bulgaria, Romania, Russia, Afghanistan, and Libya, has been between fifty and eighty percent.[30] On the other hand, the rate of approval for refugees from countries whose governments are supported by the United States at the time, for example Haiti, El Salvador, or Guatemala, has been between one and five percent.[31] These statistics clearly show that applicants from communist controlled countries have a much lower threshold of proof than is required of others from non-communist, authoritarian regimes that are American allies.[32]

A look at how asylum law has been applied to Central Americans, specifically those from El Salvador, Guatemala, and Nicaragua will demonstrate the selectivity with which asylum protections have been granted in the United States. Also, a historical view of Caribbean refugees, namely those from Haiti and Cuba will show how asylum policy is changing in the United States and being used as a political tool.

A. Central American Refugees

During most of the 1980s, Central America, specifically Nicaragua, El Salvador, and Guatemala, was involved in violent guerrilla warfare and counter-insurgency operations.[33] It has been estimated that during these years over 100,000 Guatemalans were killed.[34] Another 40,000 Guatemalan citizens remain unaccounted for.[35] El Salvador did not fare much better. Between the years of 1979 and 1985, 60,000 of its citizens were killed.[36]

The brutal fighting in Central America resulted in thousands of displaced persons. By 1989, an estimated two million Central Americans had left their homelands to seek refuge in other countries.[37] About 80% of those persons fled to the United States.[38] Many Central Americans sought refugee protection once inside U.S. territory. However, the United States was very hesitant to grant asylum to citizens of El Salvador and Guatemala. Since the United States supported the governments of El Salvador and Guatemala, the granting of asylum to those persons would have been tantamount to an admission by the United States that it was giving aid to governments that violated internationally recognized civil rights.[39] This resulted in noticeably lower asylum approval rates for Salvadorans and Guatemalans when compared to those of Nicaragua, which was then a communist country with which the United States was at war (albeit through the proxy "Contra" army).[40]

Those Salvadorans and Guatemalans who did apply for asylum had a shockingly low approval rate of about 2%.[41] The INS treated these people as similarly situated to Mexican immigrants long before there was civil unrest in Mexico.[42] That is, they were labeled as illegal economic migrants and were shipped back to their countries without being informed of their right to apply for political asylum.[43] It was estimated that 10,500 of the 16,000 Salvadorans apprehended in 1981 by the INS were returned back to El Salvador.[44] Many Guatemalans also had a similar fate.

On the other hand, Nicaraguans were treated very differently by U.S. immigration officials. During the late 1980s, more Nicaraguans were granted asylum status than any other nationality.[45] Furthermore, those persons that were denied asylum were not hastily deported.[46] Former United States Attorney General[47] Edwin Meese III ordered that no Nicaraguan be deported until the U.S. Department of Justice[48] reviewed the case, even if that alien had been denied asylum and had exhausted all appeals.[49] In 1989, 199 Nicaraguans were actually deported, while 4,731 Salvadorans were forced to leave the country.[50] In answering questions about the disparity in the granting of asylum when more civilians had been killed in El Salvador than in Nicaragua, Meese stated, "Of course, it is understandable that persons would have a well-founded fear of being returned to a totalitarian country, such as Nicaragua, than to a democratic country, such as El Salvador."[51] Experienced asylum advocates and practicing refugee lawyers had observed that the INS systematically discriminated against applicants from El Salvador and Guatemala in its adjudication of asylum applications. In response to this glaring pattern of discrimination, a lawsuit was filed in 1985 in a U.S. Federal Court on behalf of these persons by more than 80 religious and refugee non-governmental organizations against the INS.[52] They had alleged that the INS was violating the 1980 Refugee Act. In December of 1990, the INS decided to settle the dispute rather than have it go to trial for a determination of fact and law.[53] In the settlement ("ABC settlement") the INS acknowledged that foreign policy and border enforcement considerations are not proper factors in determining eligibility for asylum, nor are the government's opinion of the political or ideological beliefs of the applicant, nor the fact that an individual is from a country that the U.S. politically supports.[54]

Under the terms of the settlement, the INS would reconsider over 150,000 asylum petitions from El Salvadorans and Guatemalans that were previously denied.[55] Following the settlement, the Department of Justice created a separate asylum office in Washington, D.C., named the "Central Office for Refugee, Asylum and Parole" to take care of the reprocessing.[56] The Asylum officers assigned to this office would be trained in international human rights issues and would function independent of the immigration service.[57] Through this new asylum system, the INS sought to improve the asylum adjudication process by making it more objective and equal to all applicants. However, to this date, nothing has been done. The 150,000 cases have not yet been reprocessed, but instead form part of the 350,000 asylum cases currently pending.[58]

Despite the ABC settlement, discrimination and disparity in the treatment of refugees from different countries of origin is not over. The recent influx of Haitian and Cuban boat people proved once again that refugee protection in the United States is not free from foreign policy considerations and continues to be used as a political tool.

B. Haitian Refugees

In 1981, an executive agreement was entered into between the United States and Haiti that allowed the "interdiction and selective return to Haiti of certain Haitian migrants and vessels involved in the illegal transport of persons coming from Haiti."[59] The agreement gave U.S. officials the authority to board Haitian ships and detain those on board if found to be in violation of United States or Haitian law.[60] Under the agreement, the United States recognized its international obligations and stated that it would not return any Haitian migrant that qualified for refugee status.[61] Those not meeting refugee status would then be returned to a Haitian port.[62]

In December of 1990, Jean-Bertrand Aristide was voted into office.[63] He was the first democratically elected president in Haiti since the country gained its independence 186 years before.[64] Despite his popular support among the Haitian people, he was ousted by the Haitian military during his first year in office.[65] Aristide then traveled to the United States where he lived in exile.[66]

After the military coup in September of 1991, a consistent pattern of gross violations of internationally recognized human rights were committed by Haitian security forces, and this pattern gained international recognition. These violations included extra-judicial executions, torture, disappearances, and arbitrary arrests.[67] Supporters of Aristide were forced into hiding for fear that they would be killed by those in power.[68] Since the 1991 military coup, approximately 40,000 Haitians fled the violence of their country.[69] many of these people fled to the United States by boat. In accordance with the ten-year old U.S.-Haiti agreement, Haitian boats were intercepted and all potential refugees were screened to determine whether they were "refugees" and were therefore eligible for asylum or, in the alternative, eligible for protection from refoulement.[70]

In May of 1992, however, in a dramatic change in policy, United States President George Bush issued the Kennebunkport Order,[71] which called for the interdiction and return of all undocumented migrants on the high seas, regardless of their potential status as refugees.[72] The United States became the first country in the world to ever implement such a policy.[73] Because the Kennebunkport order appeared to violate both U.S. immigration law[74] and the 1967 Protocol,[75] refugee non-governmental organizations filed a lawsuit in federal court to enjoin its implementation.[76] Although the federal judge did find that the Kennebunkport order violated U.S. immigration law, the victory was short lived. In June of 1993, the United States Supreme Court held in the case of *Sale v. Haitian Centers Council* that the relevant portion of the INA and of the 1951 Convention (as adopted by the 1967 Protocol) applied only to actions taken by the united States within its own territorial waters.[77] Accordingly, since the questionable actions were taking place outside U.S. territorial waters, the executive order did not violate either provision, even though repatriation of Haitians with potential refugee claims may occur as a result.[78] The court's decision completely ignored the humanitarian purposes behind both the federal and international provisions and potentially stunted the further development of international human rights law and the recognition of international human rights law within the united States.[79]

Meanwhile, 14,590 Haitians had applied for asylum at processing centers within Haiti between January and November of 1993.[80] As of August 1993, only 307 Haitians were granted refugee status and permitted to immigrate to the United States and request asylum.[81] These statistics show that in-country processing is not a practical solution for most Haitians. Because Haitians are subject to persecution for merely attempting to seek asylum,[82] in-country processing is further made futile.

Restoring democracy to Haiti soon became a national interest to the United States in an effort to stop the constant exodus of Haitian boat people escaping the country.[83] In July of 1993, a meeting was held between President Aristide and Lieutenant General Raoul Cedras, the military leader following the coup.[84] An agreement was reached that called for Aristide's return to Haiti by October 30, 1993, the resignation and granting of amnesty to General Cedras, the lifting of an embargo on Haiti and a resumption of economic aid to the country. However, General Cedras failed to step down.[85]

In response to this breach, international sanctions were levied against Haiti. Also, on October 18, 1993, the U.S.. interdiction program was temporarily suspended, thus fleeing refugees would no longer be returned to Haiti.[86] On May 7, 1994, President William Clinton finally rejected the Kennebunkport Order. The new administration continues to encourage Haitians to apply for refugee status at processing centers in Haiti, rather than fleeing by boat. However, it was announced that all Haitians interdicted at sea would only be given a truncated asylum interviews[87] on board U.S. ships and at sites such as Guantanamo Bay, Cuba. No appeal is possible from these interviews.

In September of 1994, a U.S. invasion of Haiti aimed at the restoration of Aristide to power became imminent.[88] Amidst a growing threat of invasion, former U.S. President James Carter was able to negotiate a new accord with General Cedras. Cedras again agreed to step down from power on the condition that he would be granted amnesty by the Haitian Parliament. Shortly after the accord was made public, President Clinton announced that the 14,000 Haitians being detained at Guantanamo Bay, Cuba, would soon begin their return home. Jean-Bertrand Aristide regained the Presidential position in Haiti in October of 1994.[89]

It is difficult to discern the criteria that the Presidents of the United States have used to formulate their respective Haitian refugee interdiction policies. These policies do not appear to adhere to any objective goal of international human rights law or humanitarian law, but appear to result from the political motivation of halting a large influx of Haitian refugees.

C. Cuban Refugees

The best example where refugees are being used as political tools is seen in the relationship between the United States and Cuba. There, a combination of both foreign policy and the domestic policy of the state of Florida played a key role in shaping the application of asylum law to Cuban nationals.[90] Until recently, the American policy toward Cubans was best illustrated by ex-President Carter's words that Cubans are welcomed with "an open heart and open arms."[91] This welcoming policy was codified in the Adjustment Act of 1966. That Act provides for a virtual automatic granting of political asylum.[92] Additionally, the Act provided that any Cuban who was lawfully admitted into the United States subsequent to January 1, 1959, and has been physically in the territory of the United States for at least one year will be granted permanent residence status.[93] This law has been a powerful draw for Cubans to come to the U.S.

In 1984, a bilateral agreement was made between Cuba and the United States in which Cubans with close family members in the United States were legally entitled to immigrate.[94] Although 20,000 visas were allocated for Cubans each year, there have been far fewer visas actually granted. In 1993, only 964 Cubans were granted visas.[95] During the first six months of this year, 1,200 visas have been granted.[96] Because legal immigration was not very significant, and the economic situation in Cuba worsened, due in large part to the U.S. economic blockade, large numbers of Cubans felt they had no other option than to attempt to reach the U.S. by sea.

In late August of 1994, it was estimated that 4,000 Cubans had fled the island by boat since the beginning of that month.[97] Cuban President Fidel Castro was seen as attempting to dictate American immigration policy by not taking steps to stop the boat people from leaving.[98] Also, this tactic was seen as blackmailing the U.S. to have talks with Cuba on such things as the lifting of the embargo and the return of the Guantanamo naval station.[99]

On August 18, 1994, in the most dramatic shift of U.S. Policy, Attorney General Janet Reno announced that the INS would interdict all Cubans at sea and detain them at a safe haven in the U.S. naval base in Guantanamo Bay, located on the Cuban island.[100] In addition, those Cubans who reached the United States would be sent to Dade County's Krome Detention Camp in Miami, Florida. [101] Cubans, who had for years been given special treatment, were being treated like Haitian refugees. However, unlike Haiti, the U.S. does not have a repatriation agreement with Cuba, therefore, Cubans do not have the option of voluntarily returning to their country. At least theoretically, Cubans could remain in detention indefinitely.[102]

Since sending Haitians to "safe havens" had slowed the exodus somewhat, the U.S. believed it would work the same for Cubans.[103] However, news of the new U.S. policy of interdiction did not immediately stop the continued refugee flow of Cubans, as more boat people took to the sea. One day after the announcement was made, 575 refugees arrived in the united States.[104] It became clear that some additional action had to be taken by the United States if it wanted to stem the flow of refugees. Eventually, an accord was signed on September 9, 1994, between the U.S. and Cuba.[105] The Cuban government agreed to take measures to stop its citizens from fleeing by sea in exchange for a guarantee from the U.S. that a minimum of 20,000 Cubans would be admitted into the U.S. each year.[106] U.S. law places various numerical limits on the admission of refugees and immigrants. The 1994 accord with Cuba is unique in that the U.S. guaranteed that it would admit a minimum, not a maximum, number of people. This accord appears to violate established U.S. immigration law which sets a ceiling of 20,000 visas per year per country.[107]

The United States' strong anti-Cuban government attitude is based more on emotion[108] and satisfying a powerful Cuban lobby, than on any viable foreign policy argument, since Cuba no longer poses any threat to U.S. national security after the fall of the Soviet Union.[109] Other influences in this radical policy change were the strong pressures from irate taxpayers worried about costs of supporting refugees, and the impending re-election of Democratic Governor Lawton Chiles in Florida.[110] Also one must question why the United States continues to have ties with Vietnam, whose human-rights record is no worse than Cuba, or why Communist China was recently extended most-favored trading nation status.[111] Clearly, the root of U.S. immigration policy lies in its political motives. The change in the attitude of the United States has, at best, left Cuban refugees feeling betrayed.[112]

3. The Future of Asylum Law in the United States

As of 1993, the number of refugees in the world has been estimated to be over 16 million,[113] the majority of which are women.[114] In addition, the number of people internally displaced within their own countries has reached 24 million.[115] There are numerous causes for this growth in the number of displaced persons around the world, including internal strife, war, and famine.[116] However, at a time when the number of refugees has escalated and continues to grow, receiving countries in Western Europe and the United States have begun to severely restrict the number of refugees who can benefit from asylum protection. In the United States, this sentiment has taken the form of proposed legislation entitled, "The Expedited Exclusion and Alien Smuggling Enhanced Penalties Act of 1993."[117] If implemented, it could have the impact of excluding potential legitimate asylum seekers.

The Exclusion Act would amend the INA to prohibit the granting of asylum to anyone who uses or attempts to use fraudulent documents to enter the United States, unless this person has a credible fear of persecution.[118] This determination would be made at the port of entry by an immigration agent and a decision denying asylum would not be subject to judicial appeal. The only form of review available for a denial would be by a limited petition of *habeas corpus*.[119]

This provision of the Exclusion Act could have the greatest impact on refugee women because of the evidentiary problems posed by determining refugee status immediately at the port of entry. In addition to the more common forms of violence, females are uniquely targeted for gender-related persecution, such as genital mutilation, forced sterility, and systematic rape.[120] It has been recognized

The U.S. *contra* war against Nicaragua created hundreds of thousands of refugees, as the attacks were mostly against "soft targets," meaning civilians and property. This family is temporarily housed in a school building in Honduras. (photo: UNHCR / D 8044 / J. C. Constant)

that women who are victims of this type of persecution, specifically sexual assault or violence, may suffer from Rape Trauma Syndrome.[121] Thus, female claimants may have greater difficulty in communicating their story of persecution to an immigration agent, who may be insensitive to their situations. Furthermore, because the Exclusion Act offers no useful form of judicial review, a decision denying asylum will have dire consequences for female refugees.

The Exclusion Act would also allow the Attorney General of the United States to invoke, without referral to an immigration judge, the power to order the exclusion of an alien who appears to be excludable, in certain circumstances. These circumstances would include when the number of aliens en route to the U.S. or when circumstances surrounding the arrival of aliens to the U.S. presents an "extraordinary immigration situation." The Attorney General would have sole discretion to determine when such an extraordinary immigration situation exists. The addition of this provision was clearly made with the recent influx of thousands of Haitians and Cubans in mind. It is problematic however, because the Attorney General is given total and uncontrolled power to declare an extraordinary immigration situation for any reason, proper or improper.

The power to exclude could also be invoked to exclude any alien aboard a vessel outside the territorial waters of the U.S., or a vessel encountered within the territorial seas or waters of the U.S., or an alien who has arrived on a vessel into the U.S. without authority. This provision seeks to expand the scope of the Kennebunkport Order to include territorial waters inside the United States. It is debatable whether the Supreme Court would sanction such an expansion; however, given the *Sale* decision, support for the expansion is more likely than not.

If passed, the Exclusion Act could severely affect legitimate refugee seekers. The last action taken on the bill was on Feb. 28, 1994.[122] Its status is pending.

4. Recommendations

There are several actions that can be taken which will improve the outlook for refugees in the world. This section will offer the following alternatives: 1) Putting pressure upon the government for a more neutral and objective application of asylum law; 2) the international condemnation of interdiction practices, similar to those promulgated in the Kennebunkport Order; and 3) the addition of gender-based persecution to the definition of refugee as promulgated in the 1951 Convention.

A. The Neutral and Objective Application of Asylum Law

Lawsuits similar to that which produced the ABC settlement may be the best avenue yet for insisting upon the even-handed application of asylum law by the

U.S. government. Though the positive results of the settlement have been limited in that the Salvadoran and Guatemalan asylum cases have not been reprocessed, in principle the ABC settlement was a huge victory for refugee advocates. At the very least, the government acknowledged that political considerations did not legally have a place in refugee determinations.

Another possible alternative to ensure a more objective application of asylum law may arise from the international community. Article IV of the 1967 Protocol provides that disputes between States over the interpretation of the Protocol shall be referred to the International Court of Justice.[123] Since the International Court of Justice will not consider complaints filed by individuals or non-governmental organizations,[124] it is up to the international community to pressure one or more States to file a complaint against the United States. This pressure can arise in the form of intense international media criticism.

Another novel avenue for addressing the reasonableness of the U.S. asylum policies is through the Organization for Security and Cooperation in Europe.[125] One of the purposes of this organization is to resolve political disputes between *and within* member nations.[126] The United States is one of the charter members of this organization, and played a leading role in its continuing evolution since the organization's creation in 1975.[117] Here again, the international community should protest the United States asylum and interdiction practices by pressuring one or more States to invoke the mechanisms of the OSCE against the United States, including fact finding missions and mandatory dispute resolution procedures.

B. International Condemnation of the Kennebunkport Order

The United States is the first nation to adopt a policy of going beyond its territorial waters, intercepting potential refugees, and returning them to the country from which they escaped.[128] This policy was adopted by the United States in answer to the Haitian phenomenon; however, its ramifications could be much more significant. The *Sale* decision is the only judicial opinion addressing the question of whether refugees on the high seas may be returned to their originating country in accordance with the 1951 Convention.[129] Because the United States carries significant international clout,[130] the *Sale* decision may be used as influential international precedent, instead of being seen as a temporary response to an emergency. Furthermore, individual State practice is a critical component in the development and furtherance of customary international law and the interpretation of international agreements.[131] Thus, potentially, the Kennebunkport order and the subsequent actions of the United States may influence other countries in their analysis of customary international law and human rights.[132]

The international community must condemn practices such as these as violating the spirit of the 1951 Convention and the principle of non-refoulement, or other countries may soon be emulating the practices of the United States.

C. Gender-Based Persecution

Women seeking refugee status on the basis of persecution suffered on account of their gender are rarely recognized as refugees,[133] as defined by the 1951 Convention. Bride burning, genital mutilation, forced sterility, sexual slavery, systematic rape, and domestic violence have not in the past been accepted as forms of "persecution,"[134] but merely personal violence. Women seeking asylum have therefore been forced to present their claim within one of the Convention's five criteria: race, religion, nationality, membership in a particular social group, or political opinion.[135]

The United Nations High Commissioner for Refugees (UNHCR) has reported that women and girls form the majority of refugees,[136] yet they are much less likely to gain asylum than their male counterparts.[137] In response to this, the Executive Committee of UNHCR was presented with a resolution to call upon member-nations to designate women as a particular social group for refugee adjudication.[138] However, this resolution was denied because the committee believed that it "would imply criticism of certain religious beliefs or social or cultural practices."[139] Nevertheless, Canada in 1993 became the first country to address the special needs of women in adopting refugee determination guidelines that address the issue of gender-related persecution.[140]

In the United States, ideological and cultural biases[141] continue to create obstacles for women seeking asylum based on gender-related persecution. As interpreted currently, women seeking refuge on this basis have a narrow chance of success.[142] Adoption of gender-specific guidelines by the U.S. is desperately needed to create uniform standards regarding asylum adjudication[143] and to give recognition to the unique persecution suffered by women.

6. Conclusion

Asylum law in the United States has come to the forefront recently because of the ever-growing number of refugees seeking entry. Refugees are encountering opposition in many countries because they are seen as competition for resources, social benefits and jobs. However, political considerations are also influencing the determination of whether asylum will be granted, which is a violation of the 1980 Refugee Act and other international instruments. The letter of the 1951 Convention, as adopted by the 1967 Protocol, states that no signatory country shall expel a refugee to a territory where his life or freedom would be endangered due to religious, ethnic, or political persecution. Hopefully, the U.S. will someday live up to the spirit of those words.

Notes

1. Dreifus, "No Refugees Need Apply," *The Atlantic*, Feb. 1987: 32.
2. Richard Falk, "Accountability, Asylum, and Sanctuary: Challenging Our Political and Legal Imagination," *Journal of International Law and Policy*, (988): 199, 205.
3. Jay Mathews, "5,000 Immigrants Granted Legal Status," *Washington Post*, Dec. 20, 1990: A1.
4. See George J. Church, "Cubans, Go Home," *Time*, Sept. 5, 1994: 30. (Cuban refugees will be joining the 15,000 Haitian refugees already at Guantanamo Bay, Cuba).
5. Harold H. Koh, "Closed-Door Policy for Refugees," *N.J.L.J.*, Aug. 23, 1993: 26.
6. See generally, Carmen Carriilo, "The Application of Refugee Laws to Central Americans in the United States," 9 B.C. *Third World L. J.* 1 (1989) ; Michael Elliott, "How Do We Get to the Endgame?" *Newsweek*, Sept. 5, 1994.
7. "Convention Relating to the Status of Refugees," July 28, 1951, 189 U.N.T.S. 137.
8. "Protocol Relating to the Status of Refugees," Jan. 31, 1967, 19 U.S.T. 6223, 606 U.N.T.S. 267.
9. Exec. order No. 12,807, 3 C.F.R. 303 (1993) (ordering the interdiction and return of all aliens on the high seas, issued by President George Bush from his vacation home in Kennebunkport, Maine).
10. Nehemith Robinson, *Convention Relating to the Status of Refugees: Its History, Contents, Interpretation* (1953)
11. *Ibid.*
12. *Ibid.*, 3-4; *Convention Relating to the Status of Refugees*, July 28, 1951, 189 U.N.T.S, 137 (the United States did not sign this treaty).
13. 1951 Convention, art. i, paras. A(l) and A(2), 189 U.N.T.S. at 152.
14. *Ibid.*, pmbl., 189 U.N.T.S. at 150; see also, Offices of the United Nations High Commissioner for Refugees, *Handbook on Procedures and Criteria for Determining Refugee Status* 7 (1979). Hereinafter *Refugee Handbook*. (9191 2d-27) (asylum and the treatment of refugees).
15. Gunnel Stenberg, *Non-Expulsion and Non-Refoulement* 59 (1989) ; 195i Convention, art. 33, para. 1, 189 U.N.T.S. at 176.
16. *Ibid.*
17. Protocol Relating to the Status of Refugees, Jan. 31, 1967, 19 U.S.T. 6223, 606 U.N.T.S. 267; Multilateral Treaties Deposited with the Secretary-General: Status as at 31 December 1993 at 230, UN. Doc. ST/LEG/SER.E/12, UN. sales No. E.94.V.11 (1994).
18. See 1967 Protocol, *supra* note 17, art. I., 19 U.S.T. at 6225, 606 U.N.T.S. at 268-70; Andrew J. Pizor, "Comment, *Sale v. Haitian Centers Council:* The Return of Haitian Refugees," 17 *Fordham Int'l Legal Journal*, (1994): 1062, 1068.
19. *Ibid.*
20. *Refugee Handbook*, supra note 14, at 7 (¶¶, 24-27)
21. See 8 U.S.C. §§ 1101-1524 (1994).
22. *INS v. Stevic*, 467 U.S. 407, 421 (1984).
23. *Ibid.* See also *INS v. Cardoza-Fonseca*, 480 U.S. 421 (1987).
24. The INS is a government agency that enforces united States immigration laws. It is a subdivision of the United States Department of Justice. The Department of Justice is directed by the Attorney General, who is the chief law enforcement officer in the United

States. The Attorney General is an appointed member of the Presidential Cabinet.

25. Refugee Act of 1980, Public Law. No. 96-212, 94 stat. 102, codified at 8 U.S.C. §§ 1101-1525, 22 U.S.C. § 2601 (1994); Guy Goodwin-Gill, *The Refugee in International Law*, (1983): 15-16.

26. 8 U.S.C. § 1158(a).

27. Tim Weiner, "U.S. to Charge Immigrants a Fee When They Seek Political Asylum," *New York Times*, Feb. 2, 1994: A1.

28. *Ibid.*

29. Dreifus, *supra* note 1, at 32.

30. *Ibid.*

31. *Ibid.*. See also *Immigration and Naturalization Service, U.S. Dep't of Justice, Asylum Cases Filed with District Director by Selected Countries Fiscal Year 1984*, reprinted in 33 INS REP. 10 (1985). Contains statistics on grants of asylum for fiscal year 1984.

32. Sophie H. Pirie, "Note, The need for a Codified Definition of "Persecution" in United States Refugee Law," *Stanford Law Review*, 39 (1986): 187, 203-04.

33. United Nations High Commissioner for Refugees, The State of the World's Refugees 117, (Penguin Books) (1993) (hereinafter *World's refugees*).

34. Stephen F. Gold, "A Travesty of Justice," *Christian Science Monitor*, Mar. 3, 1992: 18.

35. *Ibid.*

36. Refugee Law and Policy 90 (V. Nanda, ed. 1989).

37. *World's Refugees*, *supra* note 33, at 117.

38. *Ibid.*

39. Katherine Bishop, "U.S. Adopts A New Policy for Hearings on Political Asylum for Some Aliens," *New York Times*, Dec. 20, 1990: B18.

40. *Ibid.*

41. *Ibid.*

42. Todd Howland, et al., "Safe Haven for Salvadorans in the Context of Contemporary International Law: A Case Study in Equivocation," 29 *San Diego Law Review* (1992): 671, 673.

43. *Ibid.*

44. *Refugee Law and Policy* 100 (V. Nanda, ed. 1989).

45. Nora Boustany, "Transition at Home Raises New Worry for Nicaraguans in U.S.," *Washington Post*, Apr. 25, 1990: A6.

46. *Ibid.*

47. See *supra* note 24 for a discussion of the Attorney General.

48. See *supra* note 24 for a discussion of the Department of Justice.

49. Boustany, *supra* note 45, p. A6.

50. *Ibid.*

51. *Ibid.*

52. *American Baptist Churches v. Thornburgh*, 760 F. Supp. 796 (N. D. Cal. 1991); Jay Matthews, "5,000,000 Immigrants Granted Legal Status,"*Washington Post*, Dec. 20, 1990: A1.

53. *Ibid.*

54. *American Baptist Churches v. Thornburgh*, 760 F. Supp. at 799.

55. *Ibid.*

56. Bishop, *supra* note 39, p. B18.

57. *Ibid.*

58. Bill Frelick, "Why Asylum in the U.S. Carries a Price Tag Now,"*San Diego*

Union Tribune, Mar. 31, 1994: B11.
    59. Interdiction Agreement, Sept. 23, 1981, U.S.-Haiti, 33 U.S.T. 3559, 3559 para. 2.
    60. Haitian Centers Council v. McNary, 969 F.2d 1326, 1329 (2d Cir. 1992),rev'd sub nom. Sale v. Haitian Centers Council, 113 S. Ct. 2549 (1993).
    61. Brief for Respondents at 2, Sale v. Haitian Centers Council, 113 S. Ct. 2549 (1993) (Nc. 92-344).
    62. Ibid.
    63. Lawrence E. Harrison, "Voodoo Politics," The Atlantic, June 1993: 101.
    64. Howard W. French, "Haiti installs Democratic Chief, its First,"New York Times, Feb. 8, 1991: A3.
    65. Amy Wilentz, "Love and Haiti: Can Aristide Come Home Now; Deposed President Jean-Bertrand Aristide," New Republic, July 5, 1993: 18.
    66. Ibid.
    67. Brief of Amici Curiae Amnesty International and Amnesty International USA in Support of Respondents at 101, Sale v. Haitian Centers Council, 113 S. Ct. 2549 (1993) (No. 92 344).
    68. Ibid.
    69. Howard W. French, "In Haiti, There is No Shortage of Fear,"New York Times, Oct. 20, 1993: A3.
    70. Anthony B. Beaudain, "Note, Freedom Denied: United States Policy of Turning Back Haitian Refugees on the High Seas as Upheld inSale v. Haitian Centers Council, Inc.," 15 Whittier Law Review, 537, 538 (1994).
    71. Executive Order No. 12,807, 3 C.F.R. 303 (1993).
    72. Ibid.
    73. Brief of the office of the united Nations High Commissioner for Refugees as Amicus Curiae in Support of Respondents, Sale v. Haitian Centers Council, 113 S. Ct. 2459 (92-344).
    74. 8 U.S.C. §1253(h)(1).
    75. 1967 Protocol, supra note 17, art. T, 19 U.S.T. at 6225, 606 U.N.T.S. at 268-270 (obligating parties to the 1967 Protocol to, inter alia, apply provisions of the 1951 Convention which prohibits the refoulement of refugees). See alsosupra notes 15-19 and accompanying text.
    76. Beaudoin, supra note 70, p. 538.
    77. Sale v. Haitian Centers Council, 113 S.Ct. at 2552 (interpreting the territorial application of 8 U.S.C. §1253(h) and of the 1951 Convention, art 33, 189 U.N.T.S. at 176).
    78. Ibid.
    79. Beaudoin, supra note 70, p. 572.
    80. Weiner, supra note 27, p. Al.
    81. Ibid.
    82. Michael Kramer, "Putting People Second," Time, Nov. 1, 1993: p. 29.
    83. Norman Kempster, "U.S. Sets Plans to Protect Forces Sent to Haiti,"Los Angeles Times, Oct. 9, 1993: A13.
    84. Norman Kempster, "Crisis Clouds U.S. Role as Champion of Democracy," Los Angeles Times, Oct. 13, 1993: A9.
    85. French, supra note 69, p. A3.
    86. Paul Richter, "Clinton Freezes U.S. Assets of Haitian Leaders,"Los Angeles Times, Oct. 19, 1993.

87. U.S. Department of State, Press Release, May 13, 1994: 3.
88. "Mission to Haiti: Chronology," *New York Times*, Oct. 16, 1994: 18.
89. *Ibid*.
90. Elliott, *supra* note 6, p. 26 27.
91. Church, *supra* note 4, p 32.
92. Cuban Adjustment Act OF 1966 (Public Law No. 89 -732).
93. *Ibid*.
94. Andrew Bilski, "Damming the Flood," *Maclean's*, Aug. 29, 1994: 19.
95. *Ibid*.
96. *Ibid*.
97. Tom Post, *et al.*, "Return to Sender," *Newsweek*, Aug. 29, 1994: 22.
98. *Ibid*, p. 23-24.
99. Nancy R. Gibbs, "Dire Straits," *Time*, Aug. 29, 1994: 28.
100. Post, *supra* note 97, p. 23.
101. *Ibid*.
102. Steven Greeenhouse, "Flight From Cuba," *New York Times*, Aug. 19, 1994: Al.
103. Post, *supra* note 97, p. 24.
104. Gibbs, *supra* note 99, p 30.
105. Tod Robberson, "Story of Tug's Sinking Incited Cubans: Drownings That Launched Exodus of Rafters May Be Portent," *Washington Post*, Sept. 11, 1994: A1.
106. *Ibid*.
107. 8 U.S.C. §1152 (1990).
108. Church, *supra* note 4, p. 33-34.
109. J. F. C. McAllister, "Is It Time to Lift the Cuban Embargo?"*Time*, Aug. 29, 1994: 32.
110. Elliott, *supra* note 6, p. 26; Daniel Williams & Roberto Suro, "Detention of Cubans Poses Variety of Problems," *Washington Post*, Oct. 28, 1994: A17. (President Clinton broke with a thirty-five year practice of welcoming Cubans as refugees to assuage Florida Governor Lawton Chiles' fears that a flood of rafters would spoil his chances in a tough re-election battle against Jeb Bush, the Republican challenger).
111. *Ibid*.
112. Church, *supra* note 4, p. 31.
113. *World's Refugees*, *supra* note 33, p. 11.
114. United Nations High Commissioner for Refugees Executive Committee Report (Of the 36TH Session, UN. Exec. Comm., 36th Sess., para. c, UN. DOC. A/AC.96.673 (1985), reprinted in 1 *International Journal of Refugee Law*, 255 (1989) .
115. Ben Barher, "Refugee Ranks Swell: 17.5 Million People Fled Their Native Lands in 1992," *Gazette* (Montreal), May 29, 1993: B1 (citing U.S. Comm. for Refugees, 1993 *World Refugee Survey*).
116. *Ibid*.
117. H.R. 2836, 103d Cong., 1st Sess. (U.S. House of Representatives); 103 Bill Tracking H.R. 2836.
118. H.R. 2836, 103d Cong., 1st Sess.
119. *Ibid*.
120. Kristine M. Fox, "Gender Persecution: Canadian Guidelines Offer A Model For Refugee Determination in the United States," 11*Arizona Journal of International and Comparative Law*, 117, 118 (1994) .
121. *Ibid.*, p. 136-37.
122. See *supra* note 117.

123. 1967 Protocol, *supra* note 17, art. IV, 19 U.S.T. at 6226, 606 U.N.T.S. at 270.
124. Statute of the International Court of Justice, June 26, 1945, art. 34, para. 1, 59 Stat. 1031, 1976 U.N.Y.B. 1052.
125. Formerly called the Council for Security and Cooperation in Europe, the entity changed its name in December, 1994, to the Organization for Security and Cooperation in Europe. *Main Points of CSCE Summit Final Statement,* Agence France Presse, Dec. 6, 1994.
126. Miriam Sapiro, *Dispute Resolution: General methods and CSCEMechanisms, American Society for International Law Newsletter*, Sept. 1994.
127. *Ibid.* The OSCE is composed of fifty three States, including the United States, Canada, and European States, and all of the newly independent States of the former Soviet Union.
128. Brief of the Office of the United Nations High Commissioner for Refugees as Amicus Curiae in Support of Respondents, *Sale v. Haitian Centers Council*, 113 S. Ct. 2459 (92-344).
129. *Ibid.*
130. *Ibid.*
131. *Filartiga v. Pena-Irala*, 630 F.2d 876 (2d Cir. 1980).
132. Pizor, *supra* note 18, p. 1113.
133. Deborah Sontag, "Women Asking U.S. Asylum Expand Definition of Abuse," *New York Times*, Sept. 27, 1993: A1, A10.
134. Fox, *supra* note 120, p. 118.
135. *Ibid.*
136. United Nations High Commissioner for Refugees Executive Committee Report of the 36th Session, *supra* note 114.
137. Anders B. Johnson, "The International Protection of Women Refugees: A Summary of Principal Problems and Issues," *International Journal of Refugee Law*, 221, 222 (1989).
138. *Ibid.*
139. *Ibid.*
140. Jacqueline Greatbatch, "The Gender Difference: Feminist Critiques of Refugee Discourse," *Internal Journal of Refugee Law*, 518, 524 (1989).
141. Norman L. Zucker, et al., *The 1980 Refugee Act: A 1990 Perspective, in Refugee Policy: Canada and the United States* 224-25 (1991).
142. Kristine M. Fox, *supra* note 120, p. 143.
143. *Ibid.*

Amy Goodman

A First-Hand Account of the Role of Power in East Timor and Haiti

The greatest producer of refugees in the world has always been revolution and war. As a journalist who has covered many wars in recent years, I can testify to the horrendous abuse of the rights of innocent civilians during war. In this paper, I want to discuss the cases of East Timor and Haiti because of the similarities I have seen in the effects upon the general population. These two countries may, at first, seem to have nothing in common but there is something that unites them, but it is not often discussed in the Western media: that is the superpower behind the scenes that provided the training and support for the killings and abuses, and that power is the United States. Let me begin with East Timor. It is a small island three hundred miles above Australia. It had been a Portuguese colony for hundreds of years until Portugal began the process of decolonization after it underwent its 1974 revolution. East Timor declared its independence at the end of 1975. Its next door neighbor, Indonesia which was at that time the fifth largest country in the world, invaded immediately. The date was December 7, 1975.

On the day before, December 6th, U.S. President Gerald Ford and Secretary of State, Henry Kissinger visited Indonesia's dictator, General Suharto, in Jakarta, the capitol of Indonesia and gave the go-ahead for the invasion. Suharto needed the go-ahead because he had to deal with the United States. He had purchased huge amounts of weapons from the United States with the stipulation that they not be used for offensive purposes. Clearly, that would be the case in East Timor, but he got the go-ahead anyway from the President and the Secretary of State.

Indonesia invaded by land, by air, and by see on that day, December 7, rounding up thousands of Timorees in the capitol, Dili, bringing them down to the harbor, dragging people there, forcing families and friends to count them off as the Indonesian military shot them one by one into the harbor. Also, thousands of Timorees were being gathered in the country side and the reporters who were covering the invasion at the time, six of them on that day and in the weeks leading up to the invasion, were lined up and executed by the Indonesian military.

I tell this whole story because it is so rarely told. For more than a decade after that day, December 7, 1975, Indonesia closed East Timor to the outside world and killed more than one-third of the population through massacre and forced starvation. The killing goes on today. When thousands of Timorees fled into the mountains as they tried to escape the lowlands of Dili, the capitol of East Timor, Indonesia appealed to the Untied States for low-flying planes and Bronco helicopters so that they could scrape the Timorees out of the mountains. President Jimmy Carter provided those planes and the Timorees continued to be killed.

They continued to be rounded up, put into detention camps called concentration camps, where they were starved or massacred. In 1979, four years after the invasion, some aid workers got into East Timor. They said that the people they saw had pencil-thin arms and legs, children had distended bellies, and that what they saw there was worse than the starvation in Biafra. That year there were no stories in the major papers in the United State or Europe about East Timor.

In short, more than 200,000 East Timorees have been killed since East Timor was invaded in 1975 by a military trained and supported by the United States. I went to East Timor in the summer of 1990. I was with another reporter, Alan Narin, who was a correspondent with *The New Yorker Magazine*. What we found was a people completely terrorized living under a total military occupation. Indonesian soldiers were everywhere. Timorees were arrested if they spoke to us because we were foreigners. They were arrested if they listened to short wave radios. Nevertheless, we were told over and over again by people who would come up to us and say,

"They took my mother, my father, and my sister."

We often heard stories of women who were being kept by Indonesian military soldiers and officers as "kept-women" often forced to bear their children. When we went there the first time in 1990 it was right around the time of the U.S. military buildup in the Middle East in preparation for the war against Iraq. U.S. Secretary of State, James Baker, justified the U.S. War in Iraq by saying, "Countries with powerful military machines should not be allowed to invade, ruin the lives or occupy their peaceful neighbors." There was no mention of East Timor which certainly qualified for a level of protection by the international community far greater than what Kuwait was receiving. What happened in East Timor was a proportionately larger genocide than the mass killings in Cambodia. The difference of course was that Iraq and Cambodia were official enemies of the United States. Indonesia was and continues to be a close ally of the U.S.

I went back to East Timor in October and November of 1991 because I was going to cover a UN-Portuguese delegation, the first that was to be going to East Timor in 17 years since the occupation began in 1975. The Timorees were very excited about this. For the first time they would be able to get word to the outside world about what was happening to them.

We went to a Catholic church in Dili and there we saw women wailing. This was the first day we arrived. I wasn't sure if it was just the sorrow of East Timor or if something had happened that day. It turns out that the night before we arrived, the Indonesian military had surrounded the church and shot into it killing a young man named Sebastio Gomez. His blood was still fresh on the steps. There were many young people, young men and women taking refuge in the churches in East Timor. The Catholic church was the only civilian institution left standing in East Timor. The people wanted to talk to the UN. delegation and tell what was happening to their families but they were afraid they would be arrested before the delegation came. So they hid in the churches. Sebastio Gomez was the first victim of that march into the churches.

The next day there was a funeral held for him and a thousand people turned out. The bishop held the mass. People then marched to the cemetery to bury him. On the way they did a very unusual thing. They put up their hands in the "V" sign and said "Viva East Timor. Viva Sebastio." Something so bold, that kind of demonstration, had never before been seen in East Timor by a thousand people, a whole cross-section of the society. They arrived at the cemetery, sang hymns, chanted, and buried Sebastio Gomez. They were exhilarated but they were also terrified and went home.

The next two weeks we went around the country talking to the people about how the Indonesian military was preparing for this delegation. Everywhere, we heard the same story: the military had gathered people together in the villages and said, "If you talk to the delegation when they come, we will kill you after they leave and we have already dug the mass graves to put your bodies in." The bishop told us that the line most commonly used was, "We will kill your family to the seventh generation."

A nation-wide death threat was issued to all of the Timorees. Then it turned out that the delegation was canceled. We have now learned that the cancellation was at the behest of the United States. The story that would be told to the world from that visit is not one the United States wanted the world to hear.

What were the people to do who had dropped out of school and work, the young people who had gone into the churches for the safety in order to be able to tell their stories? They were stranded. Two weeks after Sebastio Gomez' death, they held a two week commemoration for him. This time not one thousand but three or four thousand people turned out for the early morning mass.

It was November 12, 1991. We went to the church around 7:00 in the morning, just as the mass was ending and we followed the procession as it retraced its steps two weeks before to the cemetery to honor Sebastio Gomez. Thousands of people joined in this march, old women, in traditional Timoreze garb, girls in their

Catholic school uniforms, young boys, teenagers, older men, and as they marched to the cemetery, they put up their hands in the "V" sign and shouted, "Viva East Timor." They unfurled bed sheets that they had prepared for the delegation that was never to come that said things like: "President Bush, we need your help." "Portugal, we are your responsibility." They appealed to the UN. to hear their cry. They sang hymns and chanted. Just before the crowd was about to disperse, we saw ahead of us 50 Indonesian soldiers line up. Then from the same direction that the procession had come, hundreds more Indonesian soldiers marched up with their U.S. M-16s in a ready position. They marched up in front and behind the procession. The crowd got very quiet. They were hemmed in on both sides by high cemetery walls. They had nowhere to go except the people at the very back who could turn and run. The little kids in the front were whimpering. Two girls had taken my arms because they saw the U.S. as their only shield. Yes, it was the U.S. weapons that were pointed against them, yet it was a U.S. journalist they saw as their only shield.

Alan and I were standing in the middle of the crowd. Alan suggested we walk to the front with all of our equipment on because although we knew the Indonesian military had committed many massacres in the past, they had never done it in front of Western journalists. So, I put my headphones on and Alan put the camera above his head. I put my microphone out like a flag and we walked to the front of the crowd. The Indonesian military marched up and without any warning or provocation they swarmed around the corner about 10 to 12 abreast. They swept through us and they opened fire on the crowd gunning people down from right to left. A little boy about seven years old was the first to explode before our eyes.

As for us, they grabbed my microphone, and they beat me to the ground with their weapons. Alan got a snapshot of them opening fire on the crowd and as I screamed, he threw himself on top of me. The soldiers used M-16s as baseball bats and slammed them against his head until they fractured his skull. As we lay on the ground, the Indonesian military lined us up with about ten Timorees like a firing squad to execute us like they had the Australian and British journalists in 1975. Alan was in total spasm at that point because of the brutal beating he had gotten. He was covered in blood and the only thing I could say then from the ground was, "We're from America. We're from America."

They kicked me in the stomach until I lost my breath, but as soon as I got it back I would keep repeating, "We're from America."

Eventually they took the guns from our heads. I believe it was because we were from the same country that their weapons came were from. They probably know that they would have to pay a price for killing American journalists, a price that they never had to pay for killing the Timorees. I can't even say that we were lucky that day for surviving because of how many Timorees were killed. More than 250 Timorees died in the massacre. They lay all around us.

We were able to get into a civilian jeep. The driver picked up an old Timoree man whom they had beaten to a pulp right next to us and we drove off to the hospital. About a hundred yards down the road we were hailed by Timorees who were running from the military. Dozens of people climbed into the truck and we drove as a human mass that way to the hospital. From there, Alan and I went into hiding because we knew the military would raid the hospital—which they soon did. From our hiding place, we could hear continuing gunshots.

We decided the only way to stop this was to get out of the country and report the massacre to the outside world. We were able through a great deal of luck to get on the last and only plane that was going to West Timor that day, and from there to Bali and then to Guam. We were able to report that story to the outside world from Guam.

On that day 250 Timorees were killed. The only good thing that can be said is that an international grass roots movement is growing up around East Timor. In many cases it is lead by women around the world rising up against this occupation that is clearly supported by the U.S. and is also suppressed by the U.S. media. In 1994, the U.S. Congress voted to cut off weapons shipments to Indonesia and right after the massacre in 1991 the Congress voted to cut off military training of the Indonesian armed forces. At least some in the Congress are no longer accepting the administration's argument that the training was intended to instill humanitarian ideals and democratic values in the Indonesian soldiers with that training.

The story of East Timor brings me to the case of Haiti because we see the same military training going on in Haiti. I visited Haiti in the Spring of 1994 and there I saw similar scenes to what I had seen in East Timor. It was a frightening and desperate place with bodies turning up on the streets on a daily basis, decapitated, bodies hacked to death with machetes. This is the message the Haitian military sends to the people of Haiti: if you speak out you will be killed. The terror going on in Haiti is not the random violence the mass media in the U.S. reports. The people murdered are leaders of peasant movements, student leaders, and women who are fighting against politically motivated rape. The are decapitating the whole popular movement in Haiti. And who are the people that are doing it? We are taking about paramilitary forces and military forces trained, armed, and financed by the U.S. government.

Although the U.S. government denied it when the Haitian coup happened three years ago, the U.S. military continued to train the very soldiers from that military coup in the United States at places like "School of the Americas" at Fort Benning, Georgia. Activists in the U.S. call it the "School of the Assassins." When President Clinton announced that he would send U.S. troops to Haiti to force the military junta out of power, he also said that he would begin retraining the military so that it would act in a more humanitarian manner.

Now you would think that the Haitian people would be happy for this, a relief from the military oppression they have faced. But they know what role the U.S. has played in that repression and they do not trust what the U.S. will do. We are talking about two parts to this invasion, the invasion to oust General Raoul Cedras, and then the occupation that has been very clearly laid out in advance. That occupation will not remove the military but will retrain the very military that has killed more than three-thousand Haitians these last few years. The grass-roots movements and the supporters of Aristide, the President that the U.S. Government never supported and does not like, will be targeted by the American occupation forced. Everywhere I went in Haiti, I talked to leaders of the organized movements who were opposed to a U.S. invasion and they told me they remember or they have heard stories about the first U.S. occupation that occurred in 1915 and went on for twenty-years. It was during that time that the Haitian elite and the Duvalier family were established in power; no democratic institutions resulted from the first occupation.

In addition, some 15,000 Haitian peasants were killed by the U.S. Navy. The constitution written by the occupation forces permitted for the first time foreign ownership of Haitian productive resources. U.S. corporations took over a quarter of a million acres of land to use for their profit and the Haitians remember this. And the Haitians note that the modern-day Haitian military comes from the training of the military back in 1915 to 1934. Even in the U.S., Navy documents and memos that have now surfaced from the nineteen year occupation admit it was one of the most cruel chapters of Navy history. The Haitians don't expect anything different today.

As I conclude, I want to point out one thing that President Clinton said on the eve of the U.S. invasion of Haiti. He pointed out that politically motivated rape in Haiti was a major reason to go in and invade. When I was in Haiti, this issue was just being raised. I interviewed a number of women who were victims of politically motivated rape and there is no question that it is an absolutely horrendous thing when armed men come to your home at 1:00 in the morning, break in, rob you of everything, then rape you saying, "You enjoyed it when your father Aristide became president, now lie back and enjoy it."

These women were trying to get their story out and what did the U.S. do? In April 1994, a memo written from the U.S. embassy in Port-au-Prince to the State Department in Washington, DC leaked out and revealed that these allegations of human rights abuses and politically motivated rape are exaggerations and that rape is a natural part of Haitian culture. This was just a few months before the U.S. invasion. The fact is that rape was going on then when the U.S. was denying it, and the rape continued when the President underscored how serious it was. I think that what has to be looked at here is the pretexts that are used for an invasion and how issues like human rights are only stressed at times of convenience such as when a president needs to justify an invasion. Human rights violations are thrown out and discounted when they do not serve the U.S. government's interests.

The thing activists are most concerned about is the databases. The U.S. government encouraged people to apply for politics! asylum at U.S. offices in Haiti with the promise that if they are found to have grounds for persecution they will be brought out of the country. Well, the fact is, almost no one is brought out of Haiti, but what the U.S. gets from all these people applying for asylum—and we are talking about more than 60,000 people—is a computerized database of the entire political activist movement in Haiti. The man who runs asylum processing offices is Louis Moreno who comes not out of immigration but out of anti-drug interdiction, the Phoenix program in Peru, Nicaragua, El Salvador, and Colombia. We know what the U.S. military has done in these countries; it is clear that not much interdiction of drugs has gone on but hundreds of thousands of freedom fighters have been killed, imprisoned, or disappeared. A capacity for identifying enemies of the state has now been gained in Haiti in a way that U.S. government never had in El Salvador, Peru, Colombia, or elsewhere.

Now following Aristide's return, they are offering millions of dollars to Haitian human rights groups. This is dividing the human rights groups because many are saying, "How can we be independent, especially when the U.S. moves in for the occupation if we are receiving money from the U.S.?"

The U.S. has made it very clear it wants to redefine the political center and Aristide is not a part of that political center. In fact, one of the things that President Clinton emphasized just a few hours before Aristide's return was that President Aristide promised to step down at the end of his term. In exchange for his return, Aristide has also had to cede to the U.S. (and later the UN) control over his police force, military, and cabinet. Aristide can not be much more than an figurehead with the real workings of the government firmly in U.S. hands. This is something very important to Clinton because he has never been a supporter of Aristide.

I want to end just by quoting something Alan Narin published in *The Nation* about the occupation of Haiti. He interviewed many pentagon and psychological operations experts who were involved in panning the occupation and he concludes that "You will hear it in the media Called a *peacekeeping force*, but we are talking about thousands of people, mainly U.S. military who will remain in Haiti for a very long time." Alan quotes one of the intelligence officers saying that with regard to mass demonstrations "Simple, you don't let it happen. There is no such thing as a demonstration while we are there."

The occupation is not targeted at the Haitian military. It is targeted at the population. One U.S. contractor who works for the state department noted that the naval task force now standing on Haiti has replaced its stocks of anti-armored weaponry with crowd control gear, including shields, gas masks and clubs. He said fears were running high in Haiti about the possibility of U.S. troops confronting organized slum dwellers an encounter that would have obvious consequences for unarmed Haitians.

Finally, he says, "In Panama the psychological operations group [Panama was invaded by the U.S. in 1989] which is now preparing to go to Haiti to establish a denunciation hot line in which members of the public were encouraged to dial direct to Southern Command and denounce Noriega backers, criminals, subversives, and anti-U.S. fighters who were then picked up by U.S. troops and consigned to detention camps. In El Salvador, this psychological operations group that is going into Haiti helped run the army radio station which broadcast repeated threats against the Jesuits in the days prior to their assassination. These are the groups that are now moving into Haiti. As one defense department official said, "They are not talking about protecting the city slum dwellers, the masses of people who voted for Haiti [sic], but the people up in the hills, the Haitian elite and the military, who they say will be the target of attack. These are the very people whom the U.S. will now reconstitute to work with in this new 'democratic Haiti.'"

As I conclude, I think forward to the UN Women's Conference in Beijing and, once again, I am drawn to the crucial importance of women redefining the issues that dominate public discourse. We recognize that human rights issues are women's issues, that the peace movement is a women's issue, that the anti-militarist movement, the movement against the type of militarist control I've seen in East Timor and Haiti, is a women's issue.

The discussion has always been that the West has no right to impose its values on the East, especially for example when talking about human rights. Or, that the North has no right to impose its human rights values on the South because all these different regions have different human rights values. I don't think that is the case at all, and it is extremely hypocritical and divisive to accept that dichotomy. What we are talking about, and I go back to the case of Indonesia's occupation of East Timor, are elite and powerful men in the U.S. government aligning themselves with similar people in another government and its military apparatus. They share their idea of human values and these human rights values are not the idea that the populations in these countries share. So it is not a dichotomy between East and West or North and South; it is a dichotomy that is shared by Western elites and Eastern elites and North and South elites *versus* the values held by ordinary people. I think that is what we have to be very clear about in Beijing so that we are not divided and we have to understand and take back our own definition of human rights. We cannot permit the elites in the West pretend that they have a concept of human rights that is different from the criminal abuses that occur in nations, such as Haiti or East Timor, which are totally under their control.

Yvonne Deutsh

Israeli Women and the Occupation of Palestine

It is a natural reaction to hate those who have made us suffer. It is also a natural reaction to inflict pain because one has suffered pain, and to justify it ideologically. In this small land both our peoples are stuck in a fateful embrace. It believe that our finding each other here is potentially for the greater unfolding of life. In order to fulfill this poetntial, we all need to become more fully human, which, to me means activating our capacity to undersand the suffering of others through our own, and to transform pain into healing.

—Dalia Landau

I would like to stress that throughout my years of activities I do not work in a direct and concrete way with the problems of refugees within the framework of the Israeli-Palestinian conflict. In my activities against the occupation, I was mainly involved in protest actions and in an attempt to deal with the obstacles within Israeli society to reach a just solution to the conflict. The political solutions has to be based on the principle of equal political rights for both peoples. Only the political awareness by the Jewish society of the wounds of the Palestinian society and of the continuing injustice done to it can there be a reconciliation and peace between the two peoples. Since the beginning of the Intifada, I have been active in the women's peace movement. The challenge of a women's movement should be to establish a feminist political culture of peace based on the unique life experience of women throughout history.

Some personal background might be helpful. I was born in Romania, Timisoara, as the daughter of a Hungarian-Jewish family. At the age of eight, I emigrated together with my mother to Israel. Until then, I was exposed to a culture which spoke three languages—Hungarian, Rumanian, and German. Today, the Hebrew language is the only one I speak fluently, within the limits of a learned language which is not my mother tongue. The uprooting of my family from the culture in which I grew and the move to a strange land, created within me a basic living experience of cultural dispossession and lack of roots. The uprooting made me a women with an inner experience on non-belonging and strangeness. On the same level, I find myself in a constant, obsessive, and mainly fruitless search of areas of belonging. The strange land became for me the home with which I have a raging relationship of closeness and strangeness.

The Hebrew language I learned quickly. The adaptation to the society of Israeli children was also fast. In the photography album I can see myself standing with an arm during the Remembrance Day ceremony being photographed with friends on a tank at an exhibition of the army. In my desire to be part of the society to which I was brought I took upon myself the yoke of Zionism, in the way that the religious take upon the yoke of the commandments. I embraced the near-distant times of the period of the establishment of the State, the climax of the Zionist ethos. We were to embrace the heroic past and I was left feeling sorry that I had been unable to take part in the events of that period.

The awakening to the fragments of the other truth forced me to the streets by the time I reached maturity, to demonstrate against the occupation of Palestinian lands by Israelis. My search for the shadows of reality brought me face to face with the collective denial. As a woman searching to overcome the split between the inner and the outer, I could not help being exposed to the shadows of the Zionist experience, to the forgotten meanings and the brutal denial of the collective Jewish consciousness of the establishment of the State and the war of 1948. Painfully I learned that what we call "the war of Independence, is called by the Palestinians "the Disaster of 1948." The year I stopped celebrating Independence Day, I sentenced myself to not belonging, a feeling I carry within me on a daily basis. As an emigrant I have within me an ardent desire to feel that I belong and to give my children a home which will be for them taken for granted. However, the yoke of history—the painful knowledge that what is defined by the group I belong to as freedom, independence, and a solution to persecution and destruction—has within it other interpretations that of loss, destruction, and exile. And that gives me no peace.

Mourning as a Basis for Healing and Change

The establishment of the state of Israel, in the consciousness of many Jews, was a political solution to the persecutions and the holocaust in the diaspora. Building a concrete entity and denying the Jewish part which was weak and hurt was a primary way of coming to terms with the emptiness, powerlessness, and loss, but it also denied the reality in Palestine. A 'nation state' was formed composed of Jews from various cultural backgrounds speaking different languages.

The army was, and to a great extent still is, one of the main mechanisms for creating the common national identity. It was central in creating the image of the new Israel as the antithesis of the persecuted Jew of the diaspora. The building of military strength, aside from its functional role in real politique, was used as a substitute and compensation for the lack of collective mourning on the losses and persecutions we suffered through history. This was not legitimate in the new Israeli society. The image of the persecuted Jew was hidden behind military might. Refugees and survivors kept their wounds to themselves, ashamed to show their pain, trying to build a new life on the ruins of their past—and on the Palestinian existence. This new identity alienated itself from its various roots, from its different cultures, and firmly implanted itself in a dangerous male militaristic culture. In the cultural and psychological vacuum which was created, the army was used as a source for a positive male self-image, a source of personal and national pride which emphasized protection and security. The army became the symbol of the independent Jewish protector; survival was seen as a major goal of the society. Belonging to the army became a symbol of belonging to the new society. This was particularly significant in a society of immigrants and refugees.

The failure to synthesize the experience of loss, destruction and extermination is dangerous since it prevents the soul from healing the fears and traumas of the past. The use of military strength as a destructive form of compensation to that same injured and lamenting part of the psyche creates the social and moral deformities exemplified by the Israeli occupation of Palestinian territories and the monstrous and inhumane treatment of the people. This behavior becomes part of accepted military culture which influences general social interaction. One can see here the phenomena of the split, characteristic of patriarchal political structures. Today, after signing the Declaration of Principles which grants some measure of autonomy to Gaza and small parts of the West Bank, the press is filled with words of peace, but the degradation and violation of human rights in the territories continues.

Allow me to quote from Eyad El Sarraj, a Palestinian psychiatrist who has written on the subject:

> Over the years the Israelis have created a culture of fear and paranoia with a violent projection of aggression while keeping an inner image of the victim. Their paranoia was continuously nourished by the surrounding Arabs whose demagogic leaders vowed impotently to liberate Palestine.
>
> The Palestinians on the other hand are physically dispersed in exile and are emotionally traumatized. Their feeling of victimization is deep. Their experience of trauma is overwhelming and their psyche is injured. Their mood therefore is labile, quickly swayed to extremes and their reactions rapidly swing between euphoric and despair. They will never forget their suffering and perhaps may never forgive.

Limitations of the Influence of the Women's Peace Movement

The Intifada brought about the awakening of women's political activity against the Israeli occupation. During the Intifada, *Women in Black* was the most significant protest movement against the occupation in Israel. Within a few months, Women in Black stood every Friday at thirty different sites in the country and they expressed protest and mourning. In addition to the protest groups, other women's groups with varied political agendas were formed. *Women and Peace* was the first group to bring to the national consciousness the fact that there was an exceptional awakening of women's activities. This consciousness brought about the joining of women with a power base in politics and academia. Today those women are part of the political establishment in Israel.

Women went out in the streets to demonstrate when it was finally clear to them that the military action to suppress the Intifada (what Defense Minister Yitzhak Rabin termed the "Iron Fist" response) was an aggressive and not a defensive response. This was also the case during the war in Lebanon. The sight of soldiers chasing civilians, including women and children, created a shock in Israeli women's perception of the army as moral and just protectors. Some of them went to the streets because of the fear they had for the influence the military brutality would have on their children and on Israeli society as a whole, but most of them went to the streets in the name of universal values of justice. The initial awakening was related to a questioning of basic tenets concerning the image of the army a defense force. The army began to be seen as an army of occupation determined to repress indigenous peoples.

The process of political transformation from the basic national perceptions of Israeli society is especially difficult in a state of national conflict, which enhances national identity and increases the level of collective anxiety. A change in the political consciousness and an awakening of political activity of women at a time of crisis of values (due to the shattering of the image of the army as a body with the sole attributes of defense), goes together with the feminist perception of joining the political with the personal. In principle, this unity enables one to come to terms with the evil within us. The dichotomy between the personal and the public enables moral detachment from the immorality of the State's politics or of the army's actions. It enables one to see the injustice against the "other" only as the carrying out of a duty, within the framework of which one cannot raise the question of morality. The split between the inner, injured, part and the concrete building of a new reality enables the transference of the bad onto the "other" and in consequence the justification of the injustices.

In Israel the women's movement said in a loud voice "End the Occupation." Among women there has begun a political dialog, and at times a wide-ranging feminist dialogue. It is difficult to evaluate the contribution of the peace movement to the change in consciousness which seeks peace. It is clear that Women in Black, by persisting for six years to publicly protest against the occupation did not enable the Israeli public to escape in the form of convenient denial of the injustices of the occupation. However the political strength of the women's movement is limited. The women's movement was restrained from deeply pursuing its search for an alternative political theory based on women's life experience. Jewish women in Israel, mothers of soldiers, paced like caged lions and visibly aged when their sons served in the territories. What is the meaning of the mothers' experience of sending sons to the field of battle? What is the political significance of the women's experience, and mothers who on the one hand oppose war and yet send their sons to fight in them?

Since the army holds a special place in Jewish Israeli society, the women's peace movement was not capable of creating a political alternative to the reality created by the global male militaristic and patriarchal values which include war, occupation, oppression, exploitation, violence, and rape. The perception of national security as "primal" causes women to continue their reliance on the army for defense. In Israel, many women do not make the connection between the army and its masculinist culture of violence and sexism.

The division of tasks between the men as the protectors and the women as the protected is a cultural-political-patriarchal axiom. It determines the psychology of the relationships between the sexes and is a basic factor for the discrimination, deprivation, and the perception of women as sexual objects.

Carol Cohn presents a challenge for all of us: Feminists and others who seek a more just and peaceful world have a dual task before us—a deconstructive project and a reconstructive project that are intimately linked. Our deconstructive task requires close attention to, and the dismantling of technostrategic discourse. The dominant voice of militarized masculinity and decontextualized rationality speaks so loudly in our culture that it will remain difficult for any other voices to be heard until that voice loses some of its power to define what we hear and how we name the world—until that voice is delegitimated. Our reconstructive task is a task of creating compelling alternative visions of possible futures, and a task of creating rich and alternative voices—diverse voices whose conversations with each other will invent the future.

Roni Ben Efrat

After Oslo: The Roots of the Israeli-Palestinian Conflict Still Unsolved

On September 12, 1994, a commemoration of the twelfth anniversary of one of the most horrible massacres committed against the Palestinian people was held. At the massacre of Sabra and Shatila, 3,500 helpless civilians were brutally slaughtered by Christian militias, under the guarding eyes of Israeli soldiers. The Israeli invasion of Lebanon in 1982 resulted in 20,000 dead, 80 percent of whom were civilians, and 30,000 wounded. Six hundred thousand Lebanese and Palestinians were made homeless.

Last year, two months after the euphoric handshake on the White House lawn between Yitshak Rabin and Yasser Arafat, I met a member of the European Parliament. She replied to my reservations about the Oslo agreement by saying with a touch of impatience, "Oh, but we don't want to talk about the past." In other words, she was saying to me, don't spoil the party.

Some party. The Oslo agreement was from the very beginning bitter candy wrapped in shiny paper. The first victims of the Oslo party are the four million Palestinian refugees scattered in Lebanon, Jordan, Syria, and the rest of the world. The United Nations estimates that in September 1949, there were 726,000 Palestinian refugees outside the armistice lines. Since then, UN resolutions have acknowledged the right of these Palestinians to return to their homeland or their willful acceptance of another solution. The Israeli negotiators carefully plucked out this issue, the most essential and explosive for the Palestinians, and diverted it to the multi-lateral talks, not to be included in the direct Israeli-Palestinian talks.

The aim is quite clear: to define the conflict not as a conflict between the state of Israel and the Palestinian people as a whole, but as a conflict between Israel and the two million Palestinians residing in the West Bank and Gaza Strip. Under the Madrid-Oslo concept, the fate of the four million Palestinian refugees who have suffered for 46 years from displacement and dispossession has been transformed from the number one national problem, recognized internationally as a rallying cry during years of struggle and the reason for the creation of the

PLO, to a mere humanitarian issue, to be solved by the Arab states or the mercy of immigration offices all over the world.

The attitude towards the refugees of the 1967 war is slightly different. The estimate of their number as of 1967 is 322,750, some first and some second time refugees. During the war, they fled to Jordan and later arrived also in other Arab countries. Israel has agreed to discuss their right to return to the Autonomous areas in the frame of family unification but under very limited quotas. For example, from January 1st 1994 until April 30th 1994, only 676 applications were approved.

The deep concern, though, is for the fate of the 1948 refugees, the Palestinians who still have no identity cards and are denied recognition in the Oslo accords. In Lebanon the results of this policy quickly materialized. It was only seven months until the government of Lebanon released a plan, through its foreign minister, Faris Buwayez, to get rid of the 350,000 Palestinian refugees living in Lebanon. Even though Lebanon has yet to sign a treaty with Israel, it hastens to pick the fruits of the regional détente, at the expense of the Palestinians, of course. The Buwayez plan, released on April 18, 1994, proclaimed that the Palestinians living in Lebanon should leave in the following order: 20 percent should be resettled in the Palestinian Autonomous areas; 20 percent should relocate through family reunification wherever possible; the rest should be absorbed by third countries such as Canada and Australia. Added to the existing problems of the Palestinian refugees in Lebanon, who lack many basic rights and are prevented from taking many jobs, is the urgent problem of the 6,000 refugee families displaced by the last widespread Israeli bombing of south Lebanon. This attack took place in July 1993, and 500,000 Palestinians and Lebanese fled to the north.

When they could return home many found that there was no home to go back to. Today, while UNRWA is willing to locate space in existing camps, the government of Lebanon is refusing to allow them to build. In February, a Palestinian delegation went to meet Lebanese Prime Minister Rafik Hariri. They raised their concerns about the 6,000 displaced families, but they got three no's from Hariri: No to rebuilding four camps that were destroyed by war, No to the expansion of existing camps, and No to the establishment of new camps. Furthermore, camps in the Beirut area such as Sabra and Shatila are slated for destruction as part of a plan to beautify the capital. Beirut's sports city, totally ruined the Israeli invasion in 1982, will be rebuilt and expanded in the hope of hosting the 1996 Asian games. The Saudis have already earmarked 20 million dollars for this project which is likely to engulf the camp of Shatila.

The case of Lebanon is just an example. Kuwait had a population of between 350,000 to 400,000 Palestinians. As a result of the Gulf War in 1991, most of the Palestinians were expelled from Kuwait and became refugees in Jordan. Today only 30,000 Palestinians remain in Kuwait.

One of the most outstanding deficiencies of the Oslo agreement and the Palestinian negotiating team, today addressed as the Palestinian National Authority (PNA), is that it shirked its responsibility for its raison d'être—the need to find a national solution to the Palestinian diaspora.

The Palestinian national poet, Mahmoud Darwish, who wrote the Palestinian declaration of independence in 1988, resigned from the PLO's Executive Committee realizing the disaster that the Oslo agreement would cause to the Palestinian people. He especially laments the fate of the refugees in this verse:

I see multitudes of families waiting on the shore.

They are the two generations of martyrs. We walked

them to their deaths in the struggle for Palestine.

They stand there waiting for the ship of the PLO,

but the ship has disappeared.

One year after the signing of the Oslo agreement, I cannot but agree with Darwish. Yasser Arafat has transformed himself from a leader of a people to an agent implementing the Israeli Labor party's program of Autonomy. He has merely agreed to take responsibility for running the occupation for Israel and oppressing the opposition. The roots of the problem remain unsolved, and they are threatening to explode. Indeed, to answer my friend in the European Parliament, we don't want to talk about the past. We want to find long-standing and just solutions for the future. Unfortunately, Oslo is not a solution because it does not prepare for statehood but for a new way of organizing the occupation to the benefit of Israel. According to the Oslo concept of the New Middle East, while Israel will normalize its relation with all the neighboring Arab states, and will advance in the economic conquest of their markets. The Palestinians will be forced to accept a "bantustan" solution for one third of its people, while still being regarded as a "surplus people."

With the lack of democratic procedures, encouraged both by Israel and the new Autonomy, what can women expect? When an emphasis is on force, what is the role of women? When Israel is pushing the Palestinians to the verge of a civil war, what can women hope for?

The active Palestinian women's movement, which was built as a strong grass roots movement all during the 1980s, is living today in a rather dual phase. Formally, they still function as grass roots movements, united under the frame of the Federation of Palestinian Women connected to the PLO but, in effect, when the PLO does not exist as a recognized body, but instead has to be addressed as the Palestinian Authority, the relationship does not have much meaning. Allow me to give you an example of the sharpened danger of the crises that will clarify my point. A few months ago, the Women's organizations called for a meeting to announce the drafting of *The Document of Principles of Women's Rights*. This was supposed to be a major event. The document itself is, of course, very progressive, but the riot that accompanied its ratification says much more than the draft itself. The faction of the women presenting Arafat's policy wanted to invite Um Jihad, the so-called Minister of Welfare in the PNA to preside at the meeting. The head of one of the two left-wing factions, Maja Nassar, objected saying, that Um Jihad could not participate as anyone else because three out of the five of the Federation are against the Oslo agreement.

A few days later, Maha Nassar, a well known women's leader, who sat in prison during the Intifada, got threatening telephone calls. One morning soon after the event, she found on her doorstep a bloodied piece of cloth, which was a thing done to collaborators. When women wanted to publish their resentment of these practices in the daily Palestinian *El Quds*, the paper would not publish it. An interesting question faced by the Palestinian Women's Organizations in the convention in Beijing in September 1995 was the form of their participation: NGO status or semi-state status. Would they want the Palestinian Authority to represent them? Surely not. Discussions on this issue have already started.

The Intifada has also produced a peace movement among Israeli women. The grass roots movement "Women in Black" is now famous all over the world. Indeed, women took a vanguard role in calling the government to withdraw from the occupied territories and to open negotiations with the PLO. The Two State Solution was the political demand of all active women in the movement. All this was fine as long as the right wing Likud was in power. In fact, then the whole peace movement rallied around this demand. But, cracks started to appear in this united front as the Labor party got closer to power in June 1992, and Rabin, Israel's hawkish leader, was challenging the ballot. Opposition diminished in order not to spoil his chances.

Then when Rabin and Labor took power, all voices of opposition silenced voluntarily, including that of the women's movement. Criticism was replaced by an active support to "our partners for peace on the other side." The strong Zionist left-wing Meretz women came up with a strategic decision to strengthen the pro peace Palestinian women's organizations, not caring that this win would further divide the Palestinian Women's Movement. Everyone understands that the Oslo agreement does not hold any hopes for Palestinian Independence, but all factions of the peace and women's movement decided to shut up about this situation. When violations of human rights started to appear within the new Palestinian National Authority, there was no comment on the Israeli side. Their task today is to strengthen Rabin and to strengthen Arafat. The women have tuned themselves to a pro Rabin-Arafat lobby.

Another obstacle to opposition was the agreement of the Palestinian main stream bourgeoisie and Arafat's faction to play the game. It put the Women in

Black which were standing and demonstrating until April of last year in an odd situation. Are we supposed to be more religious than the Pope?

Of course, if the women's movement in Israel was more connected to the Palestinian women in the opposition, to the moods of women in the refugee camps, perhaps this wouldn't have happened. Then they could have remained loyal to the motive that got them active in the first place: the desire to find a long-lasting solution to the ongoing conflict and not to be satisfied with this false agreement which grants the Palestinians limited autonomy, with no guarantees to independence, free elections, Israeli withdrawal, and, of course, no solution for the four million Palestinians living in the diaspora. Arafat and his apparatus became today a bad joke, a little dictator in a fake kingdomship, and the whole peace movement is rallying behind Rabin, too scared to challenge him and to lose the spoils of power.

There is a third sector of women in Israel, which is hardly talked about. This sector which did not find as yet the way to express their aspirations for peace and justice. I am referring to the Arab Palestinian women in Israel (the 850,000 Arab citizens of Israel). The Palestinian Arab population living in Israel is an integral part of the Palestinian people. They were isolated and cut off from their Palestinian brothers and sisters who became refugees and lived as a minority in Israel until 1967 when Israel occupied the West Bank and Gaza. Actually until 1966, they lived under military rule. Israel always demanded their full loyalty, but treated them as an unwanted population. Underdevelopment was ever since a policy regarding the Arabs in Israel. Until this very day, they have lived under strict security surveillance. Traditional and unnationalistic elements in society were always preferred. This had a devastating effect on the Arab women.

We in the Committees for Democratic Action, as an organization of Arabs and Jews, are exploring the ways to advance Arab women, to help them turn from a passive element in traditional society into an active legitimate body in society. Today, we are facing a situation where women compose 43% of Arab academics. The average years of studying is 11, but still only 13% of Arab women work (in comparison with 46% of the Jewish women). Most girls who finish high school sit at home. There are almost no married women who work. This fact diminishes the standard of living in the Arab sector to half of the Jewish one. It causes backwardness in the child care area and confines women to the four walls of their house. No women can leave homes for education, or work without the permission of her father or brother. We know that women who don't control their own lives cannot really have a say in what goes on in society, and it is this vicious circle which we are trying to break. In the past two years, we have really opened a little revolution in the village of Majd El Krum where we have a local community center called El Baqa. In 1992, we opened a mothers' school in order to enable women who were deprived of education to learn their children's curriculum and be able to help them in school. Of course, this is also a splendid opportunity to talk about other important issues concerning women. No wonder that within a year a group of women, who were participating in the Mothers' School, organized as a working group on other social and political matters. Our next idea is to open an economic project for women. In fact, the participants will be women who took the mothers' school course and have joined through it the women's circle.

We ran a workers' advice center and have taken up many cases of young girls working in textile. They are working under conditions of slavery and we are trying to help them both on the trade union level and on the level of self awareness. A key principle in our work is that we are always seeking the women who are in most need and we hope that through our work we will be able to organize the first real grass roots women's cadres who will become leaders in the community through their own struggle to become involved.

Palestinians from Gaza line up at 5:00 a.m. to pass Israeli checkpoints. 650,000 out of 800,000 Gazans are refugees. (photo: *Challenge Magazine*)

Sean Gervasi

The Drift toward Military Intervention in Balkans: Another Vietnam?

Robert McNamara, who was Secretary of Defense from 1961 to 1968, has written a remarkable memoir which should be read by those who believe there are no dangers for the United States in Bosnia. One of the principal architects of the war in Indochina, McNamara has now declared that he and his colleagues were wrong, "terribly wrong," in pursuing a military victory there.[1] This is an astonishing admission, to say the least. But, whatever the criticisms which may be made of McNamara or of the book itself, we should be grateful that he has finally admitted the errors which carried the U.S. into war.

McNamara sheds new light on how the United States became involved in Indochina. He makes it clear that U.S. policy-makers made decisions in the early 1960s which can only be described as reckless. These decisions amounted to a determination to ensure U.S. domination of Southeast Asia based on poor and distorted information, on heavily biased analysis, on bureaucratic and personal ambitions, and on the systematic deception of the public and the Congress.

For anyone interested in the lessons of the past, and of Indochina in particular, the publication of McNamara's memoir has come at a crucial moment. For it is increasingly clear that the United States is now involved in another civil war thousands of miles away from our own shores. The media carry daily reports about U.S. concern for the future of the Bosnian government, about visiting military missions to Bosnia, about U.S. complicity in the breakdown of the UN arms embargo, and about U.S.-inspired efforts to persuade the United Nations and NATO to put pressure of all kinds on the adversaries of that government, especially the Bosnian Serbs. Are these expressions of concern and the recent deployment of more than twenty thousand U.S. troops for a so-called peace-keeping mission reminiscent of the slide into the war in Indochina? There would certainly seem to be some grounds for wondering whether the U.S. is not now on the edge of the same kind of commitment which eventually led us into the disaster that we call "Vietnam."

The Clinton administration has made Bosnia a foreign policy priority since it assumed office in early 1993. It seems determined to keep the Muslim-led Bosnian government in power—whatever, the cost. During its first eighteen months, the Clinton administration substantially increased U.S. commitments in Bosnia. Some of these have been hidden from the American public, and even from the Congress. The second phase of Clinton's involvement culminated in peace talks held on a military base near Dayton, Ohio. The "Dayton Accord" call for multi-lateral peace keeping forces but they hardly resolve the issues which brought on the war in the first place.

The bloody civil war going on in Bosnia has been under way since 1992, when a government dominated by a Muslim minority seceded from Yugoslavia. The large Serb minority in Bosnia rebelled against the idea of Muslim rule and established its own independent republic. It was the insistence of the Muslim-led government on ruling over all of Bosnia that precipitated the civil war there. What does it mean that the U.S. is taking sides in a civil war on the edge of Europe? Indeed, in a civil war which could easily become a wider Balkan war?

The U.S. government is aware that the situation in the Balkans is dangerous. As Richard Holbrooke, the Assistant Secretary of State for Europe, put it in a Congressional hearing: "I think Southeastern Europe has replaced Northeast Asia as the really most explosive part of the world."[2] Secretary Holbrooke did not reveal in his testimony that, on assuming office, he had hoped to get the U.S. "out of the Balkan mess."

President Clinton and his advisers do not appear to understand the implications of their own analysis. The Administration apparently believes that the U.S. can support the Bosnian Muslim government, and support its war against the Bosnian Serbs, without running any serious risks. There are, however, strong grounds for thinking this is an illusion. One important reason is that the Bosnian state is very weak, and in control of little more than 20 per cent of "its" own territory. If it were not for the support of a few countries and of the United Nations—and behind it, NATO—it is doubtful that Bosnia could maintain its claim to sovereignty over Serb and Croat territories. Even the recognition of Bosnia, which had never before existed as a state, was forced on a reluctant international community by Germany and the United States.[3]

Thus the U.S. has placed itself in the position, not of supporting an established state with established boundaries, but of forcing the international community to recognize and support a state whose very existence is contested by a large minority of its population. Present U.S. policy is thus headed for a dilemma in which the U.S. will have to choose between fighting to impose the Izetbegovic government on the rest of Bosnia-Herzegovina, that is, on Bosnian Serbs and Bosnian Croats,[4] or abandoning that government to its fate.

Bosnia is therefore like South Vietnam, a state which the United States created almost single-handedly in the mid-1950s in a misguided effort to "contain communism" in Asia. And our policy in Bosnia today is similar to our policy in Indochina in the mid-1960s, the period McNamara writes about when the Johnson administration began the escalation of the war in order to protect its South Vietnamese client. More than one observer has written about the parallels between Vietnam and Bosnia recently. Writing in the *International Herald Tribune* last spring, Gregory Clark argued that the U.S. was making some of the same mistakes in Bosnia that it had made in Indochina. In seeking to impose its own solution in Bosnia, he said "the West felt it could ignore a history of racial hatred, in particular the bitter Serbian memories of massacres at the hands of wartime Croatian and Muslim Nazi collaborators, and blithely establish an artificial state of Bosnia-Herzegovina to be run by a Muslim minority."[5] The recognition of Bosnia, Clark wrote, was a "regrettable mistake," and those responsible should admit that it was. He thought, at the time he was writing, that there was still time to achieve a negotiated peace, as the United States had agreed to support "West European efforts to force the Bosnians to compromise."[6]

In February of 1995, a decorated veteran of the Vietnam war, Col. David Hackworth, now a military analyst for *Newsweek* magazine, described the U.S. as sinking slowly in the Bosnian swamp."[7] He raised a key issue which is reminiscent of the U.S. experience in Indochina. Hackworth indicated that the U.S. is covertly arming and assisting the Bosnian army.[8] He pointed out that U.S. Air Force air controllers were deployed in Bosnia, officially under the UN, but in fact "ready to direct NATO airstrikes against the Serbs." He also pointed out that the "concealed U.S. taxpayer cost of the war," apart from a contribution to the UN for Bosnian operations, "has already reached almost another $1 billion a year." These and similar actions, he concluded, "could drag us much deeper into the muck." In Hackworth's view, the solution today is to learn the lessons of Vietnam and to force our politicians to act on them.

More recently, A. M. Rosenthal, a columnist for *The New York Times* pointed out that Senator Robert Dole's proposal to lift the arms embargo on Bosnia was similar to moves which had led the U.S. into the Indochina war.[9] Although Dole had been talking about both Vietnam and Bosnia, he did not, Rosenthal observed, "make plain the connection between what he condemns in Vietnam and proposes in Bosnia." The Bosnian Muslim army needed tanks and other sophisticated arms. If the U.S. military provided them, would it not also have to train Bosnian Muslims? After the Dayton peace accord, we now know the answer. The U.S. is pledged to arm and train the Bosnian Muslim armed forces.

How many Americans, Rosenthal asked, would have to go to Bosnia? And if significant numbers went, "Will America leave them prey for Serbian guerrillas and snipers?" "What power would Mr. Dole, [as] Senator or President, commit to the protection of U.S. forces?" The failure to ask and probe such questions,

Rosenthal wrote, was "dereliction of duty." American allies warned that arming the Bosnian Muslims "would prolong the war and spread it deeper and wider." Rosenthal concluded that "Between now and May, Senator Dole, really should face the Bosnian questions that compare to the unconfronted Vietnam questions."

Mr. Rosenthal has made the dangers about as clear as they can be made in a few words, and since his article was written in April 1995, much of what he feared would happen has happened. It should be added that McNamara is also well aware of the parallels between Bosnia and Vietnam. McNamara told the *New York Time's* R. W. Apple that the United States is on the wrong track in the Balkans. Asked whether the mistakes made in Vietnam could be repeated today, he replied, "Absolutely, not only can but are being repeated. . . . American difficulties in Bosnia and Somalia involved similar errors."[10]

U.S. Strategy in the Balkans

U.S. policy in Vietnam was based on far-reaching strategic aims of "containing communism" in all of Asia. In practice, this meant asserting American power and influence in the region, creating organizations like the Southeast Asia Treaty Organization (SEATO), and suppressing revolutions—linked to communism or not—which would limit or end U.S. power and influence in a particular country. Thus our policy towards Vietnam, the policy of supporting the Diems, and Khanhs, and Kys, was always part of a much wider strategy. The fact that the strategy was itself over-reaching, contradictory, or wrong was something which was rarely discussed. Even now Mr. McNamara's own discussion of the larger strategic context of the Vietnam conflict is inadequate.

Similarly, the U.S. policy toward Bosnia is also one part of a wider strategy. It is, in fact, part of a strategy which aims at re-ordering the whole of the Balkans and establishing U.S. power and influence in a large part of the region, especially the Southern Balkans. This is not at all obvious if one is looking only at events in Bosnia. The actions taken in Bosnia have, in fact, less to do with Bosnia proper than they do with larger strategic concerns. That is one reason why, on the face things, the U.S. commitment to the Bosnian government is so difficult to fathom.

U.S. policy in the Balkans has two main components. The first is a set of policies aimed at re-ordering of the Balkans and tying it to Western Europe and the U.S. The second component consists of policies aimed at using the Balkans as a base for projecting U.S. power and influence into other areas of Europe, the Middle East, and Central Asia. The U.S. policies aimed at forging a new Balkan order are complex, for the U.S. and its allies have been attempting to do two things at once. They have, first of all, attempted to create a number of diverse client states from the nations of the former Warsaw Pact. And, beyond that, they have been attempting to balance the interests of the various Western powers in the region.[11]

The U.S., however, is a world power. It could not rest content simply with re-organizing the Balkans since the Balkan region has always had enormous strategic importance for Europe, the Mediterranean, and the Middle East. The Balkans has long been the crossroads between the East and West, North and South, Islam and Christianity. The region has been a crossroads of trade and migration and a place where cultures mixed. That is, it has long been a region where powerful and competing societies—Islam, the Hapsburg Empire, the British Empire, Russia, Turkey, Greece, and the Third Reich—struggled for mastery or for political and military access to neighboring regions. That is why the World War I began there and also why the Balkans played such an important role in the Nazi strategy of conquest three decades later. Thus, just as powerful empires had vied for the control of Indochina in the past, the United States felt compelled to try to assert its control over the Balkans after the end of the cold war.

During the cold war, the Balkans—Yugoslavia in particular—were more or less neutralized. A strategic stalemate between the West and the communist bloc prevailed. Competition between the blocs in the Balkans could easily have ignited a third world war. Both the Western powers and the communist powers understood that. So the Balkans remained relatively quiet.[12] In the post-cold war world, however, the Balkans have again become the focus of political, economic and military competition, and not only for the U.S. and Western Europe but also for Turkey, Islamic nations such as Iran, and Russia. This means that U.S. policy in Bosnia and in the Balkans has been and is being fashioned with a view to its effects across a vast area of Europe, the Middle East, Central Asia, and possibly even parts of Africa.

The U.S. policy of supporting a Muslim minority government in Bosnia locked in a civil war with the Bosnian Serbs is much more than a policy aimed at shaping the future of a single nation. The stakes are much greater than that. U.S. policy in Bosnia is part of a broad strategy serving U.S. strategic interests in an area stretching from the English Channel to Siberia and from Egypt and Lebanon to the Baltic. The following appear to be the main U.S. goals in the Balkans today:

1.- to support a Muslim-led unitary state in Bosnia-Herzegovina,
2.- to install a Western-style regime in Yugoslavia and to reduce the geographic area, power, and influence of Serbia to a minimum,
3.- to assist in the creation of a Greater Albania incorporating parts Kosovo, the Sandjak, Macedonia and possibly Bulgaria, all closely linked to Bosnia, the U.S., and Turkey,
4.- to support Croatia and Slovenia, and possibly the formation of a Greater Croatia incorporating the Croat areas of Bosnia,
5.- to prevent the formation of a state or federation uniting the Serbs of Bosnia, Croatia, and Yugoslavia,

6.- to prevent the formation of any alliance between Greece and Yugoslavia or among the Eastern Orthodox countries of the Balkans (Yugoslavia, Greece, Bulgaria and Rumania),

7.- to install American power in Southern Europe and the Mediterranean in order to block the access of the European Union or Germany to Islamic markets or natural resources such as oil in the Orient, and

8.- to block the development of Russian influence in the Balkans.

This outline of U.S. policy is not speculative, although its existence cannot yet be verified by consulting the relevant National Security Council documents. However, such a picture of U.S. strategy is confirmed by interviews, some published materials, and acknowledged elements of U.S. policy in the Balkans.[13]

On the face of things, this policy seems to make a certain amount of sense. The U.S. has always premised its foreign policy on the belief that, in spite of its enormous power, it is "locked in a race for resources" around the world and that its own economic future will depend on its ability to find new markets and sources of raw materials.[14] The Balkans now present a huge crisis for this strategy. Given the premise of U.S. foreign policy, the Balkan policy would appear to be comprehensive and coherent. What more can one ask of any policy?

The problem, of course, is that the policy is also arrogant, a-historical, murderous, based on inadequate analysis, full of contradictions, and ultimately reckless. It will lead to the complete devastation of the Balkans, including its deindustrialization. The unpredictable effects are potentially enormous. In all of these things, the current Balkan policy is very similar to the strategy which carried the U.S. into Indochina at the beginning of the 1960s. After the Vietnamese defeat of French colonialists at Dien Bien Phu, peace accords signed in Geneva on July 25, 1954 stipulated a cease-fire and a two year period of peace which would culminate in free elections in a united Vietnam and the formation of a national government. South Vietnam was created as a nation by the U.S. to bypass the Geneva agreement when on October 26, 1955 Ngo Dihn Diem declared the region of the south as the Republic of Vietnam. Years after the event, President Dwight Eisenhower acknowledged in his autobiography that the Vietnamese national liberation movement would inevitably have won those elections and constituted a government, indeed, a very popular one.

Thus Vietnam would have emerged in the 1950s as an independent, Communist state in Southeast Asia. This prospect, as McNamara attests in his memoir, greatly worried U.S. policy makers. The U.S., therefore, acting in secret undermined and overthrew the Geneva agreement by establishing a U.S.-backed regime in the South, arming it, and refusing to permit scheduled elections. This led to an internal revolt in the southern part of Vietnam, which the government of "South Vietnam" sought to suppress. The Saigon regime, however, was far from popular. It required ever increasing amounts of force to suppress the Viet Minh revolt, with horrible consequences for Vietnamese civilians. Eventually, the United

States, seeing its client government threatened, decided to intervene with massive U.S. forces and bombing campaigns to put an end to the resistance. The outcome is well known.

The problem in the Vietnamese case was that the U.S. based its creation of the South Vietnamese regime, its support for it, and its eventual entry into the war to save it, on a determination to assert U.S. dominance in Southeast Asia. The U.S. pretended to wish to "save Southeast Asia from communism," but in reality it was pursuing what the Kennedys, the Johnsons, the Nixons, the McNamaras, the Kissingers, and others in the policy planning levels of government believed to be the strategic interests of the United States: control of resources, access to markets, dominant political influence, and so forth. It was only decades later that some of our more honorable leaders had the sense and the decency to admit that the strategic schemes were "wrong.". Must the same thing now happen in the Balkans?

An Artificial State

The U.S. involvement in Bosnia-Herzegovina began under the Bush Administration, when U.S. officials and agencies began to cooperate with the Muslim-led Party of Democratic Action in order to position it for taking power early in the 1990s.[16] U.S. involvement became more public in 1992 when, against the wishes of many U.S. allies, the U.S. and Germany forced the recognition of Bosnia by the international community. Since then, and particularly under the Clinton administration, the U.S. has continued to support the Izetbegovic government in Bosnia through thick and thin. The U.S. appears to be firmly committed to a unitary government under Muslim leadership, with or without Mr. Izetbegovic. The problem is that a government dominated by a Muslim minority—and one tending increasingly to fundamentalism at that—can hardly be very secure in what would, in normal circumstances, be a South Slav state.

Like South Vietnam, Bosnia-Herzegovina is an artificial creation. It was not a state created by its people. It was a state created largely by external powers working through internal clients as part of an effort to control a strategic region of the world. As Tucker and Hendrickson have written:

> From the beginning, it was evident that the independence of Bosnia and Herzegovina could only be secured if it could muster large-scale support from the international community."[17]

This is what made both states weak. They were literally forced on the people of their respective territories by the combined efforts of ambitious and opportunistic ruling groups and powerful foreign sponsors. In the case of South Vietnam, the new state was forced on the majority of the population. In the case of Bosnia, it was forced on a large minority, the Bosnian Serbs. In South Vietnam, a widespread rebellion developed. In Bosnia, a third of the population, the Bosnian Serbs, rebelled.

How did a republic of the Yugoslav federation become a putative state led by a minority government? In 1992, Bosnia was a constituent part of Yugoslavia, much like a state of the United States. Its borders were purely administrative and had no fixed historical basis. Its population in 1991 consisted of Muslim Slavs (44%), Bosnian Serbs (31%) and Bosnian Croats (18%). These three nationalities were intermingled throughout the territory of the republic. But the Serbs occupied and farmed some 60% of the land.[18] The Muslims were concentrated in the cities. From 1989, politics in Bosnia-Herzegovina were increasingly dominated by ethnic/religious issues. In particular, the leadership of the largest group, the Muslims, began to mobilize support for an Islamic awakening in Bosnia.[19] Croatian nationalism was also on the rise.[20] The combination of the two was alarming to the Serbs who had experienced the terror of the holocaust at the hands of the Croats and Muslims during the Second World War, under direct Nazi sponsorship.[21]

There had been similar divisions in Indochina, notably between Catholics and Buddhists and between Communist-nationalists and those who had made their peace with colonialism. In 1990, Bosnia-Herzegovina held the first multi-party elections in the postwar period. Ethnic-religious tensions in the country were high, and the ethnically-based political parties emerged victorious, taking well over 70 per cent of the vote. However, no single party could muster a majority, and the republic had henceforth to be governed by a multi-party coalition of Muslims, Serbs, and Croats. The League of Communists was, however, dislodged from government. Muslims constituted the largest single group in the republic and fielded the largest single political party, the Party of Democratic Action. Muslim nationalists soon began pressing openly for the creation of an ethnically-based state. They wanted the "ethnic nation" and "the state" to coincide, and they wanted independence from Yugoslavia.

The Bosnian Serbs, however, did not want to leave Yugoslavia. And if Bosnia were to become independent, they certainly did not want a unitary state dominated by an emerging coalition of Muslims and Croats, leaving the Serbs in a minority. So far as the Bosnian Croats were concerned, their coalition with the Muslims was strictly pragmatic. Ultranationalism had already swept through neighboring Croatia. Bosnian Croats dominate the western side of Herzegovina, bordering on Croatia. And they wanted to annex Herzeg-Bosna and to join with their ethnic brethren in Croatia. The coalition with the Muslims encouraged them, since both shared narrow nationalist aims which the Bosnian Serbs might obstruct. This coalition, however, was extremely fragile, as the outbreak of vicious warfare in 1993 was to prove. Even now, after the U.S.-forced Muslim-Croat "confederation" in Bosnia, there is still fighting between the two sides.

At this point it is worth expanding on what happened to the Serbs during the 1940s. Beginning in 1941, they were forced by the Nazi invasion of Yugoslavia to live under a Croat-Muslim coalition for four years. The so-called Independent Croatian State was actually a puppet state in which Hitler installed fanatical Croatian nationalists known as the Ustasha. It included almost all of what is now Bosnia-Herzegovina. With the cooperation of the Muslims—who raised two SS divisions for Hitler—the Ustasha proceeded to carry out the "racial purification" of Croatia and Bosnia. This resulted in almost unimaginable horrors, including the deaths of some 700,000 Serbs.[22] Given the past, the Serbs could not possibly accept the situation which was emerging toward the end of 1991. In September of 1991, anticipating the worst, the Serbs proclaimed a number of "Serb autonomous regions" within Bosnia-Herzegovina. In October, Muslim and Croat members of Parliament combined to pass, against Serb objections, a resolution declaring Bosnia-Herzegovina to be a sovereign republic. This was taken to be a first step towards secession. It ended the facade of a tripartite coalition government. The Serbs then established their own Assembly and declared that the laws of Bosnia-Herzegovina would not apply in the Serb autonomous regions.[23] In late 1991, both Germany and the United States were pressing their allies to recognize the various republics wishing to secede from the Yugoslav Federation. On December 19, 1991, Germany overrode the objections of its partners in the European Community and obtained their agreement to recognize Croatia, Slovenia, and Bosnia-Herzegovina.[24] The very next day, the Muslim and Croat members of the Bosnian presidency voted to request recognition of the country's independence. The Serb members refused to take part in the vote.

In January 1992, again despite Serb objections, the Muslim and Croat members of the Bosnian parliament voted to hold a referendum on independence. The referendum, held at the end of February, was boycotted by the Serbs. Only two thirds of the population, therefore, participated in the vote. But the referendum produced a very large majority in favor of independence. The EC recognized Bosnia-Herzegovina as an independent sovereign state on April 6, 1992. The Bush Administration recognized Bosnia's independence the next day. And on that same day, the Bosnian Serbs declared their own republic. The actions of both the EC and the United States thus gave international backing to the Muslim effort to dominate the whole of Bosnia.[25] Thus the EC and the U.S. played a crucial role in launching a new state over the objections of a very large minority of its population. It should be noted that Bosnia's declaration of independence was illegal, according to the constitution of Yugoslavia. There was a provision in the constitution for secession, but only "nations," not republics, could secede. The constitution of Bosnia, too, provided for secession, but only if all the parties, "the nations," were in agreement. Nor is there any unqualified right to secession in international law.[26] This was why the Yugoslav National Army intervened with units stationed in Bosnia when civil order began to break down at the time of the secession. The position of army leaders was that they were trying to prevent communal fighting. They were, of course, seen as an obstruction and were attacked by Muslim and Croat paramilitary units. Many Yugoslav soldiers were killed and wounded.

Under pressure from the European Community states and others to leave Bosnia, the Yugoslav Army withdrew in June. For a variety of reasons, then, it is difficult to disagree with the judgment of Tucker and Hendrickson that: "the recognition of Bosnia's independence itself constituted an illegal intervention into Yugoslavia's Internal affairs, to which Belgrade had every right to object."[27]

This is a short but accurate[28] summary of how and why the Bosnian state came into being. Are there parallels to the U.S. experience in Vietnam? The first clear parallel is that the U.S. played a major role in the creation of this new state. There was no South Vietnam before the U.S. intervened after the Geneva accords. And there was no state of Bosnia-Herzegovina before the U.S. and Germany intervened at the end of 1991. The second parallel is that legality and the norms of international law were ignored in both cases. In Indochina, the U.S. overthrew the Geneva accords and set up a puppet regime, pretending that it was an independent state. In Bosnia, the constitutions of Yugoslavia and of Bosnia-Herzegovina and international law were simply ignored. The United States and Germany were able to do what they did not because they had legally acceptable reasons for doing it, but because of their overwhelming power. The third parallel is that the creation of this state left Bosnia, as Vietnam before it, profoundly divided and therefore weak. In Bosnia, there was the immediate additional consequence that the new state had control over no more than twenty per cent of "its" territory. Bosnia, in other words, did not really have the attributes of a legitimate state. It was not accidental that the foreign pressures to recognize this state, for reasons which had nothing to do with the welfare of the population of Bosnia, brought about a civil war.

The Impasse

The weakness of the Bosnian state—and all the consequences which flow from it—constitutes the Achilles heel of U.S policy in Bosnia-Herzegovina. In 1994, the situation in Bosnia was very much like that in Vietnam in 1961. In 1961, General Maxwell Taylor was dispatched to Vietnam to determine whether a significant number of "advisers" should be sent there. Taylor was sent to Saigon, because things were not going as planned, and President Kennedy had to decide what to do. Taylor recommended an expanded U.S. commitment in Vietnam, and, as we know, in spite of the constant increases in U.S. aid and the eventual deployment of hundreds of thousands of American soldiers, the South Vietnamese state did not survive.

In early 1994, after two years of war in Bosnia, the West again found itself at an impasse. The U.S., Germany, and, much less enthusiastically, other Western powers had been supporting the Izetbegovic government and its claim to exercise sovereignty over the whole of Bosnia-Herzegovina. However, owing to the refusal of the U.S. to provide troops in Bosnia[29] and owing to divisions within NATO itself about what the organization should do in Bosnia, the West had not been able to defeat the Serbs and to impose a settlement favorable to the Muslim-Croat government. The Izetbegovic government was itself too weak to win the war. The U.S. and Germany, in particular, were therefore in a dilemma. They supported the Bosnian government, but the limits to their freedom of action meant that they could do little to help it subdue the Serbs.

The United States, therefore, began to seek the same solution which it had seized upon in the late 1960s in Indochina. A policy similar to the "Vietnamization" of the war in Indochina was crafted for Bosnia. That is, the U.S. began an effort to create a much larger and more effective client (Bosnian Muslim) army which could make up for the lack of Western troops with a mandate to impose a settlement satisfactory to the Bosnian government. This second phase of the war was carried out secretly. Through 1995, the Serbs were well-equipped militarily and very strong. But their pool of military-age personnel is limited. The Izetbegovic government, on the other hand, has a large manpower pool, but lacks adequate organization, training, heavy arms, intelligence and communications.[30] So the U.S. began secretly helping the Izetbegovic government to expand, re-train, and re-arm its forces in the hope that they would be able to deal a fatal blow to the Serbs or a least be able to force them to accept a "deal" such as the one proposed by the Western contact group. By mid-1995, however, it was apparent that this strategy was not working. Serb military positions could not be taken back by Muslim government forces alone. A fall-back plan, however, had been in preparation all along. NATO air forces based in Italy and on carriers in the Mediterranean had been identifying Serbian targets in case air support was needed. In the summer of 1995, that air support for the Bosnian government became essential and massive bombing raids against Serbian gun implacements, troop barracks, roads, bridges, arsenals, and so forth were carried out. Now the secret was made plain. The West had openly intervened with massive military support on the side of the Muslim government. The Serb minority was being forced to the negotiating table in Dayton, Ohio.

There are some important differences between the situation in Vietnam in the early 1960s and the situation in Bosnia in the early 1992. In Bosnia, for instance, the Serbs are a minority, although most Croats would not live in a unitary state governed by the party of Mr. Izetbegovic.[31] In Vietnam, the opponents of the government of South Vietnam were the majority. Nonetheless, as we shall see, there are very good reasons for believing that the strategy adopted to support a unitary state governed by the Muslim minority will fail, and fail disastrously.

The Vietnamization of the War in Bosnia

In the mid-1950s, the United States created an artificial state in Vietnam in furtherance of its grand scheme of containing communism. That state, however, was corrupt and ineffectual. It triggered a rebellion by the national liberation movement. By 1960, despite considerable American economic, political, and military support, the rebellion was serious enough to threaten the stability of the state. At that point the United States had only three options. It could abandon the Saigon government. It could send significant numbers of Americans troops. Or it could try to build a much more coherent and powerful "South Vietnamese" army. There was never any question of abandoning the Saigon regime at that stage. The real choices were between sending large numbers of troops, the classic imperial response, and trying to build a real "South Vietnamese" army which could defeat the Viet Minh insurrection. The idea of sending troops overseas to fight in such a war was extremely unpopular. The United States had just fought a war in Korea and gained very little by it. By seeking to occupy Korea, the U.S. had precipitated China's entry into the war. U.S. forces had been driven south. A stalemate then developed which led to the seemingly permanent division of Korea. But even during that long stalemate, which lasted nearly three years, United States forces sustained significant losses. The war in Korea came to be seen as costly and pointless. No American government could risk repeating that experience in the beginning of the 1960s.

The only possible option for the United States in Vietnam in the early 1960s was to try to provide Saigon with economic support and to build up its military. The United States would provide logistical support and training to the "South Vietnamese" military. It would also provide the advisers needed to do the job. Saigon would fight the second American war in Asia. The dead would be young Vietnamese men and women and not Americans. Time, however, revealed the flaws in the theory. One of them was that as the effort to create a viable army for Saigon expanded, more and more American advisers had to be sent to Vietnam. These advisers then became caught in the jaws of the war. The danger now in Bosnia—following the Dayton peace accord—with more than twenty thousand U.S. soldiers deployed as "peace keepers" and military advisors is the same as it was in Vietnam in the early 1960s—how can U.S. troops not become increasingly involved in the fighting.

After the war in Indochina, the U.S. military became very shy of foreign involvements. They concluded that the U.S. armed forces should not again be drawn into a protracted and unpopular war. This point was made clearly and repeatedly by General Colin Powell, Chairman of the Joint Chiefs of Staff, during the early debates about U.S. policy toward Bosnia in 1993 and 1994. Neither the U.S. Congress nor the U.S. military wanted to send American troops into Bosnia to help it. The NATO powers were deeply divided over what should be done in Bosnia. Sending arms openly would have contravened the UN arms embargo. And Germany could not risk the reaction of its European partners if it intervened itself.

And yet the U.S. and its close allies had to continue to insist that Bosnia was a "state." The existence of such a state was a key to the realization of their strategy for creating a new Balkan order. It must have seemed to U.S. officials that there was an obvious way out of this impasse. The solution, a tried and trusted one used many times in the postwar period, was for the U.S. to do secretly what it could not do openly. The involvement of U.S. forces in the Indochina war was for many years unknown to the American public. Both the Kennedy and the Johnson administrations, while openly providing training and aid to Saigon, were also waging a "secret war" against North Vietnam and the National Liberation Front at the same time. The Clinton administration appears to have made the same decision in Bosnia. It is not known when the Clinton administration made the decision to begin significant covert military assistance to the Izetbegovic regime. But there is every indication that the decision was made sometime in the latter half of 1993, possibly even at the time of the major National Security Council review of U.S. policy in the region earlier in the year.[32]

There were reports from 1993 that the U.S. was helping to provide arms to the Bosnian regime. There were even reports of the presence of U.S. Special Forces in the region and in Bosnia.[33] However, the first reliable reports of substantial U.S. military assistance to Bosnia came to light in early 1994. At that time, French officials stated that the U.S. was secretly providing arms to the Izetbegovic regime. These arms, they stated, were Communist-bloc arms from U.S. government stocks which were being shipped into Bosnia from Turkey by air.[34] French officials stated clearly that this was a major U.S. covert operation designed to circumvent the UN arms embargo against Bosnia. This was at a time when the German government was also secretly aiding the shipment of arms from stocks from the former GDR. Germans arms were being shipped by sea from Rostock to Durres in Albania and then on into Bosnia.

Arms, equipment, and more were reaching Bosnia by other channels as well. *Defense and Foreign Affairs Strategic Policy* reported from London that 400 members of the Iranian Revolutionary Guards had arrived in Bosnia with large supplies of arms and ammunition in May 1994.[35] According to the magazine, the Central Intelligence Agency (CIA) had full knowledge of this operation. According to *Strategic Policy*, U.S. agencies were also providing large quantities of weapons which had originated in China and in North Korea to Muslim forces in Bosnia.[36] Furthermore, artillery, rocket launchers, and ammunition were arriving from Iran "with the knowledge and agreement of the U.S. government." Iranian military instructors were training Bosnian regulars and special operations units in Zenica in Eastern Bosnia. More than 3,000 Mujaheddin were fighting with the Bosnian 3rd Corps in Zenica.

Numbers of Afghan Mujaheddin had arrived in the autumn of 1994, *Strategic Policy* stated, at Ploce on the Croatian coast. They then went with false papers to Split and Livno and deployed in Bosnia, with different contingents going to the Kupres, Zenica, and Banja Luka areas.[37] Most importantly, the magazine stated that the Afghan Mujaheddin, who had been used in large numbers by the CIA in the Afghan war, were accompanied by U.S. Special Forces. These U.S. troops were on a covert mission to establish a command, control, communications, and intelligence network (C3I) in Bosnia to coordinate and support Bosnian Croat, Bosnian Muslim, and Mujaheddin offensives in central, Eastern, and northern Bosnia. The Special Forces units brought their own high-tech communications equipment.[38]

Federal Rebuplic of Yugoslavia. Croat Serb refugees expelled from the Krajina by Croatian forces which also drove thousands of Serbs from Croatia. Zabalj collective center, Voivodine (Novi Sad), Serbia, September 1995. (photo: UNHCR / A. Kazinierakis / 09.1995)

All of this was very reminiscent of the war in Indochina. There allied client states, South Korea, the Philippines, Australia, New Zealand, and others, were also providing military assistance to the Saigon regime. The same pattern seems to be emerging in Bosnia, where other U.S. clients—Turkey, Saudi Arabia, etc.— are providing funds and military aid to the Sarajevo regime. Less than two weeks after the appearance of the report in *Strategic Policy*, the mainstream British press began to provide further information on the covert U.S. role in Bosnia. *The Independent's* correspondent, Robert Block, wrote in mid-November that the United States was directly aiding Bosnian forces, providing them with intelligence assistance and training.[39] In Bihac, he stated, where a new Muslim offensive was under way, Muslim military commanders had been provided with aerial photographs of Bosnian Serb troop dispositions. He reported also, citing French and U.S. military sources and a British diplomat, that retired American soldiers were helping to train Bosnian Muslim troops. One week later, the London *Guardian* reported from Vienna that U.S. policies in Bosnia were dividing the NATO powers. According the *Guardian* correspondent, Washington was about to conclude military agreements with Zagreb and Sarajevo in order to strengthen the Izetbegovic regime. And such agreements were signed a short time later.[40] The correspondent described the U.S. ambassador in Croatia as saying that the U.S. would help to make the Muslims and Croats an "effective force" in dealing with "the aggression sponsored by Belgrade."[41] The *Guardian* went on to say that U.S. officials admitted that only Croatian and Bosnian officers were training at U.S. military colleges.

Most importantly, the paper stated that both West European and UN officials claimed, "The U.S. military and the C.I.A. have embarked on [a program of] covert military aid and training for the Bosnian army."[42] At almost the same time, *The European* reported from London that "America 'has joined the war' in Bosnia," and that the U.S. was deeply involved in the Muslim war effort.[43] The report stated that a high-level meetings had been held in Gornji Vakuf between U.S. military commanders and the Bosnian army's most important field commander, Filip Alagic. Two U.S. ambassadors were present, along with General Charles Boyd, head of intelligence in the U.S. European Command and Brigadier General Mike Mirza, director of operations in the European Command. The purpose of the meeting had been: "to make recommendations about how to provide military support to the Bosnian presidency. The result was a U.S. decision to launch a covert plan to help the Bosnian Muslims."[44] According to the London paper, "small teams of non-uniformed personnel working for the CIA" were in position and directly assisting the Bosnian Muslim forces with training in tactical operations, satellite intelligence, and air traffic control. A European defense source stated that the Americans "are teaching the Bosnian Muslims how to fight the Bosnian Serbs." "The Americans are taking sides," the source was reported to have said. "They have, in fact, joined the war."[45] Finally, *The European* reported a West European

UNPROFOR official as saying that "we have seen Americans in uniform and out of uniform for months. They stay at some of the Bosnian army bases and keep themselves to themselves." According to the paper's correspondent, senior UNPROFOR officers said they knew U.S. military personnel and CIA personnel had been working as advisers to help train Bosnian soldiers and to plan Bosnian army operations.[46] There were also indications that Bosnians were being trained in other countries.[47]

The European article went on to point out that roads were being converted to landing strips in various parts of Bosnia. It quoted one Western source as saying that "The Americans are masterminding the construction of a secret airfield in an isolated valley between Visoko and Kakanj in central Bosnia, about 25 kilometers from the nearest Bosnian Serb positions."[48] Finally, the paper's correspondent expressed his own view that "the assistance of the U.S. teams has been vital in recent Bosnian army successes."[49]

It should be noted that none of these reports—and many were published in the European press at the time—was published in the United States. And this was in spite of the fact that they were based almost exclusively on Western sources, including officials of the UN and UNPROFOR. The first that was heard of these reports in the mainstream U.S. press appeared in the *Washington Post* on November 19, 1995. Citing official sources and unnamed "Western diplomats," the *Post's* headline ran, "Charges U.S. Aids Muslims Appear to be Inaccurate."[49] The story itself, however, was exceedingly ambiguous. It contained statements such as, "However, despite their alleged inaccuracies, the reports do highlight the important role played by the U.S. military in Bosnia and in the region—a role not limited to providing food or supporting UN activities."[50] The report contained additional details of the U.S. military involvement in Bosnia and Croatia. But the headline was perhaps the most important part of the story, as is so often the case in the realm of propaganda. Reports on the questions which had been raised in the foreign press stopped almost immediately. They were to resume, however, early in 1995.

In late January, *The New York Times* published information making it clear that some of the earlier reports about U.S. efforts to turn the Muslim army into "an effective force" had been correct. The paper reported that the United States would soon send General Frederick Franks, Jr., the former commander of the VII Corps in the Persian Gulf war, to Bosnia "to assist the Muslim-Croat federation here with the integration of its armed forces.[51] The paper also revealed that General John Galvin had spent some time previously in Bosnia trying to carry out the same task. He had, however, "been unable to overcome the deep mutual suspicions between Muslims and Croats."

On February 22, *The Financial Times* reported that UN officials and diplomats in Bosnia believed the U.S to be flagrantly violating the arms embargo against that country. They stated that on the night of February 10, 1995 UN observers in northeast Bosnia had seen a C-130 Hercules transport accompanied by a jet fighter drop supplies by parachute at Tuzla, the second largest Bosnian-Muslim enclave and the site of a very large military base. At the time, U.S. jets were monitoring Bosnian airspace in a NATO operation called "Deny Flight," which has been under way since 1992.[52] NATO apparently did not report any violations of Bosnian airspace that night. This report was flatly denied in Washington. NATO sources said the story was misleading. On February 25, however, *The Guardian* in London repeated the story, adding considerable detail. *The Guardian* reported from Zagreb that UN analysts believed NATO was conniving at secret flights which were being used to arm the Bosnian Muslims covertly. *The Guardian's* reporter said that, despite the NATO denials, UN officials were standing by their reports. These were based on eye-witness accounts by a Norwegian helicopter pilot and a British intelligence officer. The Norwegian pilot had described a plane resembling a C-130 as having made a drop or a brief landing at the Tuzla air base on February 10th. Nordic UN troops, sent to investigate his report, were fired on by Bosnian government soldiers and could not pursue the matter further. The British officer reported similar airdrops or landings at Tuzla on February 12th and 17th. UN analysts said they believed these flights were part of an effort to supply arms covertly to the Bosnian government. According to *The Guardian*, the NATO reports denying that such operations were under way were "absurd" and a "whitewash." It quoted one UN source as saying, "It's a covert operation. There's no doubt about it."[53] On February 26, *The Independent on Sunday* carried the story one step further. No one had yet speculated on exactly who might be carrying out the covert flights which were being reported. *The Independent*, however, reported that UN commanders in Bosnia suspected that the United States was behind the secret night flights: "The U.S. was secretly supplying weapons to Bosnia."[54] UN peace keepers believed that "transport type aircraft of C-130 or like size" had dropped or delivered high-tech weaponry at the Tuzla air base on five different occasions beginning on February 10. Senior UN officials thought that the airdrops might have been organized by the U.S.-Central Intelligence Agency, possibly using planes from Turkey, which is well within range of Tuzla. *The Independent* said that "There was frantic activity in the State Department and National Security departments dealing with Bosnia last week." Moreover, the Assistant Secretary of State for Europe, Richard Holbrooke, had visited Turkey earlier in the week.

On February 28, 1995 NATO itself issued a report denying that covert air operations were being used to deliver arms to Tuzla. The report, however, was drawn up by an American officer at NATO's Southern Command in Naples. The NATO report stated that the flights around Tuzla were either normal NATO air traffic in Bosnia or commercial aircraft in Serbian airspace.[55] According to *The*

New York Times, the U.S. officer in charge of Southern Command, Admiral Leighton Smith "was furious about the United Nations Reports." However, UN officials in Bosnia stuck to their guns. One UN official said the NATO claim that UN officers had made elementary errors in their original reports were "frankly ludicrous and insulting."

The debate on the U.S. involvement in the war seems to have come full circle. On March 5, 1995 *The Sunday Times* of London reported that "Turkey is suspected of secretly airlifting arms to Bosnian Muslims in preparation for a new round of fighting in the spring."[56] According to the paper, American intelligence officials were "convinced" that Turkey was engaged in an airlift, but they told journalists that they had no hard evidence of Turkey's assistance to Bosnia. "The flights," according to *The Sunday Times*, "were first thought to be part of a covert operation by the Central Intelligence Agency to re-arm the Muslims." But the paper said that the CIA and other Western intelligence agencies believed the flights originated in Turkey and were financed by Saudi Arabia. The paper did not note that this was a classic pattern in CIA operations in the region. Nor did it find it strange that CIA sources would point the finger of accusation away from the CIA and toward someone else, about whose role they were also "unsure."

Refugees from Bosnia-Herzegovina at the Crnomelj refugee camp in neighboring Slovenia, May 1992. Women and children are most often victims of global strategies for control of natural resources and trading routes. (photo: UNHCR / 22026 / A. Hollmann / 05.1992)

These are just a few of the reports which have surfaced in recent months about clandestine military assistance to the Bosnian government in violation of the United Nations arms embargo. U.S. and NATO officials have issued denials stating that these reports are untrue or seriously inaccurate. At the same time, it would seem that there is overwhelming evidence that the U.S. has made a major, clandestine commitment for military assistance to the Izetbegovic regime. It appears to be providing arms, training, and advisers to the Sarajevo army. And U.S. forces appear to be operating in the field as well, just as they did in Indochina long before the public knew about it.

There are several reasons for coming to such conclusions. There are many, many eyewitness accounts indicating such an involvement on the part of the U.S. The sources providing this information to journalists are, for the most part, officials, diplomats, and officers from Western countries opposing U.S. policy. And, finally, the same facts are reported again and again from a wide variety of sources. If these accounts are correct—and they should be fully investigated, not suppressed—then the United States is very deeply involved in the war in Bosnia. And this would be dangerous for exactly the same reasons that it was dangerous in Indochina.

Conclusions

As we have seen, the United States and Germany played a major role in the creation of an artificial state in the Balkans, Bosnia-Herzegovina. This state has a weak, minority-led government. It commands the loyalty of a little more than 40 per cent of its own population. It controls some 20 per cent of the land area which it claims. By normal criteria, it would have never been recognized as an independent sovereign state. Nonetheless, the U.S. is now trying to make a viable state out of Bosnia. The evidence is clear that the U.S. has provided the Izetbegovic regime with the same kinds of resources which it provided to "South Vietnam" in the 1960s and 1970s. This commitment has apparently led already to the dispatch of U.S. military and CIA personnel to assist the besieged minority regime.

It is hard to believe that the U.S. commitment in Bosnia has anything to do with a genuine concern for the Muslim population, any more than it had, thirty years ago, a concern for the people of South Vietnam. Something else is at issue. Firstly, the Bosnian intervention is part of a broad strategy aimed at re-drawing the map of the entire Balkan region. Like the strategy of containing communism in Asia, it will not be lightly abandoned. This will be true even if, as the McNamara case shows, U.S. officials realize that they have made a mistake. Secondly, the commitment is significant because it has already involved the expenditure of substantial money and resources. According to some sources, the U.S. has already spent more than $1 billion on the war in Bosnia. And it may be planning to spend as much as $5 billion in the near future.[57] As a European defense source put it last autumn, "They [the Americans] have, in fact, joined in the war."[58]

The critical question today, for the peoples of the Balkans, for the Western powers, for the Islamic states involved and for Russia, is where this U.S. policy is leading. There are two issues that must be considered in answering this question. The first, assuming that the war in Bosnia is likely to continue for some time, is whether the U.S. itself is likely to become more involved in the war. The answer here is that it probably will. The bombing campaign against the Bosnian Serbs was a huge escalation. U.S. troops now in the role of peace keepers are armed to the teeth, and their rules of engagement permit them to use overwhelming force if even the slightest threat to their safety occurs. The Izetbegovic government and the cosmetic Muslim-Croat "federation" are far from stable. Sarajevo is certainly far from being able to give a consistently good account of itself militarily.

What will happen if the Muslim army should again fail to push back the Serbs in Bosnia to the lines stipulated in the Dayton accord? What will happen if the Bosnian Serbs refuse to any longer accept the prosecution of their leaders for war crimes while others are left to go on with the war. What will be the reaction of the American officials who are, in fact, running the war? It is very likely that they will react by increasing their efforts to "Vietnamize" the war in Bosnia, that they will spend more money, send more advisers, send more arms and provide more direct logistical support to the Muslim and Croat forces.

The public in the United States does not realize what is happening in Bosnia. It does not know that American advisers and CIA personnel have been actively involved in the war from its start. Some Americans might even approve of our policy if they did know about it, as was demonstrated by the token opposition to Clinton's announcement that he planned to send twenty thousand U.S. troops to Bosnia to enforce the Dayton accord whether or not the Congress agreed with the policy. In many ways, the Bosnia war has become the center-piece of the Clinton administration, just as Vietnam became so for Lyndon Johnson. If it were not, our government would have to abandon an important element of its overall policies for global domination.

This was the answer in Vietnam for nearly fifteen years. U.S. officials from the late 1950s until the early 1970s took the view that the U.S. had to continue helping Saigon. If it did not, Saigon would fall. And then the "dominoes" would fall, and in the end "China would take over." Such were the incantations which drove us on. Thus the answer to every reversal was more U.S. assistance. After 1965, the answer was always more U.S. troops. U.S. officials were not prepared to believe that Saigon was losing the war because they were not prepared to abandon their Vietnamese clients. Robert McNamara says in his book that the U.S. government should, have abandoned "South Vietnam" in 1963.[59] In fact, rather than looking the facts in the face, U.S. officials tried to deceive the Congress, the American public, and the world about what was happening in Vietnam. And they ended by deceiving themselves as well. It is quite likely that, if a see-saw war in Bosnia continues, the U.S. will be drawn into a new quagmire. The second issue which needs consideration is whether our policy in Bosnia makes any sense. Given that the U.S. is likely to remain committed to Sarajevo, where will our present policy take us in the long run? The answer here may be found by exploring the logic of the situation. There is a war going on in Bosnia. For both the Serbs and the Muslims, the stakes are very high. In the final analysis, there are only two logically possible outcomes in the Bosnian war. Either the Bosnian Serbs will win and be able to maintain their independence on what the U.S., Germany, and Sarajevo now consider "Bosnian soil," or the Izetbegovic regime will win and be able to impose itself on the Bosnian Serbs. What would happen if it became clear that the Bosnian Serbs were about to win the war? It is certainly possible that at some point, especially if they realize that the Dayton accord reduces them to a status somewhat comparable to that of the Palestinians, the Bosnian Serbs will launch a devastating major offensive against the Muslim army. The Bosnian Muslims could not easily sustain a major defeat. They might be forced to retreat from critical areas they now hold. That could lead in turn to the collapse of the Sarajevo regime. Would the U.S. and NATO with their thousands of peace keepers in position in Bosnia merely stand by? Could they resist the enormous pressures to intervene militarily at such a time? It seems very doubtful. Open U.S. or NATO intervention would produce a major change in Bosnia and possibly Croatia.

If such a confrontation ever takes place, no one will be able to predict the consequences. The Bosnian Serbs might feel forced to carry the war into Croatia proper. NATO might very well attack military positions and installations inside Yugoslavia. The Bosnian Serbs or the Yugoslavs, depending on the Western response to Yugoslav involvement, might attack NATO bases in Italy or even in Germany. Turkey might enter the war in Bosnia, precipitating a general Balkan war. Russia might intervene directly or indirectly.

In short, without any doubt at all, the war would spread and increase in intensity. This would inevitably affect the whole of Europe, dividing it profoundly in the midst of spreading chaos. The consequences of a major conflict in central Yugoslavia between NATO forces and the Serbs would be catastrophic for all.

The other obvious possibility is that the Izetbegovic regime might win the war. What would happen if the Dayton accord were successful and the Izetbegovic regime secures actual control over the area with certain powers of autonomy reserved for the Serb faction? The initial result of a Muslim victory would be obvious. Isolated and militarily defeated, the Serbs might have to abandon their republics in Bosnia and in Croatia. They would then have the choice of staying in both countries under horrific conditions (i.e., those on par with Palestinians) or leaving for Yugoslavia. But, despite being under siege—a siege which is less and less popular with the countries of Eastern Europe—Yugoslavia would be more or less intact. It would receive covert assistance from Russia, Greece, Rumania, and Bulgaria. With half the Bosnian Serbs in Yugoslavia and half in Bosnia, what would be likely to happen? Indeed, not just likely but absolutely certain to happen? Firstly, the Bosnian government would continue with its ethnic cleansing of Serbs. In fact, the Dayton accord only abets such ethnic cleansing, as it requires Serbs to hand over five Serbian controlled suburbs of Sarajevo by March 20, 1996 to the Muslim government. Will the 70,000 Serbs living there be forced out, leaving Sarajevo a Muslim-only city? Secondly, this repression would lead to guerrilla warfare. Thirdly, Serb guerrillas would begin to operate not just in Bosnia and parts of the Krajina, but also from Yugoslavia. Finally, the Serb guerrillas would also receive assistance from Russia, Greece, Rumania and Bulgaria.

In short, a Muslim victory in Bosnia would not lead to the establishment of anything like a normal state, but to prolonged instability and conflict. When John F. Kennedy considered sending U.S. military advisers to Vietnam, he posed two conditions which would have to be met. The Saigon regime would have to achieve political stability. And it would have to be able to defend itself.[60] These conditions were never really met. United States officials ignored them. In the face of every reversal, U.S. civilian and military officials persuaded themselves that the situation could be "turned around" in the future. All that was necessary was more aid, and, later on, more troops. But the United States was never able to establish a viable regime in Vietnam, despite the expenditure of tens of billions of dollars and the dispatch of nearly half a million troops. As we now know, the entire enterprise was based on grandiose ambitions, ignorance, distorted information, self-serving analysis, and misguided personal and bureaucratic ambitions. And the tragedy of Vietnam may be attributed in part to the fact that the conditions posed by Kennedy were ignored.

The United States is now making the same mistake in Bosnia. For there can never be a stable government in Bosnia under a Muslim-led regime. A Muslim military victory over the Serbs would not produce a stable government but a repressive one. The political conflict in Bosnia would not be resolved but suppressed. And, in consequence, there would be no peace. There would almost certainly be a long guerrilla war, a war which could easily spread to other parts of the Balkans. The Sarajevo regime, therefore, would continue to be dependent on the U.S., Germany, and the Islamic states for continued security assistance. For that reason alone, Bosnia would remain an artificial state. It could achieve a minimum of stability only with foreign assistance.

The Bosnian "state" would remain an artificial one in another sense. The Serbs work most of the farm land in Bosnia. After a Muslim "victory," those lands would either be depopulated or in turmoil. Where would Bosnia be if its farmlands were in chaos? Economic development could scarcely be expected to resume. Bosnia would be largely dependent on the outside world for many of its everyday needs. The United Nations, major donor countries, and international aid organizations would be called on to supply those needs. Would they want to do so under the political conditions which would in all probability prevail? It does not seem likely.

Therefore, even if the Sarajevo regime could achieve a military or a diplomatic victory over the Bosnian Serbs, the results would bring little improvement over the conditions which have prevailed during the last few years. The fundamental issues would not have been resolved equitably. And they cannot be, as long as the United States and Germany continue to support a regime whose main reason for existence is that it serves their strategic interests in a land which belongs to other peoples

Thus U.S. policy in Bosnia either leads to a wider war in which the U.S. would inevitably be involved, or it leads to the establishment of another politically unstable client state. This is not a policy, but a guarantee of costly failure, just as our policy in Indochina was. It is, therefore, time to recognize that our policy in Bosnia is mistaken. Recently a former Secretary of State, Cyrus Vance, told reporters at the United Nations that the recognition of Bosnia-Herzegovina had been a mistake.[61] Mr. Vance was right. What is needed now is a serious national debate about U.S. policy in Bosnia and its parallels to our policy in Vietnam. This should include a scrutiny of our policy in the Balkans as well. Only if such a debate is begun will we have a chance of avoiding the same trap which killed 59,000 Americans and more than two million Vietnamese in the 1960s and 1970s.

Postscript

In the second half of 1995, U.S. policy in the Balkans carried the U.S. and NATO into direct intervention in two civil wars, one between Croatian Serbs and the new protofascist state of Croatia and one between the Bosnian Serbs and the Bosnian Muslim-Croat Federation. In both cases, the U.S. and NATO intervened against the Serbs.

In the first case, the U.S. helped the new Croatia to plan, organize and carry out the invasion of the Krajina region in Croatia, where three hundred thousand Serbs, whose ancestors had lived on the same lands for three centuries demanded autonomy in fascist Croatia and then rebelled when it was denied. U.S. and German aircraft actually participated in the attack on the capital of Krajina, Knin, in the beginning of August.

The result was the uprooting of more than 250,000 Croatian Serbs, who had to flee to the Bosnian Serb Republic. They were bombed, strafed, and shelled on the way, as Croatian forces sought to establish what extreme Croatian nationalists have always dreamed of, "an ethnically pure" Croatia. Within Krajina, many of those who remained behind, primarily the elderly, were tortured, killed, and even mutilated. More than 16,000 Serb properties, according to the U.N., were put to the torch. These extensive atrocities were reported by the United Nations, international humanitarian organizations, and even European television networks. The U. S. government's reaction to these reports was to try to keep such news off the front pages by diligently concocting such frauds as "the Srebrenica massacre," which the French television network, Antenne 2, revealed to be entirely without any basis.

In the second case, the U.S. used NATO, against the advice of many allies, to destroy the military infrastructure of the Bosnian Serb Army. Plans were being prepared at the time this article was written to use NATO air power to end the military superiority of the Serbs on the ground, or to severely reduce it. These attacks, allegedly in response to an exploding bomb or shell in a Sarajevo marketplace, caused enormous destruction, including civilian casualties. This enabled the Croatian and Sarajevo armies to invade Western Bosnia and roll back the Bosnian Serb army. This led, again, to the flight of tens of thousands of Serbs, well over 100,000 by United Nations estimates. The story of the marketplace bombing was, once again, a contrived one. For the operations set in motion in August and September were being planned at the beginning of the year and were aired in Congress in the spring.

The U.S.–NATO intervention represents a major escalation of the U.S. military commitment in the Balkans. As such, it follows, more closely than the writer anticipated last spring, the logic which was revealed in the original article, the logic which landed the U.S. in the war in Indochina.

In intervening in this manner, the U.S. and NATO not only took sides in what President Clinton himself had proclaimed a civil war. They also allied themselves with precisely those elements in European society, fascists and extreme nationalists ready to kill in the name of ethnic purity, whom the whole world fought to defeat during the last world war. Tragically, the U.S. has embraced a racist and increasingly militaristic German government as its major European partner at the very moment that German leaders are seeking revenge against Yugoslavia and the Serbs for the defeats which the Second and Third German Reichs suffered at their hands earlier in this century.

Worse still, the United States, in order to create what it thinks will be a more favorable atmosphere for the re-election of President Clinton, has now imposed an unworkable overall peace "settlement" on Yugoslavia and is enforcing it with a 60,000-person NATO task force which includes 20,000 U.S. troops This is a major step into a Balkan quagmire. For, though U.S. troops are due to withdraw next year, the Dayton pact has not secured stability in the region. And NATO troops will certainly not leave. U.S. troops, furthermore, may have to stay if only to keep the others there. The present situation indicates that the Dayton "diktat" will not work. It will not establish an independent regime in Sarajevo which can meet John F. Kennedy's conditions for sending U.S. troops to Vietnam: political stability and a capacity for independent self-defense.

There will be more fighting, and the Muslim-Croat Federation is very likely to unravel. What will the United States do then? What the extraordinary events of the last few months demonstrate is that U.S. leaders, barring perhaps some in Congress, have completely lost touch with history and reality. There can be no doubt that the U.S. and Europe, and principally Europe, will have to pay the costs of this unprincipled and vicious recklessness in the not very distant future.

Notes

This article was orignially written in April and May 1995, four months before the United States drew NATO into an open military attack on the Bosnian Serb Army, the purpose of which was to shift the balance of power in Bosnia-Herzegovina. This action, which I did not anticipate at that time—and this was a serious error—was very much a part of the logic of escalation described here.

1. Robert S. McNamara, *In Retrospect: The Tragedy and Lessons of Vietnam*. New York, 1995.
2. Richard Holbrooke, "Hearings on U.S. Policy in Europe before the House International Relations Committee," Washington, D.C., March 9, 1995, transcript, p. 13.
3. See, for instance, General Pierre M. Gallois, "Balkans: la Faute Allemande,"*Le Quotidien de Paris*, January 28, 1993.
4 The hostility between Bosnian Muslims and Bosnian Croats continues, as does the fighting between them. As an experienced Balkan hand put it recently, "The principal [U.S.] projects the so called contact group of mediating powers and the Croat-Muslim Federation—remain as flimsy as they were at their inception twelve months ago." David Binder, "Gnats for Bosnia," *The Nation*, May 8, 1995.
5. Gregory Clark, "Bosnia After Vietnam: Ignorance, Bad Mistakes,*International Herald Tribune*, May 20, 1994.
6. *Ibid.*
7. David Hackworth, "U.S. sinking slowly in Bosnian swamp," *San Antonio Express-News*, February 4, 1995.
8. *Ibid.*
9. A. M. Rosenthal, "Dole in Bosnia," *The New York Times*, April 18, 1995.
10. R. W. Apple, Jr., "McNamara Recalls, and Regrets, Vietnam,"*The New York Times*, April 9, 1995.
11. See Joan Hoey, "The U.S. 'Great Game' in Bosnia," *The Nation*, January 30, 1995. This is one of the few articles written on this crucial aspect of U.S. policy.
12. There were nevertheless extensive covert operations going on in the Balkans, especially in the early years after World War II.
13. See, for instance, General Luigi Caligaris, "Europe's New Front Line: A View from Rome," *Royal United Services Institutions Journal*, February, 1995 and U.S. government plans for a "Southern Balkans Initiative," including a railroad from Istanbul in Turkey to Tirana, the capital of Albania.
14. See C. Fred Bergsten, "The Primacy of Economics,"*Foreign Policy* Summer,

1992 and John Stremlau, "Clinton's Dollar Diplomacy," *Foreign Policy*.

15. See McNamara, *op. cit.*, chapter 7, "The Decision to Escalate."

16. Author's interviews in Yugoslavia, December 1994. This issue will be discussed by the author in a forthcoming book.

17. Robert W. Tucker and David C. Hendrickson, "America and Bosnia,"*The National Interest*, Fall 1993, p. 15. This is one of the few serious analytical articles on this subject to be published.

18. ". . . the Serbs are a largely rural population and worked nearly 60 per cent of the land before the war," wrote Tucker and Hendrickson, p. 11.

19. See Darko Tanaskovic, "Why Is Islamic Radicalization in the Balkans Being Covered Up?" *Eurobalkans*, Summer 1994.

20. Nationalist sentiment of different kinds was on the rise throughout Yugoslavia, in part owing to the effect of deteriorating economic conditions on society. See Thomas Szayna, *Ethnic Conflict in Central Europe and the Balkans*, RAND Corporation, 1994, pp. 5-18.

21. See the entries for "Croatia," "Jasenovac," and "Yugoslavia" in the*Encyclopedia of the Holocaust*, Israel Gutman, Editor in Chief, Vols. 1-4, 1990.

22. In the entry for "Yugoslavia" in *The New Encyclopedia Brittanica*, vol. 29, 1986, p. 922, one finds that "Armed resistance to the [German] occupation began in Bosnia, and there the Croatian Fascists began a massacre of Serbs which, in the whole annals of World War II was surpassed for savagery only by the mass extermination of the Polish Jews." In March, 1944, S.S. Major-General Ernst Fick in a report addressed to Heinrich Himmler stated that the Ustashi in Croatia "had butchered in Balkan fashion 600,000 to 700,000" Serbs, Jews, Gypsies and Croatian opponents. This was a year before the war ended.

23. For a careful account of the events inside Bosnia which led up to the secession of April 1992, see Robert Hayden, "The Partition of Bosnia and Herzegovina, 1990-1993," RFE/RL Research Report, May 28, 1993. See also Paul Shoup," The Bosnian Crisis of 1992," in Sabrina Ramet, ed., *Beyond* Yugoslavia, 1994.

24. General Pierre M. Gallois, "Balkans: La Faute Allemande," *loc. cit.*

25. This led very quickly to recognition by the United Nations.

26. Tucker and Hendrickson, *loc. cit.*, p. 17.

27. *Ibid*.

28. The basic facts here are no longer contested. In the early stages of the Bosnian crisis, however, few observers were aware of exactly what had happened, or indeed of much of the essential background. The result was that the early accounts which shaped public perceptions were skewed.

29. In 1992, in the middle of an election campaign, George Bush could not possibly have proposed the dispatch of U.S. troops. His opponent, now President Clinton, could not really have made such a proposal either. The "Vietnam syndrome" was still an important restraint and remains so today.

30. See James Gow, "To Win on Points—Stalemate in Bosnia,"*Jane's Intelligence Review Yearbook*, 1994, pp. 54-57.

31. Since the creation of the Croat-Muslim Federation, tens of thousands of Croats have left Bosnia-Herzegovina. In some areas, they are being driven out by the Muslims.

32. In early February, at the end of a major National Security Council review, President Clinton had decided to commit U.S. diplomacy and power to bring an end to the Bosnian war. The U.S. said it wanted to force the Bosnian Serbs to implement the battered Vance-Owen plan. It may well be that President Clinton then determined to go a good deal farther than was publicly intimated at the time.

33. *Time* magazine carried the following report on May 24, 1993: "While President Clinton goes through some very public soul-searching about whether the U.S. should send an expeditionary force to Bosnia, sources have told *Time* that U.S. Special Forces are already on the ground there, although the Pentagon officially denies it. Sources say these advanced troops are, for now, reconnaissance operatives, keeping Washington 'incredibly well-informed,' and are providing intelligence to Muslim enclaves. But they are also equipped to assist in any military action Clinton may order."

34. Author's interviews with French sources, January 1994.
35. *Defense and Foreign Affairs Strategic Policy*, London, October 31, 1994, p. 3.
36. *Ibid*.
37. *Ibid*.
38. *Ibid*.
39. Robert Block, "US accused of aiding Bosnian forces,"*The Independent*, London, November 12, 1994.
40. Ian Traynor, "US upsets allies in Bosnian deals,"*The Guardian*, London, November 18, 1994.
41. *Ibid*.
42. *Ibid*.
43. Askold Krushelnycky and Ian Mather, "America 'has joined war' in Bosnia,"*The European*, London, 18-24 November, 1994.
44. *Ibid*.
45. *Ibid*.
46. *Ibid*.
47. *Ibid* and author's interviews, Washington, D.C. 1994..
48. *Ibid*.
49. John Pomfret, "Charges U.S. Aids Muslims Appear to be Inaccurate,"*The Washington Post*, November 19, 1994.
50. *Ibid*.
51. Roger Cohen, "Retired U.S. General to Aid Muslim-Croat Federation,"*The New York Times*, January 24, 1995.
52. "Bosnia arms embargo 'broken,'" *Financial Times*, February 22, 1995
53. Julian Borger, "Bosnians 'are being covertly armed,'"*The Guardian*, London, February 25, 1995.
54. *Ibid*.
55. Robert Cohen, "NATO Disputes UN Reports of Possible Airlift to Bosnia,"*The New York Times*, March 1, 1995.
56. "Turks accused of secret flights to arm Bosnia," *The Sunday Times*, London, March 5, 1995.
57. Ed Vulliamy, "America's Secret Bosnian agenda," *The Observer*, London, November 20, 1995.
58. Krushelnycky and Mather, *loc. cit*.
59. McNamara, *op. cit.*, p. 230. McNamara states, "I believe we could and should have withdrawn from South Vietnam either in late 1963 amid the turmoil following Diem's assassination or in late 1964 or early 1965 in the face of increasing military and political weakness in South Vietnam."
60. McNamara, *op. cit.*, p. 320.
61. "Vance: Recognition of Former Yugoslav Republics Was a Mistake,"*Tanjug Wire*, New York, February 9, 1995.

Sara Flounders

Bosnian Refugees—Pawns in the "Great Game": A New US-CIA War

The history of modern Europe revolves around carving and re-carving the Balkans. It is a history of continual redrawing of borders and defining regions of influence, of arming mercenary bands and holding international conferences in Paris, in Berlin, in London, and at the Hague to confer about which power would be in control of what region. It was called the "Great Game." All this was always without any consultation with the many small nations whose fate hung in the balance.

For the last four years, the recurring media image of Yugoslavia in the U.S. and Europe shows a desperate people fleeing local war and ethnic hatred or living a precarious existence dependent on United Nations convoys for their next meal. According to the UN High Commission on Refugees, this is the largest refugee population in the world. By 1994 figures, there are over 3.7 million war refugees in former Yugoslavia. The war has taken its toll on all participants of the struggle. Of the refugees, 44% are Muslim, 36% are Serbs and 20% are Croatian. The enormous human suffering represented in these cold statistics can not begin to be calculated.

The very names Bosnia or Serbia are now associated with ethnic cleansing, mass rape, atrocities, and age-old national hatred. Whenever U.S. involvement, UN troops, or NATO forces are discussed in the media, it is in terms of peace keepers, humanitarian missions, diplomatic initiatives, and neutral forces. When UN officials, NATO generals, and U.S., British, French or German diplomats meet, it's to discuss the newest peace plan. Every measure is always described as deriving from deep concern over how to end the fighting.

Is the civil war raging in Yugoslavia a case of spontaneous combustion caused by "ancient ethnic hatreds" burning out of control? Is the U.S. government an innocent bystander? Is the real problem Washington's indecision about how to defend a small, oppressed Bosnian Moslem government targeted by the new fascists of the 1990s—the Serbs?

A closer examination of the root causes of the incredibly destructive civil war raging in the region yields a different picture. The reality is that the U.S. government lit the fire in the Balkans. At every stage Washington has acted as an arsonist pouring gasoline on the flames. The greatest responsibility for the dismemberment of Yugoslavia and the resulting civil war lies with the U.S. Government. It was not an accident or an oversight. It was a policy decision. Each step the U.S. has taken has widened the war and increased divisions in the region.

Age-old ethnic hatred among small nationalities didn't just explode into modern day barbarism. Rather, war exists in the region as a result of outside powers fighting through proxy armies for control of the Balkans. In this process, the U.S. has been neither an innocent bystander nor a neutral party.

A year before the dissolution of Yugoslavia, the U.S. Congress passed the 1991 Foreign Operations Appropriations Law 101-513 on November 5, 1990. This bill was a signed death warrant. One provision in particular was so sweeping that even a CIA report described three weeks later in the *New York Times* predicted it would lead to a bloody civil war (November 27, 1990).

A section of Law 101-513 suddenly and without previous warning cut off all aid, trade, credits and loans to the Federal Republic of Yugoslavia within six months. It also ordered separate elections in each of the six republics, requiring State Department approval of the election procedure and results before aid would be resumed to the separate Republic. The legislation further required U.S. personnel in all financial institutions to effect the extension of this cut-off policy to all credits and loans from the World Bank, the International Monetary Fund, and other international financial institutions.

There was one final provision. Only forces that the State Department considered "Democratic Forces" would receive funding. This meant an influx of funds to small right-wing nationalist parties in a financially strangled region suddenly thrown into crisis by the overall funding cut-off. The impact was exactly what could be expected—devastating.

This law threw the Yugoslav Federal government into crisis. It was unable to pay the enormous interest on the foreign debt or even to arrange the purchase of raw materials for industry. As credit collapsed, recriminations broke out on all sides, principally between the Serbians, the Croatians, and the Bosnian Muslims.

At this time, however, not a shot had been fired nor had any region attempted to secede from the Yugoslav Federal Republic. The U.S. was not engaged in a public dispute with Yugoslavia. The region was not even in the news. World attention was focused on the international coalition Washington was assembling to destroy Iraq, a war that reshaped the Middle East at a cost of a half million Iraqi lives.

What was behind the sweeping legislation directed at Yugoslavia especially when U.S. policy makers predicted that the sudden unraveling of the region would lead to civil war? With the collapse of the Soviet Union, Washington was embarking on an aggressive march to reshape all of Europe. Non-aligned Yugoslavia was no longer needed as a buffer state. A strong, united, and economically determined Europe as envisioned in the Maastrict Treaty was hardly desirable from the point of view of the U.S. government. Washington policy makers considered both relics of the Cold War.

Control of the Purse Strings

This one piece of legislation demonstrates the U.S government's enormous power. The Foreign Operations Act implements U.S. corporate control through major funding to international financial institutions such as the Inter-American Development Bank, Asian Development Fund, the African Development Fund, and bilateral assistance. The deadly restrictions imposed on Yugoslavia take up a mere twenty-three lines in the Act. More than nine pages detail the sanctions to be imposed on Iraq. As of January 1995, these U.S. and UN sanctions have killed more than half a million children in Iraq. This estimate is from Thomas Ekfal, United Nations Children's Fund (UNICEF) representative in Baghdad. (*New York Newsday*, December 19, 1994).

This law also prescribes various forms of economic strangulation for other countries deemed enemies, including Angola, Cambodia, Cuba, Iran, Iraq, Libya, Syria and Vietnam. On the other hand countries moving hastily toward a capitalist market economy in 1990, such as Poland, were to receive special funding. In all the expressions of concern and sympathy for refugees and displaced people in countries across the globe, but especially in the former Yugoslavia, no U.S. official ever mentions the terrible suffering caused by U.S. economic strangulation.

Of course, financial strings were hardly new to Yugoslavia in 1990. For more than a decade, Yugoslavia had become utterly dependent on loans from Western banks. The increasingly onerous conditions had increasingly dislocated the economy. A year earlier the price of continued U.S. loans and credits was a brutal austerity program that devalued the currency, froze wages, cut subsidies, closed many state industries deemed unprofitable and increased unemployment to 20%. The result had been strikes, walk-outs, a sharp increase in political and economic tensions and above all an upsurge in nationalistic and religious antagonisms on all sides.

Once the U.S. acted so decisively toward Yugoslavia in 1990, the European powers were hardly willing to be bystanders to the enforced break-up of a country in their own backyard. The U.S. Foreign Appropriations Bill sent a clear message to the European powers that the Balkans were again up for grabs. On their own they might never have dared to act. Now they dared not be out of the action.

European Intervention

By February 1991, the European Council followed the U.S. measure with its own political demands and explicit economic intervention in the internal affairs of the Yugoslav Federation. Their demand was similar: that Yugoslavia hold multi-party elections or face economic blockade. Right-wing and fascist organizations not seen in 45 years since the defeat of the Nazi occupation by the anti-fascist partisan movement were suddenly revived and began receiving covert support. These fascist organizations had been maintained in exile in the U.S., Canada, Germany and Austria. Now they became the main conduit for funds and arms.

By March of 1991, Croatian fascists were organizing attacks and demonstrations calling for independence, and the expulsion of all Serbs from Croatia. On May 5, 1991 the date of the six month deadline imposed by the U.S. Foreign Operations Law 101-513, Croatian separatists staged violent demonstrations and besieged a military base in Gospic. The Yugoslav Federal Government, under attack ordered the Army to intervene. The Civil War had begun. Slovenia and Croatia declared independence on June 25, 1991.

In Croatia the right-wing party, the Ustashi, came to power using fascist symbols and slogans stemming from the era of Nazi occupation. Its program denied citizenship, jobs, pensions, passports, or land ownership to all other nationalities but especially targeted the large Serbian minority. In the face of armed expropriations and mass expulsions, the Serbs in Croatia began to arm themselves. The experience of World War II when almost a million people, primarily Serbs, but also Jews, Gypsies, and tens of thousands of others, died in Ustashi death camps fueled the mobilization.

As the largest nationality and the one that opposed the breakup of the Yugoslav Federation, the Serbs became the target and the excuse for Western intervention. History was turned on its head as the media portrayed the Serbs as fascists and coined the term "ethnic cleansing" to describe the actions of the Serbs. In 1991 right-wing nationalist parties swept the elections in Slovenia and Croatia. However, in Serbia and in Montenegro the mass mood was overwhelmingly for the Federation and also against further privitizations or inroads of the capitalist market. This was an unexpected resistance to the political collapse sweeping Eastern Europe at the time.

The tactic of targeting the Serbs with UN resolutions, imposing brutal sanctions, freezing all credit, and trade also serves as veiled threat against Russia, the traditional ally of the Serbs. Reunited Germany moved aggressively in the region to consolidate its position. Germany was the first nation to openly grant diplomatic recognition to the break-away Republics, especially Croatia, its former WW II ally.

The U.S. State Department's declared position after Croatia and Slovenia seceded was to support the continuation of the Federation. But this flies in the face of the demands and the processes set in motion by the U.S. Foreign Operations Law passed in 1990 before the Yugoslav civil war began.

The Rewriting of History

The rationale behind Western intervention in Yugoslavia is based on rewriting history. Every debate about drawing and redrawing the map of Bosnia assumes the right of the Western powers as outside "neutral" forces to carve up and decide the fate of the region in the interests of "peace." The implied justification is that the small, barbaric nations of the Balkans are so torn by ethnic hatred that they are incapable of deciding anything themselves. It is true that there is a bloody history in the Balkans, but it is not of small nationalities fighting each other. Rather the true history reveals the major imperialist powers battling for control and domination of the strategic crossroads of Europe and the Middle East.

The Austro-Hungarian Empire, Ottoman Turkey, Czarist Russia, Britain, France, Germany, and Italy have all considered the Balkans their rightful "sphere of influence." World War I began in Sarajevo. Although the competition and rivalry for markets extended globally, far beyond Bosnia, this small region has always been a tinderbox for the big powers.

In World War II, the resistance movement to Nazi occupation led by Marshal Tito and the League of Yugoslav Communists united the small nations of the Balkans for the first time into an explosive political force. From scattered bands of guerrillas, it grew into the largest partisan movement in Europe, more than a million strong. Forty-three German divisions could not destroy the movement. This experience shaped Yugoslavia's history and laid the basis for the Federation. It remains a powerful heritage today.

Among the media's endless descriptions of "ancient ethnic hatred" this revolutionary partisan movement and the long tradition of struggles to unite the South Slav peoples against outside domination is never mentioned. For 45 years, the Yugoslav Federation was able to hold the Western powers at bay. From an impoverished, backward area it was able to develop industrially and raise its standard of living. The fact that the IMF and U.S. banks were able to again strangle and dismember it does not change historical accomplishment. The IMF and World Bank control access to international markets, and as the Yugoslav Federation attempted to enter the international market, it subjected itself, unwittingly, to the impositions of the world monetary system, a system devised to benefit American and western European corporations.

Casting the Serbs as Fascists

How did the Serbs come to be viewed in the western media as fascists? This has now become an accepted fact for western journalists, an issue beyond debate. It makes any discussion of U.S. motives seem unimpeachable and on the side of the victims of a resurgent fascism. An April 1993 interview by Jacques Merlino, associate director of French TV 2 with James Harff, director of Ruder Finn Global Public Affairs, a Washington, D.C. based public relations firm, explains the role of the corporate media in shaping a political issue. Harff bragged of his services to his clients, the Republic of Croatia, the Republic of Bosnia-Herzegovina, and the parliamentary opposition in Kosovo. Merlino described how Harff uses a file of several hundred journalists, politicians, representatives of humanitarian associations, and academics to creates public opinion. Harff explained that, "Speed is vital . . . it is the first assertion that really counts. All denials are entirely ineffective."

In the interview Merlino asked Harff about his boldest public relations endeavor:

Harff: To have managed to put Jewish opinion on our side. This was a sensitive matter, as the dossier was dangerous looked at from this angle. President Tudjman was very careless in his book, *Wastelands of Historical Reality*. Reading his writings one could accuse him of anti-Semitism. [Tudjman claims the Holocaust never happened.] In Bosnia the situation was no better: President Izetbegovic strongly supported the creation of a fundamentalist Islamic state in his book, *The Islamic Declaration*.

Besides, the Croatian and Bosnian past was marked by real and cruel anti-Semitism. Tens of thousands of Jews perished in Croatian camps, so there was every reason for intellectuals and Jewish organizations to be hostile toward the Croats and the Bosnians. Our challenge was to reverse this attitude and we succeeded masterfully.

At the beginning of July 1992, *New York Newsday* came out with the article on Serb camps. We jumped at the opportunity immediately. We outwitted three big Jewish organizations—The B'nai B'rith Anti-Defamation League, The American Jewish Committee, and the American Jewish Congress. In August we suggested that they publish an advertisement in the *New York Times* and organize demonstrations outside the United Nations.

That was a tremendous coup. When the Jewish organizations entered the game on the side of the [Muslim] Bosnians we could promptly equate the Serbs with the Nazis in the public mind. Nobody understood what was happening in Yugoslavia. The great majority of Americans were probably asking themselves in which African country Bosnia was situated.

By a single move, we were able to present a simple story of good guys and bad guys which would hereafter play itself out. We won by targeting the Jewish audience. Almost immediately there was a clear change of language in the press, with use of words with high emotional content such as "ethnic cleansing," "concentration camps," etc., which evoke images of Nazi Germany and the gas chambers of Auschwitz. No one could go against it with out being accused of revisionism. We really batted a thousand in full.

Merlino: But between 2 and 5 August 1992 when you did this you had no proof that what you said was true. All you had were two *Newsday* articles.

Harff: Our work is not to verify information. We are not equipped for that. Our work is to accelerate the circulation of information favorable to us, we try to aim at judiciously chosen targets. We did not confirm the existence of death camps in Bosnia, we just made it widely known that *Newsday* affirmed it. . . . We are professionals. We had a job to do and we did it. We are not paid to moralize.

Control through Division in Bosnia

The divisive U.S. role in Bosnia, the most multi-ethnic of the republics, raises other questions. Does the U.S. seek, through the breakup of Yugoslavia, to position itself in the region, or is there a more complex hidden agenda? Certainly U.S. conduct has involved many maneuvers that have prolonged the war and increased the rivalry among Britain, France, and Germany. Turkey, Greece, and Italy have also historically been involved in the region and are again maneuvering. On March 18, 1992, a negotiated agreement for a unified state brokered by the European Community was reached in Lisbon between the Bosnian Muslim, Croatian, and Bosnian Serb forces. This agreement of all three parties would have prevented the disastrous civil war of the past three years. It would have saved the hundreds of thousands of refugees who lives have been destroyed by war.

Washington sabotaged this original agreement by convincing the Bosnian Muslims that they hold out for control of a greater portion of Bosnia. The U.S. role in destroying this carefully crafted agreement is acknowledged by all sides. Even the June 17, 1993, *New York Times* described Washington's role. The U.S. government officially encouraged Alija Izetbegovic, the head of the right-wing Party for Democratic Action, to unilaterally declare a sovereign state under his presidency. Bosnian Muslim groups in two separate areas of Bosnia have challenged the government led by Izetbegovic. They disputed Izetbegovic's claim that he represents the interests of the Muslim community. They wanted a policy of cooperation and trade with the other nationalities of the region. Both groups have condemned Izetbegovic for right-wing nationalist policies and reliance on U.S. military aid.

The elected Bosnian Muslim government in the city of Tuzla, one of the wealthiest industrial centers of old Yugoslavia, claims that the U.S.-supervised rewrite of the Bosnian constitution gave power only to the most extreme rightwing nationalist forces of Izetbegovic's Party for Democratic Action and neo-fascist Franjo Tudjman's Croatian Democratic Union. Other political forces even among Moslems were excluded. The current Bosnian constitution was written by a U.S. lawyer. The draft was approved at the U.S. embassy in Vienna and the constitution was finalized in Washington on March 18, 1994. A Bosnian Muslim group in the northwest Bihac area led by Fikret Adbic declared its autonomy from the U.S. backed government based in Sarajevo. In retaliation, the Izetbegovic government launched a military attack against these Muslim forces that wanted peace with their Serbian and Croatian neighbors. This attack on an elected Moslem Bosnian government was organized by the U.S. As now revealed in numerous articles in the major media throughout Western Europe, six U.S. generals took part in planning the offensive in June of 1994. The attack violated the ceasefire and a UN declared safe area.

The Izetbegovic government's offensive was at first successful in the Bihac region. But the Bosnian Serbs, in alliance with Serbs in Croatia and Bosnian Moslem forces led by Fikret Adbic reorganized and began a strong push back. In the U.S. media, neither the U.S. role in planning the offensive or the fact that the U.S. backed forces were the ones to violate the cease fire was examined. The Bosnian Moslem forces opposing the Izetbegovic government based in Sarajevo have received only scant mention as "renegade forces."

The CIA Role in Bosnia

Another view of U.S. aims and U.S. involvement develops from reading the European press. News stories such as the following simply do not appear in the U.S. media:

"CIA Agents Training Bosnian Army," *The Guardian*, November 17, 1994
"America's Secret Bosnia Agenda," *The Observer*, November 20, 1994
"How the CIA Helps Bosnia Fight Back," *The European*, November 25, 1994
"Allies Facing Split Over Bosnia," *The Independent*, November 12, 1994
"Europe Braces for More Rows with US," *The Guardian*, November 12, 1994

These few headlines of the British press expose both the CIA role in Bosnia and the depth of the growing dispute in NATO. The media in France, Germany, and Italy has carried similar exposés of large-scale CIA involvement in the widening war in Bosnia. Coverage has included information on tactical operations, sharing satellite information, and controlling local air traffic. Units of both the Croatian and Bosnian Army have reportedly been trained within the region and in the U.S.

which has also provided assistance in building air strips and organizing large weapons shipments through Croatia to the Bosnian forces.

Also reported was the meeting of six U.S. generals with the leaders of the Bosnian Army to plan the military offensive that broke the nine month cease fire in Bosnia and opened fighting in the UN declared "safe zone" of Bihac. All of this immediately raises the question of how long the CIA has been involved? What is its purpose? The budget of the CIA is today three times the budget of the U.S. State Department.

The debate in the European press complete with Pentagon denials and clarification has received scant coverage in the media in the U.S. This avoidance in the U.S. media of an issue receiving wide coverage in Britain and France raises further questions of why the major U.S. media is aiding and abetting this operation and why the European media is exposing this information now. The exposés follow months of increasingly sharp criticisms and veiled charges by UN officials that the U.S. has sabotaged each agreement, peace plan, and even the negotiated cease fires.

It is clear that the Civil War in Yugoslavia has broken the growing unity of the European powers. They are at each other's throats over how to proceed. The struggle between the use of UN peace keepers vs. NATO bombing reflects these divisions.

UN Leaks Information on the U.S. Role

Occasionally the debate leaks out in the U.S. media. On April 30, 1994, the *Washington Post* cited two senior United Nations officials, a general and a civilian, who blame the U.S. "for the continuation of the war in Bosnia because it has given the Muslim-led Bosnian government the false impression that Washington's military support was on the way." The article explained that the officials interviewed were two of the highest-ranking UN representatives in Bosnia. Yet they feared using their names lest they be expelled from Bosnia. However, both claimed that U.S. moral and financial support of the Bosnian Muslim government was prolonging the war.

The officials accused the U.S. of leading on Izetbegovic's Bosnian Muslim forces by promising full-scale NATO intervention on his side. Gen. John Shalikashvili, chairman of the U.S. Joint Chiefs of Staff, had gone to Sarajevo to meet with Bosnian military leaders. It was a powerful incentive to keep fighting which was reinforced when, in an impassioned speech at the opening of the new U.S. Embassy in Sarajevo, U.S. Ambassador to the UN Madeleine Albright said, "Your future and America's future are inseparable." On June 24, 1994, the *New York Times* described the new supplies, including heavy weapons, have been flooding into Bosnia since the U.S. organized Croatian-Bosnian alliance.

Each "peace proposal" or map defining the areas of Bosnian Moslem or Bosnian Serb control defines a dependent, unsustainable enclave needing constant resupply which would require a military presence for many years. Industrial centers and the convergence of roads in this mountainous nation are allocated to the Bosnian government based in Sarajevo. The Bosnian Serbs have been allocated the poorest rural and mountainous regions with no connecting roads or corridors between them. The Bosnian Serbs cannot survive under these plans. Their situation is untenable and they are driven to resist.

Use of War Propaganda

The siege of Gorazde in the Spring of 1994 is one of the clearest examples of the U.S. propaganda barrage to justify and demand measures that would widen the war and give the U.S. military a blank check. Nightly news broadcasts of Gorazde focused on the Serbian bombing of a hospital and claimed casualties in the thousands. Then, after days of gory stories in the media and heavy U.S. pressure, U.S. planes flying under NATO auspices bombed Serb positions. A heated UN Security Council vote however blocked the full-scale NATO air strikes that the U.S. demanded. After the siege was lifted, the commander of UN troops in Bosnia, British Army Lt. Gen. Michael Rose, told visiting U.S. Rep. John P. Murtha, chair of the House Appropriations Committee Subcommittee on Defense, that reports of damage and casualties were greatly exaggerated. The Bosnian casualties around Gorazde "were closer to 200 than 2,000." The media had wildly exaggerated casualties in order to promote a war climate and justify NATO intervention.

The UN officials found that the hospital in Gorazde, which had been repeatedly described as all but destroyed by the Serbs, basically needed a broom to clear up the rubbish. It was still functioning. The hospital had been damaged because the Bosnian Muslim government forces had established its military headquarters next to the hospital. After the siege ended, a report in the April 24, 1994 *New York Times* referred to a giant munitions factory in Gorazde under Bosnian Muslim control. The Pabjeda Munitions Factory includes "a honeycomb of underground tunnels and storage bunkers." There were "enough explosives in the factory to flatten a city." Throughout the siege the public has been bombarded with countless stories on the plight of unarmed Bosnian Muslim forces versus a well-armed Bosnian Serb army.

Support for the government of Izetbegovic has been built mainly through horror stories of brutal Serbian attacks on unarmed civilian in Sarajevo. One of the most gruesome was an attack on an open air market that left 68 people dead on February 5, 1994. As the rift between the U.S. forces and the British and French forces under UN flag grows more heated these widely publicized Serb atrocities are being disputed. A UN analysis of the crater showed that the Bosnian Government was responsible for the explosion at the market. On November 10, 1994 the UN publicly released a crater analysis of another shell that exploded wounding a child as proof that the Muslim Bosnian Army had fired on its own civilians to gain sympathy.

Inter-Imperialist Rivalry

CIA involvement in the civil war in the Balkans has positioned the U.S. militarily in a strategic region. At the same time it has disrupted the developing unity among its European imperialist rivals, principally Britain, France, and Germany. These U.S. rivals bear the increasing burden of hundreds of thousands of destitute refugees, thousands of ground troops in position and the bitter acrimony of competing interests. What appears to be a bureaucratic dispute between NATO and UN officials is in reality a struggle between the imperialist ruling class of the U.S. and its European rivals, who fear being drawn into a protracted war. Each defends its right to carve up this strategic region in accordance with its own interests. But the Europeans have troops on the ground. If their forces take casualties while the U.S. calls the shots, opposition at home will rise.

There seems to be a great deal of information of closer German-U.S. collaboration at the expense of British and French interests. But even this may change. The fact that the U.S. has armed and is now training Croatian troops may be a sign that Washington is asserting itself in Croatia also. The debate on U.S.-controlled NATO forces helping to evacuate UN "peace keepers" reflects an expanding effort to make the U.S. the only power deciding the fate of the Balkans. Both French and British determination to again be powers in carving up the Balkans is reflected in their large commitments of troops under the UN flag, in place throughout Bosnia. But the Pentagon has been able to frustrate totally the British and French troop placements by encouraging the Bosnian government, a government totally dependent on the U.S. to sabotage any peace agreement. Washington's November 1994 decision to unilaterally and officially end the UN Security Council arms embargo by openly supplying the Bosnian forces was the most open statement to date that it would pursue its own agenda in Bosnia at the expense of the Europeans. This decision is also at the expense of the hundreds of thousands of uprooted and displaced people caught in the cross fire.

All of the imperialist powers, but particularly the U.S., recognize that Yugoslavia sets precedents for intervention in the former states of the Soviet Union. In early December 1994, the summit of the CSCE, newly formed into the Organization for Security and Cooperation in Europe met. Its first military action was to authorize a "peacekeeping mission" to Nagorno-Karabakh, the enclave disputed by Armenia and Azerbaijan. The stated purpose of the forces going into Nagorno-Karabakh is to prevent a Bosnia situation. Their track record, however, in preventing violence and war is not encouraging.

Ownership and control of the newly privatized industries and natural resources is at stake in the former communist bloc. In a war torn region all of this can be bought for a song. Who will control the markets, the rich resources, the rebuilding and the new investments? Military control of the situation will be decisive. Diplomacy is only the cover for the military balance.

The Pentagon Plan

The U.S. is determined to be the dominant power in the Balkans. This thinking is best reflected in an extraordinary 46-page Pentagon document on the Balkans. Excerpts published by the *New York Times* on March 8, 1992 assert the need for complete U.S. world domination in both political and military terms and threaten other countries that even aspire to a greater role. The public threats seem to be aimed at the European powers and Japan. Why else would the document be leaked and then not disavowed. The Pentagon policy document states:

Croat Serb refugees from the Krajina/Kragujevac collective center, Serbia. Pawns in the "great game." (photo: UNHCR/A. Kazinierakis/09.1995)

Our first objective is to prevent the re-emergence of a new rival. . . . First, the U.S. must show the leadership necessary to establish and protect a new order that holds the promise of convincing potential competitors that they need not aspire to a greater role or pursue a more aggressive posture to protect their legitimate interests.

We must account sufficiently for the interests of the advanced industrial nations to discourage them from seeking to overturn the established political and economic order. Finally, we must maintain the mechanism for deterring potential competitors from even aspiring to a larger regional or global role.

The document goes on to specifically address Europe. "It is of fundamental importance to preserve NATO as the primary instrument of Western defense and security. . . . We seek to prevent the emergence of European-only security arrangement which would undermine NATO."

No senior U.S. official, including President Bush ever denounced or renounced this document. When Bush was asked directly about the document he said that while he hadn't read the report, "We are the leaders and we must continue to lead."

Operation Balkan Storm

Just how little U.S. involvement has to do with "aiding poor Bosnia" is best seen in an OpEd piece in the *New York Times* (November 29, 1992) by retired Air Force General and Air Force Chief of Staff Michael J. Dugan entitled "Operation Balkan Storm: Here's a Plan." Dugan is best remembered for an unusually candid interview before the Gulf War where he laid out very precise plans for the aerial destruction of Iraq. He was relieved of his command for being too frank in describing the Pentagon's war plans at a time when the U.S. was claiming to the UN that it wanted to impose sanctions on Iraq only to pursue a diplomatic solution. However, four months later the war unfolded almost exactly as Dugan had described.

About the Balkans, Dugan writes, "A win in the Balkans would establish U.S. leadership in the post-Cold War world in a way that Operation Desert Storm never could." He goes on to lay out a scenario of coalition building, if possible, with Britain, France and Italy on an ad-hoc basis since the UN Security Council is deadlocked on the use of force by NATO. He describes arming the Bosnian Muslim forces and unconventional operations in Bosnia to suspend UN humanitarian operations, then massive air power against Serbs in Bosnia and Serbia. This Air Force General likes to brag about U.S. death technology. Dugan listed using aircraft carriers, U.S. F-15s, F-16s, F-18s and F-111s, Jstars and Tomahawk missiles to destroy Serbia's electricity grid, refineries, storage facilities, and communications. "But the U.S. costs in blood and treasure would be modest compared with that of Bosnian trauma." We know that, in fact, all of what Dugan predicted did come true in the air campaign against the Bosnian Serbs in late 1995.

General Dugan describes the next phase of the Balkan war. What is clear is that at each phase the flames of the conflict were fanned by U.S. policies, beginning with the legislation of November 1990 and continuing through the recognition of an independent Bosnia under a right-wing U.S. backed government rather than the compromise government acceptable to all sides in March of 1992. The U.S. brokered Croatian-Muslim Federation of March 1994 and the U.S. interventions at each stage in the growing conflict must be foregrounded in any discussion of the Balkan crisis. Whether it is the Vance-Owen plan to cantonize Bosnia into tiny enclaves early 1993 or the Vance-Stoltenberg Plan of late 1993 for a three-way partition of Bosnia, each proposal is an assertion of U.S. determination to dominate the region and keep its imperialist rivals off guard.

The defeat of the CIA-trained and now well-armed Bosnian troops in Bihac in early December of 1994 by combined Bosnian Serb, Croatian Serb and Muslim forces hardly means that the Pentagon and the war planners will slow their relentless drive to dominate the Balkans. Despite the many grim warnings of difficult terrain and low cloud cover the Clinton Administration has sent some 20,000 troops as a "peacekeeping" force. Massive use of air power is again threatened. Once committed, more and more troops will be required in a war that can quickly escalate. Clinton has already announced a $25 billion increase in the Pentagon budget. Gingrich, Dole, and Helms are demanding much more. There is a heated debate today in ruling military, corporate, and government circles, but it is not about how to negotiate peace. It is about how to insure U.S. domination of a strategic region.

The analogy to CIA advisors in Vietnam followed by 25,000 troops to prop up the U.S. puppet Diem government come all too quickly to mind. The war that is unfolding will not be fought in a Hollywood fantasy in front of computer screens as the military brass tried to make us think the Gulf War was. Rank and file soldiers of other U.S. wars know perfectly well that the war on the ground is far different than what American TV watchers see. The trauma for millions of refugees from South East Asia continues to this day. It will cost much more in blood and treasure than General Dugan so callously estimates. A further expose of U.S. war plans and involvement in the Balkans is desperately needed in order to open a debate and build a powerful opposition to the latest series of Pentagon plans for world domination.

Jemera Rone

Displacement Related to Human Rights Abuses and Aid Manipulation by the Military Parties to the War in Southern Sudan

Sudan, with approximately twenty-five million people, occupies the largest land area of any country in Africa, nearly one million square miles. Since 1983, a civil war in the southern third of Sudan has claimed the lives of some 1.3 million civilians.[1] The pre-war population of the south was five to six million. But by 1994 its population was estimated at only four and a half million, despite a typical growth rate of three percent per annum in a peaceful African country. The U.N calculated excess mortality in 1993 alone at 220,000 people.[2]

Those responsible for these deaths are the parties to the conflict, the government army and the rebels of the Sudan People's Liberation Movement/Army (SPLNVA, hereafter SPLA), who in 1991 split into two factions, SPLA-Mainstream and the breakaway SPLA-Nasir faction, which then began fighting each other. It is this three-way war, and related displacement of people, asset depletion, disease, and food deprivation, that is killing off the southern peoples.

The war has generated about 380,000 Sudanese refugees in neighboring countries as of late 1993.[3] In addition there were some 600,000 internally displaced people in southern Sudan in 1993, one-sixth of the estimated southern population. Several hundred thousand more have been displaced to northern Sudan, where there is no armed conflict.

Although the term "refugee" often is used for internally displaced, there are several important distinctions between the two categories. The war-related causes for the displacement of people are frequently the same for both internal refugees and external refugees, but by virtue of crossing an international border some come under the jurisdiction of the United Nations High Commissioner for Refugees (UNHCR), a decades-old UN. agency whose role is to assist people in foreign countries to which they have fled. There is no similar UN. agency mandated to help the internally displaced within their country of origin. Often the International Committee of the Red Cross (ICRC), not a UN. agency, is able to assist the internally displaced. Since no international law or treaty requires countries engaged in internal conflict to cooperate with the ICRC, it must resort to diplomatic and moral persuasion.

Providing assistance where war is being waged is much more difficult than helping refugees in a country at peace. When the internally displaced live in rebel held territory, the government usually resists allowing any agency to assist the displaced. The government is understandably suspicious that any aid going into rebel territory will fortify the rebels militarily or at least feed the rebel army. Similarly, when rebels control territory through which aid must pass to reach government-controlled zones or towns under rebel siege, the rebels also are reluctant to allow transit. Because of fighting and endless and often fruitless haggling over access, the war-time flow of relief to the internally displaced and needy is rarely reliable or sufficient.

The current armed conflict in Sudan is predominantly a regional war of the north against the south and other marginalized areas such as the Nuba Mountains. Issues include the role of Islam in Sudan, and Sudan's identification as an Arab or African state, questions that have been open since independence in 1956. Religion is a factor in this conflict because, since the military coup in June 1989, the Sudan government has been an Islamic fundamentalist state, run from behind the scenes by the National Islamic Front (NIF).[4] Southerners are not, for the most part, Muslims but practice traditional African religions. A minority of southerners is Christian.[5] Both traditional African religionists and Christians have resisted the attempts of the central government—whether the present one, the prior democratically-elected one (1986-89), or the Nimeiri military dictatorship (1969-85)—to apply Islamic law, or *shar'ia*, to non-Muslims and to the south.

Race or ethnicity is also a factor. Arabs are not the ethnic majority in Sudan.[6] The south is predominantly inhabited by African peoples, compared to the rest of the country where the majority claim Arab descent. The majority of southern peoples are Nilotes—Dinka, Nuer, Anuak, and Shilluk—the Dinka being the largest ethnic group in Sudan. The Nuer is the second largest group in the south.

Regional and global politics have fueled the conflict as well. Sudan and Ethiopia have had a long history of fighting and helping each other's armed dissidents for purposes of mutual retaliation and attempted deterrence.[7] Rebel Eritreans fighting for the separation of Eritrea from Ethiopia were aided by the Sudanese government. Southern Sudanese rebels were helped by an Ethiopian monarch, Haile Salasie (deposed in 1974) and then by Ethiopian Marxist military officers.[8] In the mid 1980s Mengistu Haile Meriam, then dictator of Ethiopia and client of the U.S.S.R., facilitated the creation of the SPLA in Ethiopia. Mengistu opened Ethiopia's doors not only to hundreds of thousands of Sudanese refugees but also to SPLA bases where SPLA recruits could be trained on Soviet-bloc hardware.

Cold War allegiances were by no means firm. The Sudanese's alignment with the Soviet Union was destroyed when an attempted Sudanese Communist Party coup pushed Sudan into a western affiance in 1971. Ethiopia's western alliance ended with the ascendancy in 1974 of a group of junior Marxist officers and the 1977 Ogaden War between Somalia and Ethiopia, which was the excuse for the Soviet Union to switch its patronage from Somalia to the more populous Ethiopia, with its better communications and naval facilities.

With Ethiopian, Soviet bloc, and other backing, the SPLA made major advances throughout the south. By mid-1991, the military momentum was solidly with the SPLA. It controlled most of southern Sudan except for a few major garrison towns and had access to the borders of Ethiopia, Kenya, Uganda, and Zaire. The SPLA's momentum came to a halt after the May 1991 overthrow of the Mengistu regime, and an eight-year patron-client relationship between Mengistu and the SPLA was destroyed overnight. The SPLA evacuated its bases and the three large Sudanese refugee camps in Ethiopia within a matter of days or weeks and escorted an estimated 270,000 refugees back into Sudan.

Once inside Sudan, the Sudanese refugees' (or repatriatees') fortunes rapidly changed. They joined several hundred thousand precariously subsisting internally displaced people. Relief to internally displaced people inside Sudan was not provided at the same level as it had been to the refugees Ethiopia; what came was little and late. The UN. was criticized for not acting on warnings in 1991 that a disaster was impending. It "did not prepare adequately for the inevitable suffering that [rapid repatriation] would entail."[9] The recalcitrant and hostile Sudan government put every obstacle in the way of access to the needy.

The SPLA quelled several internal efforts at dissent before 1991 with the help of Mengistu's army and internal security apparatus, but with his fall the SPLA became more vulnerable to division. On August 28, 1991, scarcely three months after Mengistu's overthrow and the enormous Sudanese refugee repatriation, three SPLA commanders called for the overthrow of SPLA Commander-in-Chief John Garang, and were joined by others.[10] The coup faded but the SPLA remained split, roughly along tribal lines, especially after the breakaway SPLA forces (mostly Nuer) captured Garang's home Dinka territory of Bor and massacred many Dinka civilians. The "Bor massacre" touched off one of the most violent periods of interfactional and intertribal fighting in southern Sudan's history. This fighting exacerbated a desperate situation for the civilian population and led directly to the creation of the 1993 "Hunger Triangle," a pocket of famine in Upper Nile province. This was only one of such pockets.

Even before the war, subsistence on the harsh clay plains environment of Upper Nile, periodically subject to drought, was never easy. Agriculture alone was unreliable due to the combination of erratic flooding, unreliable rainfall, and clay soil. A millennium ago this led to the development of a mainly pastoral economy, in which pastoralists seasonally moved their cattle, following fresh water supplies and leaving dried up areas, until they came to rest on the *toic*,[11] the river-flooded grassland along the upper Nile.

Historically the pre-war economies of the ethnic and political Upper Nile groups, mostly sections of Nuer and Dinka, were linked together and formed a wider regional system that enabled each group to survive the limitations of its specific geographical area. The groups used a variety of networks of exchange, some based on kinship obligations, some on direct trade. Through these networks, the peoples of the region have enjoyed regular access to distant resources in search of survival, crossing political and ethnic boundaries.[12] As the historian Douglas H. Johnson wrote:

> We should recognize that people go where the food is, that in this region lines of kinship frequently follow and strengthen lines of feeding. Social ties... were, and still are, the main way in which the Nilotic people survive and recover from the natural catastrophes which are endemic to their region.[13]

In times of shortage, they drew on each other's reserves, even if there was only a surplus in relative terms.[14] One tactic employed was intermarriage:[15] fathers of the bride customarily receive cattle as a bride-price, thus enabling the family wealth to be replenished by marriage into a group with more resources, also extending the kinship safety net. Trade in cattle and ivory was yet another link between the Dinka and Nuer. Raiding both cattle and grain (and women and children) occurred between Dinka and Nuer especially during the nineteenth century, when it was more common than in this century.

The SPLA split of 1991, while not tribally motivated, drove a military and political divide between the two largest groups in southern Sudan, the Dinka and Nuer. The places of greatest SPLA factional fighting of 1991-93 were in the Upper Nile "Hunger Triangle" areas including Duk Ridge and Kongor,[16] which in the past produced grain surpluses. Because of attacks targeted at civilians and civilian property, it could no longer provide a bridge in the hunger gap.

This disaster was hardly limited to the Hunger Triangle, where 165,000 people were in need.[17] In 1993 the UN. estimated that in addition to those 165,000, there were another 506,000 who would be relying almost entirely on outside relief in 1993 and an additional 830,000 who retained some survival capacity but were at great risk. The total was 1,497,000.[18] Some of the 600,000 internally displaced in the south might not have needed assistance, or did not need it in the initial stages of their displacement. The peoples of southern Sudan have long experience coping with food shortages occasioned by drought, flooding, and raiding. Historically they moved (displaced themselves) as a first step in a range of survival strategies which included migration to seek work, migration to relatives (who have an obligation to share with needy kinspeople), and sale of assets (often involving migration to a market). Other strategies included cutting back on food consumption, eating wild foods, and conducting their own raids—the last option being a rarer and a communal form of action.

During this war, southern Sudanese have fled (or been displaced) to avoid being victims of repeated raids and military attacks. It became more difficult for them to use the usual self-help strategies because military movements blocked their access to markets, jobs, or relatives, and disrupted the economy. People had to travel greater distances to any market. Two co-wives interviewed in Upper Nile province in 1993 said that they walked thirty days to and from market (from SPLA to government territory) to sell their modest amounts of jewelry. Military occupation of territory cut others off from their land and relatives indefinitely. Raiding stripped them of the cattle they could have sold to tide them over during periods of shortage.

In such cases there is still recourse to wild foods, but this is one of the few strings left on the self-help bow. In the faction fighting in Upper Nile province in 1993, many civilians ran to the flooded *toic* areas where they ate water lilies (wild foods) and tried to fish, although their fishing nets were lost or destroyed in the raids. The marshy *toic* was a wet barrier to military incursions, but the high rate of malaria in the *toic* took a heavy toll on the displaced.

The war-displaced and the needy who stay behind often are in need of emergency assistance. Therefore a very important player in the food game in southern Sudan has become the international relief community, consisting of both non-governmental organizations (NGOs) and U.N. agencies, with government and private donors. The basic principle of their African relief operations has been to define, usually according to nutritional status, the most vulnerable groups within a population and to target them with the minimum necessary food, water, and shelter to sustain life.[19] The displaced, carrying their belongings on their heads or backs and towing along small children, are immediately and visibly a most vulnerable group.

The problem in Sudan and other areas of Sub-Saharan Africa is that relief agencies are not dealing with a temporary emergency involving a normally robust and self-sustaining population which with brief supplements of food can eventually resume its former life. Frequently these displaced and needy have been looted of all their assets and burned out of their homes several times. They have lost economically active family members: almost one-quarter of the households in southern Sudan were headed by women in 1993.[20] They have been pushed by war into areas where they have no kinship safety net. The present conditions are the final result of more than 100 years of colonial and post-colonial war, traceable directly back to 1820 when Egypt invaded and took control of all Sudan. Egypt exploited the Sudanese population for 60 years until a revolution led by

Mohammed Ahmed (who called himself Mahdi, the leader of the faithful) threw the Egyptians out after a bitter fight in the 1880s. Mahdi's leadership of an independent Sudan was, however, short lived. In 1898, the British along with the Egyptians (who had been under British colonial administration since 1882) reimposed colonial rule on the Sudan which lasted until 1956, at which point the newly independent Sudan fell into the military conflict known as the Cold War. The net effect of this history has been to so disrupt traditional social and economic patterns of life that it is now nearly impossible to expect Sudanese people to be able to return to a "former life."

The most insidious aspect of colonial rule is a process of sustained asset transfer, which has taken place and is synonymous with the spread of mass impoverishment. It now continues as a feature of the factional wars. This asset-stripping usually targeted the property of "enemy" civilians. Although raiding occurred long before the civil wars, it usually was settled by negotiations between tribal leaders and payment of compensation was agreed to. The practice changed in this war when the raids became part of a larger political game in which negotiations for local compensation were not relevant (incidentally undercutting the authority of the tribal leaders in favor of younger military chieftains). The objective became to take without compensating—a practice antithetical to traditional social and economic patterns but intrinsic to colonialist practice—to win war booty, and to strip the wealth of the other side. The result has been extraordinary impoverishment of the civilian population, resulting in periodic famines and large numbers of civilian deaths.[21] The winners are those with the military power and their associates.

These abusive military practices bear great responsibility for the long history of food shortage in southern Sudan; famine can be regarded as an outcome of a political process of impoverishment resulting from the transfer of assets from the weak to the politically strong.[22]

Looting and asset stripping are violations of the rules of war, also known as humanitarian law. The rules imposed on the parties to this internal armed conflict include a prohibition on destruction of civilian assets (with limited exceptions which have been exceeded here) and on war booty. Other abuses of humanitarian law also provoke hunger, some intentionally, and others indirectly.

Among the hunger-provoking abuses committed by the government in this conflict are

1) indiscriminate aerial bombardment of southern population centers, causing people to flee and abandon planted fields;

2) army scorched earth tactics against villages around garrison towns, burning and looting the villages and killing, displacing, or capturing civilians;

3) Arab and other tribal militias' killing of southern civilians, pillage of civilian cattle and grain, and burning homes; these militias were a means for the government to carry on its counterinsurgency war on the cheap and to

"drain the sea" of peoples deemed supportive of the SPLA;

4) restriction of movement of the civilian residents of garrison towns—in Juba, forbidding them from leaving even in times of food scarcity—and placement of land mines and military patrols on the exit routes to enforce the ban on movement; and

5) severe restrictions on relief efforts destined for SPLA areas, and impunity given to army officers and others who profiteer on relief food.

Among the hunger-provoking abuses committed by one or both SPLA factions are

1) indiscriminate attacks on civilians living in the territory of the other SPLA faction;

2) pillage of civilian cattle and grain and destruction and burning of homes;

3) taking food from civilians, directly or indirectly, by force or fraud;

4) siege of garrison towns, including occasionally using starvation of civilians as a method of combat; and

5) warehousing thousands of "unaccompanied minors"—boys originally brought or lured to Ethiopian refugee camps for educational opportunities, who were segregated from their adult kin, used to attract relief food, and trained for ultimate underage military deployment.

Relief operations may, to varying degrees, help keep people alive but, at best, this is all they do. The way such programs are conceived and resourced means they are unable to tackle the process of resource depletion (war and looting) which is equated with recurring famine.[23] Nor has any relief program to date met more than a fraction of the need; the war-affected must still use self-help as the first line of defense against famine.

Externally provided relief has become an important commodity in the assistance/subsistence economy of southern Sudan and in the war. Relief agencies, targeting civilians impoverished by the conflict, inject additional and free food and non-food items (fishing nets, for example) into the economy. This becomes another factor in civilian survival strategies, despite the fact that the food delivered is often sporadic and unreliable as to amount and location. Hungry people will walk days to a source of food; they frequently flock in the thousands to the locations where rumor has it that food is being air dropped, trucked in, or barged up the Nile. A few family members will make the trip, pick up food, and carry it back—often walking for days—to dependent and less able family members.

Food and sustenance naturally play an important role in internal conflicts in any impoverished country. They are both weapons and goals. Relief food may have unintended side effects: it can attract a struggle for control. The strategic military implications of daily deliveries of tons of international food relief to the displaced inside southern Sudan are considerable. Such deliveries make it much more difficult for either side to achieve a military victory.

The large UN/NGO cross-border relief operation into SPLA territory in southern Sudan, Operation Lifeline Sudan (OLS),[24] is intended to slow population displacement and deaths in the area. It also has the side effect of making it more difficult or even impossible for the government to force a military conclusion. Some believe that such cross-border operations into guerrilla territory make the international community a participant in the effective partitioning of Sudan, a goal of many rebels.[25] The OLS/NGO provision of emergency relief to garrison towns under government control means that the relief operation has adverse consequences for the SPLA's military fortunes as well. It significantly reduces the SPLA's ability to capture those garrison towns through siege.

Although relief food is intended solely for needy civilians, frequently it is seized upon as an asset to be taxed, confiscated, expropriated, diverted, or otherwise taken for the war effort (or personal profit) by the government army and the rebel factions. They also divert food and other aid from the warehouse or barge (sometimes at gun point) before it reaches the civilians. If both sides are suspicious of relief food being delivered to the territory of their enemy, it is because they know from their own abuses how such relief can be turned into an illegal military bonanza.

Unlike the Eritrean and Ethiopian conflicts, there seems to be no reciprocity in Sudan between those who collect the food "tax"—the military powers—and the taxed civilians.[26] Rarely do the government or the rebel factions provide government services to the civilians, aside from defense and some food aid which originate elsewhere. While defense of southern peoples against government military attack is valued, and the government by its nature has more administrative infrastructure for schooling and other services, neither the government nor the factions account to civilians for their governance or even for their administration of aid intended for civilians. Neither seems to be concerned about civilian welfare except as it is necessary for the armies' survival. Shocking government neglect of southern needs was an underlying cause of the civil war to begin with.

The army's predatory practices are primarily intended to feed the troops, that is, to substitute military for civilian beneficiaries, although personal profit-taking, particularly on the government side, occurs as well. Food may be used for military purposes even when it reaches the intended needy civilians. The longer the war lasts, the more adept the parties become at manipulating civilians and the relief system.

Some in the international relief community have begun to wonder aloud whether relief operations, besides preserving some civilian lives and health, prolong the war by directly or indirectly feeding the armies. Certainly this has not been the intention of the relief community. But seeking to limit the predatory practices most directly affecting food delivery, such as diversion through theft and "taxation," while simultaneously retaining the same abusive parties' permission to have access to needy civilians on the other side, is an uphill battle.

The effect on civilians of the presence or absence of relief is not easy to measure. It is hard to know how many internally displaced civilians died in 1992, when little relief aid reached them, compared to the 220,000 excess deaths in 1993, when the U.N. had greater access to deliver food as well as to estimate the mortality rate.

While the government placed every conceivable obstacle—successfully—to prevent assistance from reaching the internally displaced in southern Sudan in the late 1980s and early 1990s, its tune changed shortly after Somalia was the subject of a U.N. peacekeeping action in late 1992. Government-approved flight access for cross-border operations to southern (SPLA) Sudan grew from seven in January 1993 to forty-five government and SPLA-held locations in December 1993, and another forty isolated locations were serviced by barge and rail convoys from the north.

In 1992, directly following the first devastating spurt of faction fighting in the Bor massacre, the Sudan government's dry season military offensive was successful in recapturing many towns. This campaign, including indiscriminate bombing, looting and burning, caused tremendous population shifts and deaths: uncounted civilians died during military attacks but many said more, particularly children, died of hunger and malaria while they hid in the *toic*.

In 1993 the nature of the conflict changed back to the two rebel factions' attacks on the others' civilian bases, as in 1991. In 1993 hundreds of millions of dollars of assistance was provided, compared to a trickle in 1992. Some fighting, although by no means all, took place where the U.N. was attempting to deliver food to prevent further displacement. Were the rebels drawn to these areas by the presence of U.N. relief food? Or were the factions attacking any "enemy" civilian locales, regardless of whether the food came from agriculture, trade, or relief? Was the presence of aid a neutral factor?

The most extreme example of rebel fighting in areas of food deliveries in 1993 was in the "Hunger Triangle" in Upper Nile province in 1993. This area, from Ayod to Kongor to Waat, began its descent into famine in 1991. It was the first location of fighting between the factions, when the breakaway SPLA-Nasir faction and a collection of Nuer raiders attacked, in two forays, the home of SPLA commander-in-chief John Garang, near Bor to the south of the Triangle. The raiders headed south through the Hunger Triangle, then back north again as Garang's forces pursued them, raiding, slashing, and burning "Nasir" civilians. The breakaway Nasir faction then made another thrust south, and so devastated Garang's Dinka civilian base that these raids were called "the Bor Massacre."

The population, raided, killed, and burned out, scattered for safety. Many found assistance far from the Triangle, usually closer to an international border. Always, however, there were thousands left behind, usually the weaker. It was almost a year and a half before relief could reach them in this area far inside southern Sudan. This aid, when it came, was a mixed blessing. One example of rather advanced manipulation techniques is using relief food as a lure to direct the movement of the starving civilian population to strategic military locations. Once civilians arrive at these locations, the army can siphon what it needs and use the thousands of civilians huddled near the airstrip or delivery point as porters, farmers, and shields. Luring or displacing civilians for these military purposes violates the important rule that civilians shall not be displaced for reasons connected with the conflict,[27] a major provision of the Geneva Conventions.

In 1993 the SPLA-Nasir manipulated the international relief program and the civilian population to create a forward garrison in Yuai, Upper Nile province. Yuai was in the Nuer (northern) area of the Hunger Triangle. The rebels accomplished their goal by ordering civilians (mostly displaced) living under their jurisdiction in Wast to move to Yuai, some forty kilometers southwest. They thus created a town of 15,000 where only 100 lived before. Yuai was right on the Nuer/Dinka border and east of the Duk Ridge, in a still uneasy area where faction fighting had raged up and down in 1991-92, a dangerous place for civilians.

The SPLA-Nasir undertook to create this mass migration of civilians knowing that concerned relief officials, aware of the desperate plight of these displaced, would attempt to airdrop food to them, and that other civilians would arrive, drawn by the magnet of tons of free food literally falling from the heavens.[28] It is likely that the SPLA-Nasir counted on being assisted in this plan by the international press. The Hunger Triangle, like much of southern Sudan, was accessible with difficulty before the war, either on the Nile or when the land was dry over badly-maintained dirt tracks. The war cut off these means of access. The relief effort had to resort to very costly air access, saving fuel when possible by airdropping fifty kilo bags of triple-wrapped maize. Food monitors and medical teams on the ground had to commute regularly, sometimes daily, by air for security reasons. The areas were more accessible than ever before, for small numbers of people. The international press had this access but logistics were so difficult and time-consuming, even with relief flights, that many journalists never attempted the trip, or stayed only a short time because of tight press deadlines. This was most conducive, especially for those journalists new to the area, to a shallow understanding, focused on images of emaciated children covered with flies, in search of the next Somalia.

The UN/NGO relief operation had no interest in blocking press access; it was dependent on the magic of the press—even a parachuted press—to attract attention to the genuine crisis in southern Sudan. The relief operation's ability to raise funds even from government donors was closely related to favorable press coverage of the extent of starvation. But because of limitations of the press and possibly because of lack of direction and understanding from higher echelons of the UN., the UN. was poorly positioned to refuse, even on food abuse grounds, to supply locations such as Yuai.

The SPLA also recognized the limits of the press. If it alleged that the U.N. was going to cut off food to starving children, headlines would portray the world bureaucracy as in the wrong again.

Therefore by January 1993, civilians were organized by SPLA-Nasir and RASS[29] to move south from Waat to Yuai, apparently by promising them that food would be delivered there. In that month, the U.N. noted that it expected some 16,000 people to move there.[30] SPLA-Nasir also moved an important military headquarters to Yuai.[31]

By January 26, 1993, a local population of 3,564 had sprung up,[32] and the U.N. started an airlift to Yuai. The displaced, as ordered and/or attracted by word of food arriving in Yuai, poured in on foot; on February 18, 1993, a total of 7,048 people were living in and around Yuai. In March, the population increased to about 15,000.[33]

There is no doubt that the airlift of food and medicine to the area created a draw for civilians. Said one displaced person who went to Yuai in January 1993 at the urging of the SPLA-Nasir commanders, "Now we are like flies. Wherever there is food that is where we go." Many displaced said they came to food delivery locations to "pick seeds from the airstrip," referring to scavenging by women of grains of maize that scatter when airdropped bags split open on the ground.[34] This harvesting of airstrips has become another survival strategy in southern Sudan.

Nasir, Southern Sudan, August 1990, Nuer women and children wait for medical care at a clinic operated by Operation Lifeline Sudan (OLS). Years of civil war and drought have disrupted the lives of some 4.5 million people in the Sudan. (UN Photo 157662 / Milton Grant)

Garang's SPLA forces made a surprise attack on Yuai on April 16, 1993. Hundreds of civilians died in the attack, their huts burned, and their cattle looted, in violation of humanity law. Under international diplomatic pressure, the two SPLA factions agreed to withdraw all their military personnel from an area encompassed by a forty-five mile radius from the aircraft landing fields at Ayod Kongor, Waat, and Yuai by June 5, 1993. This was done to create safe areas for delivery of food to the "Hunger Triangle." It did not work. When the food returned, the civilians began to return to and rebuild Yuai. A Nuer man who fled Yuai after the April 1993 attack returned a month later. "I feel safe when the UN. is here," he reported, "because of the presence of expatriates." On June 16, 1993, Garang's forces attacked Yuai again, despite the pullback agreement. Again many civilians perished, some fled to the bush and others ran to the river where they drowned. Yuai's huts were "burned to ashes."

The responsibility for civilian deaths in Yuai belongs to the attacking faction—Garang's SPLA. The attack was indiscriminate—heedless of civilian presence—if it was not actually a deliberate attack on the civilians to drive them away. It was, however, also an attack on a legitimate military target, a military headquarters of the opposing faction. That military target was near the village.

One rules of war issue is whether the SPLA-Nasir faction, in locating its headquarters so near the village, did so with the intent to use the civilian presence as a shield against attack.[35] Intent is difficult to prove. In Yuai, however, there was no village larger than 100 people until the SPLA-Nasir decided to create it. The prohibition on using human shields also prohibits using the civilian population to favor (or hinder) military operations. Certainly directing the movement of civilians to Yuai favored military operations; it helped the SPLA-Nasir move its base of operations closer to the wavering front line and made it possible to provision the soldiers from the Yuai civilian food ("taxes"). This also violates prohibitions on displacing civilians for reasons connected with the conflict.[36]

The Yuai case is a variation on the prevalent theme of predatory armies in southern Sudan. The area is very large and its enormously diverse population is not equally affected by the war. Diversion of food aid has been accomplished by frequently changing tricks, and in some areas has been more rampant than others, where civilians are better treated by some units of the SPLA and government. The Yuai case, which is by no means unique, suggests that reform of relief approaches is in order.

The OLS since 1989 (and some NGOs even earlier) has been engaged in cross-border operations in southern Sudan for the displaced southerners, expanding on the post-Cold War tendency to downplay sovereignty when faced with human calamity. This OLS operation, however, does not address the rules of war abuses committed by the parties, nor does it have effective means of preventing some of those abuses connected to food diversion that directly affect civilian welfare. The

OLS has attempted to reach and serve affected civilians without directly confronting the militaries that are increasingly adept at using international relief for their own purposes, using diplomacy, and other skills. It has been more successful than might be expected with the limited arsenal at its command. A solution cannot be found at this operational level, however, without the explicit political backing of the UN's decision makers.

It is unrealistic to expect the OLS to tackle the parties to the conflict on issues so central to their military survival without the backup of the international community. Until now, high-level concern has been lacking until the disaster is unmanageable, i.e., famine sets in. Yet the increasing number of displaced requires that their problems be faced. The twenty-four million displaced persons worldwide now exceeds the world's nearly twenty million refugees.[37]

In 1991, a step forward was taken when the UN. Commission on Human Rights drew attention to the needs of the internally displaced.[38] A report on refugees, displaced persons and returnees was submitted to the UN. General Assembly, suggesting that the Commission on Human Rights might consider creating machinery for addressing the human rights aspects of internal displacement to enable it "to deal with existing problems in this area with the necessary degree of urgency and in a concrete manner, bringing them to the attention of the international community and trying to generate the cooperation of all interested and concerned Governments."[39]

The Human Rights Commission appointed a special rapporteur on internally displaced persons, a southern Sudanese, Francis Deng, who issued a preliminary report";[40] and others' work on the displaced is continuing.[41]

Because humanitarian law violations are central causes of displacement and food shortages, human rights provisions should be specifically written into the mandate of future UN. efforts to assist the displaced. Among other things, accountability provisions should be written into the standard rules of relations between UN./NGO agencies and the local groups administering the aid. These rules should be widely announced to the affected communities, whose participation in allocation and monitoring is essential to the needed transparency and efficacy of food relief. Should these local partners administering aid fail to meet the contracted requirements, the administration of aid should be shifted to other persons or locations, after notice and explanation to the affected civilians.

It must be made clear to the warring parries that taxation of relief food is not permissible, even if "voluntary." Nor are attempts to direct the movement of the population for military advantage. Military activities or location of military equipment of troops near displaced persons locations, which often become the largest population centers in the whole province, are not permissible.

The history of international relief operations in southern Sudan shows the necessity for these reforms. Even if it is too late to enact these rules in Sudan, it is not too late to learn from this and other experiences and require rules designed to curb violations of humanitarian law relating to food in all future emerge

Notes

This essay has been adapted in part from Jemera Rone,*Human Rights Watch/Africa, Sudan: Civilian Devastation, Abuses by All Parties in the War in Southern Sudan* (New York: Human Rights Watch, June 1994). This essay does not represent the views of Human Rights Watch.

1. Millard Burr, *A Working Document: Quantifying Genocide in the Southern Sudan*.(Washington, DC: U.S. Committee for Refugees, October 1993), p. 2.
2. OLS press release, "UNICEF Preparing for Renewal Emergency in Southern Sudan," Nairobi, Kenya, January 31, 1994.
3. See U.S. Committee for Refugees, *1994 World Refugee Survey* (Washington, DC: U.S. Committee for Refugees, 1994), p. 69.
4. The fundamentalist NIF party won less than 20 percent of the vote in the last free elections in 1986.
5. The Encyclopedia Britannica, *World Data Annual 1993*, says that in 1980 73 percent of the Sudanese population was Sunni Muslim, 9.1 percent Christian, and 16.7 percent practiced traditional belief.
6. The Encyclopedia Britannica, *World Data Annual 1993* gives the ethnic composition in 1983 as Sudanese Arab 49.1%. Of the southern groups, Dinka were 11.5% of total Sudan population, Nuer 4.9%, Azande 2.7%, Bari 2.5%, Shilluk 1.7%, Latuko 1.5%. The Nuba were 8.1% and the Fur 2.1%; these are located in the transition zones and in the west. "Other" was 9.5%. The two most frequently-spoken languages are Arabic and Dinka, and Sudan has fourteen minor languages which are further divided into some l00 sub-languages. Of these languages nearly half are found in southern Sudan.
7. Lemmu Baissa, "Ethiopian- Sudanese Relations, 1956-91: Mutual Deterrence through Mutual Blackmail?" *Horn of Africa*, III-V (Washington, D.C.: October 1990-June 1991): pp. 1-25.
8. Sudan permitted Eritrean, Tigrean, Amharan, and Oroman rebels to open offices and operate from its territory and Ethiopia permitted the SPLA the same. Cross-border attacks between Sudan and Ethiopia were not uncommon.
9. Alastair Scott-Villiers, Patta Scott-Villiers and Cole P. Dodge, "Repatriation of 150,000 Sudanese Refugees from Ethiopia: The Manipulation of Civilians in a Situation of Civil Conflict," *Disasters* 17 (1993): 206. This study concludes that the returning refugees were pawns in Sudan's civil war, manipulated by governments, military forces and the media, and that the international community failed to deal effectively with their plight.
10. Douglas H. Johnson and Gerard Prunier, "The Foundation and Expansion of the, Sudan People's Liberation Army," in*Civil War in the Sudan*, ed., M. W. Daly and Ahmad Alawad Sikainga (London: British. Academic Press, 1993), p. 139.
11. "The *toic* in the dry reason becomes pasture. In Upper Nile there are four main vegetation areas: permanent swamp, river-flooded grasslands or*toic*, rain-flooded grasslands, and relatively flood-free land where the villages are built and cultivation undertaken. In the wet season or during a flood, the rivers rise, the rains fall, and th*etoic* is flooded.. Sorghum is sown during the April-November rains. During the dry season, cattle are moved away from the villages in stages, following the water as it dries up and exposes new pastures, until they come to rest on th*etoic*. Douglas H. Johnson, "Political Ecology

in the Upper Nile: The Twentieth Century Expansion of the Pastoral 'Common Economy,'" *Journal of African History* 30 (1989): 465.

12. *Ibid.*, p. 463.
13. *Ibid.*, p. 484.
14. *Ibid.*
15. *Ibid.*, p. 480.
16. The Duk Ridge—a series of sandy knolls occupied by the Gaawar Nuer to south of Ayod, the Ghol Dinka at Duk, Fadiat and the Nyareweng Dinka at Duk Faiwil—was frequently productive throughout the first half of the century. Johnson, "Political Ecology in the Upper Nile," pp. 469-70.
17. The OLS estimated that the groups in Bor (50,000), Kongor (50,000), Waat (25,000), and Ayod (40,000) lost all their livestock and failed to reap a crop during the fighting of 1991 and 1992 would be relying almost entirely on outside relief in 1993. OLS (Southern Sector), " 1992/93 Situation Assessment," Nairobi, Kenya, Feb. 1993, p. 6.
18. *Ibid.* Seventy-five percent of the food-dependent were considered "specially vulnerable," or almost entirely reliant on food assistance. The needy did not include the population of the severely besieged city, Juba. See Office of U.S. ForeignDisaster Assistance (OFDA), "Humanitarian Relief Operations in Sudan: Trip Report, July 1993" (Washington, D.C.: USAID), p. 14.
19. Mark Duffield, "NGO's, Disaster Relief, and Asset Transfer in the Horn: Political Survival in a Permanent Emergency," *Development and Change* 24 (1993): 145.
20. In the most seriously affected areas, women outnumber men by three to two. OLS Press Release, "UNICEF Preparing for Renewal Emergency in Southern Sudan," Nairobi, Kenya, January, 31, 1994.
21. Mark Duffield, "NGO's, Disaster Relief and Asset Transfer in the Horn: Political Survival in a Permanent Emergency," *Development and Change* 24 (1993): 145.
22. *Ibid.*
23. *Ibid.*
24. Operation Lifeline Sudan (OLS) is a joint UN-NGO relief operation for the needy internally displaced and war victims in Sudan, under the UN. umbrella. It began operations in early 1989, working on both sides of the civil war, in government and non-government areas, but only with consent of the parties. OLS (Southern Sector), coordinated by UNICEF from Nairobi, Kenya, provides the umbrella for relief activities for the UN. and over thirty international non-governmental organizations. About 150 international staff from UN. agencies and NGO's were permanently residing in twenty SPLA-held areas serviced from the south in early 1994. OLS (Southern Sector) press release, "UNICEF and WFP Request Urgent Funding for War-Torn Southern Sudan," Nairobi, Kenya, February 14, 1994.
25. Mark Duffield, "The Emergence of Two-Tier Welfare in Africa: Marginalization or an Opportunity for Reform?" *Public Administration and Development* 12 (1992): 151.
26. *Ibid.*
27. Article 17 (1) of Protocol II of 1977 to the Four Geneva Conventions of 1949: The displacement of the civilian population shall not be ordered for reasons related to the conflict unless the security of the civilians involved or imperative military reasons so demand. Should such displacements have to be carried out, all possible measures shall be taken in order that the civilian population may be received under satisfactory conditions of shelter, hygiene, health, safety and nutrition. The exceptions to this rule, security of the civilians or imperative military reasons, generally refer to imminent military clashes. When they are over, civilian return to their homes is required.
28. The SPLA-Nasir argued that Yuai was ideal for relocation from overcrowded

Waat, because Yuai had fishing and a dry season river.

29. Relief Association of Southern Sudan, the SPLA-United relief arm.

30. UN Special Coordinator, "Simulation Report for Period 7 January – 10 February 1993" (Khartoum, Sudan: UN, Office of the Special Coordinator of the UN. Secretary General for Emergency and Relief Operations in the Sudan), p. 6.

31. While the location of a military base near a population center is common enough and not in itself a violation of the rules of war, placing Nasir faction headquarters in this newly-created population center in a front line zone foreseeable exposed the civilians to the likelihood of an SPLA-Torit attack on the headquarters.

32. OLS (Southern Sector) Bi-Monthly Situation Report No. 33, January 22 – February 5, 1993, pp. 3-4.

33. OLS (Southern Sector) Bi-.Monthly Situation Report No. 35, February 21 – March 24, 1993, pp. 4-5 .

34. Despite this loss, it is still more economical to air drop supplies than expend expensive fuel landing and taking off. WFF or other food monitors on the ground watch the airdrop and supervise movement of the bags of grain into a storage area. Obviously the spilled food does not go to waste.

35. Article 51 (7) of Protocol I to the Geneva Conventions, to which we look for authoritative guidance in this conflict, provides:The presence or movements of the civilian population or individual civilians shall not be used to render certain points or areas immune from military operations, in particular in attempts to shield military objectives from attacks or to shield, favor or impede military operations. The Parties to the conflict shall not direct the movement of the civilian population or individual civilians in order to attempt to shield military objectives from attacks or to shield military operations.

36. See Protocol 11, article 17: 1. The displacement of the civilian population shall not be ordered for reasons related to the conflict unless the security of the civilians involved or imperative military reasons so demand. Should such displacements have to be carried out, all possible measures shall be taken in order that the civilian population may be received under satisfactory conditions of shelter, hygiene, health, safety and nutrition. 2. Civilians shall not be compelled to leave their own territory for reasons connected with the conflict.

37. James Rupert, "World's Welcome Strained by 20 Million Refugees,"*The Washington Post*, November 10, 1993, noting Sadako Ogata, UN. High Commissioner for Refugees.

38. UN. Commission on Human Rights, Resolution 1991/25 (Geneva: UN. Economic and Social Council, March 5, 1991).

39. UN. General Assembly, "Report on Refugees, Displaced Persons and Returnees, prepared by Mr. Jacques Cuenod, E/1990/109/Add 1. (New York: United Nations, June 27, 1991).

40. UN. Economic and Social Council, Commission on Human Rights, "Further Promotion and Encouragement of Human rights and Fundamental Freedoms, including the Question of the Programme and Methods of Work of the Commission, Alternative Approaches and Ways and Means within the United Nations System for Improving the Effective Enjoyment of Human Rights and Fundamental Freedoms, Analytical report of the Secretary-General on internally displaced persons," E/CN.4/1992/23 (Geneva: United Nations, February 14, 1992).

41. See Roberta Cohen, "Strengthening United Nations Human Rights Protection for internally Displaced Persons" Washington, D.C.: Refugee Policy Group, February 1993), pp. 5-9.

Jeff Drumtra

Genocide in Rwanda

The clearest case of genocide that the world has witnessed in fifty years occurred in Rwanda in 1994. Up to one million ethnic Tutsi Rwandans were systematically murdered in a three-month period by extremist political and military leaders and their followers. Even on an African continent all-too-familiar with war and death on a massive scale, the mass murders in Rwanda were shocking in their scope, intent, and efficiency. The murders were an orchestrated effort by the ruling regime to eliminate any and all political opponents, subvert planned democratic reforms, and maintain the regime's exclusive grip on power.

By the time the masterminds of the killing fled the country in mid-1994, their carefully planned genocidal campaign had come close to achieving its goal of exterminating an entire ethnic group in Rwanda. The slaughter wiped out between fifty and ninety percent of Rwanda's Tutsi population (precise estimates are difficult due to inaccurate population figures and uncertainty over exactly how many persons perished in the massive killing). In the aftermath of such coldly efficient bloodletting, Rwanda will never again be the same—the legacy of genocide will linger in Rwanda for decades, perhaps for generations.

Outsiders should not dismiss the genocide in Rwanda as merely a tragic isolated event in an obscure country of east central Africa. The stakes for the world community are great. The horrors that happened in Rwanda, and the world's failure to respond appropriately, reverberate far beyond that tiny country's borders. "Genocide"—an attempt to exterminate an entire ethnic group—is a term that carries immense legal and moral weight. It is not a word to be used carelessly. In 1951, in the wake of the holocaust of World War II, the international community solemnly proclaimed genocide to be the ultimate crime against humanity. An international agreement known as the 1951 Genocide Convention, signed by most major nations (though not by the United States until the mid-1980s, and then with certain reservations), gives the international community the legal right and obligation to intervene to prevent or suppress crimes of genocide whenever and wherever they occur. The 1951 agreement put extremists of the world on notice that genocide—an attempt to exterminate an entire ethnic group—would "never again" be allowed to happen by the world community.

In Rwanda, however, the world failed to honor its solemn pledge. Despite the brazen, horrific nature of the mass murder perpetrated by Rwanda's then-leaders, the international community pointedly refused to intervene to stop the genocide. Worse, the world's powers sitting on the United Nation's Security Council gave Rwanda's killers a sense of impunity by abruptly withdrawing some 2,000 UN troops from Rwanda when the killings started. The international community's decision to turn its back on the mass murder was a "scandal," declared UN Secretary General Boutros Boutros-Ghali.

In the aftermath of Rwanda's genocide, and the world's failure to respond to it, many observers fear that the international taboo against genocide has been broken, that the 1951 Genocide Convention has been drained of its legal and moral force. Brutal extremists in other countries have undoubtedly noticed the relative impunity with which Rwanda's former rulers perpetrated mass murder in search of political gain. Anti-democratic forces worldwide have seen in Rwanda that one tactic they can use to block multi-party, multi-ethnic government is to try to kill all political opponents, while the world stands idly by. Rulers and would-be despots around the globe have seen yet again that one method to gain or retain political power is to pit local ethnic groups against each other, artificially creating violent ethnic hatreds that can persist for decades.

In short, since the world community declined to intervene to halt a clear and massive case of genocide in Rwanda, there is reason to doubt that the world community can ever be relied upon to respond appropriately to other atrocities elsewhere. In that sense, the chilling legacy of Rwanda's genocide of 1994 will likely haunt many parts of the world for the foreseeable future.

Ethnicity in Rwanda: A Brief Review Prior to 1990

Because genocide is an attempt to erase an entire ethnic group, it is important to understand the ethnic make up of Rwanda's population and the historic relationships between Rwanda's population groups.

The estimated 7.5 million persons who lived in Rwandan prior to the 1994 genocide were almost entirely ethnic Banyarwanda. The Banyarwanda are composed of three sub-groups: Hutu, Tutsi, and Twa. An estimated eighty-five percent of Rwanda's population was Hutu, some fifteen percent were Tutsi, and one percent or less were Twa. These demographic estimates are inexact—the physical distinctions between Hutu and Tutsi are often virtually indiscernible even to Hutu and Tutsi themselves. The stereotype that all Tutsi are tall and thin and all Hutu are short and stocky is not entirely true. Hutu and Tutsi both spoke the Bantu language Kinyarwanda, shared the same culture, and lived intermingled on the thousands of hills that constitute Rwanda. Intermarriage was common. Children of mixed marriages are usually classified according to the ethnicity of their father.

In fact, referring to Hutu and Tutsi as separate "ethnic" groups is a bit of a misnomer, according to anthropologists. "Caste" and "class" are slightly better descriptions of the distinctions between the two groups. Tutsi tended to raise cattle and often held higher status in the country's feudal economic system prior to the 1950s. Hutu tended to be farmers, either on their own land or on the land of wealthy Tutsi patrons. Although Tutsi dominated the ruling class and possessed most political power prior to Rwanda's national independence in 1962, the demarcation between Hutu and Tutsi was somewhat fluid—wealthy or politically powerful Hutu could be socially "elevated" and transformed into Tutsi, and destitute Tutsi families sometimes came to be considered Hutu. The lines between the two groups were further blurred by the fact that, despite Tutsi dominance of the ruling class, the majority of Tutsi were poor and gained virtually no material benefit from the caste system.

It is for these reasons that many historians say it is wrong to speak of "age-old hatred" between Hutu and Tutsi. Although there was ethnic awareness between Tutsi and Hutu, large-scale ethnic violence was rare.

Fleeing the violence in Rwanda, an estimated 250,00 Rwandese swept into Tanzania over a 24-hour period in the largest and fastest refugee exodus ever recorded by UNHCR. Ngara, Kagera Region, Tanzania. (photo: UNHCR / 24067 / 04.1994 / P. Moumtzis)

More than forty years of Belgian colonial rule, beginning in 1919, deepened divisions between Hutu and Tutsi and produced new levels of bitterness between the two groups. Belgian rulers favored the Tutsi minority. Belgians gave Tutsi preferential treatment in education and employment at the expense of Hutu, and local Hutu chieftains were deposed by the colonists in favor of Tutsi chiefs. The most hated aspect of Belgian rule was the draconian practice of forced labor: Hutu were forced to provide manual labor under Tutsi overseers who were themselves often pressed into service involuntary. Life became unbearable for Hutu and many poor Tutsi. With Rwanda often afflicted by famine, hundreds of thousands migrated out of the country in the 1920s and afterwards.

By the late 1950s, most Hutu leaders came to view national independence and an end to Tutsi supremacy as two sides of the same coin. The struggle for independence included violent attacks against Tutsi leaders and civilians by Hutu insurgents, and reprisals by Tutsi against Hutu leaders. Several thousand persons, predominantly Tutsi, died in the unrest. By 1964, two years after independence, continued violence had pushed more than 200,000 Tutsi into other countries. Tutsi refugees mounted several unsuccessful attacks against Rwanda's new Hutu-dominated government until 1966.

Despite the violence of the 1950s and early 1960s, it is important to understand that no sustained political or ethnic violence occurred in Rwanda during the 24-year period of 1967-1990. The political party known as the National Republican Movement for Democracy and Development (MRND) ruled the country in a one-party political system. Approximately one million Tutsi (estimates of Rwanda's Tutsi population ranged from 750,000 to 1.5 million) lived in the capital, Kigali, and in Rwanda's mountainous countryside, where they were integrated among the estimated 6.5 million Hutu majority.

The government required all citizens to carry identity cards specifying each individual's ethnic affiliation, even though ethnic distinctions were often so subtle as to be arbitrary. During the 1970s and 1980s, as in pre-colonial times, ethnic awareness existed in Rwanda, but ethnic tensions were relatively low in the course of normal daily life. Most average Rwandans were primarily preoccupied by the rigors of survival and national development—Rwanda was, according to UN studies in 1993, one of the 25 poorest nations on earth and was the most densely populated country on the African continent.

Prelude to Genocide: 1990 to Early 1994

Civil war erupted in Rwanda in October 1990 when an army composed primarily of Tutsi refugees invaded Rwanda from neighboring Uganda. Known as the Rwandese Patriotic Front (RPF), the invaders asserted that their right to resettle in their homeland had been blocked for years by the Rwandan government. The RPF called for democracy, ethnic integration of Rwanda's military, improved social services, and the right of all refugees to repatriate. The RPF was not an exclusively Tutsi organization. RPF leadership included Hutu who had become alienated by the single-party political system in Rwanda, a system that perpetuated the ruling party's monopoly of all power.

The RPF force numbered some 7,000 soldiers. The Rwandan government's army responded to the RPF incursion by expanding to more than 30,000 troops, a six-fold increase. France deployed several hundred troops to support the Rwandan government and train new recruits to the Rwandan military. Government leaders also responded to the RPF attack by detaining some 8,000 persons in a crackdown against all political opposition, Tutsi and Hutu.

By mid-1993, some 900,000 Rwandans had become internally displaced by the ongoing civil war, and protracted peace talks had produced a cease-fire but no permanent peace treaty. Rwanda's government began to implement, gradually and grudgingly, a multi-party political system, but an international commission of human rights experts reported that security forces and government officials persisted in their practice of committing widespread human rights violations. Approximately 2,000 civilians, most of them Tutsi or Hutu political opponents of the ruling MRND party, had been executed since the start of the civil war, the human rights experts reported. A separate UN-sponsored investigation in mid-1993 implicated Rwanda's leaders in the deliberate and arbitrary killings of at least 2,300 civilians, as well as other human rights violations, since the civil war began in 1990. The UN investigation said that growing numbers of civilian militia were being organized to support the ruling MRND party. (A year later, in 1994, the militias were to play a key role in carrying out the campaign of genocide.) The UN report also cited human rights abuses by the rebel RPF.

With the RPF in control of the northern one-fourth of the country and clearly capable of further territorial gains, the government of Rwanda and the rebel RPF signed a peace accord in August 1993. An agreement, known as the Arusha accord because the final signing of the agreement took place in Arusha, Tanzania, committed both sides to share power within the framework of a multi-ethnic, multi-party government. The agreement provided for the installation of a new, broad-based Rwandan government by mid-September 1993. The Arusha accord pledged to allow the repatriation of all Rwandan refugees and called for ethnic integration of the armed forces. During the six months after the signing of the Arusha accord, the UN dispatched some 2,500 peacekeeping troops to monitor the expected transition to peace and democracy.

It quickly became apparent, however, that Rwandan President Juvenal Habyarimana and his political and military supporters were desperate to circumvent the power-sharing agreement they had signed. Political assassinations, local massacres, and other human rights abuses continued. The ruling MRND party violated repeated deadlines for the installation of a new government, and virulent anti-Tutsi diatribes aired regularly on *Radio Milles Collines,* a private radio station owned by members of Habyarimana's inner circle. The hate-filled radio broadcasts characterized domestic political opponents as "enemies" or "traitors" who "deserved to die," according to Human Rights Watch/Africa. Weapons training for the ruling party's armed youth militias accelerated, reportedly with French assistance.

As April 1994 began, President Habyarimana and his ruling MRND party continued to thwart implementation of the Arusha accords. Daily life in Kigali grew visibly tense. The political stalemate, combined with regular political assassinations and killings of civilians, and vehement anti-Tutsi broadcasts on the country's radio airwaves, created a pervasive sense of foreboding.

The Campaign of Genocide

The campaign of genocide that would ultimately kill up to one million persons in a three-month period was unleashed on the night of April 6, 1994. It began with a pretext: an airplane carrying Rwandan President Habyarimana was shot down by rockets as it approached Kigali airport, killing Habyarimana and all other passengers, including Burundian President Cyprien Ntaryamira. International investigators now believe that President Habyarimana was assassinated by hard-line extremists in the Rwandan government and military who were determined to retain power and who feared that Habyarimana was on the verge of implementing the Arusha peace accord for power-sharing that had been agreed to eight months earlier.

The death of the president was used as a pretext to eliminate all political opponents of the president and his party. Within minutes of the assassination, Rwandan soldiers and youth militias sealed Kigali with roadblocks and, in a well-organized house-to-house search, systematically murdered key political figures not favored by the MRND party, including politically moderate Hutu. Government soldiers killed the country's moderate prime minister, the head of the supreme court, and hundreds of key opposition figures and human rights activists in the first hours of the slaughter.

One of the "ironies" of Rwanda's genocide is that, in those first hours, the largely Hutu army and youth militia massacred hundreds of fellow-Hutu who were judged to be too politically moderate. Within days, however, the well-planned campaign of murder targeted Tutsi almost exclusively, regardless of their individual political beliefs. Rwandan military and youth militia in the countryside erected their own roadblocks and conducted house-to-house searches in small towns and rural areas to round up and liquidate the local Tutsi population. Individuals whose identity cards indicated they were Tutsi were usually slain on the spot. By mid-April, the International Committee of the Red Cross announced that the situation was "catastrophic" in many areas of the country. A UN official in Kigali described the militia killers as "demons in human form." UN officials in neighboring Uganda and Tanzania reported seeing hundreds of bodies per day floating down Rwanda's rivers. Many of the bodies had their hands tied behind their backs.

Given Rwanda's population density and its ethnically integrated settlement pattern, most Tutsi had nowhere to hide and no means of escape. Tens of thousands flocked to local churches in search of sanctuary—Rwanda is a predominantly Christian country, and as many as sixty percent of the population reportedly practice Catholicism. The churches, however, became death traps. The youth militias, who called themselves the *Interahamwe* ("those who attack together"), stormed church compounds and slaughtered Tutsi they found cowering there. Most Tutsi in Rwanda's rural hills were slashed or bludgeoned to death by machetes, nail-spiked clubs, hammers, screwdrivers, and other "low-tech" weapons carried by the *Interahamwe* and by Hutu villagers who were often forced to join in the killing. When Tutsi in some localities managed to repel the initial attacks by the *Interahamwe* militias, government soldiers moved in with more powerful weapons (rifles and grenades) to overwhelm any armed opposition by Tutsi civilians.

Despite the "low tech" nature of most of the weapons, the campaign of genocide during April and May was ruthlessly thorough and efficient. In some areas, local authorities enticed Tutsi out of hiding by announcing over loudspeakers that Tutsi should congregate at local sports fields so they could be "protected" from Hutu mobs. Local officials provided fleets of trucks to transport frightened Tutsi to designated sanctuaries. Once the Tutsi assembled for protection, they were butchered *en masse* by their government "protectors," according to the few survivors. At some massacre sites, authorities were apparently so obsessed with exterminating every last Tutsi that, after the day's massacre, officials tear-gassed the mangled pile of Tutsi bodies in a effort to find any half-dead survivors who needed to be bludgeoned or shot again. At many locations, the breasts of women and the genitals of men and infant boys were routinely cut off or lacerated. Countless babies were dismembered. The twisted logic of genocide—wiping out an entire ethnic group—required that the young in particular could not be spared.

These gruesome details are important. The international public tended to react with numb incomprehension at the news that a half-million or more persons in an obscure African country were being murdered. Perhaps it is human nature that the immensity of Rwanda's genocide can only be comprehended in the small, grisly details. Those who master-minded the genocide have not been arrested and remain brazenly unrepentant about their crime to this day. The key perpetrators are counting on the world to misunderstand what happened—they expect to escape accountability because they expect that the world will shrug off events in

Rwanda as a spontaneous tribal war beyond the ability of foreigners—especially Westerners—to comprehend or ameliorate.

The killings were not a spontaneous eruption. Nor was the motive behind the slaughter difficult for foreigners to comprehend. The carnage was organized and controlled by government officials who believed that the annihilation of all Tutsi in Rwanda, as well as of all other political opponents, would provide a political benefit. During the genocide, *Radio Milles Collines* continued to broadcast racist diatribes against Tutsi and incited the Hutu population to accelerate the massacres. "The graves are only half full. Who will help us fill them?" the radio station exhorted. Hutu residents in some areas of Rwanda resisted pressures by the government to kill their Tutsi neighbors, until the government sent in new local officials and new *Interahamwe* militia members to ensure that the killing of Tutsi got done.

By early May, one international humanitarian agency with long experience in the country, Oxfam, estimated that some 500,000 persons were probably dead. And the killing continued, as thousands of Tutsi trapped in churches and stadiums were being hunted and systematically killed daily by government troops and *Interahamwe* militia.

Katale refugee camp in Goma, Zaire, November 1994. Makeshift huts for Rwandese stretch as far as the eye can see. (photo: Jeff Drumtra)

In response to the government's campaign of genocide, the RPF rebels launched a new military offensive against the government army. The RPF captured Kigali within three months, by early July 1994, and controlled most regions of the country a few weeks later. The RPF said its military advance was intended to save any Tutsi populations that could be saved, and several thousand Tutsi were indeed rescued by the RPF. In other areas, government soldiers, *Interahamwe*, and some Hutu civilians rushed to accelerate their killing spree before they were forced to retreat by RPF forces.

As the RPF rebels advanced into eastern Rwanda, a quarter-million Hutu Rwandans fled to Tanzania in a single day in late April—the largest one-day refugee flow the world has ever seen. Less than three months later, as RPF troops seized western regions of the country, about a million Hutu Rwandans fled to Zaire in a one-week period, establishing another record. Many Hutu fled out of fear that the RPF would exact revenge for the massacres of Tutsi. Others fled because their leaders instructed them to do so. The former government's soldiers and *Interahamwe* militia members also fled to the refugee camps in Zaire and Tanzania. They remain in those sanctuaries, armed and dangerous, in 1995.

Weak International Response to Rwanda's Genocide

Rwanda presented the world with one of the greatest humanitarian and human rights disasters of modem times. It was the site of blatant genocide and produced the largest, quickest refugee flight ever seen—all in a span of three months. Such an unprecedented crisis required international leaders to respond appropriately. They didn't. The international community sent generous humanitarian assistance to the two million Rwandan refugees, but the non-response of the United Nations, the United States, and other international powers to the root causes of the genocide was, as Boutros-Ghali said in May 1994, "a scandal."

Some 2,500 multi-national UN peacekeeping troops were stationed in Rwanda when the killing began on April 6. The large UN force could have protected hundreds of thousands of persons slated for death, but did not. The UN Security Council, led by the United States and France, refused to give the UN peacekeepers in Rwanda and their Canadian commander, General Romeo Dallaire, authority or resources to stop the killing where possible. General Dallaire reportedly argued during and after the genocide that his troops could have intervened to stop much of the killing if only the international community had given him the mandate to do so.

Instead, members of the UN Security Council voted to leave Rwanda's million or so Tutsi to their fate. Two weeks after the genocide began, the Security Council responded not by bolstering its peacekeeping contingent, but by withdrawing all but 270 UN troops from Rwanda. The Security Council pointedly refused to give General Dallaire and his remaining UN troops authority to stop the killings.

During the fourth week of the genocide, the Security Council voted to condemn the massacres but blocked efforts to increase the UNs peacekeeping presence in the country. The U.S. Committee for Refugees, one of the leading American non-governmental advocacy organizations on issues affecting Rwanda, urged the UN and U.S. to declare that the killings in Rwanda constituted a violation of the 1951 Genocide Convention and recommended that UN peacekeeping troops should re-enter the country. The agency also recommended that U.S. officials should jam or shut down the inflammatory broadcasts of *Radio Milles Collines*.

During the fifth week of genocide, U.S. diplomats squelched a proposal by UN staff to send 5,000 UN peacekeepers to Rwanda. Several African countries indicated that they might provide troops for a peace-malting mission to Rwanda if wealthier countries would provide equipment and financial support for the operation. No wealthy country stepped forward with the assistance required.

As Rwanda's killing fields entered a sixth week, the UN Security Council refused to acknowledge that the mass murder underway there constituted genocide. Reportedly several African countries in particular resisted use of the term. The Security Council formally agreed that some 5,000 new peacekeeping troops might be needed in Rwanda, but U.S. diplomats insisted on more weeks of study before allowing final approval. In the seventh week of genocide, UN Secretary General Boutros-Ghali declared that the international community had failed in Rwanda. "It is genocide . . . [but] the international community is still discussing what ought to be done," he complained. In the ninth week of the emergency, the UN Security Council finally endorsed a resolution to send more peacekeeping troops to Rwanda. The troops did not arrive, however, until two months later.

In the tenth week of genocide, news reports revealed that U.S. officials were being forbidden to describe events in Rwanda as "genocide," in order to avoid pressure on the American government to intervene against the massive killings. During the twelfth week, a special UN human rights investigation declared that "genocide" had indeed occurred in Rwanda. The investigators reported that the massacres "being perpetrated at present are unprecedented in the history of the country and even in that of the entire African continent. They have taken on an extent unequaled in space and time." The investigators said they 'were "absolutely certain" that the killing "appears to be well-orchestrated." "The massacres are all the more horrible and terrifying in that they give the impression of being planned, systematic, and atrocious," the report concluded. "Whole families are exterminated—grandparents, parents, and children. No one escapes, not even newborn babies. But what is even more symptomatic is that the victims are pursued to their very last refuge and killed there." By the thirteenth week, the overwhelming majority of Tutsi victims were already dead. French troops entered the southwest quadrant of Rwanda and rescued several thousand trapped Tutsi survivors, but the French military presence also provided seven weeks of sanctuary to Rwandan government officials, soldiers, and *Interahamwe* militia who were guilty of the killing.

In the fourteenth week, a UN human rights investigator decried the international inaction. "It seems . . . quite difficult to admit that in this century you can have a massacre of up to a half a million people with everyone watching," he said. "I think if s a very, very sad event." By mid-July, during the fifteenth week of genocide, the United States finally withdrew official diplomatic recognition from the Rwandan government which had perpetrated the killing.

As the above chronology of inaction indicates, the core failing of the international community was its failure to comprehend—or its refusal to acknowledge—that genocide was occurring in Rwanda until it was too late to act against it. This massive failure—or refusal—to recognize genocide and respond appropriately against it was a shameful moment and produced international policies that were politically ineffectual and at times counterproductive. For example:

1. World leaders refused to invoke the Genocide Convention of 1951, which would have provided a legal framework to take action against the mass murders in Rwanda. The world's non-response to the killing may, in the future, have the effect of permanently eviscerating the Genocide Convention as a component of international law.

2. The UN Security Council's decision in April to withdraw most UN peacekeeping troops left hundreds of thousands of Rwandan Tutsi exposed to near certain death and gave the killers confidence that the world community would allow the genocide to proceed uninterrupted.

3. Even after the UN Security Council reversed course in May and voted to send additional peacekeeping troops, the United States delayed deployment of the troops for months, effectively giving the killers in Rwanda a grace period to complete their campaign of genocide.

4. World powers, led by the United States, refused repeated pleas from relief workers and human rights experts to shut down the propaganda radio broadcasts of Rwanda's political extremists, even though the vehement broadcasts clearly played a pivotal role in inciting and sustaining genocide and in creating a new humanitarian emergency by encouraging the exodus of more than I million Hutu Rwandans into Zaire.

5. The U.S. government continued to grant diplomatic recognition to Rwanda's self-declared government during its entire campaign of genocide. This reluctance by U.S. officials to break diplomatic relations sent the wrong message to extremists in Rwanda and to repressive regimes elsewhere in the world.

6. By failing to acknowledge in a forthright manner that genocide—the ultimate crime against humanity—was occurring in Rwanda, world leaders (particularly those in the United States) did not properly educate the international public about what was happening. As a result, much of the international public remains largely ignorant to this day about the historic nature, of the awful events that took place in Rwanda, and the lessons that should be learned from Rwanda's tragedy.

After the Genocide: Rwanda's Situation in Early 1995

Rwanda is a shattered society in the aftermath of last year's genocide. In early 1995, some 1.7 million Hutu Rwandans remained refugees outside their country, and some 1 million Hutu were still displaced from their homes inside Rwanda. Many of the 2.7 million uprooted Rwandans have not returned home because they fear that Tutsi in Rwanda will kill them as reprisal for the genocide. Many other Rwandan Hutu refugees are prevented from returning home by their own Hutu leaders, the very ones who masterminded last year's genocide.

Rwanda's former government officials and former soldiers control the refugee camps in Zaire and Tanzania and have siphoned off large amounts of relief food to support their plans for renewed warfare. Several international relief organizations have threatened to withdraw their assistance from the refugee camps because extremist refugee leaders have blocked large amounts of relief supplies from reaching the most needy beneficiaries, particularly single women and their children. "Refugees are denied the right to return to their homes, equal access to humanitarian aid, and the guarantee of basic human rights. They remain hostages" in the refugee camps, several relief groups declared in a joint statement.

The new multi-party, multi-ethnic government of Rwanda, in which the RPF plays a major role, entered 1995 lacking the resources it needs to reconstruct the country and reconcile the Hutu and Tutsi populations. The new government was struggling to establish a functioning justice system, a police force, an education system, and a functioning program to repatriate and resettle the country's immense uprooted population. Some 600,000 Tutsi refugees who had fled Rwanda in the 1950s and 1960s returned to Rwanda during the last half of 1994 and were living on property owned by Hutu, creating a potentially volatile dispute over land ownership. International donors were generally slow to give financial support to the new Rwandan government as it tried to deal with these problems.

Some 5,000 UN troops were stationed throughout Rwanda in early 1995, in a belated international effort to provide security for the population. UN agencies were continuing their investigations into the genocide and were collecting evidence needed to bring at least some of the ringleaders of the genocide to justice. A special tribunal established by the UN will attempt to prosecute individual perpetrators in late 1995. More than 120 international humanitarian relief and development agencies were licensed to operate in Rwanda, but their efforts may have only limited benefits if Rwandan society remains as physically separated and psychologically polarized as it was at the beginning of 1995.

What is clear is that Rwanda will never be the same again. In the aftermath of genocide that systematically murdered up to one million persons, a pervasive psychology of fear, paranoia, and fingering hatred may require generations to resolve in favor of true reconciliation. Nearly two-thirds of the country's population have been lulled or uprooted—an upheaval from which no country or society can quickly recover. A genocidal force of some 20,000 soldiers and some 50,000 *Interahamwe* militia, by some estimates, remain poised on Rwanda's borders and in some pockets of the country itself, intent on continuing the killing and threatening to destabilize the region of east-central Africa for years to come.

Viewed in its full context, Rwanda is far more than one of the largest, most complex refugee crises in the world. The difficult and dangerous task before the world in 1995 is getting Rwandan refugees home safely and voluntarily. Even if all refugees repatriated tomorrow, however, it is sobering to realize that many of the demons afflicting Rwandan society remain. The last time the world witnessed such a clear-cut case of genocide was fifty years ago in Nazi Germany, when the surviving victims were given their own nation in which to rebuild their community and their lives. That is not an option under discussion in the aftermath of Rwanda's genocide, even though the psychological trauma of Tutsi Rwandan victims would appear to be similar to victims of the Holocaust.

The new government of Rwanda insists that it is committed to a multi-ethnic, multi-party state. Hopefully that is true. But even if it pursues the wisest of policies and the best of intentions, national reconciliation will be neither easy, nor smooth, nor quick. Such is the legacy of genocide.

Kagenyi Camp, Ngara region of Tanzania, July 1994. The civil conflict in Rwanda has left few families in tact. Many are headed by single parents, primarily women. (photo: UNHCR / 24156 / 07.1994 / L. Taylor)

Nick Papandreou

Inequality and the Emergence of a new Global Underclass: The Refugee Woman

Today's world economic system is characterized by fundamental instabilities. At the heart of these instabilities is the profit nexus: the ever-expanding search for larger markets, cheaper labor, and higher profits. One consequence of the growth of the capitalistic economic system around the world is that the world's wealth has increased. At the same time so has poverty, both in relative and absolute terms. Individuals, as measured by a poverty index, and whole countries, as measured by per capita income and indices of income inequality, are in many cases worse off today than they were two decades ago. Indeed, many nations in the post-colonial world are worse off now than they were under the colonialism of the last century.

At the same time we are witnessing an intensified effort to globalize the market system in a way which emphasizes free markets and the dismantling of the welfare state, or rather a complete absence of the state. The neo-liberal canon emphasizes private sector growth and argues against government. The reduction of the welfare state has exacerbated the inequalities, and has directly contributed to large-scale emigration and the emergence of massive refugee populations, one of the poorest and most vulnerable group of individuals that have emerged in the twentieth century. In short, whether as a result of the workings of the economic system or not, there is a new underclass today, called the refugee, and within that underclass, a sub-caste known as the refugee woman.

We start with a global overview of the nexus between growth and increasing inequality, then move on to examine the "feminization" of the work force and the structural transformations in production that demand gender-specific hiring practices, and conclude that the next step in globalization is exploitation of the new underclass: the refugee woman.

How did we get to where we are today? How could so many well-intentioned economists be wrong?

Dream on: Conventional wisdom is that the economic globalization that has characterized recent decades is considered to be a benign process that brings multiple benefits to those who have participated in it and offers a better future to those who have so far remained outside.

A. Fantasy of small firms still holds strong as competitive reality and not the reality of multi-nationals, government directed private sectors, increased expansion of single firms which spread to control all sectors of the economy.

B. Prices, are supposed to be the ultimate regulator of human economic behavior—and thinking has it that one needs only to adjust prices to alter behavior; ignores all those things that are outside domain of prices and markets, such as unpaid labor, altruism, etc. Ignore market inefficiencies and its unequal distribution. One dollar one vote. Prices are somehow magically supposed to reflect scarcities—but how can prices reflect more than our knowledge? Maybe the price of a tree in the Amazon should be one million dollars, maybe the price of clean water should be one billion but the price tends to reflect only its immediate sale price and not some deeper construct such as serious market failures

C. All of economic thought and growth theory in particular has been based on the assumption of endless resources, and that the market mechanism will lead to efficient growth. While slow growth itself might have some benefits; high growth rates of GNP are seen as the summa cum laude of all graduates each year.

For example, policies ask for all countries to increase their exports as means to promote growth. If this were truly to occur, there would be a surplus of exported goods, which would lead to lower prices for the exports, and then the countries would enter into a vicious circle of producing more and getting less. Earlier import substitution was all the rage. Now it's export promotion and private sector "enablement."

D. At worst, traditional thinking goes, the "bad" effects of growth can be remedied, things such as income inequalities, services, etc., through taxation, redistribution, and regulation. In terms of countries, institutions and expertise, after WW II, when the concept of development really took hold were supposed to help, along with corporations and private sector and governments, in the process of development. "Numbers prosper while people suffer." Now the World Bank for example, having recognized the difficulties of development so far is turning to something called "governance," another forgotten element in the development story. If governments would govern better, than development projects would get off the ground and finally we would have development.

Moving from Theory to Reality

What really has been happening? We have been witnessing a globalization of markets, accompanied by a neo-liberal prescription for reduced government involvement. This is a new form of globalization which hasn't led to much growth.

One striking transformation in the world capitalist system since the end of the Second World War has been that more capital flows to service industries and to finance than to traditional fields of manufacturing and extraction of primary products and in particular, there has been an explosion in the financial sectors.

For example, world trade in goods amounts to around $2.5 trillion to $3 trillion per year. But the London Eurodollar market turns over $300 billion each working day, or $75 trillion a year, 25 times that of world trade, and currency trading turns over $150 billion a day, or twelve times the worldwide trade in goods and services. Capital movements unconnected to trade greatly exceed trade finance.

These sort of activities have led to enormous instability even in the industrialized countries. Yet, despite these striking transformations in the advanced countries, two major distinguishing features of the third world did not change. The chains of dependency still bind the periphery to the center, and secondly, the gap between the two continues to grow.

GDP/Capita: underdeveloped as a percent of developed countries	
1960	8.7%
1970	7.4%
1987	6.1%

What is the development story behind these numbers? During the decade of intensified globalization and the increasing dominance of market economies, the per capita GDP of Africa as a percent of the per capita GDP of core countries was half of what it had been in 1960 (from 6.9% to 3.5%) and for Latin American respective number is three-fifths.

Achievements are always extolled by market proponents: mortality declined and life expectancy has increased. But as George Papandreou once said, *the numbers prosper and the people suffer*. In Latin America, only 2% of sewage receives treatment; 1.7 billion people are without access to safe water and adequate sanitation; poor women in particular bear burden of poverty.

Mechanisms of Inequality

How do we explain that even while the governments of the industrialized countries set ambitious targets for foreign aid and joined with less fortunate third world "partners" to push through the UN resolutions and programs looking to the elimination of evils inherited from an unenlightened past, the gap between rich and poor was widening?

Well, the truth is that a system built on inequality in the command of human and natural resources works in many ways not only to reproduce itself but to increase the extent of the built-in inequality. (Sweezy quote)

Let us look quickly at one mechanism of inequality: how much the third world countries receive from abroad, exports, imports and foreign investments. (balance of payments) Between 1983 and 1990, developing countries sent an average of $21.5 billion to the North.[1] Lending by the North was intended, at first to prevent collapse of these countries, but then lending turned more and more to disciplining the borrowers, imposed chiefly through the agency of the IMF and the World Bank.

Amount issued to borrowers to the Third World (111 countries) in 1989 was $86.9 billion, while repayments for old debt (principal and interest) was $129.8, meaning, for these countries, that there was a net outflow of approximately $43 billion. The Sub-Saharan Africa is transferring 7% of its export income just to service the IMF debts. Total debt burden today: $1.7 trillion.[2]

How do these countries cope? Usually through greater lending, fewer social benefits, a squeeze on wages, a drastic reduction of imports, which affects people's ability to meet basic needs. Thus we had the severe decline of income during the 1980s in Latin America and Africa, where some of the heaviest borrowing took place.

In more than one half of the countries receiving SAP loans between 1980 and 1987, food per capita availability declined (UNDP). Cuts in public health spending forced women to spend more time caring for sick members of the family; resource shifts to the export sector threaten women's food production and thus nutrition of household; slashing of wages and calls for repeal of minimum wages (as in India) forces new entrants to accept extremely low wages and under bad conditions in order to ensure the survival of their families.

India's program of liberalization of the labor market (in tune with Structural Adjustment Programs) tends to reinforce despotic relations with greater legitimacy given thereby to caste exploitation, semi-slavery, and child labor.

IMF–World Bank reforms tend to exacerbate the poverty of the people, through devaluations, slash of wages. However, these are not so much World Bank policy as much as they are requirements to be a competitive member of the world capitalist system (see Karl Polanyi) What the Bank does is to prescribe measures to ensure that countries can remain part of the game; only a completely different world order and different ideological directions would make a difference.[3]

World Bank's real role: to prepare and equip countries with the tools and instruments needed for capitalism—accounting, environmental checks, judicial reform, transparency, procurement policies, limited military budgets, support private sector, try and make capitalism function better in those countries, probably a lost cause.

Nature of Globalization and Effects on Work Force

Chiefly through deregulation—like NAFTA—and not globalization, in the sense of growth. Such neo-liberal globalization is likely to generate greater income inequality both between and within countries, along with greater environmental destruction, especially without firm institutional settings in the various countries, which can serve to regulate and soften effects of unequal growth.

Globalization changes The structure of the work force—through the feminization of the paid labor force; internationalization of investments has caused significant adjustments in world-wide labor markets. This has led to a growing incorporation of women into the labor force, both in the US in Mexico and around the

The feminization of poverty in the developed world is mirrored in underdeveloped nations. These women in the Gaza Province of Mozambique are suffering from long years of drought and civil war which have disrupted traditional means of production. They are waiting for a delivery of food to the Macuacua Camp for displaced persons. March 1984. (photo: UN Photo 153619/Kate Truscott)

world. This restructuring has yielded large growth in jobs generally associated with women, jobs that provide only part-time employment, comparatively low wages, and reduced union membership.[4]

The proliferation of technology did not lead to reduction but to an increase in menial, low-skilled jobs, with such jobs in both the North and the South. The nature of industrialization favors the hiring of women. Jobs often include subcontracting and home working. In electronics we are seeing an acute stratification of labor, based on skill and sex.

The search for greater profits means the search for greater flexibility in production and in labor management. This means that firms target strategic labor pools formed by women and immigrants. Host governments in Asia, Latin America, and the Caribbean have provided incentives that have led to the growth of export-processing zones, where millions of workers, mostly women, now assemble products for the world market.

The maquiladores program in Mexico saw targeting by managers of women and wives and daughters who had been part of the economically inactive population.

Current development projects rely on the opening of counties that rely heavily on comparatively low wages and disciplined workers, many of whom are women. The goal of development through direct competition in the world market is on the basis of pliant low-cost labor.

Emphasis on growth of the private sector and greater reliance on the private sector means lessening of social infrastructure, health care, and the assumption is that rising wages means being better off, but wages don't include opportunity costs of women's reduction in their multiple and simultaneous roles.

Globalization, Feminization of the Work Force and the Refugee Woman

In the capitalist system's inexorable search for profits, no underclass is left unexploited. The search for markets will encourage firms to exploit the weakest underclass available, whether this be child labor or woman refugee labor. What prevents them from doing so? What refugee woman is to blame for taking a job with wages lower than local women or even immigrant women?

I foresee that the refugee populations, if not directly, than indirectly, will be exploited by the existing system of inequalities. We will see a taxonomy of the following hierarchy of exploitation: Hiring of women, lower wages for immigrant women, and the lowest to the weakest and most desperate of all, the refugee woman. Even within the confines of the existing system of economic and political institutions, we need to worry about this as well.

In conclusion, in an age when millions of working people throughout the developing world are hired by transnationals, while others migrate in search of work, others languish without employment, and still others become refugees, where does the locus of civil rights and obligations reside? The dramatic political and economic changes occurring around the world argue for a different concept of citizenship, of rights and obligations, a concept that minimizes nationalities, boundaries and frontiers, a concept that puts emphasis on basic human rights regardless, with a special emphasis for those who are the weakest and most vulnerable.

Notes

1. In 1986 selected underdeveloped countries received $5.8 billion from abroad through economic activity like exports and services. By 1990 the number had grown to $18.9 billion. But then, if you subtract the profits, royalties, fees to the multi-nationals, interest on debt to foreign bankers, bondholders, (repayments on borrowings to the IMF and the World Bank,) you find that in 1986 these countries sent out a net of $35 billion and in 1990 a net of $31 billion. (Doesn't include new borrowings)

If the country hasn't earned enough to pay back its interest, then it ends up borrowing from international institutions. This situation in the long run is untenable and not a rosy prospect for the north either which leads to the north's interest in resolving the debt crisis and deepens links of dependency.

2. Proposals: write off all African debt; write off 100% of outstanding debt of severely debt ridden countries of lowest income and 50% of next level—middle income. Write off loans which had negative impact on environment and created refugee populations.

3. Remedies: One approach: "Fifty years is enough" campaign calls for drastic cutbacks in Bank Functions. As a lender, the Bank should return to its original mandate and reduce non-project lending to under ten percent of its total loan portfolio. Poverty reduction and ecological sustainability should become the centerpiece of the institution's operations at every level. Use UNDP's Human Development Index as starting point for new indicators.

4. In their analyses of the impact of new development projects, the World Bank does not take into account the fact that women must shift work from the home to the paid market. This shift may lead to a worse situation; or, predictions about labor supply behavior may be grossly inaccurate, since higher wages may not take into account the woman's opportunity cost of reducing household (unpaid) labor. The World Bank structural adjustment programs (SAP) ignore women's unpaid labor in their estimates of the cut-backs on social services, etc. In general, the woman's multiple and simultaneous role is ignored. An analysis of the economy that measures only market activities will not provide an adequate understanding of total economic activity.

References

Ammot, Teresa L. and Julie A. Matthaei,*Race gender & work: a Multicultural history of women in the United States.* Boston: South End Press, 1991.
Anyadike, Obinna, "Structural Adjustment: No light at the end of the tunnel,"*Third World Resurgence*, No. 28, p. 28.

Bennett, Lynn, "Women, poverty and productivity in India," Economic Development Institute of the World Bank, Number 43, World Bank, 1992.
Bergman, Barbara, R., *The Economic Emergence of Women*, New York: Basic Books, 1986.
Black, Richard and Vaughan Robinson,*Geography and Refugees: Patterns and Processes of Change*. London: Belhaven Press, 1993.
Bruce, Judith and Daisy Dwyer, eds.*A home divided: women and income in the Third World*, Stanford: Stanford University Press, 1988.
Chossudovsky, Michel, "Feeding on Poverty: India under IMF rule,"*Third World Resurgence*, No. 28, pp. 24-27.
editors, "Globalization—To What End?"*Monthly Review*, 43.10 (March 1992), pp. 1-19.
Fernandez-Kelly, Patricia M., "Labor Force Recomposition and Industrial Restructuring in Electronics: Implications for Free Trade," *Hofstra Labor Law Journal*, School of Law, Hofstra University, 10.2 (Spring 1993), pp. 623-717.
_____. "Broadening the Scope: Gender and International Economic Development,"*Sociological Forum*, 4.4 (1989), pp. 611-635.
_____. "Underclass and Immigrant Women as Economic Actors: Rethinking Citizenship in a Changing Global Economy," *The American University Journal of International Law and Policy*, 9.1 (Fall 1993), pp. 151-169.
_____ and Saskia Sassen. "Recasting Women in the Global Economy: Internationalization and Changing Definitions of Gender" in*Women in the Development Process: From Structural Adjustment to Empowerment*, Christine Bose and Edna Acosta Belen, eds. Philadelphia: Temple University Press, forthcoming.
Foerstel, Lenora, ed.*Women's Voices on the Pacific: The International Pacific Policy Congress*. Washington, DC: Maisonneuve Press, 1991.
Fong, Monica S. "The Role of Russian Women in Rebuilding the Russian Economy," *Studies of Economies in Transition*, 10 (1993).
Harcourt, Wendy, ed. *Feminist Perspectives on Sustainable Development*.London and New Jersey: Zed Books Ltd., 1994.
Institute for Policy Studies, "Fifty Years is Enough," Restructuring and Alternatives Group, Informal memo, 7.11.93.
MacEwan, Arthur, "Globalization and Stagnation,"*Monthly Review*, .45.11 (April 1994), pp. 1-15.
Morris-Hughes, Elizabeth and C. Mark Blackden, "Paradigm Postponed: Gender and Economic Development Adjustment in Sub-Saharan Africa," Technical Department, Africa Region, World Bank. 1993.
Permanent People's Tribunal, "An Indictment of the IMF and the World Bank,"*Third World Resurgence*, 28, pp. 21-23.
Summers, Lawrence H. "Investing in All the People: Educating Women in Developing Countries," Economic Development Institute of the World Bank, Number 45, World Bank, 1992.
United Nations Development Programme, "Human Development Report: 1994." New York, 1994.
van den Hombergh, Heleen, *Gender, Environment, and Development: A Guide to the Literature*. Utrecht: Institute for Development Research Amsterdam, 1993.
World Bank, "Governance and Development," 1992.
World Bank, "Women's Crucial Role in Managing the Environment in Sub-Saharan Africa," Technical Note, Women in Development, Poverty and Social Policy Division, Technical Department, Africa Region, October 1991.
World Bank, *The World Bank and the Environment*. Washington, DC: World Bank, 1993.

Julia Panourgia Clones

Environment, Refugees, and Displaced Persons: The Gender Perspective

Human beings, in their quest for survival and improvement in the quality of their lives are faced with the reality of limited natural resources and the carrying capacity of ecosystems, and, therefore, with the realization that they must take account of the needs of future generations. In other words they are faced with the facts that: the growing depletion of natural resources victimizes those who depend them, forcing them to seek refuge in other areas, and creating thus the so called "environmentally displaced persons" or, as they are sometimes erroneously called, "environmental refugees."

In turn, the hardships endured by environmentally displaced persons forces them to make a living the best way they can, even if that means disregarding environmental considerations, thus making them not only victims but agents, as well, of further environmental degradation. Given the differences in the social roles played by men and women and the constraints placed on women in most societies today, women, when compared to men, are most often the micro-managers of the environment. At the same time, they have less access to and control over resources. This paradox, that is the combination of women's higher responsibilities in environmental management and reduced access to and control over resources makes a classical case of gender discrimination.

The Status of the World's Refugees and Displaced Persons

A. The Problem

Let us first take a quick look at the "refugee" problem. According to the United Nations' High Commission on Refugees (UNHCR) in 1972 there were 2.5 million refugees worldwide. Ten years later, in 1982, there were nearly five times as many or nearly 11 million. At the end of the next decade, in 1992, the number of refugees reached 18.2 million plus 24 million displaced persons. This figure does not include the waves of "internal" refugees displaced from their homes but who do not cross international borders. Many refugees from Somalia and Rwanda are internal refugees and thus not included in the UNHCR's counts.

In essence, the refugee problem is, of course, a human rights problem. We should take notice of the fact, moreover, that in the 1990s the refugee problems are characterized by their complexities; they cannot be treated in isolation from the conditions that give rise to them, nor can those conditions be isolated from refugee concerns. When we look at the roots of this problem we can distinguish two types of factors: the systemic and the strategic factors. Three basic systemic factors or constraints which affect women's performance in the short and long term are the limited supply of natural resources, the limited access women have to what resources do exist, and the ineffective management of resources.

The Basic strategic roots of the refugee problem are political, economic, environmental, ethnic and cultural. Specifically, regarding the political roots of the refugee problem, one can say that most conflicts in the world today are within rather than between states. The vast majority of refugees are fleeing not from targeted acts of individual persecution but from generalized violence that endangers civilians and radically disrupts everyday life. These conditions are the products of instability, generated internally or externally, and they are fed by political opportunism that seeks to exploit social divisions. Women and children with their limited rights are victimized more than men by displacement and civil disorder.

When we concentrate on the economic roots we notice that bitter disputes among national groups arise from efforts to preserve or advance the standing of one group at the expense of others. Disputes concerning the distribution of resources during general economic decline are the most politically explosive. Minority groups are often turned into scapegoats. And, poverty undoubtedly exacerbates ethnic and communal tensions. (Even though the number of refugees worldwide amounts to less than 2% of the destitute, the economic deprivation interacts with other circumstances to heighten instability and aggravate conflicts).

Environmental issues, just as the gender issues, are cross-sectoral, cutting across all walks of life and social and economic activities. As such they have to be addressed in coordination with all the others. Millions of people have been forced to leave their homes because the land on which they live has become uninhabitable or it is no longer able to support them. In some cases, the cause is a natural disaster; in others the catastrophe is caused by humans; and in extreme cases destruction of habitat may be used as a deliberate weapon of war (for which unfortunately we have plenty of recent examples such as the proliferation of the use of land mines or the saturation bombing of oil fields by the U.S.-led coalition during the Persian Gulf War).

The deterioration of the natural resource base, couples with demographic pressure and chronic poverty can lead to, or exacerbate, political, ethnic, social, and economic tensions, which in turn result ini conflicts that force people to flee. Africa, for example accounts for 10% of the world's population and hosts over 20% of its refugees, for the reasons just mentioned. Women and children are among the most vulnerable groups that end up in refugee camps in numbers larger than those for men.

Let me repeat that warfare, famine, and natural ecological distress have all played their part in forcing populations to abandon their places and move. But so too have certain political or ethnic repressions, urbanization, industrialization, and energy development. In general, three major factors contribute to environmental resettlement: 1.- demographic explosion (which has reached 3.1 % per annum in Africa); 2.- lack of spatial balance between population and resource distribution; and 3.- particularly fragile ecosystems, mostly tropical.

Involuntary Resettlement

A particular aspect of the refugee problem which has not received adequate attention is involuntary resettlement for environmental reasons. Involuntary resettlement is the by-product of urban programs or of the construction of dams, highways, industrial estates, ports, agri-business ventures, and so-forth. It starts by taking away land, which is the main asset for family livelihood in poor countries, and unless properly addressed by the state, it is certain to degenerate into processes of massive impoverishment and social disorganization, with women and children as the primary victims, since these groups have limited access to property and natural resources.

In China, more than 10 million people were involuntarily resettled over a period of 30 years as a result of dam construction alone. In India the aggregate numbers are of comparable magnitude about 15.5 million people over the last four decades, including displacement from reservoirs, urban sites, thermal plants, and mines. I would like to point out, however, that in many places, particularly in Africa, most forced population displacements are not caused by development programs but rather triggered by social and political strife, such as foreign wars and domestic conflicts, or by ethnic, racial and religious persecutions, or by natural causes, such as droughts and famine.

The major risk in forced population displacements is impoverishment. Many of those subjected to forced displacement for the sake of a development program, for example, are affected by poverty even before displacement, or are in a marginal economic situation. They have been working hard to overcome poverty and to improve their incomes, health and quality of life. Then suddenly here comes a development program intended to bring benefits to many people, but which is so inadequately designed implemented that it fails to protect and benefit the very people it intents to help, particularly the landless such as women, and it contributes instead to worsening their situation.

The World Bank Experience

I would like to say a few words about the contribution of the World Bank activities to the creation of the problem of environmental refugees and forced resettlement. Even though the World Bank channels about $20 billion per year in financing projects, some of them with environmental and displaced persons implications, this amount of capital represents less than 10% of the capital circulating via other private and public channels. It is private logging operations, for example, which have destroyed most forests and have displaced people. And it is the prevailing ignorance or lack of awareness of the environmental implications from various so called development projects, which has been evident in national, international decision making levels and in academic circles which has caused the depletion of our natural resource base that we witness today. Up to very recently environmental concerns were left up to engineers alone to tackle, without the involvement of social scientists.

Up to 1991 the World Bank was involved in approximately 35 development projects which resulted in involuntary relocation of 250,000 people in Africa alone.

Recommendations

No one can offer a panacea or specific formula for solutions. It is the appropriate approach that I want to emphasize. Given the complexity of the issues involved we need a comprehensive approach to the problem of refugees and displaced persons. Such an approach should include several elements.

The first priority, of course is always to deal with immediate cause of the displacement, i.e. cease-fires, negotiations, floods, etc. A second concern should be the development of structures for longer term solutions to avoid future repetitions of the calamity. In development projects the design and implementation should account for the best method to minimize or ameliorate any possible environmental negative impacts. A third element should be economic development plans to expand the economic base and to defuse issues arising from inequalities in wealth and income distribution. A fourth element should be to explicitly address the systemic gender inequalities in the socioeconomic system. And last, but equally important is the necessity to include refugees as part of the process of rehabilitation and reconciliation at every stage.

In addition, I would recommend the development of a research agenda on how women are affected by environmental degradation. The information available so far on this topic contains two major biases: 1.- most studies have focuses only on deforestation and scarcity of fuel woods, and 2.- their main concern has been with two related types of women's domestic work the collection of fuel wood and the preparation of cooked foods. Given, however, the dependence of women's domestic and economic roles on the environment, and the importance of their economic contribution in poor households, more comprehensive research is urgently needed on how women are affected by environmental degradation, such as soil erosion, salinization, loss of crop diversity, water shortages, air pollution, and household contamination.

Four key changes in the design and implementation of studies are recommended to generate better information on the effects of environmental degradation on women:

a. Increased attention to gender (i.e. gender desegregated data on agricultural work and income generation. Researchers across disciplines will need to be cognizant of how gender-based differences in economic and social roles structure women's use of and dependence on the environment).

b. More multi-disciplinary research, closer collaboration of researchers from social, health, and ecological sciences is necessary to accurately understanding of the full range of the effects of environmental degradation on women.

c. Broader sector coverage, that is beyond the energy issues (access to biomass and peri-urban households) to agroforestry, sustainable agriculture, micro-enterprise development, and health (via increased time constraints, loss of income, and poorer health status of women).

d. Integrated concern of women in project environmental impact studies. Broader conceptualization, supported by better data, is one of the best guarantees that women will not be forgotten in our concerns about environmental degradation and our efforts to promote sustainable development.

A loud word of caution, however. There is already plenty of information on the linkages between environmental degradation and gender discrimination to justify remedial action; we do not need to wait a few more years of proof in order to start elaborating out strategies for problem solution and prevention. Such responses should include several elements. The first priority is to deal with the immediate caused of displacement, i.e. cease-fires & negotiations, etc. A second is to contribute to the development of structures for longer term mediation, so that future disputes can be settled without resort to violence. A third element incorporates economic development plans to expand the resource base and to defuse issues arising from inequality of distribution. The forth is to explicitly address the systemic gender inequalities in the socioeconomic system. Last but equally important is the necessity to include refugees as part of the process of rehabilitation and reconciliation at every stage.

An Ethiopian mother and children, 1984. (photo: UNICEF 155673 / P. Magubane)

Sissy Farenthold

The Militarization of United States Foreign Policy

The growing militarization of US foreign policy has several aspects. These include the availability of military goods to "friendly" nations and the training of their defense troops. The private corporations that depend upon military contracts have also played a dominant role in keeping levels of military spending high by lobbying and influencing Congress.

We have in this country lost a great opportunity to turn foreign policies away from militarization and toward the direction of peace and economic security for the American citizen. This moment was lost in 1988 when Jim Wright was forced to resign his positions as Speaker of the U.S. House of Representatives. Wright continually antagonized the Republican administration by agreeing to negotiate with the Sandinista government in Nicaragua. Wright who had made peace his number one priority, believed it was better to encourage free and open elections in Nicaragua than to fund the Contra War. On March 20, 1984, Wright, with ten other representatives, sent a letter to Commander Daniel Ortega, coordinator of the Unite de Gobierno in Nicaragua, commending him and his government for taking steps to open up the political process. "We support" the letter stated, "your decision to schedule elections this year, to reduce press censorship, and to allow greater freedom of assembly for political parties" (Wright, 266).

Wright's involvement in the peace process also led him to support measures for economic conversion, a policy which seeks to facilitate the transition from weapons production to factories, bases, and laboratories which produce for civilian use. This is a process which would benefit the nation as a whole and the local economies which now depend upon military production. In 1988, Wright held a meeting with Seymour Melman, professor of industrial engineering at Columbia University, in which they discussed economic conversion. Melman, a long time scholar of the military-industrial complex and a staunch advocate of conversion, recognized with other Pentagon critics that "military spending is a major drain on the civilian economy, diverting vital capital, technical and human resources away from productive uses" (Yudken, 52).

In the 1970s, Rep. Ted Weiss (D-NY) introduced legislation on economic conversion, which was never acted upon by Congress. Ten years later, the issue of economic conversion again was raised in Congress when Reps. Nicholas Mavroules (D-MA), Sam Gejdenson (D-CT), and Mary Rose Oakar (D-OH) introduced legislation similar to Weiss'. Speaker Wright asked the four House members "to form a working group and to write a consensus bill for the purpose of assisting communities that would be impacted by the December 31 recommendations of the 1988 Base Closure Commission" (Bierwirth, 190). Weiss served as the chief sponsor of House Bill #HR101, which was broad in scope and placed emphasis on planning ahead in order to minimize the difficulties of economic transition.

Those members of the House who were opposed to conversion criticized Weiss as encouraging government intervention in public businesses. Other influential economic interest groups, especially the corporations working with the military, used National Security as a lobbying point to influence Congress against economic conversion. Large government loans and contracts from the Pentagon have helped to maintain firms involved in military production. "In addition to these direct forms of aid, the Pentagon has provided trade supports to its favored industries for decades and operates a large Foreign Military Sales program" (Yudken, 50).

In 1990, for example, Lockheed won a lucrative contract from the Pentagon to produce advanced tactical fighter planes. It is important to note that Rep. Newt Gingrich, now Speaker of the House, is tied in with the Lockheed industry. Following its merger with Martin Marietta, another weapons producer in Gingrich's home district, Lockheed became the nation's largest defense contractor.

Speaker Wright's support for economic conversion was obviously a threat to the interests of Newt Gingrich and the corporations he represents in Congress. Wright had to be removed. A small band of Republicans led by Newt Gingrich attacked Wright and the ten members of the House who signed the letter sent to Daniel Ortega. They claimed that the letter was illegal and unconstitutional. "These ten Congressmen," Gingrich stated, "clearly undercut the efforts of their own government to apply pressure to the Nicaraguan regime" (Wright, 67). Apparently, letters from members of Congress to foreign heads of states are not uncommon, but in this incident, Wright's letter was used by Gingrich as a means to discredit him.

Gingrich then filed formal charges accusing Wright of violating House rules in his personal finances. Although Wright was cleared of all charges, pressure mounted until he was forced to resign the Speakership and his Congressional office. At a weekly meeting of Democratic Whips, Rep. David Obey of Wisconsin told Wright that "the *Wall Street Journal* is after your economics, Mr. Speaker, not your ethics. Newt Gingrich is after your effectiveness not your ethics" (Wright, 183). Further misfortune followed when Rep. Weiss was stricken with a fatal heart attack. Therefore, any serious discussion of economic conversion for arms manufacturing was cut off.

On January 30, 1995, the Nuclear Age Peace Foundation issued an Action Alert Bulletin stating that Point Six of the *Contract with America* opposes the use of Pentagon dollars for non-defense purposes, and states a preference for using these funds for traditional defense programs. A prime target may be economic conversion programs intended to provide an economic transition for communities and defense workers cut off from defense contracts.

It is quite obvious that the weapons industries profit from war and that economic conversion is a threat to their profits. A clear example of how the weapons industry and U.S. foreign policy work together can be found in the U.S. relationship with Haiti. From 1986 to 1990, four military governments have held power in Haiti. The U.S. government would immediately give recognition to the new government by issuing military aid to Haiti. One might wonder why Haiti needed the military aid (what enemies was it defending itself from?) and ask how this figured into U.S. foreign policy. The U.S. considered the coup d'état friendly, and the military aid sent was to confirm the country's approval.

The U.S. not only provides the military weapons to foreign countries, but also provides training for their military forces. The results of this U.S. policy became clear when the United Nations began to examine the violations of human rights taking place in the Americas and particularly in El Salvador. On March 15, 1993, the UN established the Truth Commission. The Commission was given six months under the terms of the Salvadorian peace accords to carry out the task of clarifying who was responsible for the violence in that nation which had killed more than 100,000 people during the preceding ten years. Among the many cases of violence researched were the killing of six Jesuit priests, the massacre of 900 civilians in El Mozote, and the assassination of Archbishop Oscar Arnulfo Romero.

"In seeking, as mandated, the most thorough accounting possible of human rights abuses in the war, this report names the institutions and those individuals whom the Commission found responsible in the cases it studied. What they found was that the vast majority of abuses studied by the Commission were committed by members of the El Salvadoran armed forces or groups allied to them" (*Truth Commission Report*). Three years before the Truth Commission was established, the School of the America's Watch (SOAW) was started in order to monitor the role of the School of the Americas, located at Fort Benning, Georgia, in the training of Salvadoran military forces. Most Americans, even journalists, are not well educated about the extent of the impact U.S. training of Latin American soldiers has on the poor of Latin America. When the Truth Commission cited the names of soldiers who were responsible for the human rights violations in El Salvador, a member of the SOAW, Vicky Imerman, compared the cited names with the names of men who graduated from the School of the Americas. She found that 19 of the 27 officers who carried out the massacre of six Jesuit priests were graduates of the School of the Americas. Concerning the rape and murder of four nuns in 1980, five officers were cited, three of whom were graduates from the School of the Americas. The assassination of Archbishop Romero was carried out by three officers, two of which graduated from the School. The El Mozote massacre, which resulted in the deaths of 900 civilians, including 135 children, was organized by twelve officers, ten of whom graduated from the School of the Americas.

The documented results from the Truth Commission shows that 73% of the soldiers cited in the human rights abuses which took place in El Salvador were trained in the School of the Americas at Fort Benning, Georgia. Basically, what this means is that despite the official rhetoric about democracy, there are close and lasting ties between the U.S. military and the "friendly" foreign military trained in the United States. The rhetoric about promoting democracy in the developing world constitutes one track of U.S. foreign policy. The other track is the training and funding of military murderers, but this tract is too often secret and unknown by the general public in the U.S. The latest example of this two track policy is the ambivalent posturing toward President Jean Bertrand Aristide from the time of the coup which ousted him from power to his return as leader of Haiti. Recent information has revealed that the CIA funded and advised adversaries of the Haitian president as well as the terrorist gang know as FARAP.

The U.S. aggressive military intervention in foreign policy did not start with the Cold War. Intervention and the United States make for a good match. However, with the advent of the National Security Presidency which was a creature of the National Security Act of 1947, both covert and overt warfare were waged without congressional authorization, and often in secrecy. The party affiliation of the president makes not a bit of difference.

The domination of U.S. arms manufactures in the supply of arms to the Third World has played an important role in the creation of refugees particularly in Africa. Again, political party affiliation is not a criterion for arms transfer. Under President Bush arms were sold to Iraq even though publicly the president was calling Iraq a sponsor of international terrorism. All administrations have actively lobbied on behalf of arms merchants. Under President Clinton, the government's participation is even more evident. The guidelines being drafted by this administration will explicitly consider the economic well-being of U.S. weapons producing corporations when reviewing arms sales to foreign customers.

Traditionally, approval of arms sales were determined by foreign policy goals and were justified as ways to strengthen regional alliances. Encouragement by U.S. embassies of arms sales, once prohibited, is now open and insistent. The

Pentagon pays some costs to fund U.S. weaponry at international trade shows. The latest report available on conventional arms transfer to the Third World was released on July 29, 1994, by the Congressional Research Services of the Library of Congress, and is known as the Grimmeth Report after its author, Richard F. Grimmeth. Officially, It Is titled *Conventional Arms Transfer to the Third World*.

The report shows that the United States is the leading supplier of weapons to the developing world, providing in 1993 over seventy-two percent of all weapons sold for a total of $14.8 billion. The US arms agreement with Kuwait alone in 1993 amounted to $2.2 billion. Although the United States dominates arms transfers to the Third World, Europe, Russia and China serve as helpful alternatives to those countries not able to buy arms for political reasons from the United States.

In the 1980s, most of the arms transfers were focused in the Middle East. In the 1990s, the arms merchants are focusing on the Pacific Rim, and so called "Tiger" countries like Indonesia, Singapore, Taiwan, and South Korea. Indonesia, whose behavior in the field of human rights is reprehensible, is a new and fast growing market for arms.

But as U.S. arms sales continue to countries with terrible records of human rights, there are some attempts to curb this merchandising of the military. For the first tine, built into foreign aid bills, Congress has conditioned U.S. support for loans by the international financial institutions, the International Monetary Fund (IMF), the World Bank and regional banks, on the recipient country's willingness to reduce military spending.

On February 1, 1995, Senate Appropriations Committee Chair Mark Hatfield (R-Oregon) and House International Relations Committee member Cynthia McKinney (D-Georgia) introduced the "Code of Conduct on Arms Transfer Act of 1995" (HR 1561) The goals of the Code are simple. The United States will not sell or give away weapons to governments that abuse the human rights of their citizens, deny their people democratic rights, or attack their neighbors. Nor must a government undermine international attempts to control arms. In her arguments to the committee, Ms. McKinney pointed out that foreign arms sales cost American citizens $7 billion in subsidies each year and that U.S. made arms are used in 90% of the world's conflicts. Altogether, the U.S. accounts for 70% of all arms sales world-wide. Weapons that destroyed Iraq only five years ago are now on the market to nearly any nation who wishes to purchase them.

The proposed legislation would not only force countries to abide by democratic principles if they want U.S. weapons, it would also force the administration and Congress to participate in the process. The legislation would require the President to list the countries allowed, under the four criteria, to receive U.S. military assistance. Congress, on the other hand, would be required to vote to approve arms sales to countries that did not appear on the President's list.

In a vote taken on May 12, 1995, the Code of Conduct bill failed to pass the committee by a narrow vote of 18 against and 17 for. This was the first time in nineteen years that a bill proposing to subject weapons sales to congressional scrutiny even made it to a full vote of the International Relations Committee.

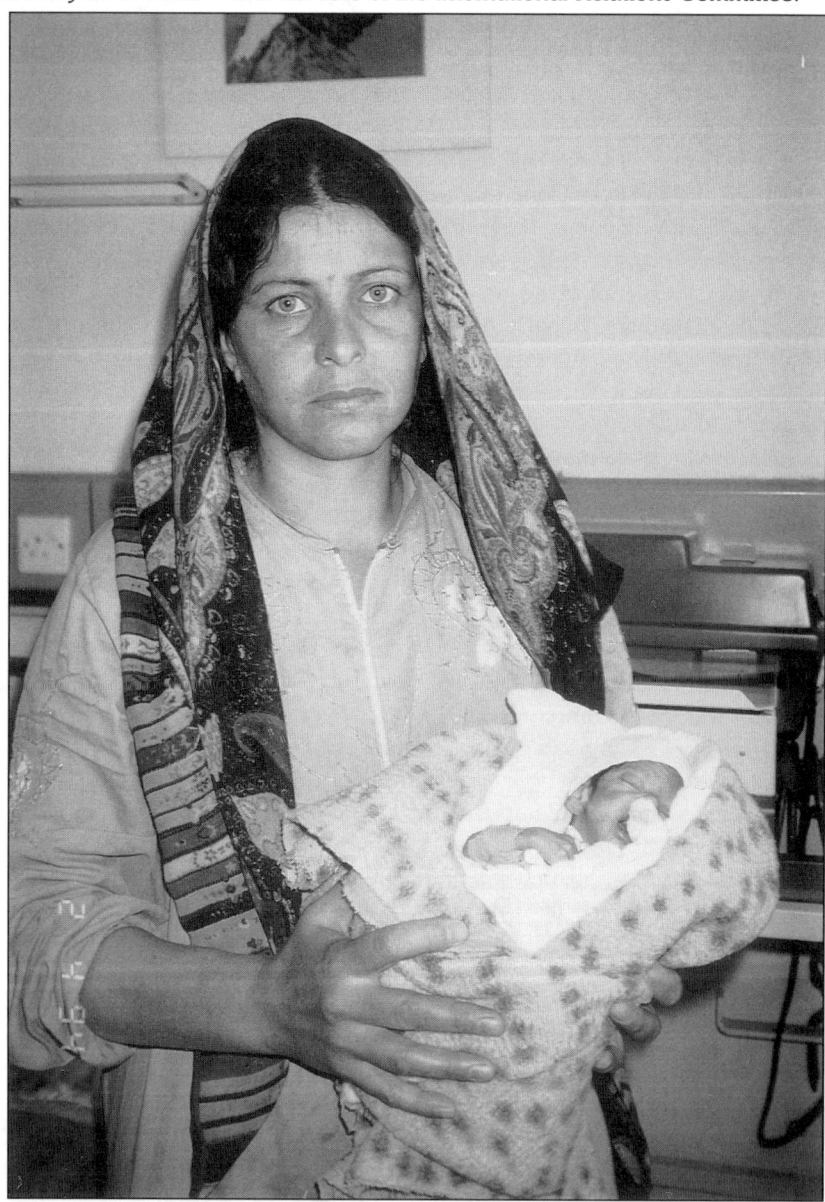

This Iraqi women with her sick child cannot get help at Baghdad Children's Hospital because of the U.S. led war against Iraq. The U.S. had until the month before the war sold weapons to Iraq. (photo: Sara Flounders)

The figures below were read into the *Congressional Record* by Representative McKinney. They are originally from a "White House Fact Sheet:Conventional Arms Sales Policy." While the numbers seem somewhat incomplete—why are there no entries for El Salvador, Honduras, Saudi Arabia, and others—they do show how U.S. weapons are playing a major role in wars and governmental repressions around the world.

U.S. Arms Deliveries to Areas of Conflict, 1984–1993

Region of the World	U.S. Deliveries 1984-93 ($ millions)	Last year of U.S. sales	% of imports provided by U.S. 1987-91/1991-93	Other Suppliers
Europe				
1. Former Yugoslavia	163.4	1991	13/0	Russia, Germany, Iran, Egypt, Saudi Arabia
2. Spain	4,003.6	1993	85/86	France
3. United Kingdom	6,318.5	1993	100/95	
4. Russia	none			
5. Moldavia	none			
6. Georgia	none			
7. Turkey	6,302.5	1993	76/80	
Middle East/North Africa				
8. Azerbaijan	none			
9. Iraq	4.4	1989	1/0	Former Soviet Union, China, France
10. Israel	9,544.1	1993	99/91	
11. Algeria	105.2	1993	1/0	Former Soviet Union, Egypt, China
12. Morocco	404	1993	26/76	France
13. Egypt	7,227.9	1993	61/89	France
14. Sudan	155.6	1989	9/0	China, Middle East Suppliers, Italy
15. Yemen	50.6	1991	1/0	Former Soviet Union, China
16. Iran	covert sales, value not known			Russia, China, other European suppliers
Sub-Saharan Africa				
17. Mauritania	1.5	1992	1/0	Former Soviet Union
18. Mali	.2	1993	1/0	Former Soviet Union, Middle East sources
19. Chad	50.3	1993	27/25	France
20. Somalia	109.3	1991	44/100	Italy
21. Senegal	13.6	1993	11/100	France, European suppliers
22. Liberia	33.4	1990	48/0	Former Warsaw Pact, Middle East suppliers

Region of the World	U.S. Deliveries 1984-93 ($ millions)	Last year of U.S. sales	% of imports provided by U.S. 1987-91/1991-93	Other Suppliers
23. Togo	1.9	1993	1/0	Latin America
24. Nigeria	82.4	1993	9/2	Italy, Former Soviet Union, Czechoslovakia, France
25. Uganda	10.6	1993	5/100	Former Soviet Union, Italy
26. Rwanda	1.4	1993	5/0	China, France, Egypt, Uganda, South Afroca
27. Burundi	.6	1993	1/0	Former Soviet Union
28. Kenya	100.2	1993	25/100	U.K., France
29. Zaire	55.9	1990	17/0	China, France
30. Angola (UNITA rebels)	250 (300)	n/a	n/a	Former Soviet Union (to Gov't)
31. South Africa	8.3	1988	n/a	n/a

Asia

32. Tajikistan	rebels receive covert weapons from CIA via Afghanistan			
33. Afghanistan	28 covert weapons to rebel factions			
34. Pakistan	1,801.7	1993	44/3	China
35. India	316.6	1993	1/0	Russia, U.K., European suppliers
36. Bhutan	.2	1992	1/0	
37. Sri Lanka	8.6	1993	7/0	China
38. Bangladesh	16.7	1993	4/5	Former Soviet Union, China
39. Myanmar (Burma)	6.2	1989	1/0	China
40. China	423.9	1993	8/1	Russia
41 Philippines	619.3	1993	93/75	Italy
42. Cambodia	covert weapons to Khmer Rouge via Thai army			
43. Indonesia	583.3	1993	38/33	Germany, U.K., Netherlands, European suppliers
44. Papua New Guinea	none			Former Soviet Union

Latin America

45. Guatemala	35.8	1993	86/0	Israel
46. Haiti	2.6	1992	25/0	Latin American sources
47. Columbia	647	1993	28/19	Brazil
48. Peru	136	1993	6/8	France, Former Soviet Union
49. Brazil	528.8	1993	35/40	Germany, France
50. Mexico	301.2	1993	77/64	

Source: *Congressional Record*, H5515-H5516, May 24, 1995.

References

Bierwirth, M. "Capital Hill and Conversion: A Summary of Recent Congressional Action," *Real Security: Converting the Defense Economy and Building Peace* Kevin J. Cassidy and Gregory A. Bischak, eds. Albany: State University of New York Press, 1993.
Hartung, W. D. *The Nation*, January 1995, p. 124.
Yudken, J. "Economic Development, Technological, and Defense Conversion: A National Policy Perspective" in *Real Security: Converting the Defense Economy and Building Peace*, Cassidy and Bischak, eds.
Wright, J. *Worth It All*. Washington, DC: Maxwell Macmillian Company, 1993.

U.S. Arms Sales Agreements with the World, 1986-1993

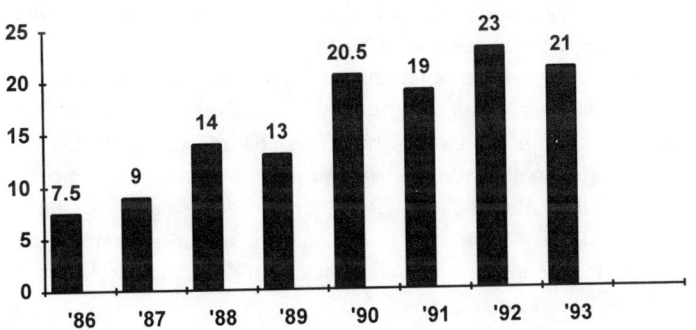

Average Arms Sales, 1984-1989, Cold War on — $10.6 Billion per year
Average Arms Sales, 1990-1993, Cold War over — $21.6 Billion per year
(Dollars are in billions, constant for 1993)

Georgina Ritchie

From Powerlessness to Empowerment: Turning the Refugee Experience into a Movement for Human Rights

To become a refugee is to lose everything. Gone are the comfortable securities, personal and societal, by which you have identified yourself. There is no longer a sense of "home" either without or within. With the loss of beloved land, property and possessions identity disappears. With the often violent loss of loved ones, a sense of purposelessness descends. Often survival itself becomes the only goal and at the same time there is a profound sense that little is left for which one could will or want to survive.

Unfortunately, examples abound. The experience of Bosnia is an endless chronicle of personal loss. An interview with a 73-year old Bosnian refugee women now living in Houston, Texas, by Dr. Selina Ahmed is typical. The woman survived two wars in Bosnia. Her husband died 30 years ago and she raised nine children all by herself. She worked at many jobs and is very proud that her hard work enabled all of her children to complete high school and, for some of them, college as well. When the current conflict began in Bosnia, she had fifteen grandchildren. At this moment she has no idea if any of her children or grandchildren are still alive. Her tragedy began when soldiers came to the door of her home insisting on knowing the whereabouts of one of her sons. She knew nothing about where he might be, and, in spite of her age, they brutally beat her and raped her. The soldiers took away her two youngest sons and two granddaughters. That was the last she knew of any of her family.

Nana Apeadu is a female chief in Ghana and has worked with refugees in Somalia and with Rwandan people in camps in Kenya. She points out that the most devastating loss any refugee suffers is the loss of beloved family members. She tells of 10,000 orphaned boys who arrived at a camp in Kenya after walking hundreds of miles. They had each lost their entire family. Those who arrived at the camps were survivors. Thousands died on the way to the camps and were either buried in shallow graves by the side of the road or left where they died. People who suffer natural disasters such as earthquake, fire, or flood have all they have built up over a lifetime taken from them in a matter of minutes or hours. Still they are given much to cling to with community and strangers rushing aid and comfort to them and often with the opportunity to rebuild their lives on the same site or nearby. What is singular about the refugees from war, military repression, or exploitative economic development is that lack of familiarity, the sense of moving into a permanent state of being in which the refugee will always be other, "a stranger in a strange land."

Even the most basic identity—such as gender specific work—disappears. Eighty per cent of refugees worldwide are women and children, and the work and protections previously provided by men are no longer available in the new environment. Women most usually have been in charge of preparing and distributing food to their families. When women and children become refugees food becomes a source of power and control. Therefore, it is usually men who are put in charge of distribution of what food is available and it is not uncommon for women and children to go without when there is scarcity. It is also often the case that women are required to submit to demands for sexual acts in order to get food for themselves and their children. Even once food has been distributed the danger is not over. Nana Apeadu was told of six women who went out to gather firewood. All but one were killed. The next day as the survivor readied herself to seek firewood again, Apeadu asked why she would embark on such a dangerous task. The answer was simple: "My children must eat."

The essence of being a refugee is victimization—most often experiencing trauma after trauma over a prolonged period of time. It begins with the terror which causes populations to flee their homes. In such an emotionally overwhelming situation people do not or cannot think clearly about what is most necessary and often may have to leave a family home and land inhabited by ancestors for generations with only what can be carried in their arms. The refugee may be in extreme terror from having been forced to witness the brutal murder of loved ones, submit to personal rape, or be horrified by the rape of a mother or daughter or by seeing family members taken into custody by police or army.

Often the trip into exile is scarred with intense physical suffering and still further loss of family not strong enough to endure the rigors of the journey. What remains of property, health and even the sanctity of one's own body can be lost in the flight to survive.

There will be many times when women and children arrive at their destination having suffered repeated rape. A woman who works with Southeast Asian refugees tells heart rending stories of some who escaped by boat. Girls as young as seven and nine were taken from their families and the boats on which they traveled. They were taken aboard "pirate" boats which sometimes doubled as fishing boats where the girls were forced to give repeated sexual satisfaction to all the men on board. When the boat was ready to come back to port, the girls were thrown overboard to drown. When some survived to tell of their subjugation, subsequent crews made sure that the girls were dead before they threw them overboard.

Even when temporary safety is reached in a camp, across a border or far from home, new and unimagined physical danger and additional trauma often await. An article in *MS* magazine entitled "No Woman's Land," states, "Females of all ages are preyed upon by guards at borders and at refugee camps, armed men in and out of uniform, officials, pirates, male refugees. . . . Fear is a fact of life in the camps as sleeping areas often must be shared by unrelated families, traditional enemies and unprotected women and children." It is reported that the newer the refugee camp is the harsher will be the conditions experienced there. Often camps are in bleak, unpopulated areas near a border, and they are surrounded by barbed wire or other prison-like barriers. Sanitation is frequently poor and there is ever-present danger of infection and illness.

Addressing the Problem

The number of unfortunate persons driven to exist in such surroundings continues to rise. The current number of displaced people and refugees worldwide is estimated to be more than 20 million. That number has risen from 8 million in the 1970s as estimated by the UN. High Commissioner for Refugees. Government and non-government agencies as well as religious and private organizations and individuals are at a loss to know how to meet even the most basic needs for food, water, sanitation, and protection from spread of epidemics. These primal lacks are inexcusable because we know their solutions are within the capacities of nations. At the very least wholesale suffering can—and it must—be attacked by strenuous applications of international willpower. Our right to call ourselves civilized depends on it.

Beyond unmet survival needs, however, there is a realm of trauma and internal privation that also lies within the power of humankind to aid by providing safety, empathy, and healing. Along with food and shelter, refugees need protection from rape, relief from fear, therapy for extreme and repeated physical and psychological violations, the re-establishment of meaningful work, the re-uniting of surviving family members and the encouragement of a sense of hope. Although solutions are available for each of these concerns, they are barely being addressed at all.

A rare exception came when professor Maja Kandido-Jaksic spoke to the 1994 Athens Conference on Refugee and Displaced Women In Times of Conflict.

Dr. Kandido-Jaksic interviewed 345 refugees and displaced persons in 47 locations in Croatia. Her work was conducted in coordination with the UNHCR. to define concrete problems, gather statistics and recommend activities, policies and solutions to the problems of those women. The two greatest difficulties presented by the vast majority of women were homesickness (92%) and separation from family and friends (83%). Many defined poverty and the impossibility of finding paid work or the opportunity to earn money to meet their needs as a major problem. They expressed feelings of loneliness, abandonment, and boredom.

Ninety-one percent of the women interviewed had under-aged children living with them. Due to the fine humanitarian aid available in these camps many of the basic needs of the women and children were being met. Yet the survival regimen proved psychologically damaging because it disrupted traditional family roles. Mothers found that their children were organized by authorities to the point where they were leading independent and completely organized lives apart from the family. Mothers felt that they were not sufficiently involved in the education of their children and that the children no longer respected or obeyed them as before. Mothers feared they were losing their deep emotional contact with their children and some stated that their children avoided them. Many women experienced depression and had feelings of uselessness because they neither worked nor cared for a household. The women perceived life as monotonous and empty.

Both physical and mental illness were a problem and the incidence of both increased with the amount of time a women had been displaced. There was some difference in response based on education. women with more education seemed more able to preserve some self confidence and self esteem in their time of loss and displacement. Yet the overall picture is overwhelmingly bleak. If displaced women living in a camp situation were to take part in the administration of facilities they would gain a sense of personal power and control over their experience. Problems of day to day life and adjustment would be dealt with by those who experience them. Women can be trained to accept responsibility, learn administration procedures and create solutions for recurring or endemic difficulties of life in exile. Through this they would become personally stronger and less inclined toward depression. Women would also learn new skills which might serve them well as they move toward resettlement.

Since the world now faces vast and increasing numbers of people displaced, often permanently, from their homes, their nation and their culture, it is vital to look at problems and solutions that extend beyond the short term. The emotional despair and lack of any possibility for escape from refugee status presents enormous long range problems. Most refugees cannot return home for political, economic, or security reasons. They cannot live productively or even safely in camps. Third countries worldwide are increasingly unwilling to accept them for resettlement. In cases where displaced persons have been resettled they face joblessness, prejudice, poor living conditions, and declining physical and emotional health. Many refugees become the target of violent physical attack by the local population which fears an influx of cheap labor, makes assumptions about criminal natures or intentions, or requires an outlet for economic and social frustration.

How can anger be converted to energy and despair moved to action against further victimization? How do we even begin to approach healing wounds of such depth and duration? Now can this victimization not only end but be turned to empowerment which will make it increasingly less possible for similar events to occur in other parts of the world?

The map is being drawn by brave women, children, and men in exile worldwide. It is all-important to heal the anger toward the enemy who has caused the loss. Untended angers of the past are the seeds of new wars. We see it now as Western Christians, Muslims, and Orthodox Christians in the former Yugoslavia act out enmities ingrained for generations. For healing to begin, victims must be able to voice rage and eventually to be able to see their personal tragedy as a part of a larger and non-specific evil of power imbalance which must be fought in every nation. It is the refusal to accept permanent powerlessness which constitutes the true end of the victimization of those who are now without a nation. They are pioneers of a new geography of recovery on a grand scale. The experiments they live will give us multiple approaches and directions within which to work.

The first and most repeatedly expressed need came from women from all over the world who journeyed to Athens, Greece, in September 1994 for the International NGO Dialogue: Refugee and Displaced Women In Times Of Conflict. The conference grew out of the need for physical protection. The rape of women and children has become a constant physical, psychological, and culturally dehumanizing threat in times of upheaval. Even when systematic rape becomes openly known about and blatantly, routinely practiced as a tactic of terror, it seems the world is slow in recognizing and attempting to put a stop to it.

Rape is a crime of power, not of sexuality. Linda E. Ledray in her book, *Recovering From Rape*, states, "Rape is a crime of violence and aggression against women. It is not a crime of passion. For rapists, sex is a weapon used to humiliate, control, and degrade women. The purpose is disempowerment and intimidation. There is a corruption of innocence which creates shame, isolation and even a sense of guilt in the victim. The process of healing is long and painful. Those who commit rape somehow see the source of women's power as sexual rather than spiritual.

But women's power lies in the ability to create love and to connect with others in love. Those who commit rape are making an attack on the soul. The soul can be defined as the ability we all have to connect with and love ourselves, other people, and that which is beyond ourselves. When a woman has experienced even one incidence of rape—let alone many—she experiences great difficulty in reconnecting with herself and others. The fear and anger experienced often immobilizes the victim.

There is movement in many countries to prosecute rapists and to make it safe for women to report such crimes to authorities with the reasonable expectation that claims will be believed and the criminal pursued and punished. There are also many nations in the world where rape is still considered to be the fault of the woman and the victim to be the one to endure punishment. Professor Catharine MacKinnon reports, "Rape was not charged in the post-World War II indictments of the Nazis at Nuremberg, although sexual forms of torture, including rape, were documented at the trials. . . . Rape in war has so often been treated as extracurricular, as just something men do, as a product rather than a policy of war."

Still, much has happened to indicate these views can be changed. Rhonda Copelon, co-director of the international Women's Human Rights Clinic at the City University of New York where she is a professor of law states, ". . . rape, forced prostitution, and forced pregnancy should be identified as crimes against humanity and war crimes independent of whether they were carried out as part of ethnic cleansing. Rape is an atrocity and a tactic of war whether it is used for ethnic cleansing or to reward triumphant soldiers. To protect women globally, we must insist that rape is an atrocity in all its contexts, in war as well as in the everyday."

In May 1993 a war crimes tribunal of eleven judges was established by the UN Security Council. However, gender-specific crimes are not now fully recognized in international law. This initial proposal for a tribunal did not contain clear procedures for prosecuting rapists and their commanders and there was no provision for compensating victims. There was no money allocated for data gathering or investigation of criminal charges and the more than one million dollars set aside by the UN. was all for administrative costs. The U.S. representative to the UN, Madelaine Albright, in May 1993 said, "We must ensure that the voices of the groups most victimized are heard by the tribunal. I refer particularly to the detention and systematic rape of women and girls, often followed by cold-blooded murder." Legal prosecution is vital both for attracting world attention and for deterring continued use of rape as a method of war. Turning light on the secrets that perpetrators of pain would keep hidden is essential to bringing about cessation of crimes against human rights, the most basic of which is the sanctity of the human body.

Some model work is being done in Zagreb, Croatia, by the Center for Women War Victims. The organization defines itself as "a feminist group of refugee, displaced and securely citizened women, working with refugee and displaced women regardless of nationality, working on psycho-social self-help and rehabilitation." They have established thirty-seven self-help groups. The center resettles some women and their children in other countries and distributes humanitarian aid in the form of food, feminine hygiene, and other personal needs. Financial aid is given directly to some 600 women each month. The center defines its main intention as giving refugee and displaced women support for psychological self-help.

The staff seeks to support women in regaining control over their lives and validating their experiences. Spokeswomen say that since the circumstances in which the women are living do not change, "feelings of uncertainty, unsafety and fear are still very much present. More and more of them are mourning over their multiple losses (close family members, friends, communities, property, former lifestyles)." They are encouraged to go through this process together in groups. The group leaders have been trained in stress management and anger release. Groups are run in the refugee camps and some are held at the center for women who are living in private accommodations in Zagreb.

The groups fill a great need as the women living privately are more isolated and more alone with their experiences and problems. They have found that individual counseling is more requested in the camps. Women who live near one another in camps are more concerned about confidentiality and are somewhat distrustful of the others at the camp. They tend to be uncomfortable with the possibility that self revelation in a group will lead to gossip. The center has found that nine to twelve months of group or individual work seems to be "long enough for women to find and strengthen their self-esteem and self-confidence and to build a support network."

A very effective way to promote healing after enduring rape is to have the opportunity to talk about the experience to someone trained to give help to victims dealing with complex feelings of anger, shame, fear and powerlessness. It can be a long process made even more difficult by the particular sexual taboos of any given society and by the way each culture regards and treats women. Open discussion about women's issues and the feeling of group support can be the beginning of women achieving self esteem which they had never in their lives before considered a possibility.

Groups set up in refugee camps and areas of resettlement can do more good than just putting women in touch with community resources and helping them deal with the trauma of their personal experiences. Coming out of the isolation of their losses and bonding with others can turn anger into the energy of empowerment. When in Somalia on a fact finding mission for the UN., Nana Apeadu was given a declaration by a group of women. It read as follows:
We women have followed behind our men in the wake of detestation and destruction of our homeland. Now understand that we leave our roll as followers and become the leaders of our people into peace. we are the most affected group of people in Somalia and now we raise up our voices in anguish and pain, but also in strength and hope that we can be the peacemakers. These women have

turned their personal loss into an energy to change their society. With hope and positive intention replacing despair, they intend to create peace for a generation of children yet unborn in a culture they hope will center on peace and human rights and the strong partnership of mutual empowerment and respect.

The world so rapidly moves from one world disaster to the next that it is important to help people connect with those who suffer through no fault of their own. We must repeatedly bring the personal tragedies of refugees and displaced women and children to the attention of the media worldwide. Their stories must be followed up in their full complexity, making connections between the glamorization of violence and the easy availability of lethal armaments. The purposeful arming of small diverse and disquieted groups either for monetary or political gain must be connected in the minds of the world's peoples with the death, destruction, displacement, expense, and ultimate difficulty on all sides which occurs when vast numbers of people become homeless and nationless.

The United Nations and World Court must focus on legal means of enforcing basic human rights everywhere and these rights and rules of law must cover people experiencing displacement from their homeland. Protection of displaced persons must be taken seriously by host countries. Groups modeled on the admirable and effective Doctors Without Borders should be created to address the mental and emotional victimization of the international homeless.

Above all, this massive displacement and movement of peoples fleeing rape, torture, murder, and persecution must be recognized as a stoppable phenomenon. Human rights education should be implemented at every level in every society. Conflict resolution skills should be taught and used in schools, government and businesses. Partnership and power sharing should be taught where and whenever possible.

When there are signs of impending armed conflict plans could be offered to share power, with economic development being underlined "using" rather than "losing" lives. Companies of all sizes from any nation which think they might do business in a area of pending conflict should be gathered together. Their contribution could be key because their corporate perspective will make it clear that it is economically counter-productive for countries to endure years of war, have their earth mined or poisoned, and vast numbers of productive young people killed only to have businesses come in afterward and develop the country. If a plan offering jobs and market development were presented early even the most power hungry might see the wisdom of prosperity in place of destruction.

Rights as defined in the UN universal covenant on human rights must become a serious value kept in the foreground for all politicians, governments and business. People must know what their human rights are and band together to see that these rights are not withheld from them. Businessmen—especially arms traders and producers—must be condemned as capable and culpable of violating human rights, just as governments have been. Victims can learn to reclaim their power through self help, helping others, and political activism. People must be taught to vote and to take voice in every country, learning to use their numbers and common need to demand attention. The massive upheaval that is experienced when all you have previously depended upon has been taken away can at beat be used to envision and create a world where victims become empowered to say, "NO MORE."

Robert Merrill

Theory and Progress of Human Rights: The UN Declaration on the Rights of Indigenous Peoples

On November 10, 1995, Ken Saro-Wiwa, Barinem Kiobel, Saturday Dobee, Paul Levura, Nordu Eawo, Felix Nuate, Daniel Gbokoo, John Kpuinen, and Varibor Bera—all leaders of the Movement for the Survival of the Ogoni People— were hanged by the Nigerian government working on behalf of Shell Oil, Mobil, Texaco, and Chevron to end the uprising of the Ogoni people against the exploitation and destruction of their homeland in southeastern Nigeria. While events such as this have been commonplace since Europeans began their conquest of the world more than six centuries ago, the conflict between western profit seekers and indigenous peoples seems now to be heading for another moment of seminal crisis. The end of corporate nationalism and the rise of global "free trade" in the last decade coupled with the collapse of the Soviet Union as a sometimes-effective restraint on capitalist adventurism in the third world has meant a exponential increase in the pressure exerted by first world banks and global corporations on the natural wealth located in parts of the world inhabited by some 300–600 million peoples whose identification is not with an artificial "state" but rather with a specific, natural land area. As resources located in developed states become less and less profitable to exploit because of depletion, pollution, population density, high labor costs, and government regulation, transnational corporations find natural resources located in lands inhabited by traditional peoples increasingly attractive.

One could say, irresistibly attractive. As the authors of *50 Years Is Enough: The Case Against the World Bank and the International Monetary Fund* show so clearly, global financial institutions (including investment banks in New York, London, Tokyo) have bankrupted governments in third-world states so that they are now engaging in what amounts to a "fire sale" of their natural resources in order to catch up on debt payments and thus remain able to borrow more cash for even more development projects. During the last ten years "debt for equity in natural resources swaps" have become common. As it so often happens, the swapped resources lie in areas inhabited by indigenous peoples, and it becomes the job of the local government to dispossess them of their land. In the 1980s, the military government of Guatemala killed nearly 100,000 Mayan Indians in an effort to drive them from their ancestral lands so that transnational corporations could raise cattle and coffee for export. Structural Adjustment Plans forced by the IMF on states which experience trouble in repaying foreign debt always make it more attractive for foreign capital to invest in the local economy. In Africa, thirty out of forty-seven states are under the control of IMF Structural Adjustment Plans. According to Kevin Danaher, these typically include:

1. Selling state enterprises to the private sector to reduce the cost of government. Often state owned enterprises are sold to foreign investors at bargain basement prices and often are in mining, oil drilling, or some other natural resource development, thus giving foreign investors control of vital national wealth.

2. Raising producer prices for agricultural goods. This increases the tax base by shifting it to the broadest sector of the population and the poorest sector as well.

3. Devaluing local currencies to make exports more competitive in foreign markets, which is, in effect, to give a pay cut to everyone who works as a wage laborer in order to widen the margin between production cost and sales price for the producers.

4. Encouraging free trade by reducing protectionist measures and regulations on the private sector, including the power of trade unions.[1]

With advantages such as these, there is almost no reason for capital to stay at home. Julian Burger, author of *Report from the Frontier: The State of the World's Indigenous Peoples*, says that natural resources located in lands occupied by indigenous peoples are functioning as a late twentieth century version of the myth of El Dorado, the legendary city of gold that led Spanish conquistadors to search and pillage over much of North and South America. In 1975, the governor of the Brazilian state which includes the traditional home of the Yanomani Indians told international human rights activists trying to defend the Yanomani that "An area as rich as this, with gold, diamonds, and uranium, cannot afford the luxury of preserving half a dozen Indian tribes which are holding up development."[2]

Massive neo-colonialist invasion is deeply resented and often bitterly and violently opposed by indigenous peoples who cannot but be acutely aware that they are losing control of their land base and lives. This is the issue Ken Saro-Wiwa and his countrymen died for. From the transnational capitalist's viewpoint, the problem is how to expropriate the natural wealth of indigenous peoples with the best possible profit margin. They are exercising what to them is a property right; they have—by one means or another—obtained a legal right to develop property. From the point of view of indigenous peoples, the problem is about survival itself, as Jason Clay writing in *State of the Peoples* points out: "No single issue affects the survival of indigenous peoples as much as the state appropriation of the resources, in particular land, that indigenous peoples require if they are to survive as recognizable societies."[3] When Mayan Indians in the Chiapas province of Mexico formed the Zapatista National Liberation Army and rose up against the passage of the North American Free Trade Agreement (NAFTA), their spokesperson, Subcommandante Marcos, said: "The North American Free Trade Agreement is the death certificate for the indigenous people of Mexico. We rose up in arms to respond to Salinas' death sentence against our people."[4]

In the case of Shell Oil against the Ogoni people, the language was blunt and clear, "Shell Oil, whose oil and gas production generates 50 percent of Nigeria's annual revenue, minced no words in 'encouraging' the Nigerian regime to crack down on Saro-Wiwa: 'Shell's operations [are] still impossible unless ruthless military operations are undertaken for smooth economic activities to commence' (Internal Nigerian military memo, May 1994)." The memo goes on to indicate that soldiers should immediately begin "wasting operations" in Ogoni-land which would include "especially vocal individuals." Saro-Wiwa was arrested twelve days after the memo's circulation. In the war of Shell Oil against the Ogoni people, 27 Ogoni villages have been destroyed, 2,000 Ogoni killed and 80,000 displaced from their homes since 1993.[5] Gavin Grant of the Ogoni Community Organization based in London charged that "Shell demonized Ken Saro-Wiwa in the eyes of the Nigerian military." Under pressure from international rights organizations such as Amnesty International and Human Rights Watch to intervene with the Nigerian government for clemency or a new trial, Shell claimed that it had nothing to do with the charges and eventual execution of Saro-Wiwa and the eight others, and, furthermore, Shell executives explained, "It is not for a commercial organization like Shell to interfere in the legal processes of a sovereign state such as Nigeria."[6] They never seem to feel that way, however, when it comes to asking the government to insure favorable social conditions for economic activity. Meanwhile, the repression of some 500,000 members of the Ogoni ethnic group who live in oil rich but desperately poor swamplands of the Niger River delta continues at full steam. To date, no state has taken meaningful sanctions against the Nigerian government, and Shell continues to sell its products around the world as usual.

Organizing International Resistance

What makes the example of ethnocide in Nigeria so outrageous—and it differs little from the practices of transnational corporations and corrupt state governments on all continents—is that it is occurring precisely as the United Nations is proclaiming the "International Decade of Indigenous People, 1995-2004" and planning for the signing of the *Declaration on the Rights of Indigenous Peoples* which, as Rigoberta Menchú, an activist for Mayan rights in Guatemala, claims, "should guarantee that the individual and collective rights of indigenous people are not violated. It should encourage its member states to permit and promote the participation of indigenous people in actively defending their own rights at the national, regional, and continental levels."[7] Resolution 49/214 commits the UN to resolving the crisis of indigenous people during the next decade:

> *Bearing in mind* that one of the purposes of the United Nations, as set forth in the Charter, is the achievement of international cooperation in solving international problems of an economic, social, cultural or humanitarian character and in promoting and encouraging respect for human rights and fundamental freedoms for all without distinction as to race, sex, language or religion . . . *Decides* to include in the provisional agenda of its fiftieth session the item entitled "Programme of activities of the International Decade of the World's Indigenous People. (General Assembly, 94th Plenary Meeting, December 23, 1994).

If the United Nations means business this time, then it will have to confront multinational capital and the state governments it controls head on. At the very least, the General Assembly will have to become the forum at which indigenous peoples can collectively confront multinational capital with newly declared rights and powers. Speaking at the official opening ceremonies for the International Year of the World's Indigenous Peoples on December 10, 1992, UN Secretary General Boutros Boutros-Ghali told those gathered in the General Assembly hall that "The really crucial role of the United Nations is to promote and protect the human rights of indigenous people. The way indigenous people are treated by states and the international community will be a major test of the seriousness of our commitment to a genuinely universal human rights regime. If we are serious about development, political participation, and human rights, we must address the special situation of indigenous people."[8]

I should confess that I have no illusions about where the United Nations stands. Even though UN conventions since 1948 have treated colonialism and neo-colonialism as crimes against humanity, it has been ineffective in challenging the imperialist actions of rich nations against poorer ones, especially those of its own Security Council member states, the United States, Great Britain, France, Russia, and China. A simple survey of the countries where the UN has chosen to send its "peace keeping" forces is enough to dispel even the most hopeful notions that the UN is on the side of people and truly abides by the principles articulated in its *Charter* and magisterial *Universal Declaration of Human Rights*. Why were peace keeping forces not sent to Nicaragua, El Salvador, and Guatemala in the 1980s instead of Cambodia and Angola? If anything, the wars in Latin America were externally financed and managed, while that in Cambodia was an internal conflict. Why not to Vietnam in the 1960s instead of the Congo? Why is it now cooperating with NATO in the former Yugoslavia instead of opposing the new attempt of western Europe to divide up the Balkans? Why has the UN done nothing about the Israeli occupation of Palestine. The UN was created to prevent war, but as William Means argues, in *Voices of Indigenous Peoples*, the same volume in which Butros-Ghali's remark just quoted appears, "The longest war in world history has been the war against indigenous peoples."[9] Indeed, Patrick Brogan's *The Fighting Never Stopped* which surveys all wars since World War II shows that the vast majority have been between indigenous peoples and the colonizers or settlers who want to take their land. Most often the wars do not directly involve first world military forces, except as advisors, trainers, intelligence providers, and financiers. The fighting is done by mercenaries and surrogate armies; the "contra," the Mujahaddin, the Khmer Rouge, RENAMO, UNITA are just a few examples of major wars funded and directed from the outside. During the Gulf crisis of 1990-1991, the UN—for all the wrong reasons—passed a series of resolutions against Iraq which were enforced to the letter. Its long past time for the UN to get serious about other matters; it would do well to adopt George Bush's ultimatum during the Gulf crisis: "This aggression will not stand." Now would be a good time to pass resolutions—for the right reasons—and make them stand.

The Evolution of Human Rights Theory

In spite of the poor record of the UN, there is no doubt in my mind that UN conventions on human rights, economic rights, and international law represent the highest moral and political thinking humans have ever achieved. And, the work being done toward the *Declaration on the Rights of Indigenous Peoples* is of utmost value, for even if the UN does nothing itself, groups of indigenous peoples will be empowered to summon states, corporations, or individuals before the International Court of Justice in the Hague for violations of the Declaration. While this is no panacea, it does add one strategy not now available. Additionally, the grass-roots organizing among indigenous peoples is having the effect of raising their own self-consciousness. The result of that is the articulation of a philosophical alternative to the fundamental principles of Eurocentric capitalism, the philosophical model which grounds nearly all economic and political thought in the world today. The philosophy of "Indigenism," as Ward Churchill has called it, represents a truly different body of theories about the position of human beings in the world, and therefore a different foundation from which economic and political theory might flow. This philosophy is built into the *UN Declaration on the Rights of Indigenous Peoples* and it is in this sense that the convention represents one of the most significant political moves in the last century—a chance to move human rights theory to a new level beyond that conceived in Eurocentric philosophy. Members of western industrial societies have nearly as much to gain from a "paradigm shift" in their own understanding of the world as indigenous people do. Such a shift is a matter of survival not just for indigenous people but for the whole world caught in a downward spiral of economic consolidation and environmental degradation. Non-indigenous peoples have a lot to learn from those who understand better their relation to the earth and the environment in which they live.

It is useful, then, to consider human rights theory in generations. Indigenism represents a fourth generation of human rights theory, and for Eurocentric thinkers the first paradigm shift in rights theory. Thus,

1st generation	—	the right to own property in one's own name (13th-14th centuries)
2nd generation	—	political and civil rights to participate in government and hold opinions in one's own name (17th-18th centuries)
3rd generation	—	economic and social rights to participate in and benefit from the production of wealth (19th century)
4th generation	—	environmental and cultural rights to a national identity and connectedness to a land base (20th century)

The first generation of human rights in western philosophy concerns property, and human rights theory in the west has never really exceeded that foundation. The right of an individual to own something in an absolute sense forms the essential paradigm for subsequent human rights theory. Superseding it is now our present challenge, since the practice of private property ownership effectively converts the world into a commodity subject to market place definitions which may have nothing to do at all with human (or animal) interests. Property has truly gone out of control. Not many people in the west understand that as little as six hundred years ago, individuals did not have the right to own anything. In early Europe, all property was held to belong only to God who loaned it to humans for their use as long as they remained without sin. Sinners must go propertyless (this, by the way, is the origin of the connection in the west between poverty and moral turpitude). The Catholic pope served as God's vicar and all property was held through him. No individual, not even kings or lords, held property in their own right. Giles of Rome (1246-1316) wrote in *On Ecclesiastical Power*, "The church is more the owner of thy property than thou thyself art." In the thirteenth century, however, this doctrine began to break down with the rise of secular power and modern states. Giles is answered by John of Paris (1250-1310) who in *On Papal and Royal Power* argues that the king, too, can serve as God's vicar (i.e., the divine right of the king) and thus hold property in his own right. This debate between church and state is the origin of property rights doctrine in the west. There is no intrinsic need for individual property rights; rather, they grew out of a rebellion against religious totalitarianism.

As a middle class of tradespersons and shopkeepers arose in the late Middle Ages and Renaissance, the right to own property in one's own power and name was extended beyond the aristocratic classes. The doctrine is finally fully articulated in G. W. F. Hegel's *Philosophy of the Right* published in the early 1800s. Hegel argues that all social, political, and legal rights, indeed, even a right to the status of being "human" derive from the ownership of property because it is only through property that an individual objectifies himself. Without property the individual is really nothing. Pierre Proudhon, forty years after Hegel, in a book called *What is Property* went so far as to suggest that all government is superfluous since property serves as the master system for organizing human communities. While called the father of anarchism, Proudhon is also the father of current libertarianism. The implications of Hegel's views were played out literally in the American experience with the native peoples or people of African descent. The U.S. Supreme Court ruled in 1857 that Dred Scott, an African-American slave, was the property of Mr. Sanford, and since he was property himself and not the owner of property, he had no legal right to himself or to sue for his freedom. In effect, the case proved that because he did not own property, Scott was not entitled to the legal privileges of a human being. He was a thing belonging to Sanford, and the law was not bound to hear arguments from things, only from persons. Hegel's point is that personhood and identity are inextricably bound to property ownership. Two hundred years after Hegel, we know how destructive such a principle can be both for individuals addicted to consumption and for the environment overwhelmed with the by-products of consumption. Property rights theory needs a fundamental revision, but it is not likely to be produced in the west where ownership functions as a fetish.

Largely because of the predominance of property rights theory, the west has never developed an adequate philosophy of the person. When it is not speaking of the human religious character, it is consumed with "economic man." While I cannot explore that issue fully here, I have searched through western literature, mythology, philosophy, and theology for a theory of the person that was not based on some contingency (such as God, an "other," or property) and have not found it. No one can be anything in and of himself. Instead, self knowledge arises only in conflict with some "other," and frequently this is a negative "other" to which the self can be the positive term. Identity based on race, sex, or class work this way. Whites are all of the qualities that blacks are not. The "haves" are everything that the "have nots" are not. Eurocentric people erroneously feel that by owning more and controlling more they will finally feel psychologically whole. Cultural critics have understood this deficiency for quite some time. At the beginning of the 20th century Thorstein Veblen in *The Theory of the Leisure Class* pointed out the dependency of "self" upon "wealth."

I am not suggesting that there is anything wrong with property ownership limited to personal property. I take that as a fundamental human right, but when self depends upon property and property extends to productive resources, natural resources, and empires far beyond anything an individual could use personally, then we should see a psychosis. As the experience worldwide proves, absentee landlordships is a disease or a perversion, not a human right. Whatever selfhood emerges from this sort of ownership is monstrous and perverse. Western literature and history are filled with madmen obsessed with owning things: J. D. Rockefeller, William Randolph Hearst, Howard Hughes, and so on. Probably the most notorious is King Leopold II of Belgium who considered the entire Congo River basin his own personal property and began a campaign of genocide against the indigenous peoples which from the 1880s to the 1910s resulted in the murder of some five to fifteen million people. Ironically, he called his property in central Africa the Congo Free State and his genocidal development policies were promulgated under the name of "Free Trade." Now a hundred years later, we have a new regime of global free trade which will likely produce the same results for indigenous peoples—unless some development in fundamental human rights theory can supersede property ownership rights. Corporations are legally defined as individuals (not as collectives such as peoples or nations) and have from the beginning demonstrated all of the same psychoses about ownership that certain individuals show. In recent years the quest to bring everything under individual or private ownership has led to the defining of information and knowledge as property to be owned by someone. Even the genetic coding of plants, animals, and humans can now be privately owned. Harley Davidson is currently attempting to trademark the sound its motorcycles make so that no one else will be able to make that noise without running the risk of stealing Harley's property. In spite of all the talk about trade, NAFTA and GATT are really more about property rights and freeing up restrictions on capital movement around the world (i.e., buying up property in foreign markets). The restructuring of the "public sector" generally means privatization. There are some in the American right wing, such as Newt Gingrich, who believe collectives and nations should not own anything. Gingrich does not believe in "the social" at all. Everything must be done privately, from private medical savings accounts to pay for health care to the running of schools, parks, and wilderness reserves—everything should be done by private property owners, except of course, the military.

The ultimate cause of this psychosis about private property lies in Christianity's view of mankind as above and essentially different from the natural world. The goal of life is to subdue nature and thereby transcend nature, the body, and time. The thirteenth century represented both a rebellion against Christian anti-materialism and simultaneously an obsessive hatred of nature. In the puritanical strains of Christian thought, nature is evil and must be tamed, subdued, or conquered. As one conquers nature, however, he comes to own it. Max Weber's classic, *The Protestant Ethic and the Spirit of Capitalism*, is essential on this point. Property rights as the foundation of western human rights is, finally, a deeply flawed doctrine, one that urgently needs transformation.

The second generation of human rights concerns civil, intellectual, and religious rights. These were first articulated by Enlightenment writers such as Locke, Rousseau, Condorcet, Diderot, Montesquieu, and others. A determination to exercise these rights fueled the French and American Revolutions of the 18th century, and while the rights initially applied only to the upper classes or land owners, they gradually have been extended to all peoples—at least in theory. Individuals were seen to have a natural right (for atheists) or a God-given right (for believers) to freedom of thought and expression, to freedom of religion, and to a free choice about the kind of government under which one lives. This last freedom, often called social contract theory, holds that political power inheres in people who may choose to transfer some portion of it to a government of their own creation in order to perform more efficiently tasks that whole groups of people chose. This is a significant advance over feudal theory which believed government itself was instituted by God and therefore had inherent powers and rights. Because people are now held to be sovereign, social goals such as justice, education, dignity, equality, peace, and freedom of conscience become thinkable and possible. It is important to recognize that such rights philosophy developed in Europe precisely as a reaction to the oppressive and unjust conditions of feudal monarchism. In other areas of the world at the same time in history, say pre-colonial North America, peoples did not develop a similar philosophy of rights because they had no need for it; they were not oppressed by brutal monarchies or inquisitions determined to torture and execute people who worshipped the creator in a different way. The *United Nations Universal Declaration of Human Rights* (signed by member nations in 1948) embodies this first generation of human rights theory. For example,

> *Article 1.* All human beings are born free and equal in dignity and rights. They are endowed with reason and conscience and should act towards one another in a spirit of brotherhood.
> *Article 2.* Everyone is entitled to all of the rights and freedoms set forth in this Declaration, without distinction of any kind, such as race, colour, sex, language, religion, political or other opinion, national or social origin, property, birth, or other status. . . .
> *Article 21.* 1. Everyone has the right to take part in the Government of his

country, directly or through freely chosen representatives.

    2. Everyone has the right of equal access to public service in his country.

    3. The will of the people shall be the basis of the authority of government; this will shall be expressed in periodic and genuine elections which shall be by universal and equal suffrage and shall be held by secret vote or by equivalent free voting procedures.

This second generation of human rights, as crucial as it surely is, however, does not go very far. It has nothing to say about the social and economic experience of people, and it does not mean that much has to change in the day-to-day lives of most people. Human rights theory needed to move beyond the Enlightenment to a next phase, for human dignity, freedom of conscience and expression, and the right to vote could not mean very much to a person excluded from the economic life of his or her community.

    The third generation of human rights theory focuses on economic and social rights; it arose in the 19th century in reactions to the industrial revolution by Luddites, trade unionists, Marxists, and utopians. Economic and social rights theory rests upon the recognition that the producers of wealth (i.e., workers, not capital owners) ought to benefit from its creation. The most important innovation of this generation is the tentative recognition of humans in collectives or groups. The resources of the world belong to all peoples of the world collectively and the exploitation of these resources should benefit all of the people. While this insight is unworkable in practical economic terms, socialist thinking at this point is beginning to understand the inherent problem in private property rights theory. The third generation of human rights are embodied in the *United Nations International Covenant on Economic, Social, and Cultural Rights*, approved by the United Nations 1966. The United States, however, has so far failed to ratify this convention. The Convention recognizes that all of the rights and powers enumerated in the civil and political rights documents cannot be truly actualized if the economy is controlled by an elite class directing economic activity for its own benefit. For example,

    Considering that, in accordance with the principles proclaimed in the Charter of the United Nations, recognition of the inherent dignity and of the equal and inalienable rights of all members of the human family is the foundation of freedom, justice, and peace in the world,

    Recognizing that these rights derive from the inherent dignity of the human person,

    Recognizing that, in accordance with the Universal Declaration of Human Rights, the ideal of free human beings enjoying freedom from fear and want can only be achieved if conditions are created whereby everyone may enjoy his economic, social and cultural rights, as well as his civil and political rights. . . .

    Article 1. 1. All peoples have the right of self-determination. By virtue of the right they freely determine their political status and freely pursue their economic, social, and cultural development.

2. All peoples may, for their own ends, freely dispose of their natural wealth and resources without prejudice to any obligations arising out of international economic cooperation, based upon the principle of mutual benefit, and international law. In no case may a people be deprived of its own means of subsistence.

Thus the *Covenant* recognizes that human freedom and dignity derive from economic sovereignty, that is, access to and ultimately popular control over the means for producing wealth. In practical terms, that means everyone has a right to a job which pays a wage sufficient to provide for a decent living for the worker and his or her family. In broader terms, this means that societies must have some control over the investment of private capital. Treaties such as GATT and NAFTA which liberate capital to abandon people in a search for lower labor costs run directly counter to the third generation of human rights. Taken together, the second and third generations confirm the point that civil democracy cannot exist without economic democracy. Put another way, economic tyranny is just as bad as civil tyranny, and both violate inherent human rights and are crimes against humanity.

The third generation, therefore, attempts to impose some limitations on property rights doctrine, without directly addressing the meaning of property in western philosophy. Thus we cannot expect economic and social rights to extend very far until some new understanding in property rights takes hold. So far, as demonstrated above, property rights theory has developed only in a linear extension forward to include more and more areas of human experience under the category of property. In a very real sense, the second and third generation of human rights arose as attempts of the "have nots" to protect themselves from the "haves." They have not been very effective. In fact, in recent years with the rise of global free trade, we have seen significant retrenchments in civil, economic, and cultural rights. Organized workers simply cannot risk making demands upon factory owners for fear that they will shut the factory down and move to a lower wage country. We are fast approaching a moment of crisis—a third of the world's population now has no access to the means of making a living. They have been driven from traditional agricultural lands and now driven from workplaces. All the while, corporate profits rise like skyrockets.

The Philosophy of Indigenism

The fourth generation of human rights theory concerns the relations people have with the earth; that is, environmental, territorial, national, and cultural rights. Individuals have an inherent right to a nationality or an ethnicity—to belong to a people, a race, or nation with roots in a specific land area. This is the most important statement of human rights made in modern times. Its implications are vast and, as we see, all other rights depend upon it.

While it is indigenous peoples who are making these demands, similar insights are driving groups of people who have long been dispossessed or exiled from their traditional homes. The basic tenet of multi-culturalism, Afrocentrism, and other efforts of people living in industrial societies is to root themselves in a history or culture that is natural rather than the artificial culture of the "nation-state" or the commodity culture of the marketplace. In this regard, the experience of United States is interesting, for the U.S. has always tried to be the perfect artificial culture, without ethnicity or differing traditions. To be "American" was to belong to a new "American race" grounded in the "nation-state." The founding fathers were quite clear about this. John Quincy Adams wrote that immigrants must "cast off their European skin, never to resume it. They must look forward to their posterity rather than back toward their ancestors." In the 18th and 19th centuries, Blacks or Native Americans were not invited to join this new race, but in the 20th century the message has generally been assimilate or die.[10] The artificiality of the U.S. as a nation-state accounts for the strikingly a-historical consciousness of its citizens; they don't know anything about their history—"their ancestors"—except for American myths. Public schooling has always been more about assimilating immigrants into the "melting pot" of non-ethnic identity (or, more accurately, Anglo-Americanism masquerading as a transparent universal non-ethnic identity for all) than about learning history. In place of ethnicity, national origins (i.e., belonging to a "people"), or natural social relations, America supplants the market place. What it really means to be American is to be identified by one's position in the market, that is, one's relation to the production of commodities or wealth. American identity is solely that of "economic man" or the "bourgeoisie." The fourth generation of human rights is, at least on one level, a right not to be bourgeois. Karl Marx's definition of the bourgeoisie is still best:

> We see, therefore, how the modern bourgeoisie is itself the product of a long course of development, of a series of revolutions in the modes of production and of exchange. . . . The bourgeoisie, wherever it has got the upper hand, has put an end to all feudal, patriarchal, idyllic relations. It has pitilessly torn asunder the motley feudal ties that bound man to his 'natural superiors,' and has left remaining no other nexus between man and man than naked self-interest, than callous 'cash payment' . . . .
>
> The bourgeoisie has stripped of its halo every occupation hitherto honored and looked up to with reverent awe. It has converted the physician, the lawyer, the priest, the poet, the man of science, into its paid wage-laborers. . . .
>
> The bourgeoisie cannot exist without constantly revolutionizing the instruments of production and thereby the relations of production, and with them the whole relations of society. Conservation of the old modes of production in unaltered form, was, on the contrary, the first condition of exist-

ence for all earlier industrial classes. Constant revolutionizing of production, uninterrupted disturbance of all social conditions, everlasting uncertainty and agitation distinguish the bourgeois epoch from all earlier ones. All fixed, fast-frozen relations, with their train of ancient and venerable prejudices and opinions, are swept away, all newly-formed ones become antiquated before they can ossify. All that is solid melts into air, all that is holy is profaned, and man is at last compelled to face with sober senses, his real conditions of life, and his relations with his kind.

The need of a constantly expanding market for its products chases the bourgeoisie over the whole surface of the globe. It must nestle everywhere, settle everywhere, establish connections everywhere.[11]

How can there be any such thing as a bourgeois identity? The fact is there cannot. As a whole, Americans tend to exhibit classic symptoms of maladjustment: aggressiveness, violence, instability, untruthfulness, fetishism with the new, acquisitiveness, drug addiction, wanderlust, and what Christopher Lasch calls in *The Culture of Narcissism* the "banality of pseudo-self-consciousness."[12] Obviously, the American experiment is not working, and yet under the terms "modernization" and "development" it is being forced upon the rest of the world.

The fourth generation, therefore, does not derive from the experience of European or American peoples, but rather from that of indigenous peoples and presents itself as a possible paradigm shift in human rights theory and therefore a potential solution to the nihilism at the root of property rights. While the stated intent of the *Declaration on the Rights of Indigenous Peoples* is to carry forward the rights and powers enumerated in previous declarations and conventions to include indigenous peoples, it grounds those human rights on a different fundamental conception of human nature and human experience in the world. This is the crucial point, and it is just as important for people living in settler or industrial societies as it is for indigenous people. By itself, western philosophy will never resolve the "war of all against all" that Thomas Hobbes in the 17th century said lay at the very foundation of human experience. Hobbes argued that human nature rests upon three essential qualities: diffidence, competition, and egoism[13]— that is, a lack of faith in and alienation from others, a struggle for scarce resources, and a unique or isolated point of view. Of course, Hobbes is only describing the conditions of bourgeois man which are not true for the huge majority of peoples, but it nevertheless forms the core of western philosophy and human rights theory and it has proved to be very useful for capitalists who are able to justify exploitation on the savage nature of the world. The regime of human rights in western philosophy arose to protect us from one another and to regulate competition, but it does not challenge Hobbes fundamental assumptions (except for certain romantics, revolutionaries, and utopians such as Rousseau, Condorcet, Owen, Fourier, and others). It is time to abandon Hobbes and begin building a philosophy on the deep and powerful sympathies humans have with each other and with the earth. There is just very little in the western philosophical tradition on which to build it.

The full text of the *Declaration on the Rights of Indigenous People* is printed in the Appendix to this volume; for the present purposes the *Declaration* stipulates that

> *Article 25.* Indigenous peoples have the right to maintain and strengthen their distinctive spiritual and material relationship with the lands, territories, waters, and coastal seas and other resources which they have traditionally owned or otherwise occupied or used, and to uphold their responsibilities to future generations in this regard.
>
> *Article 26.* Indigenous peoples have the right to own, develop, control and use the lands and territories, including the total environment of the lands, air, waters, coastal seas, sea-ice, flora and fauna and other resources which they have traditionally owned or otherwise occupied or used. This includes the right to the full recognition of their laws, traditions and customs, land-tenure systems and institutions for the development and management of resources, and the right to effective measures by States to prevent any interference with, alienation or encroachment upon these rights.
>
> *Article 27.* Indigenous peoples have the right to the restitution of the lands, territories and resources which they have traditionally owned or otherwise occupied or used, and which have been confiscated, occupied, used or damaged without their free and informed consent. Where this is not possible, they have the right to just and fair compensation. Unless otherwise freely agreed upon by the peoples concerned, compensation shall take the form of lands, territories, and resources equal in quality, size and legal status.

The core of this text is the right of individuals to understand themselves as "a people" or a nation constituted by a spiritual relationship to a specific land area and its history. In the mid-1980s the Cordillera people issued a pact to the Philippine government declaring their nationhood: "As original inhabitants of the Cordillera, we possess the inalienable and primary right to our ancestral domain. We have the right to defend this ancestral domain, and to recover and regain control over lost territories and resources. In order that this right be guaranteed, the Cordillera ancestral domain shall be constituted as an autonomous region. . . ."[14] Indigenous peoples do not see their environment as property and themselves as different or above it; rather they tend to see the environment as culture, part of the fabric within which they live, and their identity as individuals or a community is bound to their environment. Few people remember that Erik Erikson invented the term "identity crisis" in the 1920s to describe the psychological condition of Native Americans he saw living in urban areas or government provided communities on reservations. The vital connections to their traditional homeland had been broken and they suffered as a result. Without such a connection to the land, they could not have a healthy and secure identity.

The truth is that all people suffer in this way but in different degrees. Bourgeois Americans are suffering because of their disconnectedness from anything but the marketplace. Jews long for a homeland in Israel. Palestinians do the same. Edward Said in "Reflections on Exile" shows how the condition of exile has come to dominate 20th century literature, although in a way that is much distanced from the agony of real historical exiles.[15] In a seemingly odd way, the same claim is made by some obvious settler groups. In the United States, members of the Christian Identity movement who claim to be descendants of the original British colonialists call themselves "indigenous Americans" or "native Americans." Sometimes their movement is called "the nativist movement," and it forms a powerful block in the political campaigns of right-wing Republicans. A similar claim is made by white South Africans who are the descendants of the original Dutch settlers. When these two obvious settler communities make such claims, it is clear that they wish to invoke the power of Indigenism to authenticate themselves in relation to others—those others who are more recent settlers and are making claims to the land or those others who are more ancient inhabitants whose claims to the land the *new* nativists wish to negate. What, of course, we see in their claim is not validity but rather the desperation and alienation felt by exiles and settlers everywhere. The psychic conditions of abandonment are real, but the stealing of someone else's land will never resolve it. The opposite is true; they need to stop stealing and start thinking more historically. In South Africa or Zimbabwe, lands stolen from indigenous peoples will have to be returned. This will mean a reduction in wealth and political control by whites, but so be it. The same is true throughout the Americas. No indigenous group is making a claim for the return of all land or the expulsion of any settler community (the opposite is true, indigenous communities are subject to expulsion). There seems to be an acceptance of migration provided essential rights are respected. The absolutist position of expelling peoples is, rather, held by settlers who want all the land and have a history of taking it bit by bit. Jimmie Durham tells about the time he explained American Indian legal rights to a member of the Institute for Policy Studies. The answer he got was "That would mean the break-up of the United States."[16] It seems that the ideology or abstraction "United States" has more validity than the real relations of people to land. This is a sickness, let it break up. Let settlers make do with portions they have and return to Native Americans all the lands they hold by treaty agreement.

In a "Report to the Commission on Indigenous Philosophy," The International Indian Treaty Council wrote,

> The philosophy of the indigenous peoples in the Western Hemisphere has grown from a relationship to the land that extends back thousands of years. It is founded on an observation of natural laws and incorporation of those laws into every aspect of daily life. This philosophy is profoundly different from the predominant economic and geopolitical ideology which governs the practices of the major industrial powers and the operations of

transnational corporations. Its chief characteristic is a great love and respect for the sacred quality of the land which has given birth to and nourished the cultures of indigenous peoples. These peoples are the guardians of their lands which, over the centuries, have become inextricably bound up with their culture, spirits, their identity and survival. Without the land bases, their cultures will not survive.[17]

In a chapter called "I am an Indigenist," Ward Churchill gives a wonderful personal confession of what it means to live the philosophy of Indigenism. He names hundreds of places, people, and events and concludes, "In my view, those—Indian and non-Indian alike—who do not recognize these names and what they represent have no sense of the true history, the reality, of North America. They have no sense of where they've come from or where they are, and thus can have no genuine sense of who or what they are." A few pages farther on, he continues, "Like the historical figures I mentioned earlier, these are names representing positions, struggles, and aspirations which should be well-known to every socially-conscious person in North America. . . . Indigenism offers an antidote to all that [i.e., the a-historicism of assimilated Indians or non-Indians], a vision of how things might be which is based on how things have been since time immemorial, and how things must be once again if the human species, and perhaps the planet itself, is to survive much longer. Predicated in a synthesis of the wisdom attained over thousands of years by indigenous, land-based peoples around the globe—the Fourth World or, as Winona LaDuke puts it, 'the Host World upon which the first, second, and third worlds all sit at the present time.'"[18]

What people in industrialized societies desperately need is a way to place themselves in history. It is only this that will supersede the bourgeois society, the psychotic obsession of owning more and more and exploiting more and more. The implication of this argument is not, however, that settler communities should immediately pack up and move back to where ever they came from. That would be impossible. It is rather about the adoption of a different orientation, a different understanding of their place in the world, one based on an honest account of their history and one that moves beyond the western conception of property rights. I am on slippery ground here, for it has been the history of western peoples to appropriate ideas and values of others, make them over into mass commodities, and sell them to the satisfaction-starved bourgeoisie as some new fetish object. "New Age" philosophy and "whiteshamanism" are but two examples of this process in the American context, what Hopi anthropologist Wendy Rose calls the "Cults of the Culture Vultures."[19] This is not at all what I am advocating, however. These cults arise because bourgeois Americans are, indeed, starved for some deeper sense of connectedness, but in their ignorance of their own history, they continue to practice the very acts of imperialism (in this case, cultural imperialism) that created those feelings of disconnectedness in the first place. As in the case of South Africans noted above, the feelings of exile and alienation cannot be resolved by stealing more land or more anything. So too in the U.S. context. While Euro-Americans can learn a great deal from Native Americans, whiteshamanism is exactly that "banality of pseudo-self-awareness" that Lasch describes as one of the manifestations of this culture of narcissism. Narcissism destroys not only the self but the other as well. What is needed is genuine self transformation based on a genuine historical consciousness. Now this consciousness is not likely, as least for Euro-Americans, to be at all pleasant, for one has to locate himself or herself in the actual world rather than the fantasy world of the market place or the myths about civilizing natives. Part of the history of colonization is ethnocide and environmental devastation. These are not deviations from the core of western values; they reside at the deepest roots of western civilization and philosophy. What are we going to do about it? Feelings of guilt are not the answer. Guilt is only more narcissism, as the guilty one meditates upon his own wounded feelings and becomes quite impressed with his own ability to feel. If the practice of guilt had the ability to change the world, it would never have been taught to intensely by the Catholic or Jewish religions. Guilt is about keeping things just the way they have always been.

What needs to be done is to refuse to elide the great contradiction in western philosophy: the second and third generations of human rights and all of the discourse on justice or equality crash into the historical reality of exploitation, environmental destruction, and ethnocide. The great need of the west is to historicize the values it cherishes only in an abstract sense. It is no accident that students in private-property states are taught to be a-historical.

The fourth generation of human rights offers a model that just might serve as a strategy for effecting a paradigm shift in Eurocentric philosophy. Feminists have taught us to be wary of simply adding cultural elements of marginalized groups to the canon of patriarchal culture. In the same way, the fourth generation of human rights cannot just be added to the earlier generations and leave us happy with the thought that we now have more rights than before but nothing in the basic structure of rights theory changes. Feminists insist that feminism transforms patriarchy. Similarly, fourth generation rights must transform the first three generations, especially the first generation's concept of individual property rights. At the present moment, property (and here I mean land, natural resources, and knowledge, especially) is regarded as a simple commodity, something to be bought and sold. An owner has a right to exploit his property. This is the logic which must be transformed. Vandana Shiva, an anti-GATT activist and researcher in India, points out that no matter how big multi-national corporations grow, they are always too small for the logic of growth. The 1980s and 1990s have seen tremendous growth in the ownership of the world by multi-national corporations. At present, some three hundred corporations own more than one-quarter of the world. The top fifty or so corporations have "economies" larger than three-quarters of all the nation-states on earth. In the United States, the richest one percent of the population owns more than the bottom ninety percent. In spite of all this, corporations or their top management are always just as desperate for growth as the laborers, peasants, tribalists, or indigenous people they dispossess. The logic of private ownership of productive resources creates a culture of desperation for both the top and the bottom of the economic spectrum. While the desperation at the top is more psychosomatic than real, we know that psychoses often lead to more desperate acts than physical deprivation. The logic of ownership is also a logic which has no built in limitations or restraints. It cannot resolve the problems it creates. It only moves forward toward greater and greater consolidation of the earth's wealth in the hands of fewer and fewer owners. The history of King Leopold of Belgium is the archetype for this logic.

If settler communities are ever to overcome the alienation and desperation they manifest, they will have to begin to look on the regions where they live with a different thought process, a different logic. The logic of Subcommandante Marcos provides a model:

> the concept of the land for indigenous people goes beyond what the land produces, or even gives life itself. It's not the same relationship as it is with a peasant, although his relationship with the land is very similar, in that it gives him a livelihood, roots, a goal in life. For the Indian, it's also his link with history. I'm not referring to only the land he works but also the land where he lives, his community and his mountains, his rivers. It is the reference to his historic past that is not limited to something that has already passed, but it is something that is still happening."[20]

When land transcends the commodity system of marketplace, it ceases to be property-as-chattel and becomes a foundation for community. The west has always substituted the market for genuine culture and genuine social relations. For a land based community, the other is no longer on the margins but becomes part of the self. The struggle of indigenous peoples to preserve their ancestral lands and traditions must no longer be the fight of a foreign people, but must be our own fight (those of us who belong to settler communities). When all people who claim to stand for human rights make common cause to support the causes of the most oppressed, then we have transformed the human rights regime from one of self-interest to one of human interest.

Notes

1. Kevin Danaher, "Introduction," *50 Years Is Enough: The Case Against the World Bank and the International Monetary Fund* (Boston: South End Press, 1994), p. 3.

2. Julian Burger, *Report from the Frontier: The State of the World's Indigenous Peoples* (London: Zed Books, 1987), p. 3.

3. Jason Clay, "Looking Back to Go Forward: Predicting and Preventing Human

Rights Violations, "*State of the Peoples: A Global Human Rights Report on Societies in Danger*, ed. Marc S. Miller (Boston: Beacon Press), p. 66. This volume presents a very good overview of current invasions by transnational corporations into the lands of indigenous peoples.

    4. Subcommandante Marcos, *Inter-American Trade Monitor*, January 10, 1994.

    5. Mitchel Cohen, "Murder in Nigeria," *Z Magazine*, February 1996, p. 38.

    6. Paul Lewis, "Rights Groups Say Shell Oil Shares Blame,"*New York Times*, November 11, 1995, A6.

    7. Rigoberta Menchú Tum, "From This Day Forward," *State of the Peoples*, ed. Marc S. Miller. (Boston: Beacon Press, 1993), p. 1.

    8. Butros Butros-Ghali, "Foreword," *Voices of Indigenous Peoples*, ed. Alexander Ewen (Santa Fe, NM: Clear Light Publishers, 1994), p. 12.

    9. William Means, *ibid*. p. 58.

    10. Adams quoted in Arthur Schlesinger, Jr., *The Disuniting of America: Reflections on a Multicultural Society* (New York: W. W. Norton, 1992), p. 25. Schlesinger argues stridently for continuing the American process of de-racinating individuals into an eternal melting pot of American identity.

    11. Karl Marx, *The Communist Manifesto*(Chicago: Henry Regnery Company, 1954), pp. 18-20.

    12. Christopher Lasch, *The Culture of Narcissism: American Life in an Age of Diminishing Expectations* (New York: W. W. Norton, 1979), ch. 4.

    13. Thomas Hobbes, "Of the Natural Condition of Mankind, as Concerning Their Felicity, and Misery," *Leviathan* (New York: Random House, 1968).

    14. The full text of the Pact appears in Julian Burger, *Report from the Frontier*, pp. 153-156.

    15. Edward Said, "Reflections on Exile,"*Out There: Marginalization and Contemporary Culture*, ed. Russell Ferguson, Martha Gever, Trinh T. Minh-ha, and Cornel West. (Cambridge, MA: MIT Press, 1990).

    16. Jimmie Durham, "Cowboys And . . . Notes on Art, Literature, and American Indians in the Modern American Mind, "*The State of Native America: Genocide, Colonialism, and Resistance*, ed. M. Annette Jaimes (Boston: South End Press, 1992), p. 426.

    17. Quoted in Burger, p. 14.

    18. Ward Churchill, *The Struggle for the Land: Indigenous Resistance to Genocide, Ecocide, and Expropriation in Contemporary North America*(Monroe, ME: Common Courage Press, 1993), pp. 404-407.

    19. Wendy Rose, "The Great Pretenders: Further Reflections on Whiteshamanism," *The State of Native America*, p. 414.

    20. Saul Landau, "In the Jungle with Marcos,"*The Progressive*, March 1996, p. 28.

Appendix

1. Excerpts from International Instruments on Refugee Status
2. UN Declaration on the Rights of Indigenous People
3. Women for Mutual Security
4. Contributors to this book

Excerpts from
International Instruments Regarding Refugees and Displaced Persons

The Statute of the Office of the United Nations High Commissioner for Refugees

(Adopted by the UN General Assembly on December 14, 1950 as Annex to General Assembly Resolution 428.V)

Chapter I – General Provisions

1. The United Nations High Commissioner for Refugees, acting under the authority of the General Assembly, shall assume the function of providing international protection, under the auspices of the United Nations, to refugees who fall within the scope of the present Statute and of seeking permanent solutions for the problem of refugees by assisting Governments and, subject to the approval of the Governments concerned, private organizations to facilitate the voluntary repatriation of such refugees, or their assimilation within new national communities. . . .
2. The work of the High Commissioner shall be of an entirely non-political character; it shall be humanitarian and social and shall relate, as a rule, to groups and categories of refugees. . . .
3. The High Commissioner shall follow policy directives given him by the General Assembly or the Economic and Social Council.

Chapter II – Functions of the High Commissioner

6. The competence of the High Commissioner shall extend to:
A (i) Any person who has been considered a refugee under the Arrangements of 12 May 1926 and of 30 June 1928 or under the Conventions of 28 October 1933 and 10 February, the Protocol of 14 September 1939 or the constitution of the International Refugee Organization.

(ii) Any person who, as a result of events occurring before 1 January 1951 and owing to well-founded fear of being persecuted for reason of race, religion, nationality or political opinion, is outside the country of his nationality and is unable or, owing to such fear or for reasons other than personal convenience, is unwilling to avail himself of the protection of that country; or who, not having a nationality and being outside the country of this former habitual residence, is unable or, owing to such fear or for reasons other than personal convenience, is unwilling to return to it.

Decisions as to eligibility taken by the international Refugee Organization during the period of its activities shall not prevent the status of refugee being accorded to persons who fulfill the conditions of the present paragraph.

The competence of the High Commissioner shall cease to apply to any person defined in section A above if:
    (a) He has voluntarily reavailed himself of the protection of the country of this nationality; or
    (b) Having list his nationality, he has voluntarily reacquired it; or
    (c) He has acquired a new nationality, and enjoys the protections of the country of his new nationality; or
    (d) He has voluntarily re-established himself in the country which he left or outside which he remained owing to fear of persecution; or
    (e) He can no longer, because the circumstances in connexion with which he has been recognized as a refugee have ceased to exist, claim grounds other than those of personal convenience for continuing to refuse to avail himself of the protection of the country of this nationality. Reasons of a purely economic character may not be invoked; or
    (f) Being a person who has no nationality, he can no longer, because the circumstances in connexion with which he has been recognized as a refugee have ceased to exist and he is able to return to the country of his former habitual residence, claim grounds other than those of personal convenience for continuing to refuse to return to that country.

B. Any other person who is outside the country of this nationality, or if he has no nationality, the country of his former habitual residence, because he has or had well-founded fear of persecution by reason for his race, religion, nationality or political opinion and is unable or, because of such fear, is unwilling to avail himself of the protection of the government of the country of his nationality, or, if he has not nationality, to return to the country of his former habitual residence.

8. The High commissioner shall provide for the protection of refugees falling under the competence of his Office by:
    (a) Promoting the conclusion and ratification of international conventions for the protection of refugees, supervising their application and proposing amendments thereto;
    (b) Promoting through special agreements with Governments the execution of any measures calculated to improve the situation of refugees and to reduce the number requiring protection;
    (c) Pursuing governmental and private efforts to promote voluntary repatriation or assimilation within new national communities;
    (d) Promoting the admission of refugees, not excluding those in the most destitute categories, to the territories of States;
    (e) Endeavoring to obtain permission for refugees to transfer their assets and especially those necessary for their resettlements;
    (f) Obtaining from Governments information concerning the number and conditions of refugees in their territories and the laws and regulations concerning

them;

(g) Keeping in close touch with Governments and inter-governmental organizations concerned;

(h) Establishing contact in such manner as he may think best with private organizations dealing with refugee questions;

(i) Facilitating the co-ordination of the efforts of private organizations concerned with the welfare of refugees.

9. The High Commissioner shall engage in such additional activities, including repatriation and resettlement, as the General Assembly may determine, within the limits of the resources placed at this disposal.

The 1951 Convention and 1967 Protocol relating to the Status of Refugees

(The Convention was adopted by the UN Conference on the Status of Refugees and Stateless Persons at Geneva from July 2 - 15, 1951 and entered into force on April 22, 1954. The Protocol relating to the Status of Refugees was adopted by the UN General Assembly on December 16, 1966 and came into force on October 4, 1967. The Convention and Protocol are the main instruments that regulate the conduct of States in matters relating to the treatment of refugees. While the Convention does not create a right to asylum, it is important for the legal protection of refugees and the definition of their status. It attempts to establish and international code of rights for refugees on a general basis. It embodies principles that promote and safeguard their rights in the fields of employment, education, residence, freedom of movement, access to courts, naturalization, and, above all, the security against return to a country where they may risk persecution.

The importance of the protocol lies in the fact that it extends the scope of the 1951 Convention by removing the dateline of January 1951 contained in the definition of the term refugee in Article 1 A(2), thus making the Convention applicable to people who become refugees after that date. The 1967 Protocol also provides that the Protocol be applied by States Parties without any geographic limitation. However, if States have opted, when acceding to the 1951 Convention, to limit its application to events occurring in Europe [Article 1B(1)(a)], that limitation also applies to the 1967 Protocol.)

Article 1 – Definition of the term "Refugee"

A(2) [Any person who] . . . owing to well-founded fear of being persecuted for reasons of race, religion, nationality, membership of a particular social group or political opinion, is outside the country of this nationality and is unable to or, owing to such fear, is unwilling to avail himself of the protection of that country; or who, not having a nationality and being outside the country of his former habitual residence . . . is unable or, owing to such fear, is unwilling to return to it (as amended by Article 1(2) of the 1967 protocol)

Article 33 – Prohibition of expulsion or return ("refoulement")

(1) No Contracting State shall expel or return ("refouler") a refugee in any manner

whatsoever to the frontiers of territories where his life for freedom would be threatened on account of his race, religion, nationality, membership of a particular social group or political opinion.

Universal Declaration of Human Rights

(Adopted by the UN General Assembly Resolution 217 A (III), December 10, 1948)

Article 9
No one shall be subjected to arbitrary arrest, detention or exile.

Article 13
(1) Everyone has the right to freedom of movement and residence within borders of each state.
(2) Everyone has the right to leave any country, including his own, and to return to his country.

Article 14
(1) Everyone has the right to seek and enjoy in other countries asylum from persecution.

Article 15
(1) Everyone has the right to a nationality.
(2) No one shall be arbitrarily deprived of this nationality nor denied the right to change his nationality.

International Covenants on Human Rights

(The UN Covenant on Economic, Social, and Cultural Rights and the Covenant on Civil and Political Rights were adopted by the UN General Assembly and opened for signature in December 1966. Both Covenants entered into force in early 1976. The UN has set international human rights standards in some 70 covenants, conventions, and treaties. The two International Covenants noted here are among the UN treaties that impose legally binding obligations on states parties concerning the rights of people under their jurisdiction.)

International Covenant on Civil and Political Rights

Article 2
(1) Each State Party to the present Covenant undertakes to respect and to ensure to all individuals within its territory and subject to its jurisdiction the rights recognized in the present Covenant, without distinction of any kind, such as race, colour, sex,

language, religion, political or other opinion, national or social origin, property, birth or other status.

Article 12
(1) Everyone lawfully within the territory of a State shall, within that territory, have the right to liberty of movement and freedom to choose his residence.
(2) Everyone shall be free to leave any country, including his own.
(3) The above-mentioned rights shall not be subject to any restrictions except those which are provided by law, are necessary to protect national security, public order (*ordre public*), public health or morals or the rights and freedoms of others, and are consistent with other rights recognized in the present Covenant.
(4) No one shall be arbitrarily deprived of the right to enter his own country.

Article 13
An alien lawfully in the territory of a State Party to the present Covenant may be expelled therefrom only in pursuance of a decision reached in accordance with law and shall, except where compelling reasons of national security otherwise require, be allowed to submit the reasons against his expulsion and to have his case reviewed by, and be represented for the purpose before, the competent authority or a person or persons especially designated by the competent authority.

Convention Against Torture and Other Cruel, Inhuman or Degrading Treatment or Punishment

(Approved by consensus by the UN General Assembly on December 10, 1984 as Annex to General Assembly Resolution 39/46. The Convention extends the principle of *non-refoulement* and non-extradition to any State.).

Article 3
(1) No State Party shall expel, return (*"refouler"*) or extradite a person to another State where there are substantial grounds for believing that he would be in danger of being subjected to torture. For the purpose of determining whether there are such grounds, the competent authorities shall take into account all relevant considerations including, where applicable, the existence in the State concerned of a consistent pattern of gross, flagrant or mass violations of human rights.

African Charter on Human and Peoples' Rights

(Adopted by the 18th Assembly of the Heads of State and Government of the Organization of African Unity (OAU) on June 27, 1981 at Nairobi, Kenya.)

Article 12
(3) Every individual shall have the right, when persecuted, to seek and obtain asylum in other countries in accordance with the law of those countries and international conventions.

Organization of African Unity (OAU) Convention Governing the Specific Aspects of Refugee Problems in Africa

(Adopted by the Assembly of Heads of State and Government at its 6th Ordinary Session, Addis Ababa, Ethiopia, September 10, 1969. This Convention adopts a broader definition of the term "refugee" than the internationally accepted definition found in the 1951 Convention and the 1967 Protocol. It does not include any temporal or geographical limitations, nor any reference to earlier categories of refugees. The OAU Convention also regulates the question of asylum. In addition, it unambiguously stipulates that repatriation must be a voluntary act.)

Article I – Definition of the term "Refugee"
1. [Definition as in Article 1 A (2) of the 1951 Convention.]
2. The term "refugee" shall also apply to every person who, owing to external aggression, occupation, foreign domination or events seriously disturbing the public order in either part of the whole of this country of origin or nationality, is compelled to leave his place of habitual residence i order to seek refuge in another place outside his country of origin or nationality.

Article II – Asylum
1. Member States of the OAU shall use their best endeavors consistent with their respective legislations to receive refugees and to secure the settlement of those refugees who, for well-founded reasons, are unable or unwilling to return to their country of origin or nationality.
2. No person shall be subjected by a Member State to measures such as rejection at the frontier, return to expulsion, which would compel him to return to or remain in a territory where his life, physical integrity or liberty would be threatened for the reasons set out in Article I, paragraphs 1 and 2.

Article V – Voluntary Repatriation
1. The essentially voluntary character of repatriation shall be respected in all cases and no refugee shall be repatriated against his will.

Article VIII – Co-operation with the Office of the United Nations High commissioner for Refugees
1. Member States shall co-operate with the Office of the United Nations High Commissioner for Refugees

American Convention on Human Rights "Pact of San José, Costa Rica"

(Signed on November 22, 1969 at the Inter-American Specialized Conference on Human Rights, held at San José, Costa Rica.)

Article 22
(2) Every person has the right to leave any country freely, including his own.

(5) No one can be expelled from the territory of the state of which he is a national or be deprived of the right to enter it.

(7) Every person has the right to seek and be granted asylum in a foreign territory, in accordance with the legislation of the state and international conventions, in the event he is being pursued for political offenses or related common crimes.

(8) In no case may an alien be deported or returned to a county, regardless of whether or mot it is his country of origin, if in that country his right to life or personal freedom is in danger of being violated because of his race, nationality, religion, social status or political opinion.

Source for the above documents: "International Instruments and Their Significance," Annual Report of the UN High Commissioner for Refugees, 1995.

United Nations Declaration on the Rights of Indigenous Peoples

(Draft Declaration as Agreed upon by the Members of the Working Group at its Eleventh Session. Complete text.)

Affirming that indigenous peoples are equal in dignity and rights to all other peoples, while recognizing the right of all peoples to be different, to consider themselves different, and to be respected as such,

Affirming also that all peoples contribute to the diversity and richness of civilization and cultures, which constitute the common heritage of humankind,

Affirming further that all doctrines, policies and practices based on or advocating superiority of peoples or individuals on the basis of national origin, racial, religious, ethnic or cultural differences are racist, scientifically false, legally invalid, morally condemnable and socially unjust,

Reaffirming also that indigenous peoples, in the exercise of their rights, should be free from discrimination of any kind,

Concerned that indigenous peoples have been deprived of their human rights and fundamental freedoms, resulting, *inter alia*, in their colonization and dispossession of their lands, territories and resources, thus preventing them from exercising, in particular, their right to development in accordance with their own needs and interests,

Recognizing the urgent need to respect and promote the inherent rights and characteristics of indigenous peoples, especially their rights to their lands, territories and resources, which derive from their political, economic and social structures and from their cultures, spiritual traditions, histories and philosophies,

Welcoming the fact that indigenous peoples are organizing themselves for political, economic, social and cultural enhancement and in order to bring an end to all forms of discrimination and oppression wherever they occur,

Convinced that control by indigenous peoples over developments affecting them and their lands, territories and resources will enable them to maintain and strengthen their institutions, cultures and traditions, and to promote their development in accordance with their aspirations and needs,

Recognizing also that respect for indigenous knowledge, cultures and traditional practices contributes to sustainable and equitable development and proper management of the environment,

Emphasizing the need for demilitarization of the lands and territories of indigenous peoples, which will contribute to peace, economic and social progress and development, understanding and friendly relations among nations and peoples of the world,

Recognizing in particular the right of indigenous families and communities to retain shared responsibility for the upbringing, training, education and well-being of their children,

Recognizing also that indigenous peoples have the right freely to determine their relationships with States in a spirit of coexistence, mutual benefit and full respect,

Considering that treaties, agreements and other arrangements between States and indigenous peoples are properly matters of international concern and responsibility,

Acknowledging that the Charter of the United Nations, the International Covenant on Economic, Social and Cultural Rights and the International Covenant on Civil and Political Rights affirm the fundamental importance of the right of self-determination of all peoples, by virtue of which they freely determine their political status and freely pursue their economic, social and cultural development,

Bearing in mind that nothing in this Declaration may be used to deny any peoples their right of self-determination,

Encouraging States to comply with and effectively implement all international instruments, in particular those related to human rights, as they apply to indigenous peoples, in consultation and cooperation with the peoples concerned,

Emphasizing that the United Nations has an important and continuing role to play in promoting and protecting the rights of indigenous peoples,

Believing that this Declaration is a further important step forward for the recognition, promotion and protection of the rights and freedoms of indigenous peoples and in the development of relevant activities of the United Nations system in this field,

Solemnly proclaims the following United Nations Declaration on the Rights of Indigenous Peoples:

Part I

Article 1. Indigenous peoples have the right to the full and effective enjoyment of all human rights and fundamental freedoms recognized in the Charter of the United Nations, the Universal Declaration of Human Rights and international human rights law.

Article 2. Indigenous individuals and peoples are free and equal to all other individuals and peoples in dignity and rights, and have the right to be free from any kind of adverse discrimination, in particular that based on their indigenous origin or identity.

Article 3. Indigenous peoples have the right of self-determination. By virtue of that right they freely determine their political status and freely pursue their economic, social and cultural development.

Article 4. Indigenous peoples have the right to maintain and strengthen their distinct political, economic, social and cultural characteristics, as well as their legal systems, while retaining their rights to participate fully, if they so choose, in the political, economic, social and cultural life of the State.

Article 5. Every indigenous individual has the right to a nationality.

Part II

Article 6. Indigenous peoples have the collective right to live in freedom, peace and security as distinct peoples and to full guarantees against genocide or any other act of violence, including the removal of indigenous children from their families and communities under any pretext.

In addition, they have the individual rights to life, physical and mental integrity, liberty and security of person.

Article 7. Indigenous peoples have the collective and individual right not to be subjected to ethnocide and cultural genocide, including prevention of and redress for:

(a) Any action which has the aim or effect of depriving them of their integrity as distinct peoples, or of their cultural values or ethnic identities;

(b) Any action which has the aim or effect of dispossessing them of their lands, territories or resources;

(c) Any form of population transfer which has the aim or effect of violating or undermining any of their rights;

(d) Any form of assimilation or integration by other cultures or ways of life imposed on them by legislative, administrative or other measures;

(e) Any form of propaganda directed against them.

Article 8. Indigenous peoples have the collective and individual right to maintain and develop their distinct identities and characteristics, including the right to identify themselves as indigenous and to be recognized as such.

Article 9. Indigenous peoples and individuals have the right to belong to an indigenous community or nation, in accordance with the traditions and customs of the community or nation concerned. No disadvantage of any kind may arise from the exercise of such a right.

Article 10. Indigenous peoples shall not be forcibly removed from their lands or territories. No relocation shall take place without the free and informed consent of the indigenous peoples concerned and after agreement on just and fair compensation and, where possible, with the option of return.

Article 11. Indigenous peoples have the right to special protection and security in periods of armed conflict.

States shall observe international standards, in particular the Fourth Geneva Convention of 1949, for the protection of civilian populations in circumstances of emergency and armed conflict, and shall not:

(a) Recruit indigenous individuals against their will into the armed forces and, in particular, for use against other indigenous peoples;

(b) Recruit indigenous children into the armed forces under any circumstances;

(c) Force indigenous individuals to abandon their land, territories or means of subsistence, or relocate them in special centers for military purposes;

(d) Force indigenous individuals to work for military purposes under any discriminatory conditions.

Part III

Article 12. Indigenous peoples have the right to practice and revitalize their cultural traditions and customs. This includes the right to maintain, protect and develop the past, present and future manifestations of their cultures, such as archaeological and historical sites, artifacts, designs, ceremonies, technologies and visual and performing arts and literature, as well as the right to the restitution of cultural, intellectual, religious and spiritual property taken without their free and informed consent or in violation of their laws, traditions and customs.

Article 13. Indigenous peoples have the right to manifest, practice, develop and teach their spiritual and religious traditions, customs and ceremonies; the right to maintain, protect, and have access in privacy to their religious and cultural sites; the right to the use and control of ceremonial objects; and the right to the repatriation of human remains.

States shall take effective measures, in conjunction with the indigenous people concerned, to ensure that indigenous sacred places, including burial sites, be preserved, respected and protected.

Article 14. Indigenous peoples have the right to revitalize, use, develop and transmit to future generations their histories, languages, oral traditions, philosophies, writing systems and literatures, and to designate and retain their own names for communities, places and persons.

States shall take effective measures, whenever any rights of indigenous peoples may be threatened, to ensure this right is protected and also to ensure that they can understand and be understood in political, legal and administrative proceedings, where necessary through the provision of interpretation or by other appropriate means.

Part IV

Article 15. Indigenous children have the right to all levels and forms of education of the State. All indigenous peoples also have this right and the right to establish and control their educational systems and institutions providing education in their own languages, in a manner appropriate to their cultural methods of teaching and learning.

Indigenous children living outside their communities have the right to be provided access to education in their own culture and language.

States shall take effective measures to provide appropriate resources for these purposes.

Article 16. Indigenous peoples have the right to have the dignity and diversity of their cultures, traditions, histories and aspirations appropriately reflected in all forms of education and public information.

States shall take effective measures, in consultation with the indigenous peoples concerned, to eliminate prejudice and discrimination and to promote tolerance, understanding and good relations among indigenous peoples and all segments of society.

Article 17. Indigenous peoples have the right to establish their own media in their own languages. They also have the right to equal access to all forms of non-indigenous media.

States shall take effective measures to ensure that state-owned media duly reflect indigenous cultural diversity.

Article 18. Indigenous peoples have the right to enjoy fully all rights established under international labor law and national labor legislation.

Indigenous individuals have the right not to be subjected to any discriminatory conditions of labor, employment or salary.

Part V

Article 19. Indigenous peoples have the right to participate fully, if they so choose, at all levels of decision-making in matters which may affect their rights, lives and destinies through representatives chosen by themselves in accordance with their own procedures, as well as to maintain and develop their own indigenous decision-making institutions.

Article 20. Indigenous peoples have the right to participate fully, if they so choose, through procedures determined by them, in devising legislative or administrative measures that may affect them.

States shall obtain the free and informed consent of the peoples concerned before adopting and implementing such measures.

Article 21. Indigenous peoples have the right to maintain and develop their political, economic and social systems, to be secure in the enjoyment of their own means of subsistence and development, and to engage freely in all their traditional and other economic activities. Indigenous peoples who have been deprived of their means of subsistence and development are entitled to just and fair compensation.

Article 22. Indigenous peoples have the right to special measures for the immediate, effective and continuing improvement of their economic and social conditions, including in the areas of employment, vocational training and retraining, housing, sanitation, health and social security.

Particular attention shall be paid to the rights and special needs of indigenous elders, women, youth, children and disabled persons.

Article 23. Indigenous peoples have the right to determine and develop priorities and strategies for exercising their right to development. In particular, indigenous peoples have the right to determine and develop all health, housing and other economic and social programs affecting them and, as far as possible, to administer such programs through their own institutions.

Article 24. Indigenous peoples have the right to their traditional medicines and health practices, including the right to the protection of vital medicinal plants, animals and minerals.

They also have the right to access, without any discrimination, to all medical institutions, health services and medical care.

Part VI

Article 25. Indigenous peoples have the right to maintain and strengthen their distinctive spiritual and material relationship with the lands, territories, waters and coastal seas and other resources which they have traditionally owned or otherwise occupied or used, and to uphold their responsibilities to future generations in this regard.

Article 26. Indigenous peoples have the right to own, develop, control and use the lands and territories, including the total environment of the lands, air, waters, coastal seas, sea-ice, flora and fauna and other resources which they have traditionally owned or otherwise occupied or used. This includes the right to the full recognition of their laws, traditions and customs, land-tenure systems and institutions for the development and management of resources, and the right to effective measures by States to prevent any interference with, alienation of or encroachment upon these rights.

Article 27. Indigenous peoples have the right to the restitution of the lands, territories and resources which they have traditionally owned or otherwise occupied or used, and which have been confiscated, occupied, used or damaged without their free and informed consent. Where this is not possible, they have the right to just and fair compensation. Unless otherwise freely agreed upon by the peoples concerned, compensation shall take the form of lands, territories and resources equal in quality, size and legal status.

Article 28. Indigenous peoples have the right to the conservation, restoration and protection of the total environment and the productive capacity of their lands, territories and resources, as well as to assistance for this purpose from States and through international cooperation. Military activities shall not take place in the lands and territories of indigenous peoples, unless otherwise freely agreed upon by the peoples concerned.

States shall take effective measures to ensure that no storage or disposal of hazardous materials shall take place in the lands and territories of indigenous peoples.

States shall also take effective measures to ensure, as needed, that programs for monitoring, maintaining and restoring the health of indigenous peoples, as developed and implemented by the peoples affected by such materials, are duly implemented.

Article 29. Indigenous peoples are entitled to the recognition of the full ownership, control and protection of their cultural and intellectual property. They have the right to special measures to control, develop and protect their sciences, technologies and cultural manifestations, including human and other genetic resources, seeds, medicines, knowledge of the properties of fauna and flora, oral traditions, literatures, designs and visual and performing arts.

Article 30. Indigenous peoples have the right to determine and develop priorities and strategies for the development or use of their lands, territories and other resources, including the right to require that States obtain their free and informed consent prior to the approval of any project affecting their lands, territories and other resources, particularly in connection with the development, utilization or exploitation of mineral, water or other resources. Pursuant to agreement with the indigenous peoples concerned, just and fair compensation shall be provided for any such activities and measures taken to mitigate adverse environmental, economic, social, cultural or spiritual impact.

Part VII

Article 31. Indigenous peoples, as a specific form of exercising their right to self-determination, have the right to autonomy or self-government in matters relating to their internal and local affairs, including culture, religion, education, information, media, health, housing, employment, social welfare, economic activities, land and resources management, environment and entry by non-members, as well as ways and means for financing these autonomous functions.

Article 32. Indigenous peoples have the collective right to determine their own citizenship in accordance with their customs and traditions. Indigenous citizenship does not impair the right of indigenous individuals to obtain citizenship of the States in which they live.

Indigenous peoples have the right to determine the structures and to select the membership of their institutions in accordance with their own procedures.

Article 33. Indigenous peoples have the right to promote, develop and maintain their institutional structures and their distinctive juridical customs, traditions, procedures and practices, in accordance with internationally recognized human rights standards.

Article 34. Indigenous peoples have the collective right to determine the responsibilities of individuals to their communities.

Article 35. Indigenous peoples, in particular those divided by international borders, have the right to maintain and develop contacts, relations and cooperation, including activities for spiritual, cultural, political, economic and social purposes, with other peoples across borders.

States shall take effective measures to ensure the exercise and implementation of this right.

Article 36. Indigenous peoples have the right to the recognition, observance and enforcement of treaties, agreements and other constructive arrangements concluded with States or their successors, according to their original spirit and intent, and to have States honor and respect such treaties, agreements and other constructive arrangements. Conflicts and disputes which cannot otherwise be settled should be submitted to competent international bodies agreed to by all parties concerned.

Part VIII

Article 37. States shall take effective and appropriate measures, in consultation with the indigenous peoples concerned, to give full effect to the provisions of this Declaration. The rights recognized herein shall be adopted and included in national legislation in such a manner that indigenous peoples can avail themselves of such rights in practice.

Article 38. Indigenous peoples have the right to have access to adequate financial and technical assistance, from States and through international cooperation, to pursue freely their political, economic, social, cultural and spiritual development and for the enjoyment of the rights and freedoms recognized in this Declaration.

Article 39. Indigenous peoples have the right to have access to and prompt decision through mutually acceptable and fair procedures for the resolution of conflicts and disputes with States, as well as to effective remedies for all infringements of their individual and collective rights. Such a decision shall take into consideration the customs, traditions, rules and legal systems of the indigenous peoples concerned.

Article 40. The organs and specialized agencies of the United Nations system and other intergovernmental organizations shall contribute to the full realization of the provisions of this Declaration through the mobilization, *inter alia*, of financial cooperation and technical assistance. Ways and means of ensuring participation of indigenous peoples on issues affecting them shall be established.

Article 41. The United Nations shall take the necessary steps to ensure the implementation of this Declaration including the creation of a body at the highest level with special competence in this field and with the direct participation of indigenous peoples. All United Nations bodies shall promote respect for and full application of the provisions of this Declaration.

Part IX

Article 42. The rights recognized herein constitute the minimum standards for the survival, dignity and well-being of the indigenous peoples of the world.

Article 43. All the rights and freedoms recognized herein are equally guaranteed to male and female indigenous individuals.

Article 44. Nothing in this Declaration may be construed as diminishing or extinguishing existing or future rights indigenous peoples may have or acquire.

Article 45. Nothing in this Declaration may be interpreted as implying for any State, group or person any right to engage in any activity or to perform any act contrary to the Charter of the United Nations.

Women for Mutual Security
Statement of Purpose

Women for Mutual Security is a network of women's organizations and individuals committed to making a paradigm shift in the world from the dominant hierarchical and violent model of society to a new cooperative and peaceful model.

We specifically oppose nuclear weapons, the arms race and the militarization of international relations which express the mentality of patriarchal thinking. We take an organic view of humanity and nature, stressing the oneness of all life and the interconnections of all phenomenon. This kind of society involves the sharing of global resources across classes, nations, ethnic groups and the sexes.

WMS develops projects on issues involving conflict resolution, environmental protection, and human economic development, new institutions for peace and justice. We do not duplicate the efforts of our member groups, but work with them on world community objectives, believing in the strength of integrated action and initiative.

We believe that common security cannot be achieved without the leadership of women. We see women, and men who share our vision, as the true agents of social change in the coming century.

We support the *Universal Declaration of Human Rights* and other international covenants protecting civil, political, social, economic and cultural rights. Our struggle for change is creative, holistic and appeals to human needs which celebrate nature, life and the spirit of community

(This revision of our 1986 statement was made in March 1993)

Global Coordinator: Margarita Papandreou, Greece

Vicki Rutter - Australia; Leona Detiege - Belgium; Jacqueline Pitanguy - Brazil; Rosalie Bertell, Madeleine Gilchrist, Kay MacPherson - Canada; Stanislava Hybnerova - Czech; Hilkka Pietila - Finland; Cecile Goldet - France; Lilo Klug - Germany; Joyce Aryee - Ghana; Dessima Williams - Grenada; Margaret Alva - India; Roni Ben Efrat - Israel; P. M. Asiyo - Kenya; A. Van Melle-Hermans - Netherlands; Helen Clark - New Zealand; Bianca Jagger - Nicaragua; Berit As - Norway; Isla Jad - Palestine; Louise Aitsi - Papua New Guinea; Elena Kamenetskaya - Russia; Nomonde Ngubo - South Africa; Anna Balletbo I Puig - Spain; Hema Goonatilake - Sri Lanka; Najah Atar - Syria; Blanche Cooke, Lenora Foerstel, La Donna Harris, Ellen Ray, E. Faye Williams - U.S.A.; Hilda Lini - Vanuatu

1, Romilias Str., GR. 14671 Kastri, Greece (301) 88.43.202 / (301) 80.12.850

A list of Women for Mutual Security's activities includes the following:

The International Assembly of Women, Athens, November 1986, with complete representation of East-West bloc countries participating on an equal basis, and of other countries from all regions of the world. This was the founding meeting of an international women's peace network.

The Women's Defense Dialogue with NATO, Brussels, June 1987, under the auspices of WMS and NATO Alerts Network, when women from 14 countries met with the NATO ambassadors to discuss nuclear disarmament. Special session with Lord Carrington, general secretary of NATO.

Congressional Hearings, Washington, D.C., December 1987, with women from twelve countries who gave evidence to U.S. congresswomen on the occasion of the signing of the INF Treaty.

The Warsaw Pact Women's Dialogue, Sofia, Bulgaria, March 1988, organized by WMS and the NATO Alerts Network and the Oxford Research Group to bring women leader from East and West for a discussion with the foreign ministers of the Warsaw Pact countries in an effort to break down the barriers between the two military blocs.

Women Leaders and the NATO Defense Ministers Meeting, Brussels, April 1, 1988 when women from seven NATO countries pursued their defense ministers with demands for more rapid nuclear disarmament and a review of the political developments in Europe and the Soviet Union in connection with the raison d'être of NATO.

The Women's Summit, Greece, April/May 1988, organized by WMS and attended by women leaders from the U.S. and the USSR and resource people from nine other countries. The group produced a Peace Platform which was presented to the Soviet Foreign Minister and the US Assistant Secretary of State in Moscow at the super-power summit, June 1988.

Women Leaders at the Moscow/U.S. Summit, Moscow, June 1988. International women leaders held meetings with Raisa Gorbachev, Mikhail Gorbachev, Rozanne Ridgway from the U.S. State Department, Soviet General Nikolai Chervov and Foreign Minister Shervenadze to discuss militarization, nuclear disarmament and peace initiatives.

NATO and Warsaw Pact Women, in Brussels, December 1988. Organized in conjunction with NATO Alert Network. This was a "first" in NATO history when NGO women from Eastern Europe were brought in by their counterparts in Western countries to meet with NATO authorities and ministers to discuss East-West problems.

Environment and International Security, in Athens, April 21-24, 1989, organized by WMS to formulate, along with W.I.D.F. and UNIDO and representatives of 15 countries, a women's environmental platform for use by governments and political activists.

NATO Dialogue - Comprehensive Concept, Brussels, April 28-30, 1989, to launch proposal for NATO to take a dynamic initiative in arms control and security policy.

International Meeting, "Women, Peace, Ecology," Moscow, May 31-June 7, 1989, for international cooperation in the field of environmental protection. WMS participation and leadership.

NATO Defense Dialogue, Brussels, May 21-23, 1990, under auspices of NATO Alert Network in collaboration with WMS, with women from 13 NATO countries and 6 Warsaw Pact countries to discuss the developing problems of a post-Cold War Europe.

Women's International Gulf Peace Initiative 1, trip to Iraq, January 7-11, 1991, by women representing international organizations in all parts of the world, to work out a peace plan with the Federation of Iraqi Women in an attempt to avert war.

South Pacific international Policy Congress, Vanuatu, January 6-12, 1991. Book on the Congress published in the Fall, 1991, called *Women's Voices on the Pacific* describing how the meeting dealt with the problems of nuclear testing in the Pacific and women's role in confronting this problem. Women from the islands, Australia, New Zealand, Europe and North America participated.

Women's International Gulf Peace Initiative II, May 16-24, 1991, post-war fact-finding mission. Film makers from England and Belgium documented the findings in an attempt to mobilize humanitarian aid and to stop the sanctions. A team of five women from WMS, some of whom were in the first Initiative, organized this trip in conjunction with WILPF and the Federation of Iraqi Women.

Campaign for a Woman Secretary General of the United Nations, June-November 1991. In addition to letters and articles, and mobilization of other women's organization, an international group of women visited the United Nations to meet with representatives countries in the Security Council to gain support for this campaign.

Palestinian - Israeli Women's Negotiation Seminar, "Palestinian Women and Children under Occupation: Humanitarian and Political Solution," May 21-26, 1992, Athens. This seminar, with Palestinian and Israeli women, was facilitated by two qualified persons in conflict management, and was followed by a three day fact-finding trip in Israel, the West Bank, and the Gaza Strip, by a team of WMS members. Book about seminar in process.

First International Minoan Celebration of Partnership, October 4-11, 1992, Crete, Greece, a conference of 450 persons from 41 countries. The Minoan civilization was a peaceful society with a great reverence for nature. The conference reconnected with these early traditions in order to explore healthier and more balanced alternatives for the present and for the future. The work done at this Celebration, designed primarily for social change activists provided an urgently needed positively vision for our future. Book in process. This unique event was intended, also, to furnish a sample format, both in substance and in organizational style, for the UN International Women's Conference in China in 1995.

Panels UN, March, 1994, WMS conducted two panels in conjunction with the NGO preparatory activities for the China Forum. One panel was on "Women and the Mass Media," the other on "Refugee Women in Times of Conflict." WMS joined with other organizations to hold workshops in the Peace Tent on these subjects at the Forum of the UN Fourth International Conference on Women.

Human Rights of Women, April 20-22, 1994, WMS group of four women participated in this conference in Baghdad, Iraq, organized by the Iraqi Federation of Women. The Group of Four presented a program for lobbying in the States for ending the sanctions on the people of Iraq. Activities are ongoing.

Pre-China Forum Dialogue, "Refugee and Displaced Women in Times of Conflict," Athens, Greece, September 15, 16, 17, 1994. Collaborating agencies: Sisterhood is Global Institute (SIGI), Refugee Women in Development (REFwid), WILPF, jointly with the UN High Commission on Refugees (UNHCR). Organized locally by Center Research and Action on Peace (KEDE). Purpose of Dialogue was to give women refugee and refugee advocates from around the world a voice in the international arena, starting with this Dialogue in Athens and carrying on to the UN Forum in Beijing in 1995.

Second International Athens Conference Against the Embargo on Iraq. WMS played leading role in organizing this conference, bringing high-level women and men from a over the world to participate. This was part of the ongoing project for ending sanctions o the people of Iraq.

Demonstration outside United Nations, New York, March 13, 1995. Organized with Ramsey Clark's IAC (International Action Center) at the time of Security Council deliberations on sanctions on Iraq. Speakers Ramsey Clark, Tariq Aziz (deputy prime minister of Iraq), and Margarita Papandreou spoke at a meeting "The Silent War Against Iraq."

Contributors

Roni Ben-Efrat is a member of the editorial board of *Challenge/Etgar* magazine, published and written by Israeli and Palestinian journalists. Ben-Efrat is one of the founders of both Women in Black and the Women and Peace Coalition. After the 1987 outbreak of the Intifada, she served nine months in an Israeli jail on charges of having illegal contacts with the Democratic Front for the Liberation of Palestine. She is also on the Board of Women for Mutual Security.

Ward Churchill (Creek/Cherokee Métis) is a coordinator of the Colorado Chapter of the American Indian Movement, Director of Planning, Research and Development for Educational Opportunity Programs at the University of Colorado, and is co-director of the Institute for Natural Progress. Author of numerous books, including *Fantasies of the Master Race: Literature, Cinema and the Colonization of American Indians*.

Julia Panourgia Clones is an economist and environment and gender specialist with over 35 years of experience in Africa, Europe and North America. She was the Economic Minister at the Greek Embassy in the U.S. and served as Permanent Representative of Greece to the World Bank Group for nearly eight years. She is the Acting Chair of World Women in Development and Environment Network. WorldWIDE is a global nongovernmental organization with chapters in numerous countries.

Yvonne Deutsh is a social worker and coordinator of the feminist center Kol Ha Isha (Women's Voice) in Jerusalem. She is among the organizers of Women in Black and is on the board of the Association for Women of the Mediterranean Area based in Malta. Ms. Deutsh lives with Andre Rosenthal, one of the few Jewish lawyers who defends Palestinian human rights.

Jeff Drumtra is an African policy analyst for the U.S. Committee for Refugees (USCR). He has conducted site visits to assess refugee issues in Somalia, Kenya, Mozambique, Zimbabwe, Malawi, Rwanda, Burundi, Zaire, Thailand, Cambodia, and Burma. Drumtia also works as the USCR's Congressional liaison on U.S. budget issues affecting refugee programs, and regularly testifies at Congressional hearings on budget issues affecting international refugee assistance. The USRC is a nongovernmental, nonprofit organization located in Washington, DC.

Frances Tarlton Farenthold is a Distinguished Visiting Professor at the Thurgood Marshall School of Law at the Texas Southern University in Houston, Texas. She served in the Texas House of Representatives from 1968-1973. In 1972, Farenthold's name was placed on the nomination ballot for Vice President of the United States at the Democratic National Convention. She became the first chair of the National Women's Caucus in 1973, and served as President of Wells College from 1976-1989. She is also on the Board of Women for Mutual Security.

Sara Flounders is co-director of the International Action Center, an organization established in 1991 by former U.S. Attorney General Ramsey Clark to oppose U.S. militarism and war. She was coordinator of the International Commission on U.S. War

Crimes in the Middle East in 1992, which brought leaders from 30 countries together for the International War Crimes Tribunal on the Gulf War. This commission held hearings in 20 countries and 30 U.S. cities. She edited the book, *War Crimes: A Report on U.S. War Crimes Against Iraq* (Maisonneuve Press, 1992) and coordinated research for Clark's book, *The Fire This Time*. She is a Board Member of WMS.

Lenora Foerstel is a cultural historian whose research on the South Pacific included extended field work with Dr. Margaret Mead in Papua New Guinea. She has written numerous articles, produced several films, and recently co-authored a book, *Confronting the Margaret Mead Legacy: Scholarship, Empire and the South Pacific*. She has been the North American Coordinator for Women for Mutual Security since 1990. She has served as a delegate to the First International Conference on Women, Peace, and the Environment, held in Moscow in 1989. She coordinated and convened the 1991 International Pacific Policy Congress in Vanuatu, and served as a delegate to the Population and Development Conference held in Cairo, Egypt, September, 1994.

Sean Gervasi is an American economist and political scientist. He has taught most of the last thirty years in England and France, at the London School of Economics, Oxford University, and the University of Paris. He has spent fifteen years as a consultant in various organs of the United Nations. He is presently Research Professor at the Institute of Internal Politics and Economics in Belgrade.

Amy Goodman is a radio journalist working for Pacifica Network News, WBAI in New York and WPFW in Washington, DC.

Teresa Gutierrez is the Director of the International Peace for Cuba Appeal. She has traveled to Cuba many times and has organized medical aid to Cuba. She was the main organizer of the New York Javits Convention Center Rally in Solidarity with Cuba in 1992. She was also co-director of the Commission of Inquiry on the U.S. Invasion of Panama and has participated in two delegations to Chiapas, Mexico.

Jocelyn McCalla is Executive Director of the National Coalition for Haitian Refugees (NCHR). McCalla also serves on the Board of Human Rights Watch/Americas, the National Immigration Forum, and the Haitian Studies Association. Under McCalla's leadership, the NCHR has actively worked to protect the rights of Haitian asylum-seekers under international and U.S. law and helped promote human rights and democratic leadership in Haiti. He has edited, authored and co-authored numerous works and is considered a major authority on the issues concerning Haitian refugees.

Robert Merrill the chief editor of Maisonneuve Press and has written on postmodernism, terrorism, as well as literature. In 1988, he founded the Institute for Advanced Cultural Studies, a non-profit organization committed to social change through cultural analysis. He has taught at the Catholic University in Washington, D.C. and at Penn State University. Currently he is coordinator of the Liberal Arts Division at Maryland Institute, College of Art in Baltimore, MD.

Margarita Papandreou is president of the center for Research and Action on Peace (Greece) and is Global Network Coordinator for Women for Mutual Security (international). As the former First Lady of Greece, she helped found the Women's Union of Greece in 1976, a nationwide, independent feminist organization. She was influential in pressing for numerous reforms enhancing the legal and social status of women in Greek society, abolishing the dowry system, introducing civil marriage, legalizing abortion, and securing pensions for farm women. The network she created (WMS) was represented at all of the former US/USSR Summits, as well as at several NATO and Warsaw Pact meetings. She is the author of "Nightmare in Athens" which documents the rise and fall of the Greek military dictatorship. More recently, she has published Excerpt from "A Political Wife"

Nicholas C. Papandreou is an economist and author who served as the Chief Economist at Asia Capital Management. Between 1989-1991 he collaborated with a multi-divisional World Bank team on solving issues covering the Middle East and North Africa. As a financial analyst in Athens, Greece, he worked on a five-year plan for the Ministry's foreign exchange needs. Mr. Papandreou was also a columnist for the Greek weekly *Economicos Tachydromos*. He is well known for his publications on economics, as well as his literary works.

Georgina Ritchie has researched and taught alternative healing for 17 years. She presented a paper on Psychic Healing at the First European Congress of Hypnosis in Psychotherapy and Psychosomatic Medicine. As a counseling practitioner, she works with doctors, lawyers and commercial firms on resolving conflicts. Ms. Ritchie is also a Board Member of Women for Mutual Security.

Jemera Rone has investigated human rights and rules of war abuses for over ten years as council to Human Rights Watch, during five years of which she was based in El Salvador. H.R.W. is a nongovernmental organization established to monitor and promote the observance of internationally recognized human rights. She has investigated abuses in Angola, Sudan, Azerbaijan, Georgia, Philippines, Iraqi Kurdistan, Brazil, Croatia, Yemen, Guatemala, Nicaragua, and El Salvador, as well as abuses during the Gulf War. She practiced law in New York city for ten years. She has authored and co-authored many books and articles.

Amartya Sen, Lamont University Professor at Harvard University, is a Fellow of the British Academy and an Honorary Member of the American Academy of Arts and Sciences. He has taught at Cambridge, Calcutta, Delhi, London, and Oxford where he was the Drummond Professor of Political Economy. He is past president of the Econometric Society, the International Economic Association, and the American Economic Association. Sen has published widely. Among his many books are *Collective Choice and Social Welfare* and *Economic Inequality*.

Lilia S. Velasquez is an attorney in private practice specializing in immigration and nationality law in San Diego, California. She is an adjunct professor of law at California Western School of Law, where she teaches Immigration and Nationality Law, and is the Consulting Attorney in Immigration Law for the Consulate General of Mexico in San Diego. She has lectured extensively on immigration and asylum law in the United States and Mexico, and has delivered conferences on refugee women in Athens, Greece and Vienna, Austria. She was featured in *Citizens Stories*, an educational video produced by the Smithsonian Institute and the Close Up Foundation for services rendered to the immigrant community; and in *The Barrister* "20 Young Lawyers Who Dare to Be Different." She is the recipient of the State Bar President's Pro Bono Service Award and the San Diego Volunteer Lawyer Program Pro Bono Attorney of the Year for her work on behalf of indigent clients. She is also on the Board of Women for Mutual Security.